GOING NATIVE IN MURCIA

FOURTH EDITION

DEBBIE JENKINS, RUSS PEARCE

Going Native in Murcia

All You Need To Know About Visiting, Living and Home Buying in Murcia and Spain's Costa Cálida

FOURTH EDITION

Debbie Jenkins
Russ Pearce

NativeSpain.com

First Edition Published in Great Britain 2005 by www.BookShaker.com
Second Edition Published in Great Britain 2006 by http://www.NativeSpain.com
Third Edition Published in Great Britain 2012 by http://www.NativeSpain.com

© Copyright 2020 Debbie Jenkins & Russ Pearce
http://www.NativeSpain.com

All rights reserved. No part of this publication may be reproduced, stored in or introduced into a retrieval system, or transmitted, in any form, or by any means (electronic, mechanical, photocopying recording or otherwise) without the prior written permission of the publisher.

This book is sold subject to the condition that it shall not, by way of trade or otherwise, be lent, resold, hired out, or otherwise circulated without the publishers prior consent in any form of binding or cover other than that in which it is published and without a similar condition including this condition being imposed on the subsequent purchaser.

Cover image copyright © Russ Pearce, used with permission.
Back cover images copyright © Russ Pearce & Bob Shoesmith, used with permission.
Map data copyright © OpenStreetMap contributors, CC-BY-SA.
Typeset in Garamond.

Book Interior and E-book Design by Amit Dey | amitdey2528@gmail.com

Praise for Going Native in Murcia

Fabulous book. A must read if you are going to the area. Beyond a guide book. Insider info is invaluable, it added to our holiday.

Dianne Louise - 5 Star Review on Amazon

There is nothing else like it; travel guides re Murcia are generally poor however this one is a great read with lots of pertinent info.

Stef – 5 Star Review on Amazon

Very thoroughly researched with a bright, chatty but not irritating style. I find a lot of guides rather snotty and written from only one viewpoint (the most politically correct one) - Lonely Planet are a prime example - they tend never to look below the surface or understand that different people like different things. This book is a breath of fresh air. I would thoroughly recommend this guide for anyone interested in holidaying and/or investing in this area.

Amazon Review

I bought the first edition of this book when I put a deposit down on a property in Murcia some years ago and it became my Murcia bible, and now that I live in the Murcia region part of the year I bought the updated version. It is probably the most informative book I have on the Murcia region, and I have a few, but this one stands out as it gives information on the whole of the region and not just the Mar Menor and the La Manga area. There are so many beautiful places to see in Murcia that are hidden little gems and this book is fantastic at helping you find all those lovely places.

Bryan Crookston - 5 Star Review on Amazon

This guide was detailed and factual but also written in a personal style which encouraged us to explore an area which is a second home to us. We ventured further afield and enjoyed our forays to new areas. Looking forward to many more visits and opportunities to explore many more towns and villages in this lovely part of Spain.

Lynda - 5 Star Review on Amazon

Excellent book on Murcia. I have found many villages, restaurants which I would not have found otherwise. The authors really know the area can't wait to discover the area and try out some of the suggestions.

Kezar - 5 Star Review on Amazon

Been living in the Murcia region for almost 2 years now, and have found this book most useful. Not only is it informative and well written, it is also entertaining, with nice short stories of every day life in the region. Have recommended to many of my friends, who also share my opinion. A must buy, if you are planning to visit or live in Murcia.

Maru - 5 Star Review on Amazon

The book is literally packed from cover to cover with the most incredibly well researched and pertinent, up to date and relevant information that anyone, and I mean anyone, interested in buying property in Murcia, living in the region or just travelling around Murcia will ever require.

If you're about to become a new expatriate and move to Spain and in particular Murcia, this book can act as your guide, you won't want to go anywhere without it! In fact, the information contained therein will become your life map! There is information on every single conceivable topic, nightlife, the property buying process, shopping, the population and map reference of towns, airlines and hire cars, vocabulary, fiestas, money, making concrete! Every scrap of information gleaned over the past ten years is in this book! I love it! It makes fantastic, interesting and even entertaining reading for anyone with even just a modicum of interest in Spain!

Rhiannon Williamson

I just wish I had got this book two years ago, when I was buying my house in Murcia! The Spanish house buying process can be a bit daunting for the average Brit... but the flow charts really make the steps and the roles of the associated people... absolutely clear! As the book is full of very relevant web-site addresses, the content is actually much larger than presented... and will remain fresher... longer! Expat... would be expat... or just visiting Murcia for a holiday... this book is essential reading... don't go without it!

John Mellor (Cheshire/Estrella de Mar)

We purchased your book via Amazon and have found it a most useful guide to the area. We are about to start a property search in preparation for a permanent move with family to Spain at the end of the year. Had enough of cold, damp, dreary days (and nights) in Redditch and the general social decline and rising costs in Britain. So the 'Buying in Murcia' flowchart and viewing checklist are going to be most useful, as are the town/village guides. Congratulations again on a brilliant, practical book.

Rosemary Clarke

Thanks to your book I have already started the ball rolling towards our move to Murcia and have had a meeting with an agent's representative who happens to be here in Cowes to spend the holiday with relations.

Ken Meynell

I purchased Going Native in Murcia, prior to our first visit to that region in September of this year. The book is well researched and covers a whole range of information and many excellent website addresses. A must for anybody considering visiting or purchasing in the Murcia region.

Paul McGloin

This book is brilliant and has given me a good knowledge of Murcia, in preparation for my holiday there. It is very difficult to find any literature on the area and although this book is really aimed at people living or planning to live in the area, it is also invaluable for people planning to visit and who wish to make the most of their holiday.

Lin Cruickshank

I am so glad I tripped over this, a guide that concentrates on the Murcia area, which is somewhere that most books gloss right over in a page or so. This is THE only book that anyone living, touring, visiting or contemplating spending some time in the region needs. Murcia is one of the few remaining up-and-coming areas in Spain. Get in there quick, but don't go without reading this! Covers everything anyone needs to know. I love the fact that it's so easy to get it too!

Jude

Murcia is the up and coming region in Spain for British buyers, and this is the definitive guide to the area. I only wish we had bought it before we started looking for property in the area, it would have saved us a lot of time and effort! However this book is still proving to be indispensible as we explore the region and discover yet another delightful town off the tourist trail. Well done Debbie!

Sue Walker author of Retiring The Olé Way

I am more than happy to recommend it. It is very informative and although there are plenty of books about living in Spain this tells you everything you need to know about Murcia. I have found it very useful when venturing out to new towns and villages that I might not have otherwise gone to. An excellent read.

Mr. G Brown

This book is packed full of useful information and tips on how to live life in Murcia and avoid the pit holes many ex-pats fall down. It also includes useful contact information and excellent recommendations on places to eat and things to do in the various towns within Murcia.

Fred Bear

Having now read both the first and second editions, I am full of praise for the authors. They have captured the essence of this unique Region of Spain. I just love Los Alcázares and their review is spot on. Don't hesitate, buy it!

David Goodall

Although I had been living in the area over six months, this book was recommended to me and I am delighted I took their advice and bought it. The description of Spanish everyday life is hilarious; I thought it was only me who observed their unusual drinking habits! A true, honest and informative account of life here in Murcia. Whenever we have friends or family over I leave it in their room, invaluable.

Mrs J M Lewis

Having visited the Murcia region, I liked the area and the people but had great difficulty in getting any information. In fact this was the only book I could find that concentrated on the area. It told me all I wanted to know. It's a great area and the book takes the hard work out of discovering the best part of Spain.

Don Mowl

This book is an excellent reference book for people spending holidays or permanently living within the Murcia region. My wife is Spanish and is very impressed as reading the book will greatly assist in settling in to the Spanish way of life. Recommendations for eating out and recipes were good choices and all worth a visit

Mr. Brian Tennant

Contents

Foreword xiii
About This Book xiv
Updates, Changes and Your Feedback xvi
    More For You! xvi
What do *you* want? The Highlights! xvii
Overview 1
    A Brief History 1
    Language 3
    Culture 4
    Food and Drink 5
    Wine Guide 14
    Flora and Fauna 15
    Transport 19
    Climate 22
    Fiestas 25
    Activities 26
    Health & Beauty 39
Town & City Guide 47
    Where To Stay And Eat 49
    Águilas 50
    Aledo 59
    Alhama De Murcia 60
    Archena 64
    Bolnuevo 67

Bullas 68
Cabo de Palos 72
Calasparra 75
Calblanque 78
Caravaca De La Cruz 80
Cartagena and Surrounds 85
Cehegín 121
Ceutí 123
Cieza 125
Costa Cálida 127
Fortuna 128
Fuente Álamo 134
Jumilla 139
La Manga del Mar Menor 145
La Unión 150
Lo Pagán 152
Lorca 154
Los Alcázares 159
Mar Menor 167
Mazarrón 169
Molina De Segura 177
Moratalla 180
Mula 189
Murcia and Surrounds 193
Around Murcia 215
Ojós 223
Pliego 224
Portmán 226
Puerto Lumbreras 228
Puerto de Mazarrón 230
Ricote Valley 238

- San Javier 246
- Santiago De La Ribera 249
- San Pedro del Pinatar 252
- Sierra Espuña 261
- Torre Pacheco 264
- Totana 268
- Yecla 273

Essential Information 277
- Brexit 277
- Students 277
- Retiring 278
- Working 278
- Buying a House 281
- Moving To Murcia 287
- Living in Murcia 288
- Building Work & Permissions 290
- Alternatives 292
- DIY 292
- The Garden 292
- Pets (Mascotas) & Animal Ownership 293
- Smoking 295
- Entertainment 296
- Law & Order 297
- Crime 298
- Health 300
- Driving 301
- Shopping 303
- Emergency Telephone Numbers 307
- Local Charities 308

Home Comforts 312
- Home Sickness 312

British Food 314
Internet Shopping 314
Resources 315
Learning Spanish 317
Recommended Reading 319
About The Authors 320
Debbie Jenkins 320
Russ Pearce 320
Maps 322
Águilas Map 322
Caravaca Map 323
Cartagena Map 324
Lorca Map 325
Moratalla Map 326
Murcia Map 327
Connect with us and keep in touch at: 328
Full Table of Contents... 329

Foreword

Most people have heard of Murcia, one of Spain's undiscovered corners, but few know much about it: ask a Spaniard what they know about Murcia and they'll probably mention La Manga and agriculture before they dry up. Put the same question to a foreigner and they're likely to get as far as the Mar Menor, golf and cheap property. But this is just a tiny fraction of what Murcia really has to offer and as this books shows, there's a hidden land out there waiting to be discovered and enjoyed.

The authors open the window onto a world of fascinating contrasts: verdant mountain tops and desert rock formations; bustling Murcia city (one of Spain's up and coming must–see destinations) and fabulous sandy beaches that you could well have to yourself; busy expat enclaves and tiny Spanish hamlets. This is a land of Barbary sheep and Montpellier vipers, delicious Zarangollo and Carrascalejo, the Spanish Teleclub and expat bridge clubs.

When you arrive somewhere new, you need all the help and information you can get. If that information is first–hand, accurate and bang up to date, so much the better. 'Going Native in Murcia' is all of these. This gem of a guide contains vital facts, useful suggestions, top tips and helpful websites as well as plenty of valuable advice.

Joanna Styles - Freelance writer and author specialising - in Spain and relocation generally. - www.joannastyles.com

About This Book

This book has taken 15 years to research and has been a real pleasure, taking me around the whole region that I now like to call our home.

The first three editions were written by me, Debbie Jenkins, with input from my ex-husband Marcus. The first edition came out in May 2005, when we had to force ourselves to stop adding information and get the book out there! The second edition included most of the stuff we couldn't fit into the first one plus almost a year's worth of extra experience and knowledge as well as the invaluable contributions from readers. The third edition, published in 2012, was a complete reworking of the content. We added thousands more words, maps, case studies, restaurant reviews, going native suggestions and experiences.

The fourth edition, 2020, comes at a time when everything is changing or has changed. I have divorced, moved a couple of times and finally bought the #DisasterFarm near La Pinilla. My friend and colleague, Russ Pearce, an English as a second language teacher, has helped update and add new content (especially around football!) His photographs adorn the cover and our website. Places have opened (for example, the new airport – really it is OPEN!) and the housing market has changed. Brexit is causing consternation and will leave a trail of chaos in its wake. In fact, we waited an extra year to get this version in print, so we could provide the most up-to-date Brexit information.

The biggest criticism of previous editions has been our lack of images in the book (also that I forgot to mention a town, La Puebla, I've fixed that, sorry Amaroo!) I agree about the lack of images, but haven't been able to find a solution for print that's economical (books on Murcia don't get on the bestseller lists, we don't get any economies of scale). Pretty much everyone has the internet on their phone now, so we've put even more photos on our website for you: www.NativeSpain.com – go and take a look.

The book was originally borne out of the frustration of none of the major guides covering the region, or at best only dedicating 4 or 5 pages to it. When they did mention Murcia they focused entirely on the golf complexes and housing estates. In fact, the only guides we could find that covered the Murcia region in any detail were in Spanish, interspersing flowery language with inaccurate information. So we felt it was time for someone to put this major region firmly on the map. I am sad to say that this hasn't changed over the last 15 years – and I'm proud we're still the only printed guide for the whole of the Murcia region!

Murcia is a beauty, with warm and welcoming people, wonderful food and fantastic weather. Our goal for you as you read this book is that you'll be able to enjoy visiting this region in all its glory, with us as your equally wide–eyed guides. If you're thinking of investing here or even making this region your new home then the sections on buying and visiting will tell you all you need to know.

We have tried to make the information available as accurate as possible. Russ Pearce spent months going through all the town information, updating the golf courses, etc. In general when it says "I", the (frequently sarcastic) "I" in question is Debs. We accept no responsibility for loss, injury or inconvenience sustained by anyone using this book.

Although inclusion in a guidebook usually implies a recommendation, we cannot list every good place. And we apologise in advance if we missed you out, get in touch and let us know. In addition, exclusion does not imply criticism. In fact there are a lot of reasons why we might exclude a place, for example it might not be appropriate to encourage an influx of visitors!

Updates, Changes and Your Feedback

Stuff happens, prices go up, restaurants end up under concrete (no really they do!), places change hands, bad things get better and great things go bad! So if you find things have changed, please let us know. Pop us an email via www.nativespain.com.

Perhaps you have a story to share for the Native's Section? Or maybe you've visited a museum, gone scuba diving or had a wonderful meal. Get in touch, let us know. Everyone who contributes at www.nativespain.com will find their name listed in the next edition as well as author discounts on future guides.

More For You!

For loads of articles, notifications and photos head on over to www.NativeSpain.com and remember to sign up to get notified of new photos and articles as we add them.

Follow Debs Jenkins on twitter - https://twitter.com/debsjenkins or make friends at facebook www.facebook.com/debsjenkins

Follow Russ Pearce at http://www.anythingbutpaella.com or http://www.rt-english.com

What do *you* want? The Highlights!

Before we get started on the details here's our quick guide to some of the best things for you to do depending on your tastes, likes and needs. Go to the appropriate section for the details. Everyone is different, let us know what you enjoyed... and if you found something extra to include!

Sporty people: Along the Mar Menor or Mediterranean coast you'll find cycle routes. The sports section covers football, scuba, horse riding, golf, etc. Climb a mountain - try the Sierra Espuña Parque Regional with some of the highest peaks in the Murcia region (Espuña mountain at 1585m) or the highest mountain in the Murcia region, Los Obispos at 2027m in the Moratalla area. Most towns and urbanisations have tennis or padel courts you can hire for an hour. There are about 320 days of sunshine so outdoor sports activities are abundant, remember your sunscreen!

Walkers: There are mountains, you won't miss them (the big things) – the Sierra Espuña, Carrascoy and coastal mountains all have walking routes. With its large tracts of wilderness, mountains, coasts, cliffs and forests, Murcia offers unrivalled opportunities for treks, short half day walks or longer excursions. There is an extensive network of long distance walks throughout Spain, with a number crossing into Murcia. These are called the Senderos de Gran Recorrido (GRs). We have the GR7 all the way from Andorra, as well as many shorter footpaths called the senderos de Pequeño Recorrido (PRs). There are also walking groups and guides. Check out Bob Shoesmith who organises walks for charity www.facebook.com/bob.shoesmith.

Divers: I am a lapsed advanced diver, who learnt to dive right here in Murcia, in 2007. The diving in this region is awesome, the safety standard is high. Whether you're a qualified diver or an enthusiastic snorkeler, the Costa Cálida has some great dive sites. Everything from wrecks, rocks and reefs. Scuba diving is relatively inexpensive, fun and accessible for all. Beginners can get some great diving around the Mazarrón area. Advanced divers can get some thrills diving around Cabo de Palos (you need to book).

Golfers: If you like your golf you are in luck! We have loads of golf courses, with plenty of variety. There's the La Manga courses, and newer ones are well-established throughout the region. Hacienda del Alamo near

Fuente Alamo or El Valle, just off the RM19 near Corvera Airport are worth a try.

Adventure-seekers: Downhill cycling (or freewheeling) in the Sierra Espuña? Potholing in Pliego? River rafting or kayaking on the Rio Segura from the gorgeous town of Blanca in the Ricote Valley? *The speleological group* in Lorca (www.espeleomurcia.es) will help you find cavities and caves to explore, by hiking, canoeing or mountaineering.

Little kids (or little kids at heart): Try out either of the region's water parks – Aqua Natura in Murcia or Parque Tentegorra in Cartagena. Take a boat ride round the bay in Cartagena on the Tourist Boat and see the James Bondesque gun outposts and the fortresses dotted along the bay. Visit the Cartagena castle (Castillo de la Concepción) and take the panoramic lift up the 45m elevation. It's quite an exciting view if you're scared of heights.

Geologists: We have mountains and valleys, dry river beds and mines. Have a look around the mines at La Unión, which produced lead, iron, silver, and zinc from Roman times. Take a walk around Aledo with it's fossils and rock formations and join a "Walk Through Time" if you want more information.

Archaeologists: The Romans came through here a while ago, so there's plenty of Roman remains to keep you busy. Cartagena is a great bet, follow the Archaeological Route, or try Alhama, Archena, Águilas, Calasparra, Caravaca De La Cruz... pretty much all the interior towns have something interesting to see. Visit the **The Lost City**, Begastri, one of the most important late-Roman sites in Spain, 3km away from the centre of Cehegín. Pop to Lorca and see the **Columna Milenaria** which is a Roman milepost from 10 BC. There are a lot of archaeological museums!

History lovers: Get away from the beaches and the touristy areas and have a wander around some of the most beautiful villages and towns in the interior of Murcia. There's the Sierra Espuña Parque Regional, the wine towns of Yecla and Jumilla in the North East, the Ricote Valley area with the Sierra de la Pila and over to the far North West there's Caravacca de la Cruz and Moratalla. All of these places are great for a walk around the medieval towns, people watching in the beautiful squares or catching up on your cultural activities. You'll find mountains, rivers, castles, watermills, bodegas and friendly curious locals.

Rainy day activities (only about 20 days of the year!): The shopping malls in Murcia and Cartagena have plenty to keep you occupied – see the shopping section for details. There are also a lot of museums and galleries in the cities. Why not go and visit a bodega in Jumilla (and buy a few bottles to take home)? Or keep warm at one of the spas or balnearios.

Music lovers: We have a quite few music festivals during the year, including the Jazz Festival in San Javier and Mar de Músicas and Jazz Festival in Cartagena. There are theatres in Murcia and Cartagena cities. Cabo de Palos nightlife is especially noisy from Friday to Sunday and from June to September. There are a lot of places to go and drink, listen to music and dance. Lorca has a great music scene too. Try going to a local fiesta (turn up late!) and listen to live music (though frequently it's better for the next category – music haters!) www.muchomasmayo.com

Music haters (aka karaoke – sorry, I am the tone deaf member of a singing family who all love karaoke): Throughout summer the bars and urbanisations will have plenty of entertainment, and quite frequently you can join in. Karaoke is available along the La Manga strip, at Camposol and other tourist destinations. Sing along to medleys of 80s music at any of the village or town fiestas.

Nature lovers: Calblanque is a remote and almost untouched stretch of coast, just south of the Mar Menor. This designated natural park enjoys secluded bays, solitude and an abundance of wild birds and flowers. The mountains and plains in the north of the region are wonderful for wildlife.

Naturists: Let it all hang out in El Portús where there's the naturist resort: www.elportus.com. There's a gym and spa on site too.

Foodies: Try a tapas route – Cartagena and Murcia have regular ones - plenty of the small towns do their own version too. You're spoilt for choice in Cartagena as there are so many brilliant restaurants. Techos Bajos is one of our favourites for an excellent value menú del día – they are a fish restaurant though, so be prepared to eat fish, fish and more fish. Or try Bodegas Nicolas. They have a terrace out the back and seating along the front, so enjoy people watching as you sample their ample tapas selection. Try the michirones, a great example of Murcia cooking. In Murcia city you have to visit Los Zagales, who have produced excellent local tapas, including Zarangollo and Morcilla since 1926.

Shopaholics: Shop till you drop on a Saturday evening and watch the Cartagena women pose. Cartagena is a great place for shopping and people watching. All the brand shops are here – Zara, Stradivarius, Mango – plus plenty of designer and unusual shops selling hand made items. Or for the shopping-mall-experience get over to any of the shopping malls dotted around the area. Look out for

Going Native in Murcia

the markets around the Murcia area: as well as the regular weekly market days there are special artisan and medieval markets where you can find traditional products such as sausages, salted meats, pickles, honey, artisan bread, homemade sweets, cheeses and liqueurs.

Photographers: Around the Mar Menor you can watch the sailing boats from many of the little ports as they float out across this inland sea. At Lo Pagan capture the crazy kite surfers catching air. Enjoy a magnificent sun set or sun rise looking out across the two seas, *dos mares,* from any of the interesting small towns – San Pedro del Pinatar, Los Alcázares, San Javier, Los Nietos. Tilt at the windmills at Lo Pagan. If you're lucky, you'll catch the Patrulla Águilas planes flying over and get a fantastic airshow for free too!

Those who like being photographed: If you are looking for some heady Spanish nightlife then the area called El Zoco on the La Manga strip is the place to go. It has a mixture of bars, restaurants and clubs and all are open well into the early hours of the morning. Visit La Muralla cocktail bar, **underground** right in the centre of the Murcia, you can drink a large gin and tonic lounging against the fully restored Arabian city walls. And of course, the beaches – chillax, stretch out, take a selfie of your toes as the sun sets on the Mediterranean!

Overview

Murcia, covering 11,000 square kilometres making up 45 municipalities is home to just over 1 million inhabitants. The new airport near Corvera, around 20 kilometres from the city, was opened in January 2019. Due to the present location of Murcia airport the city is hardly a well–visited tourist attraction. However, spend a few days there and you won't regret it; it's a great example of Spain and all its character.

Murcia is located on the Mediterranean Sea and forms a small sea of its own, known as the Mar Menor. Some of the beaches of the Mar Menor include: San Javier, Santiago de la Ribera, Los Alcázares and La Manga.

If you're looking for more than a swim and prefer hiking, we recommend the Natural Park of Calblanque and the beautiful coves and coastal parts that surround this area. For the nature lover, there are a number of activities in the mountains of the Sierra Espuña.

A Brief History

It is widely believed that Murcia's name is derived from the Latin words of Myrtea or Murtea, meaning land of Myrtle (the plant is known to grow in the general area), although it may also be a derivation of the word Murtia, which would mean Murtius Village (Murtius was a common Roman name). Other research suggests that it may owe its name to the Latin Murtae (Mulberry), which covered the regional landscape for many centuries. The Latin name eventually changed into the Arabic Mursiya, and then, Murcia.

The city in its present location was founded with the name Medinat Mursiya (market of Murcia) in AD 825 by Abd ar-Rahman II, who was then the emir of Al-Andalus. Moorish planners, taking advantage of the course of the river Segura, created a complex network of irrigation channels that made the town's agricultural existence prosperous. In the 12th century the traveller and writer Muhammad al-Idrisi described the city of Murcia as populous and strongly fortified. After the fall of the Caliphate of Cordoba in 1031, Murcia passed under the successive rules of the powers seated variously at Almería, Toledo and Seville. In 1172 it was taken by the Almohades, and from 1223 to 1243 it briefly served as the capital of an independent kingdom.

The Castilians, with forces led by King Alfonso X, took the city at the end of this period of autonomy, whereupon large numbers of mixed immigrants from north Catalonia and Provence resettled the town. As with much of the Spanish Reconquest, these Christian populations were brought to the area with the goal of establishing a Christian base here, one that would be loyal to the Crown of Castile and whose culture would supplant that of the subjugated Moorish peoples. During the process of Christianization, many of the city's mosques were destroyed or converted into Catholic churches. In 1296, control over Murcia and the surrounding region was transferred to the Kingdom of Aragon and, in 1304, was finally incorporated into Castile under the Treaty of Torrellas.

Murcia flourished in the 18th century, benefiting greatly from a boom in the silk industry. Many of the modern city's landmark churches and monuments date from this period of nascent mercantilism.

However, this was to be followed by nearly a century of mishap. In 1810, Murcia was looted by Napoleonic troops; it then suffered a major earthquake in 1829. According to contemporaneous accounts, an estimated 6,000 people died from the disaster's effects across the province. Plague and cholera followed.

The town and surrounding area suffered badly from floods in 1651, 1879, and 1907, though the construction of a levee helped to stave off the repeated floods from the Segura. A popular pedestrian walkway, the Malecón, runs along the top of the levee.

Murcia has been the capital of the province of Murcia since 1838 and, with its creation by the central government in 1982, capital of the autonomous community (which includes only the city and the province). Since then, it has become the seventh most populated municipality in Spain and a thriving services city.

Famous People

Muhyī al-Dīn Ibn al-'Arabī (1165–1240) a Sufi thinker.

Abul Abbas al-Mursi (1219–1286) a Sufi mystic.

Diego de Saavedra Fajardo (1584–1648) a writer and diplomat.

Francisco Salzillo (1707–1783) a Baroque sculptor.

José Moñino, Conde de Floridablanca (1728–1808) a statesman, minister of King Charles III of Spain.

Isaac Peral (1851-1895) inventor of the electric submarine.

Juan de la Cierva (1895–1936) the inventor of the autogyro, a forerunner of the helicopter.

Francisco Sánchez Bautista (1925–) a poet.

Julián Romea (1818–1863) a theatre actor.

Ramón Gaya (1910–2005) painter and writer.

Alejandro Valverde (1980–) a cyclist.

Luis León Sánchez Gil (1983–) a cyclist.

Nicolás Almagro (1985–) a tennis player.

Charo (1951–) a musician, actress and entertainer.

Maria Teresa Chicote (1935–) a notable scientist.

Language

The language in Murcia is Castilian Spanish, the standard Spanish you'd be taught in school (not Catalan).

However, the Spanish spoken in Murcia is quite different from other areas of Spain. Murciano tends to eliminate many syllable–final consonants and to emphasise regional vocabulary, much of which is derived from old Arabic words. For example, swapping the diphthong ai for ei, so instead of seis you get sais (saayis). And of course the addition of the diminutive ico, for example bonico.

Some Murcian countryfolk still speak a separate dialect, called Panocho, which is virtually unintelligible to speakers of standard Castilian Spanish.

What you'll most likely notice is the lack of 's' at the end of many words, for example 'do' instead 'dos' (two).

English	Spanish	Pronunciation
Spanish (Castilian)	español	(es–pahn–YOL)
Hello, hi	castellano	(kah–steh–YAH–no)
Goodbye	hola	(OH–la)
Please	adiós	(ahdy–OS)
Thank you	por favor	(pore faah–VOR–e)
Sorry	gracias	(GRA–thyahs)
That (thing)	perdón	(pair–DON)
How much?	eso	(EH–saw)
For example	cuánto	(KWAHN–to)
English	por ejemplo	(pore eh–HEM–ploh)
Yes	inglés	(ing–GLESS)
Spanish	sí	(see)
No	no	(noh)

English	Spanish	Pronunciation
I don't understand	no entiendo	(noh en–tYEN–do)
Where's the bathroom?	¿dónde está el baño?	(DON–deh es–TAH el BA–nyo)
Cheers! (toast)	¡salud!	(sah–LOOTHE)
Do you speak English?	¿habla usted inglés?	(AH–blah oos–TED ing–GLESS)

For advice about where to go to learn the language see the Resources Section at the end of the book.

Culture

Reading the history books you'd be forgiven for thinking Murcia doesn't actually exist. From the Romans, to the Muslims, the Visigoths to the Spanish Inquisition, Murcia remains resolutely unmentioned. Murcia's cultural heritage bears an impression of old battles and recent political machinations; however, it remains clearly removed from the limelight. Signs of the influence of all of these invaders and aggressors litter the whole region, from aqueducts, castles, fortifications and Roman roads lined with olive trees to the stunning architecture of the grand buildings in the cities.

Murcia is a friendly region, a warm "Buenos Días" upon entering a shop or restaurant is uttered to all, followed by an "Adios" or "Hasta Luego" upon departure. At the coast, they don't expect visitors to speak much Spanish, however in the villages a lack of Spanish can create difficulties as few rural Spaniards learn English.

The Murcianos are a gregarious bunch, taking great care to include children and the older generations in their social activities. They enjoy making an effort in their appearance. A walk around the Murcian capital on a summer's Saturday evening will show a decadence in dress that us Brits generally reserve for weddings! Even the children will be dressed in their finery.

Murcians works on the same timetable as most of the rest of Spain, relaxed! The heat for most of the year encourages a long lunch break, followed by chatting and snoozing during the afternoon (siesta). The shops mostly close between 2pm and 5pm for most of the year, reopening at 5pm and staying open until 8 or 9pm.

During the hottest months Murcianos take advantage of the cooler evenings, sitting and chatting outside till well past midnight. It's not uncommon to see young children racing round outside restaurants at 2am, while their parents and extended family drink slowly and cool down.

In August Murcianos take a well needed 1 month holiday. Many shops and restaurants (outside of the tourist destinations) will shut down or work reduced hours, while their Murciano proprietors enjoy the beaches and the mountains.

Murcia is a very sociable region, respect for elders and enthusiasm for children leads to a relaxed atmosphere, full of life and parties. Daily Murcianos can be found at their afternoon paseo or playing dominoes in the bar.

In addition to the native Spanish population in Murcia you will find the usual pockets of immigrants and expats from the United Kingdom, Ireland, Portugal, Germany, Poland, Eastern Europe, North Africa and many from Latin American countries.

Religion

Basically Spain is a staunchly Catholic country and Murcia is no exception, remember that Caravaca de la Cruz is one of the Vatican's five worldwide holy cities.

Bull Fighting

Bull fighting is still a major interest in Spain. Many bars sport a bull's head as a trophy, surrounded by photos of famous toreadors. In fact in Murcia near the ayuntamiento there's a bull fighting club, with the colours and symbols of all the Toreros who've ever fought in the region.

Food and Drink

Throughout the book you'll find many references to the food and drink of the region. We make no apologies for dedicating a lot of time to this subject. As we researched the book our favourite pastimes were checking out bars and restaurants, tasting different wines, going on cookery courses and eating with our neighbours. Our waistlines have suffered but we did it for you, our very special readers!

The Spanish, like many Latin cultures, make the mid–day meal their biggest, stretching it out for hours. From midday to mid–afternoon, everything shuts down, except of course for the restaurants. Then, after this long, leisurely meal (and sometimes a nap) they return to their workplaces and continue into the night.

The evening meal is late, anywhere from about 9pm to midnight. While most of us are not accustomed to eating dinner so late you might consider indulging in the Spanish favourite, tapas, as a light supper, although no real Spaniard would ever do this.

Restaurant hours are typically 1:00pm to 4:30pm for lunch and 9:00pm to 12:00 midnight for dinner. Though this may vary in the tourist areas, so always check your chosen restaurant.

Ventas, an excellent opportunity to eat reasonably priced meals almost any time of the day or night. These are motorway or roadside service areas. Often attached to a petrol station they are popular with lorry drivers and coach tours. There is usually a shop where you can buy local bread, vegetables and meat. And if you're lucky homemade sausages.

Menú del Día, though not usually very exciting, this fixed price meal is required of restaurants. It's a great way to taste some standard Spanish food, without the worry of a long menu. The prices for a menú del día almost always include bread, water and wine or beer, with a coffee at the end. They are very good value.

Menú, the principal ingredients of local Murcian dishes are the fresh produce of the Huerta (market garden, the fields of Murcia) and rice, fish and seafood from the nearby Mar Menor and the Mediterranean Sea. Excellent choices are the king prawns and the huevas de mújol which is a local variety of caviar. The region also produces fine wines among which the most known are Jumilla and Yecla.

Eating Like A Spaniard

You may have noticed that Spanish restaurants seem awfully quiet… …when you go in. This is probably because you haven't worked out how to eat like a Spaniard yet. Read on to find out how to go native and eat like a Spaniard and understand how military–precision timing can be all–important (doesn't sound like Spain, does it?)

Breakfast

First Breakfast: in Spain, most people actually have two breakfasts. The first breakfast is to get you started. Since most Spaniards start the day early, the constitution is only ready to receive something light at this stage, around 7:30. So first breakfast usually comprises any of the following:

- Brandy (not necessarily a small one)
- Coffee (typically a milky one for breakfast)
- Bizcocho (a sponge cake often homemade (casero), rather like Madeira cake)

- Costillas (not pork chops!, a thin, sugar–crusted cake with a fruit jam layer)
- Pastel (a large, fresh pastry or a pre–packaged, long–life cake (the last choice))

Second Breakfast is akin to elevenses and is usually around 10–10:30. These are typically very social affairs and rather more substantial than the first breakfast. If you go into a bar at this time in the morning you may find it difficult to hear yourself think. Second breakfast will comprise any of the following:

- Brandy (not necessarily a small one)
- Beer or red wine (white wine is a woman's drink (according to ever–so–slightly chauvinist Spanish men))
- Tapas (no holding back here, could be anything from tortilla to testicles)
- Bocadillo
- Orujo from the freezer to finish

The second breakfast sets you up nicely to last through to lunch as you spend the rest of the morning operating heavy machinery, driving an HGV, approving planning permissions, etc.

Lunch

Lunch is eaten late. If you turn up at a restaurant and ask to eat at 12:30, you can expect slow service and a limited menu that may comprise left–over tapas from second breakfast. The majority of Spaniards start lunch at 2–2:30 (possibly an hour later at weekends). In fact, if you want to eat at some of the most popular restaurants, you'd be advised to turn up at about 1:45 unless you have reserved a table in advance, at 2:30 the place will be heaving. Like second breakfast, lunch is often eaten out at a restaurant with work colleagues during the week. At weekends, lunch is an opportunity to catch up with extended family, you'll usually see three generations (or more!) at the table.

During the week (and at other times in holiday areas), you will be able to get a menú del día, a set menu at a very reasonable price that includes drink (where 'drink' could mean water, beer or house wine), salad, three courses and a coffee (which may include brandy, if that's what you fancy).

Be aware of the word menú here, this is a false friend, when you ask for the 'menú por favor', expecting to get the list of things to eat, the waiter will probably say '¡si!' and walk off, and start bringing you food that you didn't order. The thing is, you did just order, you ordered the fixed–price set menu (menú del día). You wanted the carta.

Spaniards typically don't have tapas at lunchtime. Lunchtime is the main meal of the day, to fill up and take your time (in order to help you feel sleepy enough for a few minutes' siesta afterwards).

At weekends the same establishment that served you a good–value, inexpensive menú del día during the week will pull out all the stops and serve you an a la carta meal that will cost you twice as much for the same thing. The difference is that the cut of meat will be better quality and twice the size, the wine will be better and the desserts more varied.

A typical lunchtime meal has the following:

- Brandy
- Salad (even in the depths of winter)
- A starter that is frequently larger than the second course. Starters include: soup (consomé con albóndigas con un pocito fino is one of our favourites), stew (guiso), pasta or rice (arroz / paella).
- The second course is usually something like meat / fish / eggs plus chips plus a grilled pepper.
- Dessert can include fruit or a pudding. Puddings to look out for are casero (home made): flan (crème caramel), arroz con leche (rice pudding) and pan de calatrava (crème caramel with a thin sponge base).
- Coffee (frequently without so much or any milk at this stage, carajillo, bel monte or cortado are usual)
- Orujo from the freezer to finish

Supper

Supper during the week is usually eaten at home with the family, at any time between 8pm and 10pm. At weekends (starting Friday), suppertime is tapas time. This evening meal is (yet another) time to socialise, chat, flirt and speak very loudly.

Eating and drinking and drinking and eating, these activities are inseparable in Spain. A bartender will be shocked if you order so much as a caña (small glass of beer) without something to eat, even if something to eat is only a handful of olives.

Eating tapas (they even have a verb for it, tapear) requires you to do a bar crawl. Although lots of alcohol will be consumed over the course of the evening, it will always be accompanied with some food. This is why it is very unusual to see Spanish people drunk, in fact appearing drunk is very bad form in Spain. The only exception to this rule might be at fiestas, then the booze flows freely!

The Spanish might not take timing seriously for anything else, but for food and drink, timing is important. If you don't want to stick out like a sore thumb, get there at the right time and eat and drink the right things. Soon enough you'll know all the waiters and bar staff by their first names and they'll have your usual ready before you even get to the bar. ¡Te aproveche!

Tapas Guide

Tapas are snacks designed to be served with your drink. It's widely believed that the name comes from the custom of the barman covering your glass of sherry with a slice of bread, cheese, or salami to keep the flies from drinking too much, tapar means to cover in Spanish.

However research suggests that the King Alfonso X el Sabio, who is said to have refused to serve his glorious wine to visitors unless they also had something to eat, introduced the term, he would tapaba them.

Madrid is probably the best known tapas destination, but the tradition is observed in many parts, especially in the southern half of the country. There are two approaches to tapas: one is a freebie, a mouthful that comes with the price of your drink (often called a pincho). The second is a side–order snack purchased to accompany your glass of local wine.

It can be confusing at first, is this a free tapas or will the price be added to your bill? Generally, if the waiter passes you a small plate of something it's usually free. If they ask if you'd like something, then you will most likely pay.

Murcia is the Spanish Capital of Gastronomy 2020! The Spanish Capital of Gastronomy is an annual event created by the Spanish Federation of Tourism Journalists and Writers (FEPET) and the Spanish Hospitality Federation. Its objective is to recognize the city and community that has stood out most in the promotion of gastronomy as one of the main attractions for tourism in Spain. Murcia has been endorsed by 200 specialist journalists and writers.

Spaniards go to bars to chat, meet friends, argue, joke and flirt. Tapas are provided to keep them going and encourage the sales of drinks. Tapas are rarely eaten instead of a main meal but are good for soaking up the wine. Some of the best tapas bars can be found by universities and where commuters might congregate. This makes Murcia city a haven of tapas, especially around the Plaza de las Flores and Plaza Santa Catalina.

Each region has its own specialities; in fact each bar also has its own favourites. Here is a selection you might meet (or eat!):

Jamón, ham off the bone, cut to order in almost all bars and restaurants. You'll see the leg on a special holder at the bar and often you'll see many legs hanging from the ceiling (with their little upside down umbrellas to catch the fat). The jamón is taken seriously in Spain, with a number of varieties including Iberico, Serrano and Bellota.

Patatas Alioli, boiled potatoes in a creamy Alioli sauce (raw garlic mayonnaise) topped with a sprinkle of parsley.

Patatas Bravas, potatoes with a hot mustard, tomato and Tabasco sauce.

Tortilla, a fat omelette made with potatoes which sometimes includes peas, meat, tuna, peppers or mushrooms.

Magras con Tomate, fried pork cooked in a sweet tomato sauce.

Calamares, fried, beautifully fresh calamari, that melts in your mouth and calamares en su tinta, squid in their own ink.

Aceitunas or Olivas, olives, big, fat olives, often with stalks intact, firm to bite.

Pollo al Ajillo con Vino, garlic chicken with wine.

Caldo con Albóndigas, meatballs in a watery soup (consommé).

Gazpacho, cold tomato soup, almost like a salad, only usually available in the summer, unfortunately!

Rutas de Tapas

You can enjoy tapas in all the towns of the region, just pop in and point at what you want. However, many towns and cities are showcasing their bars and restaurants by hosting Rutas de Tapas, where participating bars offer their best tapas and drink for between €2 and €2.5. Here's a list of some of the ones to look out for.

At the end of January Cehegín kicks us off, then February sees Cartagena demonstrating their foodie prowess, take a look on www.rutadelatapadecartagena.es for dates, locations and previous winners.

March has tapas in Puerto de Lumbreras and Yecla, April Los Urrutias and May Los Belones.

Not really a tapas route, the Ruta del Vino de Jumilla is available all year, but in the summer they combine it with music events and even more food. Well worth a visit; take a look on their website for more details and the program: www.rutadelvinojumilla.com

From July through to the end of September Águilas offers a drink and a tapas, then in August visit Bullas, September Molina de Segura and Lorca and October Lorquí and Calasparra. November sees Moratalla host the tapas route along with Murcia city. Then in December try San Javier or Archena for some yummies, www.archena.es/rutadelatapa.

Local Food Specialities

Revuelto, is a common name for another tapas counter staple, eggs scrambled with runner beans, garlic, onions and ham.

Zarangollo, is a Murcian dish combining the concepts of ratatouille and omelette. It is made from tomatoes, courgettes, onions and eggs. Every tapas bar worth its salt in the region should have a plateful in the chiller. Menestra is similar, a dish of sautéed vegetables.

Ensalada Murciana, a wet salad of cooked red peppers and tomatoes, garlic, aubergine and onions. Always served cold and frequently with some fish (tuna or cod) thrown in. Almost always on the tapas counter.

Pastel de carne, little pasty or pie shaped pastries, filled with delicious meat, tomato and egg. Very good, give it a try. These are often bought to take to the Condomina bullring in Murcia, where they always have a merienda (snack) after the 3rd bull.

Arroz, rice is grown in the Calasparra region, with its own quality standards.

Among the wide variety of rice dishes are:

- Arroz y conejo, rice with rabbit
- Arroz de verduras, rice and vegetables
- Arroz y costillas, rice and ribs
- Arroz marinero, seafood rice
- Paella huertana, a vegetable paella

Potaje, a rich stew dish.

Habas con jamón, ham and broad beans.

Caldo Murciano, local soup dish.

Michirones, a spicy bean stew with pork and sausage (usually eaten with a toothpick).

Chuletas al ajo cabañil, garlic chops.

Pescado a la sal, baked fish in salt.

Fresh vegetables & fruit, known as the market garden (huerta), the Murcia region boasts an extensive and year round fruit and vegetable selection. Many of the fruit and vegetables you'll find in supermarkets in the UK will have come from Murcia, particularly tomatoes, melons and oranges.

Jabalí, wild boar, is available as a delicacy throughout Spain, and Murcia is no exception. The boar is served in a number of dishes (including the famous wild boar with figs) as well as just roasted.

Cheeses, the best cheeses in Murcia are granted a DOC rating, just like the wines of Yecla, Jumilla and Bullas. There are two categories of the Murcia DOC cheese, Queso de Murcia and Queso de Murcia al Vino. The Murcia DOC cheeses are all produced from whole milk from Murciano–Granadina goats.

The Queso de Murcia DOC comes in two varieties, fresh and semi–cured. The fresh variety is mild, white and has a woven texture on the rind from the tall, cylindrical mould. The cured variety is cured for at least 60 days, is rather more flavoured with a firmer texture, some holes and a smooth rind.

The Queso de Murcia al Vino DOC is a richer cheese with a characteristic reddish colour which comes from the wine that the cheese is soaked in while maturing. The cheese is matured for at least 45 days for large moulds, and 30 days for smaller cheeses.

Caviar, a locally–produced variant of caviar (huevas de mújol) is produced on the Mar Menor. It's available in jars in most local supermarkets at a very reasonable price compared to 'the real thing', but tastes pretty good!

Spanish Village Cooking - Winner of 2015 Gourmand World Cookbook Awards: BEST LOCAL CUISINE in Spain

In December 2013, after the success of my last cookery book project with *Spanish Cooking Uncovered: Farmhouse Favourites,* I (Debs) came up with an idea to work with my local village ladies and the fiesta committee to collate all the delicious recipes I'd eaten over the last 9 years of living in the small farming village of La Murta, Murcia in southern Spain.

The book, *Spanish Village Cooking – Recetas Del Campo*, was published in March 2014, three months after the initial idea. It is written in Spanish and English, with more than 80 photographs. Thirty five cooks offered their family recipes to produce more than 150 traditional Murcian dishes.

Spanish Village Cooking - Recetas del Campo: Enjoy over 150 simple, family recipes from a small village in Murcia. These recipes have been handed down through generations, grandmother to mother to daughter, making use of local, homegrown ingredients and traditional cooking methods. The chefs of La Murta generously share their secrets, so you can enjoy fresh,

Spanish food from the heart of the Sierra del Carrascoy.

Buy your copy, or gift it: www.NativeSpain.com or Amazon.

Vegetarians

Being a vegetarian in Murcia can sometimes be a little challenging. Local culture celebrates the pig and ham as a staple food, to be consumed at every opportunity. Here is a list of the top 3 vegetarian options:

Revueltos, scrambled eggs, you could ask for them with mushrooms, setas, or with asparagus, espárrago. Remember to specify sin jamón to have a better chance of having scrambled eggs without the ubiquitous ham!

Patatas Bravas or Patatas Alioli, potatoes with spicy hot sauce or garlic mayonnaise.

Huevos con patatas, egg and chips!

SIN CARNE? When ordering for a vegetarian friend in a long–established restaurant in Murcia, we ordered the safe option, revueltos sin carne. When it arrived we had to explain that even the little bits of ham in the eggs weren't appetising to our friend and asked if they wouldn't mind starting again without meat, and without jamón!

Local Drinks

Asiático, The Asiático variant of coffee is a speciality of the Campo de Cartagena. It's made from coffee, condensed milk, Spanish brandy, a liqueur called Licor 43, a pair of coffee beans, (optional) sugar and a sprinkle of cinnamon powder. In the best bars you will get a tiny wedge of lemon zest and it will be served in the 'original' glass, a miniature, vase–shaped, ornate affair resembling a milkshake glass.

The drink was created in a bar in El Albujón (a small town just north of Cartagena) called Bar Pedrín, according to legend, the drink was originally called a 'ruso' but was changed to 'asiático' during Franco's times since a communist drink was not exactly flavour of the moment.

Belmonte, you will notice the locals in Murcia most often drink a strange coffee concoction called a Belmonte. It comprises a good shot of condensed milk (more often than not from a special dispenser mounted by the coffee machine), followed by a shot of café solo and finished off with a shot (or two) of Spanish brandy.

BELMONTES: Possibly the most versatile drink in the world. Taken after dinner as a digestif, the brandy bottle is always left for regulars to add an extra slosh, to swill down the coffee and clean out the glass (just to help with the washing up, of course). Taken after lunch, it's a great way to induce the siesta and taken at breakfast to warm the blood, you'll find office workers, doctors, truck drivers and policemen enjoying its healthy properties.

Orujo, is not a speciality of Murcia (it's principally from Galicia, actually) but that doesn't put the locals off from drinking it fairly liberally after meals. This digestif comes in a number of varieties, from the plain (a colourless, 40 percent spirit), to a wide variety of flavoured varieties of a lower strength. Local favourite flavourings are coffee and herbs.

Wine Guide

There are two classifications of Murcian wine: Vinos de la Tierra and in Murcia these are from Abanilla and Campo de Cartagena; and DOC, which implies that the wine only comes from a particular area, with a particular set of grapes and that the conditions of production are controlled.

The DOC (Denominación de Origen) wine region encompasses Jumilla, Bullas and Yecla. It gets incredibly hot here in the summer, which inevitably raises the sugar levels in the grapes. The higher the sugar levels the higher the alcohol content. For many years the wines of this region were strong and heavy and mainly exported to other regions for blending. However, cooperatives are persuading the growers to develop new ways of working that are producing some very drinkable and attractive wines.

Red wine grapes are Monastrell, Granache (Garnacha), Tempranillo, Cabernet Sauvignon, Merlot and Shiraz (Syrah). White wine grapes are Airén and Macabeo. Go the region section for more details of bodegas and their websites.

Jumilla

In particular Jumilla wines are making an impact in the UK. The Jumilla DOC comes from a number of towns: Jumilla, Montealegre del Castillo, Albatana, Ontur, Hellín and Tobarra. They produce a number of varieties, the king of these being the Monastrell grape.

To the north of the Murcia region, there are many bodegas selling top quality reds, whites and rosados.

Bullas

The north west of the region is an upcoming wine producing area supported by the European Vinest

Project. The wine is produced in the towns of Mula, Calasparra, Ricote, Caravaca, Cehegín, Moratalla, Lorca and Bullas itself.

Yecla

In the far north east of the region, neighbouring Jumilla, the Yecla wines are only produced in the local region around the town itself and characterised by a more subtle balance between strength and acidity.

Campo de Cartagena

Bodegas Serrano (www.http://bodegasserrano.es) in the Finca La Cabaña 30 in Pozo Estrecho, 968 556298 is worth a visit. The owners are Manuel Martínez Meroño and his wife Carmen Inglés Inglés. Sampling these wines is quite an experience. The wine doesn't have its DO, however, there are some lovely reds and rosados, quite subtle.

See the food and drink cheat sheet in the resources section at the end of the book, or visit www.NativeSpain.com for a printable version.

Flora and Fauna

The best website for flora and fauna in the region is:

www.regmurcia.com/servlet/integra.servlets.ServletLink?sit=c|365|m|1039

Copy the link exactly, this will get you straight to the correct section. There are great photographs, excellent descriptions and useful geological information, all in Spanish.

Mammals

Weasels are just about everywhere in the region. Martens can be found mostly in the mountains, with wild cats in the Sierra Espuña and the Sierra de Moratalla and other mountain forests. You'll find badgers around the areas of Lorca, Águilas and Mazarrón. Otters are very rare but can be seen near the embalses of Cenajo and Mulata and the rivers Benamor and Quípar. At the smaller end of the scale are garden dormouse and red squirrels.

JABALÍ: Walking along the rambla at the back of the caves (on the way to the bar in the village), with our 3 teenage nephews we were accompanied by a baby wild boar (jabalí). The tiny wild boar cheerfully followed around our ankles, snuffling and playing with the boys, chasing after sticks that were thrown for it, while we adults nervously watched for its larger mother to appear, tusks bared! Luckily the baby got bored and wandered off. We got a large brandy.

Barbary sheep (Arrui or Muflón del Atlas) can be spotted in the Sierra Espuña if you're very lucky. Wild boar (Jabalí) can be found around Águilas, Mazarrón, Sierra de Carrascoy and the Mar Menor. And in every village a cacophony of cats can be found at the bakery door with a pack of dogs cheerfully wandering the streets and making friends with visitors.

SIERRA ESPUÑA: While driving to the top of the Sierra Espuña on a bright January afternoon, we were shocked to see before us in the road a beautiful Barbary sheep staring at us, resplendent with long antlers. We stopped and watched it run into the undergrowth where it joined a family of about 30. Later that same trip we spotted the entire family grazing on the hillside.

Birds

Pied Wagtails can be found in patches throughout the region, Great Bustards, Blackbirds and Long Tailed Tits are just about everywhere. Flamingos live in Salinas del San Pedro del Pinatar; Shelduks in Embalse de Santomera, Salinas del San Pedro del Pinatar and Salinas del Marchamalo; Stone Curlews in Saladares del Guadalentín; Little Owls, Eurasian Eagle Owls mostly in the mountains.

Hoopoes, Partridges, Barn Owls, Golden Orioles (incredibly beautiful), Golden Eagles, Common Buzzards, Peregrine Falcons (Sierra de Cartagena, Mazarrón and Sierra de Almenara), Bonelli's Eagles (Sierra del Altiplano, Calblanque and Peña del Águila) and Eurasian Kestrels can also be found here.

Reptiles

The Horseshoe Whip Snake, around 1 metre long can be found throughout the region, mostly around Yecla; the Viperine Water Snake grows to 50–80cm and is normally found near water; Montpellier Snakes, up to 2 metres in length, can be found around the region, they eat insects and small mammals.

Lataste's Viper at 50cm has very fast movement and is found in wooded areas. The Ladder Snake found around the whole region, in woods and natural areas, grows to about 1 metre.

Jewelled Lacertas (eyed lizard), around 60cm at their largest, can be found in the northwest of the region; Bedriaga's Skink which looks a bit like a snake, but with short legs and a very cylindrical body is fairly small, can be found around the Mar Menor. Lizard Podarcis Hispanica, which are typically only 5cm long, can be found around the whole region. They were almost extinct until 1970 when they were reintroduced.

Tortoise (Testudo Graeca) from North Africa can be found around most of the region and Mediterranean Pond Turtles at 15cm in length can too.

Turkish Geckos or Salamancas are common in the whole region, especially, it seems, in our cave house.

THE SLITHERING INNER TUBE: While driving along the road near Corvera we drove over what we thought was a bicycle inner tube, kerdunk, kerdunk, only to notice as we drove away that the inner tube also slithered away into the grass. We believe it was a Montpellier snake, fairly common in the region.

Amphibians

The Spanish Ribbed Newt usually around 20cm though can grow up to 32cm is found near Yecla; European toad whose male carries the fertilized eggs wrapped around its hind legs until they hatch, are very small (only 4cm); Natterjack Toads and Common Toads are common around most of the region too.

The Mediterranean Treefrog and Iberian Spadefoot Toad are found in the north of the region while the Spanish Painted Frog at just 7cm and the tiny Common Parsley Frog are dotted around the entire region.

Salamandra Salamandra, the largest in the family, prefers woodland. It has a shiny black body, with yellow splashes and is found only in the northwest.

Fish

The following sea fish are all common: Grouper (up to 1.4 m), Striped Sea Bream (30cm), Gilthead Sea Bream (60 cm), Atlantic mackerel (up to 60 cm), Atlantic Horse Mackerel (40 cm) and Fartet (4 cm).

Trees & Herbs

You'll find Small–leaved Elm, White Poplar, Apricot (Cieza), Plum (North–West), Peach (North and North–West), Strawberry (Mula and Segura valleys), Walnut, Almond, Carrascoy Pine, Carob, Stone Pine and Olive.

RIPE FOR THE PICKING: Take a walk along any rambla in the springtime and you'll find a huge array of herbs just waiting to be picked. Often you'll see a family returning from their afternoon paseo with bunches of rosemary. At the #DisasterFarm we get to pick wild asparragus and wild spinach. Just make sure you know what you're collecting!

Chumbo, can reach up to 2m in height, with beautiful flowers and wonderful fruit, though take care when harvesting them, the chumbos tree is also known as the prickly pear. They grow throughout the region and are often used as a natural waste eater!

Vitis vinífera are vines to make grapes that make wine! There are a number of varieties, including Monastrell, Garnacha Tinta and Cencibel, Tempranillo to make the red wines and Macabeo and Airén for the white wines. They are also cultivating a Cabernet Sauvignon. The grapes have other properties too, including as a tonic, a decongestant and a laxative, now who told us wine was good for you! The region is also home to some rare but beautiful flowers including the Butterfly Orchid, Sea Daffodil and Sea Holly.

Protected Zones

The United Nations has designated the Mar Menor as s Specially Protected Area of Mediterranean Importance. In addition it is a wetland of international importance with RAMSAR Wetland (Convención Relativa a los Humedales de Importancia Internacional especialmente como Hábitat de Aves Acuáticas).

Open areas and islands of the Mar Menor, the protected landscape includes the five islands of volcanic origin: La Perdiguera, La Mayor (del Barón), El Ciervo, La Redonda and Sujeto. Also included are three low mountains: El Carmolí, San Ginés and Cabezo del Sabinar, and the beaches of La Hita and La Amoladeras; and the salt marshes of Lo Poyo and Marchamalo.

Calblanque, Monte de Las Cenizas and Peña del Águila, LIC (Lugares de Importancia Comunitaria) are declared as Natural Park.

Sierra de la Muela, Cape Tiñoso and Roldán, are also declared as Natural Park, by LIC and ZEPA (Zonas de especial protección para las aves).

Sierra de La Fausilla, Parque Regional de Sierra Espuña, Sierra de Ricote y La Navela, Almenara-Moreras-Cabo Cope, Sierra de Moratalla, Monte El Valle and Sierras de Altaona and Escalona and Sierras de Burete, Lavia and Cambrón are all declared protected by ZEPA.

Islands of the Mediterranean Coast, including Isla Grosa (in the municipality of San Javier), Islas Hormigas, Isla de Las Palomas and la Isla de Escombreras, are protected under ZEPA.

Cabezos del Pericón and Sierra de las Victorias between the towns of Cartagena and Fuente Álamo are LIC protected.

For more details: www.murcianatural.carm.es

Transport

Road Network

Murcia has an excellent network of motorways and main roads. Murcia, Águilas, Jumilla, the Mar Menor and Cartagena are all well interlinked.

Unfortunately, there is a toll motorway in Murcia, the one between Cartagena and Águilas. Since this can add of the order of €5 to your trip each way many locals eschew this and take the back road. It's probably the quietest section of motorway in Murcia. Be warned that roadside speed cameras are in use, and the police do put out fixed and moving radar speed traps. This has had a noticeable effect and now most people stick to the speed limit (or 10km/h above, this is still Spain after all, so 'slightly' complying with the law is ingrained). For those new to the area it's recommended to use an app like Google Maps on your phone, or a GPS gadget with an up-to-date map for trips where you are unfamiliar with the road. The fixed speed cameras are nondistinct grey cabinets at the side of the road or behind overhead signs.

Airports

Región de Murcia International Airport finally opened in January 2019. It is located to the south of the town of Corvera, hence it is often referred to by that name. This is much closer to the city of Murcia itself (some 20km to the south) than its predecessor at San Javier. It is hoped it will grow to rival Alicante's El Altet and Málaga for the capacity, duty free shopping and range of fast food franchises, but throughout 2019 it has struggled to attract the passenger numbers that San Javier had.

www.aena.es will allow you to see live arrivals and departures, in English.

The runway is big enough to take a 747 Jumbo (we are prepared to bet that nothing this large will ever run a scheduled service) and will operate 24 hours. The airport should in time increase the capacity for flights, ensure lower prices and offer greater flexibility to travellers. Dozens of golf complexes have sprung up around the area in anticipation. (Ironically, we note in the local press that one of the local golf complexes was complaining to the authorities that they would be in the flight path of the new airport, at the same time as proclaiming proximity to the airport as one of the virtues of buying a house in that housing estate…)

Alternative airports for Murcia are, in order of convenience, Alicante (El Altet), Almería and, if you want the best connectivity, Madrid (Barajas). From Murcia city, with no traffic and a lead foot, you can get to Alicante in an hour, Almería in two and Madrid in four hours.

Many of the travellers coming in to Murcia airport (RMU) stay on the Costa Cálida and do not visit the city of Murcia. The closest train station is in Balsicas. A taxi all the way into Murcia city costs €29, or you can get a bus direct to the city's bus station for €5. Be aware that their timetable could be described as sporadic at best. See www.interbus.es/murcia for more details. Bus routes are also available to Cartagena, La Manga, Los Alcazares, San Pedro, Mazarrón and Águilas.

Car Rental

Unless you live full–time in Spain and have bought/brought your own wheels, car rental is probably the most cost–effective way of getting around Murcia. For week–long rentals you can often get a small car for as little as €15 a day.

Car Hire Companies

Centauro, www.centauro.net, 968 572185

Europcar, www.europcar.es, 968 335546Goldcar, www.goldcar.es, 918 344064

OK Rent-a-Car, www.okrentacar.es, 902 360636

Flamenca Cars, www.flamencacars.com, 661 086403

You can also use a rental search engine like Rental Cars, www.rentalcars.com

The main rental companies operating in the EU: Avis, Europcar (Goldcar), Hertz, Sixt and Enterprise, have signed an agreement to provide clearer and more transparent tariffs. This was due to pressure from consumer organisations caused by an increasing number of complaints, and as petitioned by the European Commission. It's highly recommended that you buy extra trip or annual car hire insurance for your own peace of mind.

Trains

Waiting for Murcia's long-awaited improved rail link with Madrid to go into service evokes memories of jokes about waiting for British Rail. There are currently 13 trains a day linking the cities and journeys take around 4 hours. The government also plans to link the city up to the high speed national rail network, AVE trains (locally called 'patos') ensuring trips from Murcia to Madrid will be reduced from 4 hours to just 2.5 hours. This is a project that has been talked about for years but work finally got underway in 2019 and should be running in 2020 (maybe!). The AVE trains run at up to 350km/h (200 mph) and are very similar to the 'bullet trains' running in France and Germany.

Unfortunately for those nearer Cartagena, you shouldn't get your hopes up of getting an AVE train to Madrid any time soon. You can check timetables and book RENFE tickets on the Internet at www.renfe.es (there's an English version there, too). If you can plan ahead, there are discounted fares available (some special Internet-only) which really do knock the prices down, albeit with some restrictions on changes and refunds. Prices are refreshingly reasonable compared to the shocking standard prices in the UK.

It is possible to get train access to the southern Mar Menor coast with the line that trundles between Cartagena and Los Nietos (on the Mar Menor near Los Alcázares), www.renfe.es.

Buses

Buses in Murcia make up for the lack of train connections around the region. From Murcia's main bus station (see the Murcia town section for details), you can get buses to just about anywhere in the country. For example, if you wanted to go to Málaga by train, you would have to go almost all the way into Madrid and then back down south to the coast. In contrast there are buses from Murcia going straight there. The long–distance coaches are good value, for example a return ticket from Murcia to Madrid is €43.

Most long distance routes are serviced by the ALSA bus company: www.alsa.es. For buses around the region, you can try Latbus 968 250088 and www.latbus.com.

However, the services between outlying towns could hardly be called frequent. For example, there are only 3 buses a day during the week from Fuente Álamo into Murcia and none on Sunday. If you do ever see such a bus, the journey would only cost you €2.20.

Taquilla Tickets run coach excursions all around the region at reasonable prices. www.taquillatickets.com/

Taxis

For getting around within a city such as Murcia or Cartagena, assuming you don't want to walk, a taxi can be a reasonable option. You want to look for taxis from a taxi rank or one that you have phoned in advance, see individual town entries in this book for specifics.

Taxis are certainly very reasonably priced per kilometre, but as soon as you start getting out of the city, then the kilometres start to mount. There are plenty of travellers who have bagged a bargain basement flight to Murcia and then caught a cab into town only to find that it would probably have been cheaper to hire a car for the weekend.

Climate

You can enjoy the coast practically year-round in Murcia, from the Easter holidays and well into autumn. There are a great variety of water activities, from sailing to windsurfing to water-skiing, scuba diving and kayaking. The average temperature during the year ranges from 11°C in winter to 25°C in summer. The climate is dry, hot in summer and mild in winter. Murcia receives the most sunshine per year in Spain.

The region of Murcia has the typical Mediterranean semi-arid subtropical climate: namely an average annual temperature of 18°C, with hot summers (registering peak temperatures of 40°C) and mild winters (though you still might see some snow higher up) with an average temperature of 11°C in the winter months of December and January.

There are between 120–150 days per year with clear skies and 2,800 hours of sun. Rain is scarce throughout the region (approx. 300–350 mm/year), falling mainly in the spring (April) and autumn (October), leaving the summer wonderfully dry. However, due to geography, the temperature differences between the coast and the interior are much more extreme in the winter. On the coast temperatures tend never to fall below 10°C, while inland at higher altitudes (in the Sierra Espuña for example) they may not exceed 6°C. Areas at higher altitude also show a higher average annual rainfall, which reaches 600 mm/yr.

Fiestas

The Murcian enthusiasm for Fiestas rivals the Madrileños (Madrid inhabitants). Each town or village has its own Patrimonio day, which you can find by looking on a calendar. You can read through the town guides to find specific fiestas but below are some of the more well-known ones of the region. www.fiestasdemurcia.es

January

- Los Reyes, the Three Wise Men, on 6th January the Spanish children receive their Christmas gifts. Most towns and villages will do something special in social clubs and town squares. Murcia and Cartagena have extra special fiestas. Look out for the televised celebrations of Madrid with massive floats, and the three kings parading through the city.
- Carnaval de Águilas in Águilas.
- Fiestas de San Sebastián in Ricote.

February

- Carnaval in Cabezo de Torres, Cartagena, Mar Menor, San Pedro del Pinatar, San Javier and Los Alcázares.

- San Blas de San Javier Romería in San Javier.

March

- Semana Santa, Easter Week (sometimes in April, check your dates), being a mainly Catholic country, Easter is a huge celebration. All towns and villages will hold celebrations, with at least 3 or 4 working days lost. Some of the best festivities can be found in Cartagena, Jumilla, Lorca, Murcia and Moratalla.

April

- Fiesta de la Primavera (Spring festival) in Murcia includes: Bando de la Huerta (Orchard procession) and Entierra de la Sardina (Burial of the Sardine).
- Certamen Internacional de Tunas Costa Cálida is an international music festival. Running since 1988, tunas (student music groups) gather from all over the world to perform. There are many night performances and street concerts to attend. Usually takes place at the end of April.

ONLY VISITING ONCE? Then make sure you come for Spring Festival. The flights will be cheaper (after Easter holidays), the weather should be great (not too hot, plenty of sunshine) and the partying is not to be missed. The floats, costumes, excitement and general friendliness in the city, will ensure you have a great time. Park on the outskirts of the city, walk in along the river and enjoy Murcia doing its thing!

May

- Santísima y Vera Cruz in Caravaca de la Cruz.

June

- Jazz Festival in San Javier, www.jazz.sanjavier.es
- Fería Sevillana at the Mar Menor.
- San Juan in all towns and villages.

July

- Jazz Festival in San Javier and Mar de Músicas in Cartagena.
- Virgen Del Carmen in Cartagena.
- Santiago Apostle in Cartagena.

August

- San Gínes de la Jara Procession in San Gínes.
- Festival of International Theatre, Music and Dance in San Javier.
- Mar Menor Folk Festival in San Pedro del Pinatar and Lo Pagán.
- Fiesta de la Vendímia in Jumilla with a wine fountain to celebrate the wine harvest.

September

- Murcia September Fair with the Moors & Christians in Murcia city.
- Mediterranean Folklore Festival in Murcia.
- Romans and Carthaginians in Cartagena.
- Rice Festival, celebrating the harvest of the rice, the usual partying and bull fights in Calasparra.

October

- Regional Horse Fair in Caravaca de la Cruz.

November

- Romería de San Clemente in Lorca.
- Jazz festival in Cartagena, www.jazz.cartagena.es

December

- Fiestas Mayores in San Javier
- Tours of the Nativities (Belenes) in Yecla.

Exact dates cannot be given for many of the above fiestas due to ever changing dates. If you want to plan your holiday/trip at fiesta time then contact the Murcia tourist office for exact dates. Murcia Tourist Office, www.turismodemurcia.es/en 968 799694.

Going Native: Magenta Slipperz Entertains The Crowds

My name is Hartley, I'm originally from Letchworth (the world's first) Garden City. My wife Jackie and I moved to Puerto de Mazarrón because we love the beautiful coastline, the mountainous backdrop and how it's still so underdeveloped and very Spanish.

We love the laid back lifestyle and the low cost of living. History is all around us and can be found in great little museums in almost every town and village. Driving out to Puntas de Calnegre is one of our pleasures. It has remote beaches and wonderful bars and restaurants within 5 metres of the sea. There's a great Chiringuito at Bahia Beach, Puerto de Mazarrón, which is a perfect spot in the summer for a coffee or a *caña* (beer) and some great views. We are thoroughly enjoying exploring the beautiful Murcia Region, learning and using our newly acquired Spanish language and meeting lots of new people.

I encourage people thinking of moving here to pause for a moment. What you think your needs are from a property and a location can change substantially over a year. Our advice would be to look around extensively and then to rent before you buy.

We are looking forward to discovering the many fiestas and events that happen throughout the year. My plan is to continue to establish my singing act. I am an entertainer, performing as my persona Magenta Slipperz. I've spent the last two years getting her out and about as much as I can. I've performed over 200 gigs in my first two years. It's been a challenge as after many years performing in the UK, it's a bit like starting again. As a drag performer I don't fit your stereotypical bawdy comedy show. I'm more of your family friendly sing along, dance along Danny La Rue type of drag performer.

You can find all my details by searching Hartley Hartley Music on Facebook. There you'll find lots of pictures and videos and over 100 independent recommendations. You can contact me via the page or via WhatsApp. I'm available for fiestas, bars, restaurants, social groups, private parties, product launches, beer festivals, Octoberfests etc.

Hartley: facebook.com/hartleyhartleymusic/

How To Fiesta

Fiestas are serious business in Murcia. It's important that you know when your local fiesta (fiesta patronal) is, check in your local teleclub or bar. Preparations start weeks in advance (depending upon the scale of the celebrations intended) with roles assigned for many of the villagers.

Usually the festivities are spread over a week or even more, with a program of activities planned. In many bars you'll find a guide to these activities along with lots of adverts from local traders.

For larger fiestas the lights will go up in the streets a few weeks ahead and often a marquee will be erected in the town square. Sometimes there will be competitions, football, sport, fruit and vegetable growing and of course, the paella cooking.

A BAD DAY FOR PIGS: November 11th is the traditional day to kill pigs for the winter and make sausages. You are only legally allowed to do this if you have a permit, but few people observe this 'law'.

Never expect evening festivities to begin much before 10pm or finish much earlier than 6am.

On top of the local fiestas there are national holidays, which include Día

Del Año Nuevo, 1st January, Reyes Day on the 6th January, San José on 19th March, Easter in March/April, Trabajador on May 1st, Corpus Christi May/June, Santiago there is 25th July, Asunción 15th August, National Day on 12th October, Constitution Day on 6th December, Inmaculada Concepción 8th December and Navidad on the 25th December.

Be prepared to take many days off for fiestas throughout the year. Shops close, people party, everyone gets merry. Don't stress about it. Hey, that's why you're here!

INVITADO: Once you are truly accepted in your little patch in Spain, there may be times when you go to the till to pay your tab and find someone has beaten you to it! This custom is known as invitar, and you will find that the barman will say, you have been invitado, nodding towards the smiling benefactor at the other side of the room. Doing an invitado first can be a bit of a challenge and requires a game of stealth to be played for the rest of your lifetime in that neighbourhood.

Activities

One of the best sites we've found to help you locate sporting activities all over Spain, including Murcia, is www.yumping.com, you can search for whatever crazy sport you're interested in and contact the companies directly.

The tourist offices in the towns, in Murcia city or on the Internet can provide more information about the many sporting activities in the region, including hiking, walking, cycling, riding, wind surfing, water skiing, scuba diving, bird watching or golfing. We outline some of the more popular ones below. For sports equipment in general, you can try the El Corte Inglés department store (Murcia and Cartagena) and any of the viral Decathlon sports supermarkets that have opened up all over the region (Cartagena, Murcia, Alcantarilla, Dos Mares). These two shops combined provide supplies for just about everything from shooting to scuba, but, as always, specialist shops will offer more choice.

Special Report: Football

It's been a while since top flight Spanish football was last seen in the region of Murcia. When Real Murcia were relegated back in 2008, few would have predicted that ten years later, no Murcian side would have graced the higher reaches of La Liga again. The 2018/19 season saw the region without even a representative in the second tier. For football fans visiting the region, that means there are a lot of games and frequent derbies. Don't think there is a lack of passion though, as even semi-professional teams in the third and fourth tiers have a loyal fan base and it's good fun to join in. Games begin towards the end of August at all levels and the regular season is usually over by the end of May with the play-offs limping on well into June.

Without a doubt the region's biggest team is Real Murcia, who play in red. Their home is the spectacular 31,000 seater Nuevo Condomina stadium just off the A7 motorway close to the shopping centre of the same name.

UCAM, owned by Murcia's Catholic University, play in dark blue. Their ground, *La Condomina*, is located in the centre of Murcia city very close to the bullring.

Cartagena, who play in black and white stripes, have frequently frustrated their fans by failing to win the *Segunda B* play-offs in almost every year since their relegation from *Segunda* in 2012. Their *Cartagonove* stadium can be found just outside the city's centre. Fans feel that their day is coming soon so they are definitely worth following closely.

Jumilla FC were a new club who worked their way up the league but following relegation from the third tier in 2019, they succumbed to their debts and the club sadly no longer exists after a mere 8 years in the league system.

If you are looking for a comprehensive list of Spanish football fixtures, they can be found at *soccerway.com*.

Women's football is alive and well in the region too. The region is currently without representation in La Liga Feminina but hopefully this will change one day. It can be hard to find information about local women's games but The Murica Football Federation do have the information lurking in the depths of their website but good luck finding it first time!

Russ Pearce

Rugby

Rugby is a new and developing sport in the Murcia region. The city's team XV Rugby Murcia, *https://xvrugby-murcia.es/*, are currently playing their first season (2019/20) in the Spanish league. They are well out of their depth in División Honor B but these are early days and they will surely continue to grow. Men's teams are also present in Cartagena and Lorca but playing at a much lower level. All three clubs also have women's teams who play regularly in regional tournaments.

Motor Sports

Cartagena has a motor sport circuit just outside the city. Circuito Cartagena, www.circuitocartagena.es/, host bikes, touring cars and classic car races from time to time.

Walking, Trekking & Hiking

With its large tracts of wilderness, mountains, coasts, cliffs and forests, Murcia offers unrivalled opportunities for treks, short half day walks or longer excursions.

There is an extensive network of long distance walks throughout Spain, with a number crossing into Murcia. These are called the senderos de Gran Recorrido (GRs). We have the GR7 all the way from Andorra, as well as many shorter footpaths called the senderos de Pequeño Recorrido (PRs).

The best books, covering the whole of the region are a range from Natursport, www.natursport.com, which can be bought online or from Murcia city (see the city guide pages for the local bookshop). Their publications include walking and cycling routes along the River Segura, into the Sierra Espuña and along the miles of coast. For hiking boots and equipment sold by somebody who actually uses the kit they sell, try SUR, Calle Vara de Rey 5, Murcia 968 220848, good prices and selection.

The Federación de Orientación de la Región de Murcia www.form–orientacion.com organises orienteering in the region.

If you want a walking tour of the city of Murcia or to visit the mines in La Unión try www.alide-interpretes.com 666 839333 or www.aldabacongresos.com 968 219099.

Going Native: Bob Walks For Charity – Join Him!

My name is Bob Shoesmith, I came to Spain in 2005 and lived on Camposol, Mazarrón. I recently moved to Bolnuevo. I had two very different and successful careers in the UK. I worked for 21 years in the Information Technology arena, then decided to take a break from work and travelled the world for 16 months with my wife Kathy. During the trip I became a Scuba Divemaster and renewed my love of photography. I returned to the UK, worked with Essex Police, where I was awarded two Chief Constables commendations and Officer of the Year award for my work in Crime Reduction.

In Murcia I did quite a few different jobs - villa management, pool cleaner and local mountain guide before wanderlust hit again. We spent a year in a motor home traveling through Spain, France, Italy and the UK. We then spent two summer seasons working on a campsite in Catalunia, that was a lot of fun. And we spent a year pet and house sitting along the East coast of Spain.

I love walking and probably average 100km a week. When I first arrived in Murcia very few walks were waymarked so I started mapping them myself, and then guiding others to see the sights. Every New Year's Day I go to the top of the Sierra Espuña at 1444 metres, it's become a bit of a ritual now.

I had conducted a few fund raising events in the UK, jumping out of planes etc., and a London to Shoeburyness 50 mile walk raising money for Mulitple Scerosis. I started raising money for MABS (see the charity section for contact details) cancer charity and in 2017 raised 1685 euros by walking the second circuit of 4kms backwards in the Race for Life event (this is the highest amount raised by one person in a single event).

I've also raised money for Noah's Arc, and more recently for Friends of Mazarron Animals. I honestly don't know the exact amount I've raised but it's in excess of 15,000 euros. I've raised thousands by doing guided tours of the Mazarrón mines, the Sierra Espuña, Carrascoy, the Mazarrón Guns and coastal walks. If you want to join me on a walk, have a great day out and raise money for charity get in touch on facebook: www.facebook.com/bob.shoesmith

I setup and ran the Camposol security group for a number of years. I love hot food and Indian cooking and I've made gallons of Chilli sauce (The Dogs Bollocks) and sold it for charity. I also cheffed a couple of nights in a restaurant in the port cooking an Indian meal.

I love taking photographs and making videos of the local area. Have a look on my YouTube channel www.youtube.com/channel/UciioOgU8FJEy4jdb-blsJxRA or my Instagram page www.instagram.com/bobshoesmith/

Segways

Of course, if you prefer a more relaxed way of getting around then you can hire a Segway. The website has a number of routes in the area: including Cabo de Palos, Fuensanta (Murcia), Calblanque and the mines of La Unión. www.consegway.es or www.natouralsegway.com, 659 255176 or 655 449876

Horse Riding

Horses are a major part of life in Murcia, though you're more likely to find your neighbour riding a mule or donkey than a pure breed Spanish horse. Safety is taken quite seriously, especially for youngsters, hats are compulsory and safety jackets often available.

La Manga, El Rancho de la Fuente, La Manga Club has its own Equestrian Centre. The Centre offers riding lessons for all standards. More accomplished riders can trek through the local foothills of the Calblanque or along the beach coves of Cala Reona. A one hour climb of the La Fuente hills to the summit will reveal splendid views of the Mediterranean and the Mar Menor, 968 137239.

Club Hípico Maipe, Carretera la Palma km 2, 5 Cartagena. Have indoor and outdoor schools, and plenty of stables.

Picadero Pascualón, Moratalla, towards Camping de la Puerta, 968 706078 or 616 142638.

Los Belones, Cuadras el Puntal, Campo del Golf, 636 067218.

Hípica de Shelly, El Palmar, Murcia, www.hipicadeshelly.com, 666 676147, caters for plenty of youngsters as it sits right next to a private school.

Complejo Aros, Altoreal, La Alcayna-Murcia, www.facebook.com/ClubAros/ or http://clubaros.es/, 968 292942. This is the most expensive and one of the newest horse riding clubs in the region. They have superb facilities and host regular competitions for dressage and show jumping.

Club Hípico de Murcia, Torre Guil, Near Murcia, www.facebook.com/Club-Hipico-de-Murcia-878365352218472, 968 868136 (also known as Carrascoy Riding club) have a large centre with plenty of outdoor areans for riding and good local hacks.

For more information have a look at the Federación Hípica for Murcia, www.fhmurcia.es or the Spanish online magazine, www.ecuestreonline.com.

Cycling

Spain is well known for producing some of the best cyclists in Europe and if you go out on the Murcian roads on any Sunday morning, you will see why. Cycling is a very popular sport, in groups as well as individually. If you are interested in joining a club you can get in touch with the Murcia branch of the Federación de Ciclismo on 968 302846, https://www.murciaciclismo.com/.

Debbie Jenkins, Russ Pearce

Location Report: Athletics Tracks & Sports Facilities

As a committed (some would say obsessive) competitive athlete, it is important to me to find good training opportunities and facilities wherever I am.

I am located in El Mojón, just outside San Pedro del Pinatar, and I have an abundance of cycle paths and relatively quiet roads at my disposal, as well as several kilometres of usually clear and flat sandy beach.

Less than 3km away from me (by cycle path) is the athletics track at Pilar de la Horada (not strictly in Murcia, as it's just across the border into Alicante province), which can be used from 8 a.m. to 10p.m. free, most days except fiestas. There is rarely anyone else on the track, but sometimes there is football training going on on the infield, so you have to keep an eye out for errant balls. There is an indoor swimming pool on the site, also climbing walls, pádel and tennis courts, a big indoor sports hall, studios for classes, a Bolas de Cartagena pitch, and a chiringuito. I belong to an athletics club in Torrevieja, about 20km away, where similar facilities are available.

The nearest athletics track to me in the Murcia region is at San Javier. Again, the track sits amidst a plethora of other sports facilities and is free to use. I once encountered members of the B wheelchair athletics team training there, and every afternoon there is a group of physically or educationally disabled young people being coached there, as well as members of the local athletics club.

Having access to these amazing facilities (and I haven't mentioned that there is a huge sport facility in San Pedro del Pinatar too, but it doesn't have a track) is just so different from where I lived in England, where track facilities were few and far between and very expensive to use.

It is also impressive how many people you see out here just walking, jogging, or running around the paths – maybe that's why you never find a crowded track, as the emphasis for the majority is on fitness and health, rather than competition.

About 5 minutes easy walk from my house is Pinatar Arena, a football training centre which also has a gym and spa facilities that members of the public can use. There is a range of membership packages available. I use the "Express" package, which gives me access to the gym, spa, and classes between 11 and 5 on weekdays and from 9-9 at weekends and on fiesta days, but there are also early and late options, and all day anytime memberships. There is a nice bar and restaurant there, and often the opportunity to watch matches between resident football teams on training camps, frequently national representative youth sides. http://pinatararena.com/

There is barely a weekend goes by without the opportunity to take part in a race of some sort. These are excellent value for money, nowhere near as expensive as races in England, and there is usually a T shirt (of specified size) for every participant and a goody bag with at least water and a cereal bar. Often there is free beer, Coca Cola and other goodies available at the finish too. Also, unlike in England, races, except for the really big city events, do not open their entries and get booked up months in advance; usually you can leave it until the Thursday evening before the event to put an entry in. A good source of information about races in the Murcia region is run by the Correbirras club. http://www.correbirras.com/Carreras_agenda.html

Although I usually like to use Spanish suppliers and services, I do need a sports physio with whom I am sure I can communicate my needs clearly. While I have had some excellent "emergency" treatment, notably at Pinatar Arena and the Virgen de la Caridad centre in San Pedro del Pinatar, I hadn't really settled myself with any one maintenance treatment person. Then I found Sheryl at Squirrel Yoga and Fitness based in the Las Velas CC in Los Narejos www.squirrellyoga.com. As well as offering excellent physio services (Sheryl and Sarah) they also offer a range of excellent classes, suitable for various abilities and largely conducted in English, though they try to accommodate Spanish class participants too.

Cath Duhig: https://www.facebook.com/cath.duhig

Gliding, Paragliding and Skydiving

Extreme aerial sports are very active in Murcia, especially paragliding. Get in touch with Federación Deportes Aéreos de la Región de Murcia: www.famur.org for details or phone 868 910796.

Shooting

The main target shooting club network in Spain is Real Federación Española de Tiro Olímpico, don't worry you don't need to be an Olympian to join, has its central branch just outside Murcia city, towards Molina de Segura. Annual membership is €150, plus a joining fee. This may seem rather steep, but consider that this does include insurance plus access to a number of ranges that provide for trap shooting, pistol and smallbore. Contact them at 968 430194.

There are also private clubs providing clay and target shooting facilities. Target (paper punching) is available for a €100 annual membership just outside Corvera on the road to Baños y Mendigo (run by Armería del Carmen in Murcia, 968 251152).

If you are interested in hunting, try the Federación de Caza de la Región de Murcia: www.federacioncaza.com. They can also help regarding the laws in Spain.

In practice, there are two ways to get a Spanish firearms licence. If you already had one elsewhere in Europe (e.g. in the UK), the easiest way to get your Spanish licence is to get your resident's permit (residencia) and take that along with your permit from the other EU country down to your nearest licensing department (intervención de armas) of the Guardía Civil. A few months later, if everything checks out OK, you should be able to pick up your Spanish equivalent permit. If you don't have a permit from another EU country you have to do some swotting in Spanish to be able to answer a multiple choice test which is picked from 400 questions that are helpfully posted, with answers, on the Guardía Civil web site.

For shooting provisions there are gunsmiths (armerías) in just about every major town, but the best we have found is in Murcia, Armería de Carmen, Calle Floridablanca, 24, 968 251152. They also have a small branch in Cartagena, Avenida de America, 8, 968 521857. www.armeri-adelcarmen.es

Go Karts

There are a number of go–kart tracks in the region. One of the best and most professional is in Bullas. Prices range from €6 for children for 10 minutes to €15 for a larger kart for adults for a 10 minute drive. Chicano–Kart, Paraje Cabeza Gorda, 699 907014. Also try the Complejo Rural, North of Los Almagros, €10 for 10 minutes for adults. A full list can be found at https://en.yumping.com/karting/murcia.

Probably the biggest is close to Cabo de Palos and you'll see it from the motorway (MU-312). They hold large events here during the year and have been around since 1970. www.lamangagokart.com, 968 563643

Scuba

Murcia is a great place to learn and explore scuba diving. The Mar Menor's shallow, calm and warm waters are great for beginners and the Mediterranean itself has loads of opportunities once you've got your certificate. The Federación de Actividades Subacuáticas de la Región de Murcia, www.fasrm.com, provides a central point of contact for most clubs in the region www.fasrm.com/quienes-somos/clubs/. Also, have a look at the PADI web site for accredited dive centres in Murcia: www.padi.com.

Around the whole Mar Menor region there are extensive beaches used for diving: el Mojón beach, Torre Derribada, La Llana, Las Salinas, Barraca Quemada and Punto de Algas, all in the Salinas Regional Park. The seabed offers a surprising range of attractive sands and the remains of Roman shipwrecks.

On the Med, all along the south coast there are Scuba clubs. Have a look on www.yumping.com for more details of all the clubs in the region, plus an easy contact form.

Águilas, Buceo Águilas, Calle Isaac Peral, 13, www.buceoaguilas.com, 968 493215 or 617 910973.

Águilas, Escuela de buceo ESTELA, Paseo de Parra, 38, www.escueladebuceo.com, 627 522233.

Cabo de Palos, Islas Hormigas Club, 968 145530, www.islashormigas.com.

Cabo de Palos, Planeta Azul, PADI Dive Centre, 968 564532, www.planeta-azul.com.

Cartagena, Carthago Diving, Muelle Alfonso XII, 640 113954, www.carthagodiving.com

La Azohía, Andrómeda, 968 150328.

La Azohía, Rivemar, www.rivemar.com, 968 150063.

La Manga, Mundo Activo, PADI Dive Centre, 968 337087

La Manga, Deep Impact Diving Center, PADI Dive Centre, 968 337 220

Puerto de Mazarrón, Zoea, Plaza del Mar, 20– PADI Dive Centre, 968 154006

Scuba Diving Villa de San Pedro, 676 745022, www.buceosanpedro.com

Scuba Diving Pinatar, 699 121523, www.caspinatar.com

Scuba Diving Turkana, 617 355636, www.turkana.org

For gear, there are scuba shops around in Puerto Mazarrón and La Manga. However, the best we have found is in Murcia, Armería de Carmen (yes, we know it's a gunsmith, they also sell fishing tackle!), Calle Floridablanca, 24, 968 251152. They also have a small branch in Cartagena, Avenida de America, 8, 968 521857. www.armeriadelcarmen.es

Watersports

Windsurfers will love La Mota beach, a completely natural course for speed, taking advantage of the wind without taking any risks. Throughout the year, early in the morning the Mar Menor is a mirror, where canoeing is a safe sport for any age.

Nautical Sports Clubs San Pedro, 968 186969, https://clubnauticolopagan.es/

La Manga, Manga Surf, 968 145331, www.mangasurf.com

Fishing

For local fishing clubs, contacts and legislation, get in touch with the Federación de Pesca y Casting, 968 221012, www.fepyc.es

Again we have to mention Armería de Carmen (not only the best gunsmith and scuba gear, but also the best fishing tackle), Calle Floridablanca, 24, 968 251152. They also have a small branch in Cartagena, Avenida de America, 8, 968 521857.

Sailing

Murcia offers a good variety of sailing, with the shallow Mar Menor being great for beginners and the Mediterranean itself for the more experienced sailor. Sailing as a sport in Murcia comes under the umbrella of the Federación de Vela de la Región de Murcia: www.fvrm.es

Águilas, Club Náutico de Águilas. Paseo de la Parra, 44, 968 411951, www.cnaguilas.com

Cartagena, Club Náutico, Puerto Marítima, 968 133355, www.rcrct.net

Club Nautico Islas Menores, Cartagena, Paseo Maritimo, 968 133 344, www.clubnauticoislasmenores.com/

La Manga, Manga Surf, 968 145331, www.mangasurf.com

Mazarrón, Club de Regatas de Mazarrón, Calle Cabezo de Cebada, 968 594011, www.serconet.com/usr/chicoyij

Santiago de la Ribera, Club de Regatas Santiago de la Ribera, Paseo de Colón, 968 570250

Lo Pagán, Club Náutico Lo Pagán, 968 186969, www.clubNáuticolopagan.com

Los Nietos, Club Náutico Los Nietos, 968 133300, www.cnlosnietos.com

If you want someone else to organise your children for you then get in touch with Arbolar, Cartagena, www.arbolar.com, 968 521400. They offer sailing training programs for 6 to 17 year olds in Los Urrutias on the Mar Menor. It's a ten day camp for kids while you enjoy your golf!

If you prefer to be skippered around and to just enjoy the views then try one of the many tour boats. A good value company is Solaz, solazlines.com, based in Club Dos Mares (La Manga), 606 806 795. They run two lines, one from the quay at El Pedruchillo Promenade (La Manga), km 8, exits 80-82-83 (near the bus stop at the promenade) and also from Mazarrón, Puerto Deportivo de Mazarrón on Plaza del Muelle.

Through the summer months they have scheduled trips from both these ports taking in any of the following destinations Isla Grosa, the La Manga strip, the five Islands of the Mar Menor, Bolnuevo, Isla Cueva de Lobos, Cala Cerrada, Cala Abierto or El Arco, depending on the boat and departure time. The prices range from €8 for a 1 hour ride for the scheduled departures. You can of course hire them yourself for a private trip. One of their boats has a glass bottomed viewing area. They have refreshments onboard!

If you fancy trying your hand at Chinese-style Dragon Boat racing, Club Nautica Santa Lucia in Cartagena do this as well as conventional sailing. Dársena de Pescadores, 968 43 60 06, http://cnsantalucia.es/dragon-boat/

Golf

Unless you have been living in a cave for the past few years, you are probably aware that Murcia is a golf mecca, in fact, even most troglodytes and hermits are fully aware of this, too. The local federation is: www.fgolfmurcia.com

A great golf guy who can book your game and get excellent green fees is Mike Probert. He has written a book, The Golfing Guide To Murcia, which will give you loads of details on each course. You can find Mike at: www.costa-blanca-greenfees.com

Club de Golf Altorreal, Avenida Del Golf, Urbanisation Altorreal, Molina de Segura, 968 648144, www.golfaltorreal.es

Close to the town of Molina de Segura, this 18 hole championship course was designed by Dave Thomas and opened in 1994. Although this course in not located close to the beach resorts favoured by many tourists, recent commercial developments such as Thader, Nuevo Condomina and IKEA (see shopping section) are within a few kilometres, meaning that non-golfers can be fully occupied while doing some serious damage to the credit card. Alternatively the historic City of Murcia is within a short driving distance.

Condado del Alhama Golf Resort is part of the GNK Golf family of courses, Condado de Alhama, 968 157 236, http://www.gnkgolf.com/campos/alhama

El Valle Golf Resort, Autovía Murcia, San Javier km 4, Baños y Mendigo,

968 033 002, http://www.gnkgolf.com/campos/elvalle

El Valle Golf Resort is another GNK course, located in a natural park area situated near to the Sierra Carrascoy mountains and was the third course opened of the nine courses planned for the Jack Nicklaus trail which follows the 'corridor of golf' along the C-3319 Murcia to San Javier highway. It's an 18 hole course.

Hacienda Riquelme Golf Resort, Los Riquelme, https://haciendariquelmegolfresort.com/

The Hacienda Riquelme Golf Resort was opened to the public in May 2008 and is located in the area adjacent to Peraleja Golf and is approximately 15 minutes drive from the C-3319 Murcia-San Javier highway, near the small village of Avileses and the town of Sucina. It is also a GNK course.

Hacienda Del Álamo Golf Resort, Avenida Hacienda Del Álamo, 10-12, Fuente Álamo, 968 157 236, http://haciendadelalamogolfresort.es/

Close to Fuente Álamo in the centre of the region of Murcia with views of numerous fruit, almond and olive plantations but still less than a half hour drive from the City of Murcia and the nearest airport which is located at Corvera. The golf course was designed by Dave Thomas and at 6,724 metres (7,400 yards) is claimed to be the longest golf course in Spain and currently boasts Ryder Cup player, Miguel Ángel Jiménez as their golf ambassador. There's also a golf academy.

La Manga Club, Los Belones, Cartagena, 968 175000, www.lamangaclub.com

The world famous La Manga Golf Resort was originally created by American Gregory Peters as a 9 hole complex on only 500 acres in February 1971. It has since been expanded to the current 1400 acres with 3000 palm trees. The resort has consistently been voted as one of the leading golf resorts in Europe. To highlight the profile of the resort in the 1980's the great Severiano Ballesteros was their touring professional.

The resort has three excellent courses with the North, South and West plus a par 47 pitch and putt course and superb practice facilities.

La Serena Golf, Avenida Principe Felipe, Urbanisation Torre del Rame, Los Alcázares, 968 575576, www.laserenagolf.es

The La Serena Beach and Golf Resort is located close to Los Alcázares. The new airport at Corvera is only 30 minutes away and it is a relatively short drive to major cities such as Murcia and Cartagena. The main feature of the course is the 500 year old Torre del Rame, which was originally built as a watch tower for pirates from North Africa.

La Torre Golf Resort, Roldán, 968 03 19 70, www.latorregolfresort.com/

The La Torre golf resort is located close to the town of Roldán and is one of the Polaris World Nicklaus Trail of golf courses and is situated on the C-3319 San Javier to Murcia. The course is unique in that it is only a par 68. The resort is now well established with an excellent clubhouse and practice facilities plus bars, restaurants, shops, supermarket, beauty salon, gymnasium, tennis courts and swimming pools. In December 2008 the 5 star hotel, spa and convention centre opened.

Caleia Mar Menor Golf Resort, Las Conquetas, Torre Pacheco, 968 041 840, www.caleiamarmenorspahotel.com/

This golf resort is located only 30 minutes drive from Corvera airport and the beaches of the Mar Menor and close to the small town of Torre Pacheco on land that was previously a fruit orchard. It includes a nine hole golf course that was designed by Dave Thomas.

Peraleja Golf, Finca la Peraleja, Carretera Avileses-Sucina, 968 60 75 75, www.peralejagolf.com

Located near to the town of Sucina and not far away from the C-3319 San Javier-Murcia highway the course, designed by Severiano Ballesteros, has good transport links and is close to Murcia airport.

Roda Golf, Carretera F-27 de San Cayetano a Los Narejos, Roda, 968 173093, www.rodagolfcourse.com It was designed by Dave Thomas of The Belfry fame.

Camposol Club de Golf, Carretera Mazarrón-Alhama, km9, Mazarrón, 968 97 88 86, https://camposolclub-degolf.com/

This golf course opened in the summer of 2002 as a 9 hole layout which has subsequently been extend to the current 18 hole layout. It bills itself as one of the most affordable golf course in Spain. The Camposol Urbanisation on which the golf course is situated is very British in many ways and comprises a 4 star hotel, banks, shops and restaurants and is only a relatively short drive from the town of Puerto de Mazarrón which has some wonderful beaches.

Terrazas de la Torre Golf Resort, This 18 hole golf course is yet another of the Polaris World Nicklaus Trail golf courses and is located close to the town of Balsicas and not too far away from the sister course of La Torre.

Club de Golf Torre Pacheco, Escuela de Golf Municipal, Calle Gregory Peters 1, Torre Pacheco, 968 585111, http://web.golftorrepacheco.es/

This course is a 9 hole pitch and putt course which is located in the town of Torre Pacheco. You can play golf at night due to the use of floodlighting. The municipal Escuela de Golf based here is very active particularly with local children.

Lorca Golf Club is an 18-hole complex co-designed by Dave Thomas and Jorge Soler and is situated close to the historic town of Lorca. 968 11 35 35, www.lorcaresort.com/

New Sierra Golf Club is an 18 hole, par 72 course situated close to the town of Balsicas which is positioned just off the C-3319 San Javier-Murcia highway. 635 06 92 43, www.newsierragolf.com/

Health & Beauty

Mud is famous for its beauty and curative qualities. The muds of Las Charcas and Lo Pagán are particularly good due to the high salination of the waters of the Mar Menor. When the mud is applied to the skin it is reputed to have a great therapeutic value for all types of ailments, including: rheumatism, arthritis, gout, skin disorders and bone fractures.

Thalassotherapy Centres

Spa Aguas Salinas, Crucero Baleares, 2, Playa de Villanietos, San Pedro del Pinatar, 968 184136, www.aguassalinas.com

Thalassotherapy Barceló Lodomar, Calle Río Bidasoa,1, Las Charcas, San Pedro del Pinatar, 968 186802, www.barcelo.com

Thalasia, Avenida del Puerto, 327-329, San Pedro del Pinatar, 902 334330, www.thalasia.com

Entre Mares, Segunda Avenida, La Manga del Mar Menor, 902 258282, www.entremares.es

Balnearios

Balneario de Leana, Calle Balneario, Fortuna, 902 444410, www.leana.es

Balneario de Archena, Carretera Del Balneario, Archena, 902 333222, www.balneariodearchena.com

Spas

Hotel Mangalan, Gran Vía, km7, La Manga del Mar Menor Murcia, 968 337000, www.hotelmangalan.com

La Manga Club, La Manga Club, 968 331234, www.lamangaclub.com

Intercontinental Spa & Golf Resort, Torre Pacheco, 968 041822, www.intercontinental.com/marmenor

Hotel Don Juan, Avenida Puerto Deportivo, 1, Playa de Poniente, Águilas, 968 493493, www.hoteldonjuan.es

Location Report: Spas, Balneariums, Thalassotherapy And The Mar Menor Mud

Balneariums, Thermal Mineral Spas or Thermal Baths are spas with thermal mineral springs that have been declared of benefit to the public, medical services and appropriate facilities for carrying out prescribed treatments. Thermal baths facilitate the absorption of some of the mineralizing elements from the water by the skin and their subsequent integration by the various parts of the body.

Thermal waters are not just preventative; they also have curative properties. They are highly recommended for trauma, rheumatic and respiratory complaints.

Bathing or taking a treatment using thermal mineral spring water infuses the body with mineral salts and provides a pleasant sense of relaxation and well-being that extends throughout the entire body, with a knock-on effect on the state of mind.

The Region's hot springs produce water at a temperature of roughly 50° C.

Thalassotherapy comes from the Greek Thalasso meaning sea water and Terapeia meaning healing, in Spanish Thalassoterapia. Sea water contains over 80 essential elements for the body and a particular concentration of calcium ion, magnesium, sodium, silicon, iodine and other trace elements. The therapeutic effects of sea-water are produced in a variety of ways: via contact with the skin, via direct contact with the mucous membranes or via inhalation through the dynamic action of waves.

Saturated with micro-droplets of sea-water in suspension, sea air is rich in iodine and negativeions, which give it antibiotic properties, have a calmative effect on the nervous system and stimulate the body's defences.

Sea water is rich in oligoelements: chloride, sodium, sulphates, magnesium, calcium, potassium that are absorbed through the skin into the body (transmineralization).

The therapeutic properties of mud have been known since Hippocrates (460-337 BC) suggested its use in treatment due to the benefits of essential mineral ions to your health.

The particular climatic conditions of the Mar Menor with a high percentage of hours of sunshine a year and a high salinity have resulted in the extreme north of the lagoon in the area known as La Puntica becoming famous for its mud. The mud has a high percentage of cations, calcium, magnesium, potassium and fluoride, as well as anions, chloride and sulphate.

The mud is found in abundance at a number of beaches along the Mar Menor. So, why should you cover yourself in mud and bake in the hot sun? Well the mud has all those positive and negative ions, which combine with extraordinarily fine sand to create a unique mud that has healing properties.

For a DIY mud bath the best thing to do is follow anyone with a trowel and see where they get their mud from. Dig yourself a handful, you won't need much it goes a long way, and slather yourself with it. Bake for 20 minutes and rinse!

For a more luxurious experience visit one of the many specialist centres in the region and indulge. To find out more about the health benefits visit: www.turismurciasalud.com

Fitness, Aerobics, Dance, Yoga & Pilates

Most towns will have a municipal building for sports activities where you will often find aerobics, dance, Pilates or yoga classes. Depending upon your town you might find that the average age at an aerobics class is closer to 65 than 25, but hey, it's all good fun.

You may also find gyms in town, which will have the usual power machines and plenty of free weights. Take a look at the golf courses for fitness rooms and look on noticeboards for dates of classes.

Towns closer to the coast or near tourist areas can probably enjoy more regular fitness classes often run by Brits. Take a look at the following.

Murcia Dance & Theatre, www.murciadance.co.tv, based near Mazarrón, offers all sorts of dance classes for children and adults. If you fancy a bit of ballet, street dance or the latest craze, zumba, then these guys can help you.

If zumba is your thing then there's a dedicated dance company, www.zumbamurcia.com, who hold classes in many tourist towns for example Los Alcázares, La Torre Golf and Santiago de la Ribera.

For Pilates there are a number of places to try, Pilates Murcia, www.pilatesmurcia.es in the centre of

Murcia and Marqueta Pilates, www.marquetapilates.com, in Cartagena.

For yoga and Pilates (and mosaic making) then Tara Casa is an excellent choice, www.taracasa.com. She holds regular classes and also special offers, for example a mother and daughter event and pamper days.

Location Report, Geocaching: What To Do When It's Too Cold To Go To The Beach

Murcia has 320 days of sunshine a year. Right now, as I write this, it's snowing here (in January 2020), only half an hour away from the Mar Menor. So, whilst Murcia's weather is usually some of the best in Europe, there are times when going for a swim in the sea is definitely out.

Murcia is blessed with fantastic countryside and one of the best ways to get out to places, that you would otherwise only wonder about as you drive by on the motorway, is a new pursuit called geocaching. Geocaching came about when gadget freaks wanted an excuse to go out and buy the, then, newfangled latest gizmo, a handheld GPS receiver. On 1st May 2000, the U.S. government switched their satellites on to a new, higher accuracy service for civilians. What this meant was that those hand-held GPS gadgets could now place themselves on the earth to within a dozen metres or so of accuracy. Great. Now what? Nice for surveyors, great for shipping and aviation, but what's the hobbyist going to do with the gadget? Geocaching, that's what!

Geocaching is, basically, hiding things in interesting places around the globe and publishing your stash or 'cache' on a web site: www.geocaching.com. On this web site, which is free to browse and join up as a member (membership necessary to publish a cache), you can search for all caches near a town, near your home, in a country, etc. It's great fun for families, especially, since it gets everybody outdoors and it's educational too (mapping, nature, etc.).

Murcia has about 20 caches at the moment, and that number is rising quickly. They are mostly in places of great natural beauty, perhaps with sea views or really off the beaten track. There are caches near Cartagena, near Murcia, Mazarrón and even way off in the mountains on the Almería border.

So this is a really expensive hobby, right? Not really, the GPS receivers can now cost as little as a good pair of hiking boots. Of course, as with all gadgets, you can spend more (up to €500 for an all-singing, all-dancing, colour display model with built–in maps, electronic compass and barometric altimeter (gadget freaks can stop drooling now)). Garmin and Magellan are the makes to look for when shopping. The other things you will need are those that every sensible hiker owns anyway: good boots with ankle support, water bottles and a mobile phone in case of emergencies (and for snapping those all important selfies).

For each published cache there will be, at a minimum, coordinates of the cache that you can punch into the GPS receiver to use as your guide to the hidden treasure. There will usually be a general description of the area, what kind of things were originally stored in the cache and usually some clues on how to get to the cache, such as where to park and marked footpaths to follow. Often the cache listing includes a 'spoiler' which spells out exactly how to find the cache, but needs to be deciphered by hand so you don't spoil your fun unless you really want to give up looking.

Remember that the GPS receivers are great, but not perfect. You will get very close to the spot with the help of the gizmo, but the next fun part is grubbing around under rocks and around trees to find the cache itself, which is usually hidden away from prying eyes. When you get to the cache, you will often find a Tupperware or metal container (usually an old army–surplus ammo box), which is clearly marked as being a geocache. Inside you will find a log book where you can make a note of your visit (remember the pen?) and some knickknacks. The protocol is to swap knickknacks and take a photo of you on your visit. When you are done, seal up and hide the cache back as you found it. When you get back to the house, you can record your visit to the cache, describing your experience, giving some hints or tips for future visitors, and even upload that photo you took while you were there!

The Game of Caliche

The game of caliche is particular to the Murcia / Levante region of Spain, based on a nationally–played game called herrón. If you, as we did, look up caliche in the English–Spanish dictionary (after seeing it in the itinerary for the local fiesta), you might be confused or even horrified. Caliche (in our 4 inch thick Collins mega–dictionary) means saltpetre, or echar un caliche means something really quite surprising, and I'm not going to reproduce the translation here (we were getting prepared to watch from a distance!).

Caliche is a game rather like skittles in Britain. 'Rather' as in very loosely indeed. It is played on a flat surface (say, the road outside your local teleclub) that is 35m long and 6m wide. A wooden baton (called the caliche), 20cm long and 3cm diameter is placed 7m from the end of the field. A 2cm disk (moneda) is placed on top of the baton. The end of the field is blocked off with a stout table or similar, turned on its side to stop the moneo disks which you throw at the baton. A moneo is a weighty metal disk of 8cm diameter (could be square, too) and about 2mm thick.

The objective of the game is to throw the moneo at the caliche in such a way as the moneda and moneo end up as close as possible to each other (after displacing the moneo from the caliche.)

The game is usually played with two teams of two. Each game has 8 throws, 4 per team and 2 per player. For a throw to be considered valid, the moneda must end up closer to the moneo than the caliche. If the moneo ends up nearer the caliche, the throw was invalid and is called a 'ganga'.

A more usual way of playing is as individuals, with the goal being to use nine disks (moneos) to knock over the caliche as many times as possible. You will often find this game played at fiestas patronales. It can get quite competitive and is fun to watch.

A Selection of Beaches

The following beaches are amongst the most beautiful in the region:

1. Villa Nanitos, near the mud baths of San Pedro del Pinatar, with various sporting facilities such as wind surfing, volley ball, kayaking and waterskiing.
2. La Llana, long, sandy, blue flag beach, with foot showers during the main season. Mild water, with some waves in parts.
3. El Espejo, another blue flag, sandy beach on the Mar Menor with wind surfing, volley ball and kayaking. Calm waters.
4. Euromanga, typical beach of the La Manga stretch, sandy and pleasant with calm waters.
5. Los Nietos, 4km long grey, sandy beach with showers, lots of restaurants and calm waters.
6. A group of 3 beaches, Cala Medina / Las Melvas / Levante, small beaches, with slightly wavy water, ranging from sand to gravel to rock, great all round beaches. There are restaurant services and some good opportunities for snorkelling.
7. Cala de las Mulas, a nudist beach with fine sands and no services.
8. Cala Cortina, a calm sandy beach with toilets and showers, and a life guard service.
9. El Portús, a quiet, sandy beach with showers, difficult to reach.
10. El Belonte Grande and Salitrona, a pair of short, sandy beaches only accessible by boat or on foot.
11. La Calera and San Ginés, gravel and sand beaches with calm water and reasonable facilities such as showers in places and a few restaurants and shops.
12. El Rihuete and Puerto de Mazarrón, sandy beaches, with plenty of local shops and restaurants.
13. El Cabezo de la Pelea and Las Covaticas, sand and gravel beaches which are great for snorkelling. Some of the coves in this area are frequented by nudist bathers.
14. Baño de las Mujeres and El Ciscar, this pair of quiet, short beaches offer great fishing as well as swimming and snorkelling.
15. Abejerro and Las Pulgas, sand and gravel beaches, quiet, with no facilities.
16. Punta del Fraile, only accessible by foot, with good clear water for snorkelling.

The town guides have more details on other beaches in the area or take a look at Murcia Turismo web site (www.murciaturistica.es) for more details on every beach along the coast.

In 2019, 25 beaches were awarded the Blue Flag: Las Delicias, Levante, La Colonia, Poniente, Calarreona, Matalentisco, La Higuerica, La Carolina, La Casica Verde, Percheles, Rihuete, El Puerto, Bahía, Nares, Grande-Castellar, El Alamillo, El Mojón, Cala Cortina, Isla Plana, Levante in Cabo de Palos, San Ginés, Playa del Cuartel, Marina Salinas, Calnegre and La Ensenada del Esparto.

Town & City Guide

All cities will have the following shops and services. Many of the towns will have a selection and some of the villages will have a bakery! It's useful to know what you can expect to find in the local areas.

Ayuntamiento: The town hall in Spain is called the Ayuntamiento. While this is a bit of a tongue–twister, it's well worth learning since just about everything to do with officialdom revolves around your local ayuntamiento. From registering to vote (empadronar) which in turn enables you to register your car and ask Telefónica for a new telephone line, to making planning applications for a patio (yes, patios need planning permission in Spain), you will have to involve the ayuntamiento.

Fortunately, for many things, you can get a gestor (runner) to do the job for you, and this will save you a lot of time in queues and frustration trying to find the right department. Here is a directory with addresses and telephone numbers: www.infoayto.es.

Correos: The post office in Spain is called the Correos and has signs in bright yellow. The larger towns will have PO boxes (apartado de correos) for rent for around €70 a year which is useful for those who have a place out in the sticks where the postie on his/her little yellow Vespa fears to travel to. It should be pointed out that the Spanish postal system isn't as good as the UK (even these days, no, really!) and post even within the country often takes more than a week to arrive and frequently disappears. It's also quite expensive to send post outside of Spain.

Plaza Mayor: Almost every town has a central square, and it's almost invariably called Plaza Mayor, however, there are some curious exceptions where Plaza Mayor isn't actually the best–known square in the town (such as in Murcia itself). The most useful aspect of the Plaza Mayor is as a meeting place, e.g. to meet the builders or delivery drivers who don't know where your house is in the village. Also you will get some vans making weekly deliveries of bottled drinks and Repsol gas passing through the Plaza Mayor.

Teleclub: The town and village senior citizen's club (Salon de Mayores or Centro de Mayores) is sponsored by the Ayuntamiento and is often referred to as the 'teleclub' (on account of the clubs being one of the first places to have TV's in villages in days gone by). Some villages don't have any bar as such, but do have a teleclub. Sometimes they are rather hard to find (no garish neon signs) but there will always be one… somewhere. You don't really have to be a member to use the facilities, although it's very good form to enrol as a member of your local; it only costs a few Euros and you don't have to be a pensioner! You will find that village meals for Christmas, Easter and other fiestas will be held here, along with a healthy Sunday pre–lunch crowd, often eating caldo de albóndigas (meatballs in consommé, best with a dash of fino sherry into the bowl) from the pot.

Turismo: The tourist information offices (the 'i') in Spain are called the Oficina de Turismo, or simply el turismo. Their usefulness varies wildly from town to town, some handing out just one leaflet (after you have persuaded the council employee to stop chatting on their mobile for a minute) through to ones that will deluge you with information. At the very least you should be able to get a free town plan here. Don't expect the turismo to be open on Sunday, fiesta days or during siesta time.

Centro Médico: If you're lucky your local medical centre will be open 24 hours. Whilst they don't have doctors on hand during the night they do have trained nurses who can administer first aid or tell you to get to a hospital. These centres are often the local ambulance station too. Most will allow you to book a doctor's appointment online. The system is much the same as in the UK: make an appointment, turn up 10 minutes before your allotted time and wait 1 hour before being seen! The medical centres can usually do blood tests.

Farmacia / Parafarmacia: Don't be confused, one sells drugs the other sells tampons, cosmetics, nappies and handcream! It can be frustrating at first, but after a while it seems to make sense. Most generic drugs that you would pay for on prescription in the UK you can probably buy here for less than the prescription price. Bring your empty packet and save some cash. Farmacia's have the same opening times as most other shops, a morning shift followed by a lunch break and siesta, then the evening shift. There is a 24 hour farmacia rota in the local newspaper (La Verdad) if you need some paracetamol in the middle of the night! And of course if you need nappies the Parafarmacia can help.

Ferretería / Almacén: The ferretería sells your usual small hardware shop stuff, lightbulbs, kitchen pots and pans, flyscreens, antpowder, screws, nails, hammers, you get the idea. The almacén will sell you a tonne of sand, a couple of olive trees or 100 breeze blocks.

Where To Stay And Eat

Each town section includes some advice on where to stay and eat. The problem with a printed book is that things change and we can't keep up with the changes very easily. Always do your homework before booking and read what other people think about the place you want to stay! Restaurants change hands, the chef might move and what was great one week might be bad the next.

The prices for hotels are for one room with 2 people sharing unless otherwise stated. We have included three or four different places to stay at different price breaks in each town section. If you want to find more then take a look at:

www.expedia.com, www.tripadvisor.com, www.booking.com, www.destinia.com, www.trivago.com

These sites have regularly updated reviews on accommodation around the world. Take care of astroturfing, when people with a vested interest in a hotel post their own review, which of course is favourable. They're usually easy to spot, look for many reviews to have a better statistical chance of truthfulness.

We have included three or four restaurants for each town. These are almost always places we have tried ourselves with friends and family. There are some recommendations from other people mixed in here too (we have to think of our waist lines!) it's also worth having a look at the following websites; they have reviews from recent visitors.

www.buscorestaurantes.com, www.restaurantesmurcia.com, www.verema.com, www.murciagourmet.com, www.tripadvisor.com, www.thefork.com, www.foursquare.com

Take a look at http://www.Native-Spain.com for useful apps for your phone that will help you find food and drink in the region of Murcia. Also there's maps.google.com, you can type in your location and search for restaurants and hotels nearby, then click on the markers to see if there are any reviews.

Many of the cities (Murcia, Cartagena, Lorca, Águilas, Caravaca de la Cruz, Archena, Mula etc) and larger seaside towns have cafés that produce a café culture, offering opportunities to pose on a Friday and Saturday night. In the more rural areas, there will be one or two bars that are the hubs of social activity, where you will see any family member from time to time, though mostly the men!

Population data for each town is taken from www.ine.es (Instituto Nacional de Estadísticas) and is for 2017, the latest data available at the time of publication. Most towns have increased in size since the 2012 edition of this guide.

Maps for Águilas, Caravaca de la Cruz, Cartagena, Lorca, Moratalla and Murcia can be found at the end of the book. Map references for points of interest in those towns are provided within the text.

Águilas

Population: 34,750

Map Reference: 1.57°W, 37.40°N
This southwestern city near the Murcian coast has an arid and mountainous landscape, extensive beaches with crystalline cliffs and small, little-frequented coves.

The hill where the **Castillo de San Juan de Águilas** (Map: C4) is based (17th century) was a refuge to a population afraid of pirate attacks. Its dilapidated condition prevented access to the interior for many years, but it has recently been reformed and also has a small museum. It offers an excellent viewpoint of the town and the surrounding coast, making the steep walk worthwhile. Of course, in true Spanish style you can drive to the top too, though parking is limited.

The castle has its origins in Carthaginian times and went through a number of renovations over the centuries. Legend has it that there are underground tunnels connecting this castle with the Tébar fortress. The castle is open Tuesday to Sunday: 11:00 to 13:00 and from 18:00 to 21:00. Closed Mondays and for Christmas on December 25 and the 1 and 6 January. Entry is just €2.

There's the **Plaza de España**, a garden with a considerable variety of trees and plants, laid out in 1874. Two of the four ficus trees located in each corner of the square are over a hundred years old. They were imported from Brazil. Eight streets converge on this square and you can find the tourist information office very close to here.

In the centre of the square there's a fountain At the end of 1887 a small sculpture was placed in the middle representing a white swan with a reptile biting its neck, whose beak emitted a jet of crystalline water, piped from the Tébar and Chuecos springs. In time, and thanks to locals' idiosyncrasy, the small sculpture of the swan was transformed into a Pava (turkey), known from then on as La Pava de la Balsa.

In the square there's also the **Iglesia de San José** (19th century), in sober Neo-Classical style, combining grey and white stones inside.

There's the **Museo Arqueológico** in the centre of town. Created in 2000, the museum houses materials from prehistoric to the Islamic period, including collections of Roman debris removed from excavations in recent years documenting the Roman settlement of Águilas. Calle Conde de Aranda, 5.

The **Centro de Interpretación del Mar**, a few kilometres to the east of the centre, has a small permanent exhibition showcasing an aquarium with fish from the area and artefects related to the sea. Entry is free. Hours: Tuesday afternoon through Sunday and holidays: 10:00 to 13:00 and from 17:00 to 19:00. In July / August: Monday afternoon to Sunday and holidays from 10:00 to 13:00 and from 18:00 to 21:00 h. 968 493287. Av Dr Bernard, 413.

Visit the **Termas Romanas de Águilas**, the Roman baths. They opened in 2001 and are situated in the basement of the building located in the Calle King Carlos III. There are remains of Roman baths dating from the first century AD, in particular part of a caldarium (hot bath room). You can also see the preserved archaeological remains and the reconstruction of the spa building. Free entry, with limited opening hours, Monday: 17:00 to 20:00, Wednesday and Friday: 10:30 to 14:00 and 17:00 to 20:00, Closed holidays, but open in July and August: from 10:00 to 13:00 and from 18:00 to 21:00.

A stroll to the port, dominated by the lighthouse, leads to the wholesale fish market, where at 5pm there's a fish auction.

On a small hill overlooking the port is the recently restored **Molino de Sagrera**. The views from here are amazing and the visitor centre provides an insight into some of the town's agricultural history and its association with windmills. It can be visited on Saturdays and Sundays throughout the year from 11:00 to 14:00 (until 13:00 in July and August) and on Saturday afternoons from 16:00 to 18:00 (17:00 to 19:00 April to October and 18:00 to 21:00 in July and August). Weekday visits can be arranged by calling 670307818. http://www.infoturmolino.com On your way there be sure to look for the beautifully decorated stairways which from afar are like murals.

Águilas also boasts a **football museum** which enthusiasts of the game will enjoy. It houses a substantial collection of football memorabilia from around Spain including a replica of the European Cup won by Real Madrid. Their then president made a promise at the opening of the museum that next time they won the cup, the replica would be given to the museum. Many years later, he made good on his promise. https://www.facebook.com/Museo-del-Futbol-Aguile%C3%B1o-desde-1896-451898951575834/ Nearby is the football stadium which is, according to the museum, the oldest continually used stadium in Spain. That claim is hotly contested by Sporting Gijon in Asturias.

In February you can enjoy Carnaval, which has a Rio de Janeiro feel about it, with 3 days and nights of floats, processions and fancy dress. In March/April, there's the patron fiesta for Águilas, La Virgen de los Dolores and on 16th July a celebration for the sea patron, La Virgen del Carmen.

The first Sunday of the month hosts the local flea market on Plaza Alfonso Escámez, in Winter from 9:00 till 14:00 and Summer 17:00 a 22:00. You can find all sorts of interesting local items, haggle for good prices.

There's also the sports marina, Club Náutico de Águilas, where you can learn to sail, windsurf or canoe, www.cnaguilas.com, 968 411951.

If you want to dive, try Zoea Aguilas at Puerto Juan Montiel, 646 412795, www.zoeaaguilas.es

Visit **Rincón del Hornillo**, a lovely spot with its characteristic flight of wide mosaic-covered stairs, opposite the Hornillo beach. Its creator was Juan Martínez Casuco and work begun in 1985. Juan Casuco worked on both the design and the actual building till his death, laying the myriad pieces of tile and creating the wrought iron work, all of which overlook the Mediterranean. When visiting, look out for the shields of the towns of Águilas and Lorca, the silhouettes of the Castle, the Mill, etc. The wrought iron work on the main railings and the weather vane showing the profile of the artist himself are notable too. There's a bar run by his son which is open in the summer time.

If you travel on from the beach at Poniente, you reach a group of coves, Cuatro Calas. These are in a protected area and so are not only great places for quiet sunbathing but also good for walks.

Tranquil beaches with fine sand, huge cliffs and beautiful coves can be found at San Pedro, Blanca and Los Hierros. Los Hierros is dominated by the tower named **Torre De Cope**, which has been attacked on numerous occasions by pirates. Close by are the beach at Calabardina and the natural park of Calnegre–Cabo Cope.

Here's an overview of some of the 28km of beaches in Águilas:

- Playa de Levante: 400m, urban, family, high occupancy, calm waters, golden sand, parking, bus, toilet, showers, anchoring area, disabled access, Club Náutico de Águilas 1km.
- Playa Poniente: 600m, urban, family, high occupancy, mild waves, sand-gravel dark, parking, bus, toilet, showers, anchorage area, disabled access, close to Club Náutico de Águilas.

- Playa Calarreona: 270m, semi-urban, high occupancy, golden sand, calm waters, parking, bus, toilet, showers, anchoring area, disabled access, Club Náutico de Águilas 5km.
- Calarreona or Playa Las Tortugas: 230m, protected area, isolated, high occupancy, golden sand, calm waters, parking, bus, toilet, Club Náutico de Águilas 5km.
- Playa Calabardina: 100m, urban, high occupancy, golden sand, moderate waves, parking, bus, toilet, showers, anchorage area, disabled access, next to the Club Náutico de Águilas.
- Playa del Arroz: 200m, isolated, vegetation, high occupancy, golden sand-gravel, moderate waves, bus, parking, Club Náutico de Águilas 4km.
- Playa del Hornillo: 600m, urban, high occupancy, golden sand, moderate waves, anchoring area, bus, parking, toilets, showers, Club Náutico de Águilas 1.5km.
- Playa de las Delicias (Map: E2): 800m, urban, high occupancy, calm waters, golden sand-gravel, parking, bus, toilet, showers, anchorage area, disabled access, next to Club Náutico de Águilas.
- Playas del Isla Fraile: diving.
- Peñón Cabo Cope: diving
- Playa de la Colonia (Map: A3): 1050m, high occupancy, semi-urban, sand-gravel-rock gold, moderate waves, parking, bus, Club Náutico de Águilas 5km.

Services

Tourist Office, Plaza Antonio Cortijos, 968 493285, www.aguilas.es, www.aguilas.tv

Ayuntamiento, 968 418800, www.ayuntamientodeaguilas.org

Taxis can be found at: 968 411470 or 968 449988, Calles Isaac Peral.

Buses, the bus station 968 441961 is at Paseo de la Estación and they also stop at the bar on the corner of Avenida Juan Carlos 1 and Calle Carlos Marín Menú. Buses go to Almería, Madrid, Cartagena, Mazarrón, Lorca and Murcia.

There are trains to Murcia and Lorca, with several daily trains to each. The RENFE station 968 411068 is at Paseo de la Estación.

Location Report: Day Out In Águilas & Diving With Dolphins

We've been to the port town of Águilas (you pronounce it with the stress on the very first A) a couple of times over the years and we've always had a wonderful time. Diving around the Cabo Cope area you'll find wooden fishing boats sunk to provide an artificial reef, in conditions that are usually calm and clear with good visibility. You'll see damsel fish, grouper and many moray eels, in fact huge moray eels, probably bigger than me! We also saw barracudas nipping about in the gloom.

We did a cave dive at La Cueva de la Virgin where a shrine has been built with an image of Mary and her child. It's not exactly a cave, more a short tunnel, where good buoyancy control is essential. On the final day of diving, on the boat on the way back to the port, we saw a dolphin. Our dive master said that only a few years ago he would routinely see six or eight dolphins on every trip, but this is the first he's seen this year.

Águilas is right down on the coast in the South West of the region. The castle of San Juan has been restored and is open to the public. It was built to ward off pirate attacks. It's worth visiting the garden at Plaza de España which is full of a collection of rare plants and shrubs, rubber plants and palms and elderly men whiling away a few hours. There's the 19th century Ayuntamiento and the parish church of San Jose where the effigy of the patron saint is kept. The town's food market and the railway monument are other places of interest.

There are a number of local towns in the area of Águilas: Barranco de los Asensios, Barranco del Lobo, El Labradorcico, Los Melenchones, Peñaranda, Los Collados, Todosol, Las Zurraderas, Los Geráneos, Los Arejos, Calarreona, El Cocón, Huerta de Abad, Los Gallegos, Las Lomas, Calabardina, Las Casicas, Cuesta de Gos, Cope, El Garrobillo de Águilas, Rincón de la Casa Grande, Las Cruceticas, Hornillo and Tébar. Some details about the larger ones follow.

Los Arejos

With just 78 inhabitants, this is a small town north-west of Águilas, at the base of Cabezo de Los Arejos. During the weekend closest to the feast of San Isidro, around May 15th they celebrate their fiesta with many activities, musical performances, comedians and a giant paella.

The rambla of Los Arejos is filled from the Sierra de la Carrasquilla, producing an area with a great variety of fauna and flora. Designated an SPA zone (Special Protection Area) for birds you'll see eagles, eagle owls and peregrine falcons. There are also tortoise colonies, which are very rare.

Los Gallegos, a neighbouring village shares their fiesta with Los Arejos.

Los Geráneos

Los Geráneos (The Geraniums) urbanization was started in the 1980s and is linked to the urban growth of the coastal areas. There are two types of activities in this area, tourism and agriculture, both buoyed by the improved road system. There are also two types of residences around town, houses surrounded by large areas of countryside (that did not follow planning guidelines) and new developments following the pattern of contemporary construction, with several residences on each floor and surrounded by gardens and terrariums. It's a pretty urbanization, with lovely views and a pine forest.

Calarreona

Calarreona is located three miles from the centre of Águilas and next to one of the most beautiful protected landscapes in the region of Murcia, Las Cuatro Calas, on the border with the province of Almería.

Coastal villages during the Berber attacks were generally abandoned and it wasn't until the 18th century that the population increased. One of the main industries was the production of esparto (grass) items, using the curve of the beach to create caves where the esparto was 'cooked' before use.

There's the remains of a bunker related to the defence of the coast during the Civil War (1936-1939).

The tourism boom of the 60s and 70s created demand for more housing and the urbanization was built. There's a population of about 100 people, which increases massively during the summer months.

There's also a Youth Hostel in Calarreona, built in the late 80s, this is the only regionally owned accommodation. It is part of the Spanish Network of Youth Hostels, and has capacity for 87 people. It also has a garden, activities room, full hall, two meeting rooms, a TV lounge, roof terrace and classrooms for training.

The beauty of the landscape and beaches have made Calarreona a major tourist enclave, so its economy is based primarily on tourism and the services sector, especially in summer. The construction of new housing is also creating jobs in this sector.

See the beaches section for details of the beautiful beaches near this town.

Calabardina

Another beachside town Calabardina is a perfect location for diving around, as it is in the Parque Regional de Cabo Cope and Puntas de Calnegre. The seabed is characterised by the abundance of wrecks and the species that inhabit them, from underwater flora of posidonia and gorgonians, to octopus, shrimp and sardines as well as grouper and sunfish.

Although there is still a small fishing port in town the main industry is in tourism and the service sectors.

They celebrate their local festival during the first weekend in May, dedicated to Santa Cruz. The first night is a joint meal of sardines and beer, the next day a procession to the Virgen del Carmen, followed by a giant paella. All rounded off with dances, folklore festivities and music.

Cope

Seven kilometres from Águilas lies Cope, a coastal town whose history is reflected in one of the most significant buildings of the town and around the coast of Murcia, Cope Tower, built in 1573.

Cope tower has its origins in the Lorcan council's (this area was owned by Lorca for many years) decision to control their coastline. Some coastal areas potentially housing a considerable wealth through their livestock or fishing activities were at the mercy of attacks by North African pirates.

So in 1530 they began the first trials to build a small fort north of Cabo Cope. For many reasons the tower wasn't completed until 1573 and was manned by three or four people to defend against the repeated violent attacks by the Barbary pirates. The fortress was ruined at the end of the sixteenth century.

The tower was rebuilt in 1663, when the economic, social and political scenes were quite different. Since the 16th century there has also been a small chapel (ermita) near the tower, which was discovered during the renovations to the tower during the 1980s.

The coastline is full of coves and beaches of great interest, especially for diving enthusiasts who can enjoy the wide variety of caves rich in marine fauna.

Cope based their development in the agricultural sector, specialising in the intensive cultivation of vegetables in a greenhouse with drip irrigation systems that take advantage of poor rainfall in the area.

Festivities are held during the month of December in honour of the Immaculate Conception and in February dedicated to farmers.

The Regional Park of Cabo Cope-Calnegre is part of the tourist attraction that doubles the local population during the summer months.

Todosol and Los Collados

The Todosol and Los Collados urbanisations can be considered pioneering developments dedicated to accommodate residential tourism and second homes (homes that are lived occasionally in the summer period) and now has a stable population throughout the year. Its unique architecture adapts to the terrain between small hills and slopes crossed by the ramblas, where you can find figs and prickly pears, wild herbs such as thyme and rosemary, and other woodland species. They are pretty coastal towns, with 250 and 150 inhabitants, respectively.

Hornillo

Protected at its western end by Punta del Caballo, its eastern end by Punta del Cambrón, with a view to the island Isla del Fraile lies Hornillo just 1.5km from Águilas.

Embarcadero del Hornillo is a pier like structure on the eastern coastline, it was built by the LBA Railway Company in 1903 in order to ship iron ore from the Sierra de Bacares y Serón, in Almería. The Embarcadero has been declared of cultural interest (since 2007). The minerals were transported by a railway line. It has been restored and free visits are possible on Monday and Wednesday to Saturday 11:00 to 14:00 and 17:00 to 19:00, plus Sundays and holidays 11:00 to 14:00.

Sleeping

There is a wide range of accommodation which includes camping in Águilas 968 419282, www.campingaguilas.es; Camping Los Geráneos, Urbanización los Geráneos, Carretera Cabo Cope, 968 419205 and Bellavista 968 449151, www.campingbellavista.com, Carretera de Vera, km3. Prices rise by about €12 in summer. Remember in summer and during fiestas you must make reservations well ahead of arrival.

Casa Roja, El Garrobillo 15 Alto, is a bed and breakfast, with self catering options available through www.casa-rurales.net

Águilas de los Collados Apartments, Urbanización Los Collados Zieschang, Calabardina Road, www.

Águilasdeloscollados.com, has 87 apartments with 2 bedrooms for four people sharing. Large swimming pool, between Calabardina and Águilas. Pets are allowed. Prices start from €80.

Hotel Puerta Juan Montiel, Avenida Puerto Deportivo, 1, Playa de Poniente, 968 493493, http://www.hotelpuertojuanmontiel.com, has 56 double rooms, 16 single, 26 doubles with living room and 30 suites. This is the luxury end of the scale, with reasonable prices. Right in the port area and close to all amenities and beaches. From €120, though you can get discounts, search online.

Eating

Águilas is a great place to eat fish and seafood, including prawns (red prawns are expensive, but really quite yummy!), octopus and sea bass.

El Faro, Calle José María Pereda, does typical local dishes at reasonable prices, recipes have been passed down through the generations, menú around €15.

Las Brisas, Explanada del Puerto, offers rich paella and fried fish. It's the bright blue restaurant in the port, you can't miss it.

La Veleta, Calle Blas Rosique, 6, good but pricey, menú is around €15 and good value, they also have a menú degustación. www.restaurante-la-veleta.negocio.site

Casa del Mar, Explanada Del Muelle, see location report for more info.

Others to consider:

- Rey Carlos III, Calle Rey Carlos III, 22, good fish and seafood.
- Café Bar Felipe, Plaza Alfonso Escámez, 1. Has a nice terrace for people watching. Dried octopus, prawns, and mixed fried fish.
- Café Bar Peña Aguilera, Avenida Juan Carlos I, 17. This bar offers some delicacies that are for the more adventurous, such as snails, baby squid and some more challenging meat dishes like morcilla (Spanish black pudding).
- Café Bar Sol Y Mar, Plaza Antonio Cortijos. Outside seating with the usual variety of seafood.
- Taberna Típica El Pimiento, Calle Joaquín Tendero. Meat–lovers only: snails, fried rabbit, fried liver and black pudding.

Night Life

In summer there are a lot of bars, discos and ice cream parlours (heladerías) along the beach front, especially recommended are Mar Azul and Colonia. The centre of the town has a number of pubs and bars, a lot of which have terraces.

In the early hours of the morning the night life gets busy around the Plaza de España. Good night spots include La Glorieta, Dakota, and Tuareg.

Aledo

Population: 950

Map Reference: 1.57°W, 37.80°N
Situated at the foot of the southern slope of the Sierra Espuña, at a height of over 800 meters, bordered to the north, south and east by the town of Totana, and west by Lorca lies Aledo.

The highest elevations are located north and south of town, on the slopes of the Sierra Espuña and the hills of the Sierra de Tercia. The cliffs that surround it are La Fontanilla and Borrazán. Also in the area is the Estrecho de la Alboleja of great natural beauty and the Cueva de la Mauta.

Aledo retains many vestiges of its historic past including the Torreón Árabe, Torre de Aledo, El Castillo and la Iglesia de Santa María.

The **Castle of Aledo** still surrounds and characterises the village, and is relatively well preserved thanks to recent renovations. Nestled in an impregnable place, well supplied with water through an integrated system of fortification, the castle has its origins in the Middle Ages. It was at this time that the Andalusian Muslims shaped the spectacular fortress, providing it with walls that surrounded the population and a strong fortress.

One interesting monument that remains today is the **Picota Aledana** (a pillory, a framework used to expose criminals to public humiliation). It's the only monument from the Middle Ages that remains in the region of Murcia and has a curious history. The name comes from peak because peaks were nailed to the heads of people who were convicted of a crime. In the Middle Ages prisoners were tortured to extract confessions and then exposed to public shame and tied in the pillory for the villagers to throw stones and insults at them. On May 26, 1813 Cadiz courts ordered the destruction of all the pillories to ensure the freedom of the villagers.

The Aledo pillory was built in the late sixteenth century (1592) when the King authorised the town to free themselves from the jurisdiction of the Order of Santiago and gave permission to imprison and pillory convicts. Originally surrounding the pillory was a simple block of wood nailed to the floor, later it was covered with brick walls for more strength, and this is how it continues today.

Shackles still remain along with the protruding peaks where prisoners were tied or nailed.

The Fiestas Patronales are in honour of Santa María la Real and San

Agustín and take place between the 25th and 28th August.

Thanks to the location of Aledo in the natural park and the surrounding Sierra Espuña there are loads of places to discover, and you'll find multiple paths and trails for walking, hiking and cycling.

Walks around Aledo are part of the PR-MU 64 and 65 and start behind the Monastery of La Santa, on to Camino de Los Molejones, Senda del Barranco de La Santa, and finally back to La Santa. Also located in the Rambla de Lébor is a canyon of several meters in length with waterfalls and ponds. You can descend a staircase visible from a wooden bridge. Access is via paths and ponds.

Services

Tourist Office, Plaza del Castillo, 696 962116, www.aledo.es

Sleeping

There's camping nearby in Totana, Carretera Nacional 340, km614, 968 424864, www.campingtotana.es

If you're looking for a natural getaway, then try the wooden houses on the outskirts of Aledo. There are four houses, with space for five people in each. There's also a shared swimming pool. Aledo Rural, Calle Estación de Servicio, 670 345326 or 609 808532, www.aledorural.com Prices start from €500 for a week for one house.

For other local hotels see the Totana section.

Eating

If you can't find anywhere to eat in Aledo then pop into Totana, where there are more choices.

Bar Restaurante Hermanos Mandola, Carretera Aledo km11, a large restaurant with open fires, that specialises in grilled meats, paellas and roasts.

Alhama De Murcia

Population: 21,450

Map Reference: 1.42°W, 37.85°N

The Arabs built a castle to defend Alhama (which the Arabs called Alhamman) where the thermal waters made famous by the Romans can be found. Today Alhama is a city with fruit in the valleys and pines on the mountains lying at the foothills of the Sierra Espuña. The road leading into the town is a hive of activity with new warehouses and office complexes going up. The town signpost shows a castle sitting artistically on top of a rock. It's not until the castle actually comes into view that it can be verified as an accurate representation.

The Ayuntamiento is an early 20th century building in the Plaza de la Constitución. There are a number of parks in the centre near the ancient house, **Casa De La Familia Saavedra**. Nearby is the **Iglesia de la**

Concepción, which is a Baroque church, restored in the 18th century.

In **Plaza Vieja** at the end of Calle Larga there are some 19th century stately houses with brightly coloured façades and the old town hall, which houses the museum (open week days, closed for siesta).

You can go up to the **Arab Castle**, perched on an isolated peak, using side streets off Calle Vergara. The castle, with its splendid view of the surrounding countryside, provided visual protection (and early warning of the next invading wave of civilisation) for the changing cultures that have all left their signatures on the land. The occurrence of archaeological remains belonging to the late Neolithic period, bronze and Iberian ages indicate an almost continuous occupation of the hill from the late eleventh or early twelfth centuries.

In the same area you will find the baroque **Iglesia de San Lázaro**. Also nearby you'll find the famous bathhouses of the town. These baths, sympathetically restored to reflect the more than 2000 years that have passed since they first attracted the attention of the Romans, are constructed over a natural spring that, due to a geological accident, provided hot mineralized water that became famous for its rejuvenating and invigorating potency.

The area is largely devoted to the cultivation of citrus fruits (oranges, lemons and grapefruit), almonds, olives and peppers, and more interesting (to me) vines. Cattle, swine, sheep and goat husbandry has significantly increased and has led to booming pork industry in the region. The El Pozo Meat Industries factory, mainly devoted to the preparation of pork, has in recent years expanded to other areas. Polígono Industrial Las Salinas, located next to the Mediterranean motorway, has several factories engaged in the footwear, ceramics, clothing, metallurgical, pharmaceutical and horticulture industries.

Alhama hosts an outlet fair, on Calle la Fería. Local clothes, shoe and household shops sell off their end of season stock near the end of October. You can grab a bargain if you're into that sort of thing. www.turismo.alhamademurcia.es

Alhama de Murcia has five parishes: El Gebas, El Berro, El Cañarico, Las Cañadas y la Costera.

El Berro, located in the heart of Sierra Espuña, 14km from Alhama and at 600 meters, is the fourth parish in population. It has a rural guesthouse and a campsite with swimming pool, camping areas and wooden houses. The festival in honour of Nuestra Señora de los Dolores is celebrated in August, where everyone is out in the streets. It is the only parish of Alhama which holds its own processions at Easter.

Gebas is located 9km from Alhama and is the least populated hamlet. The census has about 24 inhabitants, but it is very active with regard to rural tourism. Water erosion has created a lunar landscape of ravines that are well worth exploring. For a fun day out get in touch with www.espuna-adventure.com who offer all sorts of activities, accommodation and food.

El Cañarico is found in the foothills of the Carrascoy Regional Park. It has just 251 inhabitants and their celebrations in honour of San Antonio are held in June.

Las Cañadas is 10km from Alhama, bordering Fuente Álamo de Murcia. In April they have their fiesta in honour of the Virgen de la Cabeza, with a procession through the streets accompanied by the Banda Municipal de Música de Alhama.

La Costera is 6km from Alhama, at the foot of the Sierra de Carrascoy.

Many people pass through Alhama de Murcia on their way to the Sierra Espuña, see section later in the book. But it's well worth a stop for some site-seeing.

Around October 7th Alhama celebrates Nuestra Señora la Virgen del Rosario. Festivities last about a week and include masses, festivals, folklore exhibitions, music and cultural activities.

Los Mayos festival, declared of Regional Tourist Interest in 1990, is a traditional Alhameños fiesta during the first weekend in May. This festival is associated with pagan fertility rites of the earth, and the inhabitants of Alhama make rag dolls, called Mayos who take to the streets. The corremayos are people who dress up as clowns, with bells and hats, to visit the various Mayo or, in the case of young people to go out and enjoy the music concerts! There's also the Cruces de Mayo, an authentic floral altar, which is the Christianized version of the pagan festival. And there's a rice cooking contest!

La Semana Santa de Alhama is worth visiting to see the streets and floats adorned with flowers and baroque images. On February 2nd there's the feast of Candelaria which commemorates the purification of the Virgin Mary and the presentation of Jesus in the Temple. There's a pilgrimage to Collado to accompany the Virgin to the chapel built in 1981. They make a special cake for this fiesta, tortas al horno; you can have them with or without pork rind!

The book *Sierra Espuña from Alhama de Murcia: Excursions on Foot and by Bicycle* edited by Natursport written by Angel Ortiz Martínez and Lázaro Martínez

Giménez provides some excellent walking and cycling routes. For more information www.natursport.com

Services

Tourist Office, Plaza de La Constitución. Open every day apart from Sundays and during siesta. 968 633512, www.alhamademurcia.es

You can arrive by train on the Águilas to Murcia line and also the Lorca to Barcelona line. There are frequent buses to Murcia, Mazarrón, Cartagena and Lorca.

Taxis, Tomás Moro, 609 782925, 968 639143, www.taxisenalhamedademurcia.es

Sleeping

Camping can be found in El Berro. Try www.campingsierraespuna.com, 968 668038. They have 11 wooden lodges of different sizes with a camping area divided into plots. There's a swimming pool, café, playpen, barbecues, sports grounds, tennis courts, mini–golf, table tennis, public phones, 24–hour hot water, laundrette, fountains with drinking water, power points and first–aid box.

For great rural places to stay then Alhama and the surrounding towns have lots to offer. If you want your own country house or apartment there's Casa El Palomar, 646 894363, www.elpalomarcasarural.com in La Costera. In Gebas there are a number of houses to suit your needs as part of El Mirador de Gebas, 968 633644, www.elmiradordegebas.com, and Casa Rural Cueva del Grillo in Las Cañadas, 696 680787, www.lacuevadelgrillo.com

Hospedería Bajo el Cejo is a large hotel (in physical size, not number of rooms, at just 10 doubles, 2 superior and 1 suite) just outside of town in El Berro, Calle El Paso, 968 668032, www.bajoelcejo.com Prices start at around €100.

Hotel Los Bartolo on Calle Alfonso X el Sabio, 1 is a modern hotel with 18 rooms and 4 apartments, often full during the week. Prices start from €47 per night, great value. There are also two restaurants/bars and you can buy food to take away. 968 631671, www.losbartolos.com/hotel

In Gebas you'll find the La Casa del Estanco, the Hospedería La Mariposa. This is a great countryside hotel with rooms and apartments with a restaurant on site. Double rooms from €59 per night. 968 631008, www.hotellamariposa.com. They also offer quad biking, horse riding, walking, mountain climbing, kayaking and adventure stuff in general. Take a look at www.espuna-adventure.com

Eating

Specialties are rice / paella with rabbit, snails and migas. Due to the location you also get good seafood around here. Look out for stews called de cucharra, gypsy stew la olla gitana and pork stew la olla fresco. There are plenty of good value bars and restaurants, pizza places and heladerías.

- Los Bartolos, Calle Alfonso X El Sabio, 1, one of the best quality restaurants, with good fish and local specialities.
- Hospedería La Mariposa, Casa del Estanco, great value and excellent food. It has a beautiful location, great service and a good selection of veggie options. Book during peak season.
- Julian, Carretera N340, Restaurant and bar which has hearty food at a good price and is very popular with local workers.
- El Chaleco, Avenida Bastarreche, 9, high quality restaurant, specialising in fish and desserts. Slightly more pricey.
- Casa El Lobo, Carretera Cartagena, km58, popular homemade food.

The village of El Berro has just over 100 inhabitants. It is situated at an altitude of 650m and has an array of services, such as restaurants, supermarkets, cafés, and bakeries. Some of the best restaurants in the Sierra Espuña can be found here. It is also a great base for starting a walk or cycle ride.

Nightlife

In summer everyone goes to Mazarrón, however the rest of the year you'll find people in the city. A more rowdy bar is Ruta on Calle Vidal Abarca, a large place, open all night. Another bar to try is Ninfas on Calle Postigos. Avenida Ginés Campos also has many bars and clubs.

Archena

Population: 18,800

Map Reference: 1.29°W, 38.11°N

Archena, the regional capital of the Valle de Ricote, can be found on the last natural part of the Río Segura, before it heads into the city (Murcia). Archena is used as a base for visiting the Balneario de Archena and also for walks and excursions up the Valle De Ricote.

Archena is a fertile agricultural settlement at the lower end of the Ricote valley. Considered as the region's oasis, views are dominated by the rugged nearby mountains.

The history of Archena dates from Iberian times and it has archaeological remains including the Warriors Vase, now in the National Archaeological Museum. Many historians place the origins of Archena in 234 BC, during Carthaginian control of the area. The present site, however, is of Roman origin as is the name for the town. After the Reconquest

Archena passed into the hands of the Order of San Juan Bautista until the 19th century, evidence of which is to be found in the church dedicated to the saint.

Its excellent spa baths, in use since Roman times are one of the main attractions. The waters that spring from the ground at 50ºC have healing properties. The church dedicated to **La Virgen de la Salud** (Our Lady of Good Health), the patron saint of Archena, stands within the grounds of the spa complex and is also one of the town's visitor attractions.

One of the most characteristic monuments of Archena is the **Don Mario Castillo** (Torre de Archena), a square fortress on the hill between the roads from Murcia and Madrid.

Semana Santa in Archena is worth visiting, there's a great website dedicated to it: www.semanasantadearchena.es

Balneario Archena

Balneario is based about 2km from the centre of Archena, where there are a number of hotels and pleasant walks along the Río de Segura. The thermal baths at the Balneario have therapeutic properties, with temperatures around 50º centigrade.

The Balneario website has loads of information on the qualities of the water, the services available, what products you can buy and special offers! Prices for the baths are around €16 for a full day during weekdays in summertime, and during the weekends and fiestas prices increase to €22 for the day. You'll find a multitude of jets, whirlpools and Jacuzzis.

There is also a "spa circuit" for €25 during the week and €35 at weekends and fiesta time. This includes various types of sauna, an ice cave (don't touch the walls!) and even the opportunity to swim in a pool full of lemons - sensory overload!

Whilst undergoing development, further Roman ruins were found on the site of the Spa, which are now being painstakingly excavated, with minimal disruption to visitors. The car parking has been massively improved too, with a huge underground complex, which you have to pay a few Euros for.

The Balneario offers a wide range of packages, special offers, deals and discounts, look on their website for more information. The best value is "escapeterapia" which gives you a spa circuit, access to the baths, a swimming cap and lunch for €48.

There are three hotels on the site, all offering good value for money, and including deals for use of the spa.

There is also an 18th century church, Iglesia de San Juan Bautista and the Casino. The Casino is worth a visit, enjoy a coffee and watch people play with the giant chess set, or go inside and marvel at the height of the doors. The Casino was created to entertain the nobility and the bourgeoisie who came to visit the spa. 902 366 902, www.balnearioarchena.com

Services

Ayuntamiento on Calle Major, 968 670000.

Tourist Office, Parque Palacete de Villarias. Open every day including Sunday mornings. www.archena.es, 626 241 884.

Buses to and from Murcia can be found in Avenida del Carril. Also you can get the bus from here to the Balneario.

Taxi rank at Calle Paraguay 29, 968 670076, 968 475288, 968 475287.

Sleeping

Most people choose to stay at the hotels in the Balneario. However, there have been many mixed reviews online, with some people saying these hotels purport to be 4 star but in reality they are far from it. As with all bookings of hotel rooms in Spain it may be best to go and visit the hotel before making a firm commitment. You are at liberty to see a room before making a booking. This is less useful during peak season when availability is very low and advance booking is required.

Prices of all the hotels at the Balneario can be found on www.balneariodearchena.com

Prices for Hotel Termas, Hotel Levante and Hotel León start from around €130 per night for a couple, and includes access to the pools.

There's also the Hotel La Parra, Carretera del Balneario, 3, 968 670444, www.hotellaparra.com, which is a family style accommodation which is more economical. €45 for a double room.

There's the four storey (and four star) Hotel Hyltor www.hotelhyltor.com, 902 46 16 46 on Carretera del Balneario with prices starting from €70 which offers a happy medium and seems mainly to cater for Spanish.

Eating

Typical cuisine features rice with rabbit, stews with local vegetables (fennel, beans), migas (breadcrumbs mixed with meat) and michirones (beans and bacon stew). There is a tapas route through the town, usually at the end of November. More information can be found at the tourist information website.

Try Bar La Tapia on Calle Juan José Marco Benegas, a tapas bar specialising in seafood which is very popular at weekends. Or El Aboroque, Avenida del Carril, a tapas bar with high quality seafood, ham and cheeses. There's also El Internacional, Carretera del

Balneario, a modern, functional restaurant with a terrace.

Night Life

In Archena itself there are a number of options, like Torres del oro on Alfonso Sabio. A bars with a terrace is Deja Vu in Calle Alejandro Medina. Other bars to try include are El Carril and La Mar.

In the Balneario de Archena you shouldn't miss the Bar Azul, which is a pleasant place to pass an evening with a giant chess set amongst the palm trees on the terrace with a medley of cats around your feet.

Bolnuevo

Population: 1,200 (2008)

Map Reference: 1.31°W, 37.56°N

Bolnuevo is an upmarket seaside resort near Puerto Mazarrón. Bolnuevo has one of the most recognisable landmarks of Murcia, the weathered sandstone formation that adorns most of the region's brochures and tourist guides, the **Gredas de Bolnuevo**. Sometimes called **Ciudad Encantada**, the enchanted city, the bizarre rock formations have been eroded by the wind and sea into extraordinary shapes. In the summer they're often used as the backdrop for music festivals. Don't expect them to be right on the beach though. A car park separates this unusual natural phenomenon from the sands.

In the north there's the Sierra de las Moreras and also La rambla de las Moreras, where you'll see ficus, fig and eucalyptus, rosemary and thyme plants, the Bonelli Eagle, turtles, Ocellated lizard, the natterjack toad, bee-eaters, the yellow-legged gull, blackcap and zarzera and a great variety of fish and marine life in the rocks and seabed.

La Romería de Bolnuevo, around the 17th November, sees a miasma of different groups get together to celebrate the miracle of Virgen de la Inmaculada Concepción. You'll see the fishermen, the choir, the Moors and Christians, the Maestro Eugenio Calderon band, and of course lots of peñas (groups of friends).

Following the coast road to the south west brings you to miles of beautiful and often secluded coves and beaches, including a number of nudist spots. The road is very narrow and pitted so keep your wits about you as it's mostly only wide enough for one car.

Carrying on further towards Águilas, you reach Punta Calnegre, where there are more organised beaches, with a family orientation. These are best reached by car from the Mazarrón to Águilas road.

Location Report: Bolnuevo

Bolnuevo is a small town, with a long sandy beach. It's main attractions are the Sardine run in November and the famous sand erosions. It is served by an excellent supermarket, chemist and numerous bars and restaurants.

I recently relocated here and purchased a house with views over the beach and erosions. It's a stunning place to live. Being able to get up and walk along the beach each morning is fantastic, it's only a 45 min walk into Puerto de Mazarron too. In the other direction is my favorite area to walk to, Percheles, the next main beach. You see nothing but mountains to your right and sea to your left, I never tire of doing that walk. Unlike many Spanish resorts the town is kept alive by the almost full, all year round campsite.

Bob Shoesmith

See Mazarrón section for where to stay and eat.

Bullas

Population: 11,550

Map Reference: 1.66°W, 38.05°N

Bullas is one of the five regions which makes up the area called Comarca del Noroeste, the natural access to the north east of the region.

The old 19th century wine cellar is now a wine museum, located in Balsa Street (balsa means pool as there was a very big and old pool which collected the water coming from the town's main channel). The building is in a perfect state of conservation, with its brick vaults and earthenware jars which are half buried in the ground. It belonged to the Melgares de Aguilar family, who were very powerful in the middle of the 19th Century. Opening hours are Tuesday to Saturday 10:30 to 14:00 and 17:00 to 20:00, Sundays and fiestas 10:30 to 14:00, closed Mondays. €3 entrance fee. www.rvbullas.es/museodelvino

Another house belonging to the traditional powerful families of Bullas (the Marsilla - Melgares) is located behind the parish church. It was reformed in 1900 by Don José Marsilla; commonly known as Don Pepe and it was inherited after his death by his son Don Blas Rafael. It has a big wine cellar, perfectly preserved. The decoration of the main rooms is in the Art Nouveau style.

Our Lady of the Rosary Parish Church is located in the central square of Bullas (Plaza de España). Its construction began at the end of the 17th century. The tower (baroque), the side naves and the sacristy (neoclassic) were finished in 1803 after the needed enlargement and reformation works. The Tabernacle Chapel, in Neo-Gothic style, dates from 1905.

Torre del Reloj (The Clock Tower) is also called the Tower of Santiago and was built in 1900 in one of the highest points of Bullas. Since the Town Council did not have enough funds to repair the public clock the construction of this tower was a private initiative of the Mayor of Bullas, Joaquín Carreño Góngora, who wanted to cover the need of regulating the irrigation time in the orchards. The clock was assembled in Switzerland and Moisés Díaz from Palencia was commissioned for its installation. The owner Joaquín Carreño donated the building to the Municipality in 1916.

Melgares House was built in 1925 on the site of an ancient inn. It belonged to one of the richest and most powerful families of Bullas, the Melgares. It was the site of several unions and parties during the Spanish Civil War and also the Amor de Dios religious school between 1954 and 1981. Then the building was acquired by the Municipality as a location for the Youth House (later named Culture House). It is an Art Nouveau house with some interesting elements typical of the Arabic style and also a beautiful balustrade. The Public Library and the Municipality's Historical Archives are situated in this building too.

There are very few preserved remains of the ancient **Castle of Bullas**. Only part of a tower and several big projecting stones can be seen. The houses situated under the old fortress still have some parts of the old wall as big stones located underground.

Plaza Vieja, although commonly known as Old Square, is officially named Teniente Flomesta, after a local hero of the Morocco Wars in the 1920s. The colourful façades are where the Encuentro (Meeting) of Easter Morning and the street market **El Zacatín** every month take place.

Olive and almond trees grow next to the vineyards. The economy of Bullas depends to a large extent on the wine-growing industry and the most representative wines come from grapes grown here and also in Caravaca, Cehegín, Moratalla, Mula, Ricote and Calasparra.

The winters here are cold and although white and rosé wines are produced, perhaps the most famous are the wines produced from the sturdy dark grapes, which can endure the frost and snow as well as the blistering summer sun. From these grapes a full-bodied red wine is created which goes so well with many of the hearty local dishes.

The most characteristic dish of Bullas is talvina, a sort of pancake fried in an earthenware bowl with garlic, peppers, bacon, tripe and sausage. Various thick soups featuring a mixture of meats and beans are popular, especially during the winter.

The first Sunday of every month on Plaza Vieja (until lunchtime) there is a comprehensive market, selling not only the usual fare of fruit, vegetables and dodgy watches, but also local arts and crafts, including ceramics and wood carvings. It's called, El Zacatín and every month a demonstration of an old craft or trade is carried out, for example, plaiting the esparto grasses, demonstrations of spinning and weaving, making fresh cheese and in October wine making (and tasting!)

Their fiesta patronal is in October, starting the night of the Friday before the first Sunday of October and finishing on the following Tuesday (did you get that?). There is also a fiesta on the 17th January, San Antón (in La Copa, a little village in the municipality and well worth a visit).

And of course, a wine town has to have a wine fiesta. Bullas celebrates its wine during the last weekend of September. There are guided wine route tours, commented tastings and the award of the Master of Wine that goes to a person devoted to viticulture. In addition in the central square of Bullas on Sunday morning, there's the inauguration of the wine fountain, the traditional grape treading and the First Juice's Blessing.

Services

Ayuntamiento, Plaza de España, 968 652031.

Tourist office, Avenida de Murcia, 75, Open Mondays to Fridays 10:00 to 14:00, Saturdays and fiestas 10:30 to 13:30, and the first Sunday of the month at the market 9:00 to 14:00. 968 652244

www.bullas.es s one of the best local websites in the region, perhaps in the whole of Spain! You'll find a lot of tourist information on this site.

Taxis can be found on Avenida de Murcia, next to the restaurant Avenida, 639 038632 or 618 053769.

Bodegas

Carrascalejo belongs to the Pidal family and was founded in 1850. It's located between Bullas and Cehegín; you can just spot a sign for it as you drive out of Bullas on the main motorway. The winery is situated underneath the family noble house from the early 20th century. The special care of the vineyards, the vintage process and the traditional winemaking method guarantees excellent quality wine. We make special efforts to visit this bodega (frequently), their everyday drinking red is excellent, and great value for money. The crianza is well worth the 50 cents more. And you must try their Rosado, at around

€2.30 per bottle its great value. There's a small kiosk on the road outside the bodega where a friendly chap will help you choose your wines and load the car. www.carrascalejo.com, 968 652003.

Bodega Cooperativa San Isidro is a cooperative winery producing high quality red wines (mainly from the Monastrell grape variety) and also white wines (Macabeo variety). The combination of tradition and modern technology produces wines with a strong personality and intense colour, bouquet and flavour. You can't fail to see this cooperative, which is on the polígono just as you reach town on the motorway from Murcia. www.bodegasanisidrobullas.com, 968 652160.

Bodega Balcona is a family winery whose vineyards are situated in the Aceniche Valley, a very beautiful area that has the best conditions for the cultivation of vines. This is where they produce Partal, one of our other favourites. Partal is a very deep red wine, rich and fruity, made from Monastrell, Tempranillo, Cabernet Sauvignon, Syrah and Merlot grapes. www.bodegabalcona.com, 968 652891.

Bodega Cooperativa Nuestra Señora del Rosario is a cooperative winery founded in 1950. In the Rosario winery the effort and dedication of the growers is combined with the most advanced techniques in wine-making. It is the most important winery of the Bullas Origin Denomination area, with 85% of the total production. You'll probably have seen their wines in most supermarkets, Señorío de Bullas, Las Reñas and Tesoro de Bullas are three of the most famous. www.bodegasdelrosario.es, 968 652075.

Sleeping

For camping try Complejo de La Rafa, E–30180–Bullas–Murcia, www.larafabullas.es, 968 654666, This is a comprehensive camp site with apartments for rental as well as plots to camp. There's a swimming pool and restaurant.

For rural accommodation in the old town there's Pensión Flipper on Calle Paragüay, 968 652163 and Pensión San José on Calle Aragón, 968 653282, www.pensionsanjose.com.

On Paraje Molino de Abajo, 968 431383, www.castillico.com, there's a group of traditional houses, wooden houses and a hospedería. There's also a restaurant on site with a good wine list (well you'd expect that being in Bullas!)

In town on Calle General Antonio Sánchez, 38 there's the Hotel SG Bullas, 902 220203, www.hotelsg.net. Doubles start at €60. They also have a restaurant and cafe on site. Look on their website for offers and deals.

Eating

There are plenty of places to try, plus some Chinese restaurants and small cafes:

- Restaurante Avenida, Avenida de Murcia, 19, specialities include seafood, fish and sirloin.
- Restaurante–Bar Borrego, Avenida Luis de los Reyes, 7, homemade cooking and various tapas.
- Restaurante Flipper Avenida de Murcia, 48, paella and roast chicken.
- Restaurante La Rafa Camping La Rafa, local cooking.
- Restaurante–Bar Mateo Avenida de Murcia, 77, meat, fish and various tapas.
- Restaurante Polideportivo Avenida de Murcia, meat, fish and various tapas.
- Restaurante–Bar Las Peñas Calle Nicolás de las Peñas, 56, roast octopus, fish and meat.

Cabo de Palos

Population: 1,150 (2010)

Map Reference: 0.70°W, 37.63°N

Across from the Marchamalo salt flats Cabo de Palos is a small point of land jutting out into the Mediterranean. It is part of the Cartagena municipality in the district of Rincón de San Ginés. Naturally equipped with many small bays and inlets, it has always been a centre for fishing and the main port area is one of the prettiest on the entire coast. Using fresh local fish and vegetables some of the best restaurants in the area line the traditional quayside and offer very reasonable prices. Today it is primarily a tourist resort known for its gastronomy (especially for its Caldero del Mar Menor a local recipe based on rice and fish from the area).

Cabo de Palos is part of a ridge of volcanic hills that form a small peninsula including the islands in the Mediterranean Sea: Isla Grosa and the Islas Hormigas, as well as the five located in the Mar Menor.

Its famous lighthouse is up on the hill, from where you can expect to have great seafood. **Faro de Cabo de Palos** (the lighthouse) was first lit on January 31st 1865. The building rises 80 metres above sea level as planned by Leonardo de Tejada. It has an illuminated range of approximately 24 miles. It was built on the site of the watchtower, **Torre de San Antonio**, which was one of the best defences in the area against pirate attacks.

Sunday is a good day to visit Cabo de Palos. There is a large market in the morning (9:00 to 14:00) just a few minutes' walk from the seafront and there are numerous harbour front restaurants where you can sit in the sun and watch the world go by. There are also two large ceramic shops nearby which are well worth a visit.

A heaving, trendy place in the summer it's best to visit off-season to enjoy the food. But beware, in off-season many of the restaurants close.

You can hire a segway and take a route on the pavements and along the beach and visit the lighthouse for just €30. See the section on segways. Or enjoy the go karting track just off the motorway (MU-312), www.lamangagokart.com.

Each year in July there's the festival of Habaneros held up by the lighthouse for the Fiestas de Santa Maria del Mar. Choirs from across the region celebrate with music and free concerts for the public to enjoy in the atmospheric setting of the lighthouse. There's usually a market, stalls and often a greased pole stuck out over the sea, with a prize on the end for the most athletic to win.

Scuba Diving

One of the main reasons (apart from the seafood) to come to Cabo de Palos is for the diving. Founded in 1995, the Cabo de Palos Marine Reserve is one of the best places for diving on the Mediterranean coast. During recent years the development of the marine park has been spectacular, becoming an example of sustainability for all the marine reserves of the Mediterranean on account of its biodiversity and great ecological value. For this reason there are restrictions about where people can dive and the numbers of divers and their qualifications. The dive companies will be able to advise.

There are a number of sunken ships in the area many caused by the dangerous rocks that rise at least 3.5m above the sea bed. They form jagged crests which were unknown to ships of old. More recently during the First and Second World Wars the tranquil waters of Cabo de Palos were turned into an authentic battlefield on account of the German submarines and the merchant ships that were bound for America.

Try BalkySUB on Paseo D. Dimas Ortega 22, Cabo de Palos, 661 492143, www.balkysub.com

The shipwrecks include:

- Naranjito, Island of Gomera: Cargo ship 64m length, sunk in 1946. Minimum qualification required is an Advanced Diver certificate from any examining body.
- Standfield: Cargo ship of 110m length, sunk in 1917.
- Sirio: Steamship of 100m length sunk in 1906.
- Nord America: Gunned cargo ship of 120m sunk in 1883.

- Minerva: Cargo ship of 100m sunk in 1899: Minimum qualification Dive Master from any organization.

There are plenty of dive clubs to choose from who use the sports port.

Naranjito, www.naranjitobuceo.com, 968 564836.

Atura Sub, www.aturasub.com, 968 564823.

Islas Hormigas, www.islashormigas.com, 968 145530.

Puerto de Cabo de Palos, 968 563515, is a small sports port with moorings.

Sleeping

Many people visiting this area will stay in the local towns (see Cartagena section for more details), La Manga or in the urbanisations. However, there are a couple of places to stay down here. Try www.apartamentosmariaguerrero.es, 608 410462, or www.laestanciadelrincon.es, 636 972327.

If you prefer camping, then take a look at Camping La Manga, 968 563014, www.campinglamanga.es There's space for tents and caravans, there are bungalows, a supermarket, cafe and swimming pool.

Eating

Restaurante La Tana, Paseo de la Barra (facing the entrance of the port) has a reputation for good fish and rices. Its dish Rice La Tana (a caldero type rice made with minced squid and shrimps, with no heads and no bones) is delicious. They do a menu del día for around €16. www.la–tana.com.

Mesón el Mosqui, on the way up to the lighthouse. One of the really good caldero rice places in the area. Closes Thursdays.

- Restaurante el Pez, c/Los Palangres, Balcony over the port. Good fish.
- Miramar, Paseo de la Barra, 14, excellent fresh fish.
- Restaurante Miramar, Beginning of Paseo de la Barra.
- Restaurante El Navegante, End Paseo de La Barra, corner El Faro/Palangre Streets. Fish and rices.
- Restaurante La Sartenica, Tavern–Restaurant, in the way up to the Lighthouse, wide selection of typical Murcian snacks.
- Restaurante Katy, Fish and rice in the first bend on the road up to the lighthouse.
- Restaurante El Faro, Fried fish, in the port Avenue.

Night Life

Cabo de Palos nightlife is tremendously full of activity and noise especially from Friday to Sunday and from June to September. There are a lot of places to go and drink, listen to music and dance, open from 23:00 to 4:00, 5:00 or 6:00 the following morning. Then you can go somewhere else for breakfast!

There are several main areas where many of these music pubs are concentrated. Here are two of them.

Central Cabo de Palos where most of the places are located within the triangle made by three adjacent streets: Calle Salero, Calle Marín and Plaza de Los Arcos. You get there following the road that drives from the Port of Cabo de Palos to the lighthouse, just before reaching El Mosqui Restaurant. On the edge of town is the summer club Trips Discoteca, Carretera Cabo de Palos, Km. 2, www.tripalamanga.com, 968 146215.

There is a lot of activity in summer, but in winter pretty much everything stops.

Calasparra

Population: 10,250

Map Reference: 1.70°W, 38.23°N

Calasparra is noted for its excellent rice growing which is due to the proximity of the rivers Segura, Quípar and Argos.

Iberians, Romans, Arabs and Christians have left a deep and indelible mark on the history of Calasparra, which thanks to them has a rich history of archaeological and monumental art. Take a look at the cave paintings of Abrigo del Pozo, Santuario Nuestra Señora de la Esperanza, the ruins of an old town at Villa Vieja, San Juan Castle and the Palacio de la Encomienda de la Orden de San Juan de Jerusalén (Palace of the Knights of the Order of St. John of Jerusalem).

In the centre of town you can find the remains of the Arab castle, **Castillo de San Juan**, off Plaza de la Constitución. Getting to the castle is easy, go on foot from the centre of town along a stepped and landscaped street. It's currently being renovated.

One of the most visited highlights of the region is the **Santuario de la Esperanza**, located six kilometres northwest of the city in Lomas de la Virgin. It's a beautiful location overlooking the River Segura, with well tended gardens and monumental arches. The building, reminiscent of Gaudí's architecture, is a beautiful combination of nature and art and was started in the 17th century. The river has created a small valley and in a natural, river-made cave is the shrine. There are a lot of steps so make sure you wear good shoes. The shrine can get busy during peak periods.

Calasparra has a fiesta of Virgen de la Esperanza which is between the 2nd and 8th of September which is visited by many people in the region.

There is an **archaeological museum** in the old Palace House of La Encomienda, there are a number of old churches such as Iglesia de la Merced, Iglesia de san Pedro (18th century) and Iglesia de los Santos (18th century).

Calasparra specialities such as rice, sweets and cheeses can be found in Calle Teniente Flomesta.

Around Calasparra you can go up to **Las Lomas de la Virgen** to get a fantastic view of the mountains, the river and the rice fields. Nearby you'll find the natural reserve of **Cañadaverosa** which was devastated by fire in 2010. Another nearby beauty spot is **Cañón de Los Almadenes**. For cave lovers there's the **Puerto del Cueva**, located in the Sierra of the same name, which is one of the most interesting and most horizontal run. Its interior is divided into various sections, rooms and galleries.

The Youth Environmental Initiatives Center (**Centro de Iniciativas Ecológicas Albergue**), located in the hills of the sanctuary, has living areas for up to 56 people and additional camping areas. It develops a schedule of sports and adventure on a strictly educational basis aimed at teachers, environmental education courses and seminar leaders.

Friday is market day in Calasparra. The streets are filled with the aroma of sun-ripened fresh fruit and vegetables, chicken, chorizo and children.

Fiestas focus around the end of August and first week of September with bull running through the streets (encierros), solemn processions, music, food and drink, and a Romería.

The Rice

Calasparra rice is the first in the world to have been awarded a Denominación de Origen, DOC, which symbolises a guarantee of high quality.

The rice is grown in a special environment, both sunny and mountainous, ranging from 340 to 500 metres in altitude, and irrigated with fresh water from the River Segura.

The cultivation uses a unique irrigation system allowing the fresh water to be continually renewed. The clever use of crop rotation ensures the land is allowed to rest. The traditional seeds (Bomba and Balilla X Sollana) are almost unique to this region and are the only ones ever used.

The ripening process takes much longer than with other rice varieties (approximately 30% longer) and this natural drying gives the rice a distinctive taste and texture. The grain is especially hard and Calasparra rice needs more water for cooking, which means the rice never sticks together and always looks fluffy!

The rice comes in sealed packs often made from cotton, each one carrying a numbered label issued by the Consejo Regulador, guaranteeing its authenticity and quality. You can buy the rice in most large supermarkets throughout the Murcian region and from shops in Calasparra and surrounds.

Museo del Arroz was officially opened on June 1st 2007. This rice museum is based in the first and second floors of the Casa-Granero on Calle Major that belonged to the Condes del Valle de San Juan. It's a beautifully restored building with balconies, barred windows and a coat of arms above the imposing front door.

The first floor has displays on the process of rice cultivation and a number of recipes where rice is the predominant ingredient. There are also old photographs showing the work of rice farmers. The second floor houses machinery from the nineteenth century rice mill which was part of the Condes del Valle de San Juan. Visiting Hours: Tuesday to Sunday from 11:00 to 14:00.

Services

Tourist Office, in Casa-Granero, Calle Major. Monday to Fridays 9:00 to 14:00 and 17:00 to 19:00, www.turismocalasparra.es, 968 745325.

Ayuntamiento, Plaza Corredera, 27, 968 720044, www.calasparra.org

Buses from the corner of Calle Teniente Flomesta.

Taxis on Avenida Juan Ramón Jiménez, 968 720959.

Train station is 4km out to the north of town.

Sleeping

Just 4km outside of Calasparra there's the Camping Los Viveros site near Santuario de Virgen de la Esperanza. 968 735889, www.campinglosviveros.com. You can camp or stay in one of the wooden houses. There's an onsite restaurant, supermarket and swimming pools. If there's a big group of you consider renting the whole house, the Caserío Las Tinajas, which sleeps up to 12 people.

Another casa rural is the Palmera Moya on Paraje La Palmera, 968 746143, www.palmeramoya.es, which can sleep up to 8 people.

Albergue Las Lomas, on Paraje de Las Lomas, 1km from Santuario de Virgen de la Esperanza offers 7 wooden cabins in this youth hostel (albergue), 968 723000.

You could stay at the out of town Hotel Argos, Carretera Caravaca-Calasparra, km1080, 968 720707. Prices around €60, 6 rooms and a large restaurant. www.h-argos.com

Eating

The typical dish of the town is the Caldera. The tradition dates back to the fifteenth century, when the bulls, after the fight, were sent to slaughter and the locals flocked to the square to buy the meat from the animals. Typical ingredients include bull meat, knuckles of ham, peas, pepper, salt, egg and oregano.

The Caldera shares the limelight with the rice. Eating rice in Calasparra is just about compulsory! Try some of these good–value places:

- Las Lomas, Carretera del Santuario, modern restaurant with fantastic views and rich paellas (which you may need to pre–order).
- Virgen de la Esperanza, Santuario de Virgen de la Esperanza, rich paellas mixtas are available on the fixed price menu.

They have a tapas route (Ruta de Tapas) at the end of October, look out for details on the website: www.calasparra.org

Night Life

In the fiesta period Calasparra really shines with lots of live music. A lot of bars have quite a relaxed, sophisticated nature. Places to try include Mejorano, Pinver, Cantero and Rialto which are on Calle Miguel Hernández.

Calblanque

Map Reference: 0.78°W, 37.62°N

Calblanque is a remote and almost untouched stretch of coast, just south of the Mar Menor. This designated natural park enjoys secluded bays, solitude and an abundance of wild birds and flowers. Boardwalks criss–cross the sand dunes leading down to the beaches, with paths along the coast. The area is completely protected from the uncontrolled building which has affected other coastal destinations.

For places to eat and stay see Cabo de Palos, La Manga or the Cartagena sections.

Location Report: Calblanque Revealed

On a damp Sunday afternoon in February the beach is secluded. The sun is just about breaking through the low clouds, the sound of the sea crashing into the fossil-rich rocks acts as our backdrop and we once again marvel at how lucky we are to be living in Murcia. Our peace is only broken by the call of birds, the smash of the sea and the sound of a couple of 4x4s zipping around on the dirt roads.

We visited the natural park of Calblanque, a little bit of Murcia that I'd never visited before and wish I'd gotten round to sooner.

The beaches are great for scuba diving and snorkelling as the waters are very clear, though I must say that only the very hardy would be in the water at this time of year. You are more likely to bump into a herd of goats than see an armada of pedalos sailing past, as was proven by the hundreds of cloven footprints and little black droppings on the trail we followed. These beaches are also of interest to surfers, kitesurfers and windsurfers.

The area is abundant in wildlife and you may see: cypress groves, badgers, sea turtles (if you're very lucky), Bonelli's eagle, the eagle owl, the green woodpecker, flamingos and several varieties of heron and plover and many varieties of wild flowers.

Areas to visit include: Salinas de Rasall (salt flats), Playa de Calblanque, Playa Larga (long beach), Playa Negrete (nudist beach, though it was a little too cold!), Playa de las Cañas and the old mines (abandoned tin, silver and copper mines).

Best reached by car access is via a bumpy road, off the main road to La Manga. Head for the Information Point and if you're lucky you'll meet the same highly enthusiastic and knowledgeable young woman we did. When we visited they also had a small exhibition of photographs on display in the adjoining room. Call on 968 298423, open 10:00 to 14:00, 15:00 to 18:00 Tue–Sun. The information point has some useful leaflets.

There is an extensive network of long distance walks throughout Spain, with a number crossing into Murcia. These are called the senderos de Gran Recorrido (GRs). We have the GR7 all the way from Andorra, as well as many shorter footpaths called the senderos de Pequeño Recorrido (PRs).

The best books, covering the whole of the region are a range from Natursport, www.natursport.com, which can be bought online or from some tourist information points. Their publications include walking and cycling routes along the River Segura, into the Sierra Espuña and along the miles of coast, including here in Calblanque. There is the PR1, PR2 and the GR92. The Federación de Orientación de la Región de Murcia www.regiondemurciaorientacion.com organises orienteering in the Murcia region.

If you enjoy walking, cycling, nature, swimming, snorkelling or relaxing then this is the place to come.

Caravaca De La Cruz

Population: 25,600

Map Reference: 1.86°W, 38.10°N

Caravaca de la Cruz (or more commonly Caravaca) is a beautiful medieval (12th and 13th century) town, with many historic, traditional properties in the old quarter. The town has been declared by the Vatican (in 1998 by the then Pope John Paul II) as one of the world's Holy Cities, along with Rome, Jerusalem, Santiago de Compostela and Santo Toribio de Liébana, thus giving Spain three out of five. Caravaca de la Cruz is also allowed to celebrate the **Perpetual Jubilee** once every seven years the first being in 2003, when it was visited by the then Cardinal Ratzinger, now Pope Benedict XVI. The next time will be in 2017.

Eight mountains exceed 1000m: sierras de Gadea, la Pinosa, la Serrata, la Zarza, las Cabras, Mojantes and Vicario. You'll find many types of birds including Montague's harriers, curlews, grouse and small mammals, wild boar and, to a lesser extent, goats threatened by poachers and all terrain vehicles.

Narrow streets and alleys lead towards the castle, built in the 15th century and commissioned by the Knights Templar. Parking is a nightmare, park wherever you can find a space and walk! Once out and about, you'll quickly find a number of museums, such as **Museo Sacro de la Vera Cruz** (religious artefacts), **Museo de los Festejos and also Museo Arqueológico**. A handsome ensemble of medieval and Renaissance mansions and churches are clustered in the old town.

Down in the centre of town the main attractions are the **Iglesia del Salvador**, the monastery at **Iglesia de San José** and **Ermita de San Sebastián** (Map: C4) with interesting murals. Also the Ermita de Santa Elena (Map: B3) and the Iglesia de la Concepción (Map:B5). Around the area you can find the spring at Fuentes de Marqués and various archaeological sites at Cueva Negra, Palacia de Armas, Los Villares, Cerro de la Ermitas and Cuevo del Rey Moro.

The bull ring (Plaza de Toros, Map: D1) is used for music gigs, events, the Medieval market, concerts and theatre, as well as for some of the largest bull fights in the region. It can hold over 3000 people. It's a beautiful building, the red colour of the gypsum, the ochre of the walls and the unmistakable Arab and Muslim influences with arches and plasterwork makes it unmissable.

Up the hill, you'll find the most photographed church in the area, **El Santuario de Vera Cruz** (Map: F2), with a pink marble façade. The church houses the cross used in the Easter celebrations, Semana Santa. The Santuario de la Vera Cruz also houses a relic of the True Cross, brought here according to legend by two angels in 1231. This is commemorated annually on 3 May when the relic is carried through the streets.

At the beginning of May Caravaca has very famous and popular fiestas, Santísima y Vera Cruz. Book your accommodation well in advance. On May 3rd the Holy Cross is bathed at Templete (Map:A5), a hexagonal, Baroque building.

Another popular part of the May fiesta (2nd May) is los **Caballos del Vino** (wine horses) in commemoration of a tradition that took place in the 13th century. The Christians besieged in the fortress by the Arabs managed to break the siege and search for water. When they failed to find any water they returned to the fortress with the wineskins on their horses filled with wine. The commemoration consists of decoratively harnessed horses galloping up the steep slopes to the Castle.

Every Monday is market day (Map: C5), there's the fruit and vegetable part located in the adjacent streets to the Plaza Juan Pablo II and the general market in the streets: Corredera, Poeta Ibañez, Cuesta de las Herrerias, Rafael Tejeo and Cuesta de la Plaza. On the third Sunday of the month there's the **Mercado del Peregrino**, an artisan market with lots of local produce and merchandise, held in the Plaza del Arcos.

Around the first weekend in December (6th to 8th December), in the Plaza de Toros, sees the **Medieval Artisan Market**. More than 100 artisans from all over Spain dressed in costumes of the era with medieval-style decorated stalls descend upon Caravaca. Specialities include: decorating and painting, stone carving, lace making, distillation of aromatic plants, silkworm rearing, wine making, esparto grass craft, puppets, cut glass, confectionary and bakery, the pork-butcher, turrón, carpenter, beekeepers, cheese maker, rug weaver, makers of homemade soap, ceramics, jewellery, natural cosmetics, leather, cardboard, wood and stone, etc. There are also demonstrations of their work; several of these activities may directly involve visitors. Check on the tourist information site for the actual dates each year.

The other most important towns in the Caravaca municipality are Archivel, Barranda, La Almudema and La Encarnación (where the Santuario de la Encarnación has its origins). Other towns are Benablón, Pinilla de San José, Singla, Los Royos, Caneja, El Moralejo, Navares, Los Prados, El Moral and El Hornico.

Archivel

The small town of Archivel includes the villages of Casicas and Noguera, plus a number of scattered houses. It consists of 627 dwellings, of which around 20% are empty or just temporarily used. Archivel is located specifically in the corridor that leads to the Campo de San Juan (Moratalla) in the Argos river basin, at the western end of Caravaca de la Cruz. It's at 905 meters above sea level with a population of 1208 inhabitants.

Much of the town rests on a Celtic-Iberian necropolis near which were found many archaeological sites. In the **Cerro de la Fuente**, commonly known in town as 'The Saint', they have excavated a Roman castellum dating from the era of civil wars between Pompeii and Julius Caesar.

This town is shaped as an irregular circle. It is bounded by the foundations of a wall that included a defensive tower next to the entrance. It's surrounded by mountains covered in pine and juniper trees, Serrata de Caneja, Sierra de Mojantes and Majada de las Vacas.

There's a flour mill built in the early part of 1500 called **Molino Harinero del Río** with a horizontal water wheel to take water from the Río Argos. This is worth a visit and has been completely restored.

From the 4th to the 8th of December they celebrate their fiesta in honour of Santa Bárbara.

Barranda

The central zone of the town in its main square known as El Muelle is where every year pregón (literally translated as street cry) is staged, which is a satirical burlesque of the main events that have taken place during the year. This event belongs to the program of events in honour of the Virgen de la Candelaría, that are celebrated from the last Sunday of January to the 2nd of February.

Barranda celebrates the famous Fiesta de las Cuadrillas, a folk festival which takes place every last Sunday of January and attracts more than twenty thousand people to enjoy folk music in the streets. www.fiestadelascuadrillas.com

Thanks to this deeply rooted cultural tradition in 2006 they opened the **Museum of Ethnic Music** with a collection of over four thousand instruments from around the world. Open Tuesday to Friday from 10:00 to 14:00 and 16:00 to 18:00 and Saturdays, Sundays and holidays from 10:00 to 18:00. Museo de la Música de Étnica de Barranda, www.museomusicaetnica.com, Calle Pedrera, 968 738491.

La Almudema

According to some the name of this town, 12 kilometres from Caravaca, comes from the Arabic, Al-Mudayna, the citadel. The history of this town is fully linked to the history of the Christian reconquest. This is a small population nearly 800m above sea level with a landscape of pine and scrub.

La Almudema celebrates its patron saint on January 14th, for San Antón a hermit from the fourth century, who retired to a hill near the Red Sea. As well as the usual processions and parties, there are often greased pig catching contests and also a pilgrimage across the Roman Bridge.

La Encarnación

This small population 750m above sea level enjoys significant ancient sites, highlighting the Iberians and Romans. There are guided tours through these ruins.

The **archaeological complex of La Encarnación** is located a few kilometres from Caravaca, just over a mile from the hamlet Los Prados. The archaeological site consists of a sanctuary from the first century BC, built over an earlier Iberian temple and an extensive stone quarry.

La Cueva del Rey Moro is an interesting fortress that was built around the twelfth or thirteenth centuries, using a small cave or natural shelter open on the west side of the hill of Villaricos. The construction consists basically of a wall built with excellent mud mortar that closes the opening of a natural shelter located on the rocky slope formed by the narrow valley, called Estrecho de las Cuevas. La Cueva del Rey Moro is declared of Cultural Interest.

On the 25th of March they celebrate their local fiesta dedicated to Virgen de la Encarnación.

Services

Tourist Office, Calle de Monjas, 17, www.caravaca.org, click on the link which says callejero for a map or try www.turismocaravaca.org.

Ayuntamiento, Plaza Del Arco, 1, 968 702000.

Bus Station on Carretera de Granada and every hour you can get a bus to Murcia (takes 1 hour and 30 minutes). Daily buses also run to Lorca.

Taxi ranks on Calle Incomienda and at the corner of Gran Vía and Juan Carlos I, 646 223009, 622 936524.

Sleeping

In the centre of town there's the Hotel Central, Gran Vía, 18 with prices from €70 per night in low season. www.hotelcentralcaravaca.wixsite.com 968 707055. There's also a restaurant on site, but it's pricey and there have been mixed reviews.

Casa Pedro Barrera, 1 Calle el Pinar, La Almudema, 687 118450, www.casapedrobarrera.com has 5 rooms, a swimming pool and ample outside space. Prices start from €90, you can book dinner and there are a variety of interesting courses that can be included.

For a larger group, the El Molino de Río sleeps up to 32 people (smaller groups are welcome too) and is a large country house from the 16th century, 606 301 409, www.molinodelrio.com.

For plenty more casas rurales try the website: www.guiarural.com.

Eating

Generally the best food around here is migas and tocino de cielo a very sweet pudding made with egg yolk and syrup. Another speciality is Yemas de Caravaca, again very sweet. For tapas visit El Arco and La Bodega.

The casa rural, El Molino de Río, has a restaurant and they make their own beer, lager and bitter: www.cerveza-elmolino.com or 968 433381. And if you fancy making your own lunch they offer cookery courses.

Whilst it doesn't look like much from the outside, the restaurant El Cason de los Reyes, Carretera Granada, 11 (next to the hospital) is worth a visit. It opened in 2008 and has a great tapas bar along with all the usual suspects.

Others to try:

- Casablanca, Paraje Casablanca, typical dishes of the region including rice.
- Contamos Contigo, Calle Dos de Mayo, 8, cold and hot tapas.
- El Burladero, Calle Severo Ochoa, 18, meat and bulls tail.
- El Malena, Near to the Polígono Industrial Venta Cavila, game, fresh fish, and Mediterranean food.
- El Zorro, Pedanía de Barranda, traditional cooking on the grill.
- La Granja, Pedanía de Archivel, horse meat prepared like steak on the grill, with peppers and whiskey or Roquefort.
- La Paz, Calle Simancas, 12, baby goat with garlic, leg of lamb, fish.
- Fuentes del Marqués, Paraje Fuentes del Marqués, www.fuentesdelmarques.com, game, rice and fish.
- Restaurante–Bar–Cafetería, Plaza Constitución 5, Pedanía de Archival, rice, migas, various tapas.
- Rincón de Paco, Calle Lonja, 5, www.rincondepaco.com, large selection of Spanish sausages and various tapas.
- Sierra de Mojantes, Pedanía de Archivel, roast meat, rice, migas.
- Sol, Avenida Juan Carlos I, 24, cold and hot tapas, octopus, and seafood.

Night Life

Dancing clubs are found throughout the length of Calle Trafalgar. More clubs can be found in Calle Pedro Martínez such as Blanco y Negro (20s to 30s). You could also try El Hospicio on Calle Hospicio.

Cartagena and Surrounds

Population: 214,200

Map Reference: 0.98°W, 37.60°N

Situated in the south east of the region, it's the second city of Murcia. It's a maritime town with a history stretching back to Roman times. The Cartagena region can be viewed as a great plane inclined slightly in the direction NW-SE, bordered at the north and the northwest by pre-coastal mountain ranges (Carrascoy, El Puerto, Los Villares, Columbares and Escalona), and at the south and southwest by coastal mountain ranges (El Algarrobo, La Muela, Pelayo, Gorda, La Fausilla y Minera, with its last spurs in Cabo de Palos). The dominant geology of the region is metamorphic (slate, marble) and sedimentary (limestone).

The old town is limited by five small hills (Molinete, Monte Sacro, Monte de San José, Despeñaperros and Monte de la Concepción). In the past there was an inner sea between the hills called the Estero that eventually dried up. On this site the Ensanche (expansion or new town) was built at the beginning of the 20th Century.

The main road is Paseo de Alfonso XIII, to the south of which lie most areas of interest, including the city's port (pedestrianised area) and tourist sites.

The majority of tourist attractions have a maritime theme, perhaps the most obvious example being the submarine from 1888, which is installed at the port end of the main pedestrianised shopping area.

There is a naval museum, an underwater archaeology museum and a large arsenal down by the port. Near the bullring there's a recently re–discovered Roman amphitheatre.

If you have a car you'll be able to drive to many fortresses, castles, fortifications and battlements, ranging from Roman construction through to abandoned 20th century projects. Cartagena's military importance is charted by numerous installations including huge guns on the hilltops, submarine tunnels straight out of a James Bond film set and 16th century pirate lookout towers.

El Palacio de Deportes, over by the Eroski shopping mall near Tentegorra, has finally opened and currently hosts sports like basketball and handball. The outside of the uilding is already looking worse for wear, with some panels falling off. The covered swimming pool has, however, fallen victim to the continued delays with the project and requires substantial renovation before it can open to the public.

Tourist vouchers can be purchased that give substantial discounts. Reduced prices apply to children under 12, students, retired people, disabled people and the unemployed. Take a look here for prices www.cartagenapuertodeculturas.com. Or buy the Cartagena Card. Both tourist offices sell the Cartagena Card; price €18, which is valid for two weeks and covers admission to eight cultural sites as well as free travel around the city on the tourist bus and the harbour ferry.

Depending upon your interests there are specific tourist routes suggested. Here's an overview of each route and what you can see. Individual entrance to attractions is generally between €2 and €5.

Tourist Bus: takes you to Cartagena's most historic sites.

Tourist Boat: sail through the city port and get a closer look at the castles and fortresses that protected the city.

Location Report:
Tentegorra Park

Coming on holiday to the Murcia region with your kids and you'll no doubt be looking for a water park to visit. Of course you could zip up the coast and head into Benidorm for the Aqualandia experience, at about 23 euros per person, or to Aqua Natura in Benidorm for about the same price. Or you could stick around the Murcia area and enjoy one of our two water parks – Aqua Natura Murcia (covered in the Murcia section) or the little known Parque Tentegorra near Cartagena.

I don't really want to tell you about Tentegorra water and adventure park because I'd prefer to keep it to myself, but that's selfish, as this park is by far the best value for money you will find in the Murcia area. It's situated out of town near Cartagena, in the area called Tentegorra – which itself is a great place to have a drive around. It's more than a water park – there's a full blown adventure park here too, with death slides and trails through the wonderful parkland, a huge maze, a kids play area (sometimes they have a bouncy castle), football, tennis & padel courts, and of course 3 swimming pools with slides and water features. The water slides aren't nearly as big as Aqua Natura, but they are plenty of fun for big kids and little ones – there's a height restriction for the largest slide.

To use the swimming pools the prices are around (it changes a little in different seasons) 5 euros for adults & 3 euros for children – yes that's right – a family of 4 can enter the park and use the swimming pools for just 16 euros – less than the price of a single entrance to Aqua Natura. The restaurant in the park is excellent value – Spanish staples, paella at lunchtime, bocadillos, drinks all at exceptionally reasonable prices, you can sit inside or in the gardens. The changing rooms are fine, clean and plenty of space. Parking is free.

If you want a relaxing, inexpensive family day out, with plenty to do and see then come to Tentegorra.

T: 689 250 179 & Location of Parque Tentegorra – http://parquetentegorra.es/ubicacion/

Prices & hours – http://parquetentegorra.es/tarifas/

Their facebook page where they sometimes have offers: www.facebook.com/ParqueTentegorra

More information about the project – Mancomunidad de los Canales del Taibilla – La Mancomunid (MCT) http://www.mct.es/es/

Tentegorra Park & Waterpark versus Aqua Natura Murcia

Now for my money I'd choose Parque Tentegorra, especially for younger kids. It's so much cheaper, the surrounds are nicer, the food is better quality & value, parking is easy & free and access is easy. You don't have the big scary slides at Parque Tentegorra but you could go every day for a week, eat lunch there and still save money on a 2 day entrance to Aqua Natura!

Archaeological Route

Municipal Archaeological Museum. This is the base of all archaeological activity in the city. Opened in 1982 the museum is built over the late 4th century Roman necropolis of San Antón; it contains one of the most important collections of tombs in the country. There are also remains from pottery, mining, ceramics and sculpture. It's very close to El Corte Inglés shopping centre, you'll spot the remains as you walk past. Calle Ramón y Cajal, 45, 968 539027, www.museoarqueologicocartagena.es. Open from Tuesday to Friday: from 10:00 to 14:00 and from 17:00 to 20:00. Saturdays and Sundays: from 11:00 to 14:00.

Muralla Púnica (Map: E2). The Punic rampart was discovered in

1989 on the south side of the hill of San José, or Aletes, as it was known in Roman times. The construction dates back to 227 BC, with the founding of the Punic city and the conversion of Cartagena (then called Qart-Hadast) into the capital of the Carthaginians. The fortifications are in the Hellenist style, with two parallel walls spaced 18 feet apart that are linked together by other walls. The rampart enclosed the Punic city, and this particular stretch covered the isthmus, the only entrance to the city. Calle San Diego, 25, 968 500093.

Casa de la Fortuna. On either side of a stretch of Roman road lie the remains of two dwellings dating from the first century BC, known as the House of Fortune. You can see the pavements, the walls with the entrance threshold and the opus signinum decorated flooring. The most impressive feature is the fresco painted decoration of the dining room walls of the Casa de la Fortuna. Calle Duque, 29, 968 500093.

Augusteum. This is one of the best-kept archaeological sites in the city, and it is composed of the remains of two public buildings from Roman times in the Cartago-Nova area, dated from the 1st century AD. It may be one of the first locations used for religious purposes identified as a meeting place devoted to the worship of the Emperor Augustus. It has an interesting exposition hall dedicated to the Roman Forum. Calle Caballero, 2, 968 500093.

Decumanus. Excavated in 1968, this is the site of a paved Roman road, the main thoroughfare through the city, linking the port to the forum and a series of thermal baths stretching along Calle Honda as far as Molinete hill (which is also worth a visit). Plaza de los Tres Reyes, 1, 968 500093.

Roman Theatre Museum. The theatre was discovered by pure chance. The northern side of the hill known as La Concepción was the location where stands were erected. The commemorative inscriptions indicate that construction began in the late first century BC in the heyday of the Roman Colony's urban development. Right on the Roman Theatre and making up part of it lie the ruins of the Ancient Cathedral. Plaza del Ayuntamiento, 9, 968 504802 www.teatroromanocartagena.org/.

The Castle of la Concepción, Centre of Interpretation of the History of Cartagena (Map: D3). On the hill of the same name is the Centre for the Interpretation of History and Medieval Cartagena. Most of the materials used to build the castle were taken from structures built when the city was a Roman colony. Further rebuilding was undertaken in the 14th century. A number of the castle's old rooms have been refurbished. Parque Torres, 968 124000.

Amphitheatre (Map: C3). The amphitheatre was situated beneath the old bullring, built in 1854. One of the oldest monuments of its kind in Spain, it was built in the 1st century BC following the model of earlier Italian buildings. Much of it has now been excavated and can be seen from the outside. Visiting is currently impossible because the structure is unstable. Plaza del Hospital.

ARQUA - National Museum of Underwater Archaeology. Two sets of items from the Phoenician era stand out: the tusks of an elephant and the remains of boats from Mazarrón, as well as items found in the Roman shipwrecks of the Isla de Escombreras. Paseo de Muelle Alfonso XII, 22, 968 121 166, www.culturaydeporte.gob.es/mnarqua/home.html.

Baroque and Neoclassical Route

Campus Muralla del Mar. The old military hospital and the Antigones Barracks, both Neoclassical buildings constructed in the 18th Century when Cartagena had become the principal Spanish naval base of the Mediterranean, have been renovated and adapted for university use. The characteristic military architectural features of the outside of these buildings remain intact. Part of the Hospital is the Autopsy Building, where classes on anatomy were held. Plaza del Hospital (next to Universidad Politécnica).

Arsenal Gate (Map: B3). The sole remaining entrance to the ramparts of Cartagena built in the 18th century. In 1865 a clock tower was built over the gateway, highlighting the importance of the area to which it gives access. Calle Real.

Church of Santo Domingo. Once part of the Dominican Convent of San Isidoro, built in 1695 and recently restored, it houses a baroque altarpiece of multi-coloured wood featuring a variety of Holy Week images. Calle Mayor, 28.

Church of Santa María de Gracia. Built during the 18th century and renovated in the 19th and 20th centuries, its façade remains unfinished to this day. The original plan was to build a church of cathedral proportions, the natural successor to Santa María la Vieja. The most architecturally significant sculptures inside are the medieval image of the Virgin of the Rosell (former patron saint of the city) and the figures of the Four Saints, the work of Salzillo. The Holy Week processions have begun from this building ever since its construction in the 18th century. Calle Aire, 28.

Naval Headquarters Palace. The Capitanía was built in 1740 over part of the space occupied by the King's House. The façade was reconstructed in the 19th century and renovated in the 20th. The interior is richly decorated with its imperial staircase being especially notable. Puertas de Murcia, 1.

Church of El Carmen. The church was once part of the former Convent of San Joaquín, the home of the Barefoot Carmelite Order. The façade combines elements of classical and popular architecture and the interior has a single nave with side chapels. Calle Carmen, 14.

Artillery Headquarters (Map: C1). Its architecture is typical of the 18th century military constructions so widely represented in the city. The building, which was virtually destroyed by an explosion towards the end of the canton uprising in 1874, was not rebuilt until the beginning of the 20th century. The side walls best retain the original building's appearance. It is currently the headquarters of the Municipal Historical Archives and the Military Museum which, through its maps, models and documents, illustrates the history of this military arm and its links with the city since 1508. Plaza del General López Pinto, 968 501300.

Location Report: The Spanish Army

The Historical Military Museum of Cartagena is actually dedicated to the land forces of Spain's military. The building itself is worth visiting and the museum has been beautifully developed within its courtyards and two floors. It is within the confines of the old artillery park and today holds the largest collection of artillery in Europe. There are various examples of military hardware from around the world on display including tanks and mobile missile launchers. There is also a gallery full of uniforms through the centuries, but photography is strictly prohibited in that section.

You can also view the world's biggest collection of military models as verified by Guinness World Records. It consists of 2,815 pieces! Of particular interest was the story of the SS Castillo de Olite, a ship carrying Natioanlist troops at the very end of the civil war. She was sunk by Republican artillery having not received an order to retreat due to a broken radio. Nearly 1500 people died and this incident represents the greatest loss of life from the sinking of a single ship in Spanish naval history.

Modernist & Eclectic Route

Interpretation Centre of Defensive Architecture, Fuerte Navidad. The fort, built during the 1860s to defend the interior of the harbour, the city and the Arsenal from attack by enemy fleets, is located at one of the points on the coast flanking the harbour entrance. The building, of Neoclassical style, has materials explaining the importance of Cartagena along the Mediterranean axis throughout the centuries resulting from its geographically strategic position. Carretera De La Algameca, Faro de Navidad.

Railway Station. The modernist decorative details, such as the ironwork on doors and columns, the cantilever roof and the Roman window on the façade, are of special interest. The interior was also decorated along modernist lines, though all that remains today of the design are the ticket counter, the doorframes, the ceiling and the lamp. Plaza de Mejico, 1.

Palacio Aguirre houses the Regional Museum of Modern Art, MURAM (Map: D2). The tower crowned with a spectacular dome bears down over the building from which two extravagantly decorated façades emerge. The museum unites the concept of modernity in both its appearance and its content. The exhibitions are focused on artistic works produced from around 1870 to 1960. Check on the website to see what's coming next. Plaza de la Merced, 16, 968 501607, www.museosregiondemurcia.es/museo-regional-de-arte-moderno-de-cartagena/, free entry.

Caridad Church (Map: C2). Once the church of the Caridad Hospital, in its present form it has a Neoclassical style and a metal structure. The interior is dominated by the dome, a typical feature of many Neoclassical buildings, whose model was Agrippa's Pantheon in Rome. The church is the home of the city's patron saint, the Virgin of Sorrow, an 18th century image sculpted in Naples. There are several sculptures by Salzillo and his school, including the Crucifixion, the Rococo altarpiece in the Comunión Chapel and the canvases painted by Manuel Wssell de Guimbarda in 1893. Calle Caridad, 15.

Maestre House. The façade is the only reminder of the house's original design and was inspired by the Casa Calvet by Gaudí with a few touches of Baroque. The Rococo decorations around the main door, the belvedere and windows in the central section are especially notable. Plaza San Francisco, 5.

Consistorial Palace. A triangular-shaped building with three different façades, the official nature of the edifice is underscored by it eclectic construction. Inside, the modernist style is evident in the paintings and decorative details in the grand entrance hall and on the second floor. Plaza del Ayuntamiento.

Casino. The 18th century doorway is the only reminder of the building's origins as the house for the Marquis of Casatilly, which was finally remodelled by Víctor Beltrí around 1897. Inside the highlight is the patio ringed by a second floor gallery. Decorations and furnishings are modern. Calle Mayor, 13.

Casa Zapata. The house was built in the Gothic-inspired modernist style typical of Catalonia, the birthplace of architect Victor Beltrí. Outside, you can see the columned doorway and crenellated tower, as well as the Viennese-style mouldings on the walls. There is an Arab-style glass-covered patio inside but sadly it is currently closed to the public. Plaza de España, 9. You can see a video of what you are missing at www.memoriadecartagena.es/patio-de-la-casa-zapata/

Contemporary Route

Civil War Shelter Museum. These galleries, excavated out of the Cerro de la Concepción to serve as air-raid shelters, were still to be completed at the end of the Spanish Civil War. They were part of the works carried out to construct shelters able to hold 5,500 people during the heavy bombing that Cartagena was subjected to, as it was the naval base for a great part of the Republican fleet. Calle Gisbert, 968 500093.

Lift Gangway. Built across the Cartagena hill the gangway was opened in 1878, thereby connecting Cartagena to the sea. A lift now carries passengers up the 45m elevation, replacing the natural route which was swallowed up with the excavation work. Calle Gisbert, 10.

Location Report: The Spanish Navy

Located just a few minutes walk from the cruise ship terminal, the museum dedicated to the history of Spain's naval forces will take you a couple of hours to get around. There are, as you might expect, many models of ships, and a large collection of nautical paintings. Of particular interest is the video dedicated to mine clearance where you can learn how these awful weapons are dealt with at sea.

The star of the show though, is located in a separate building away from all the artillery and navigational displays. The submarine, the Peral, was one of the first electrically powered submarines to be built. It is named after its designer, Lt. Isaac Peral y Caballero, and dates all the way back to 1888. It only saw service for two years but somehow escaped being scrapped. Many years later it was placed on public display near the port before being moved to its own specially designed housing in 2013. The video showing the relocation of the submarine is fascinating.

Whilst the museum is free to visit, the staff guarding the entrance are quite firm when it comes to asking for donations! Opening times are Tuesday to Saturday, 1000-1400.

Naval Museum (Map: A1). Devoted to naval topics the museum occupies part of a modernist building built in 1926. Of special interest are the collections of model ships and maps, and the room dedicated to Isaac Peral.

Asamblea Regional. Built in 1987 for its present use, the building has a façade which displays a number of influences: the Venetian Renaissance and a certain modernist air linking it to the typical Levantine architecture. Inside, the most impressive sights are the Patio de los Ayuntamientos (Court of Town Halls) and the Patio de las Comarcas (Court of the Districts). Paseo Alfonso XIII, 53.

Shopping

The shopping area stretches along Calle Major. Most major European shops can be found here, including Zara, Mango, Bershka, Massimo Dutti, Oysho, Tintoretto and Stradivarius. They have two independent bookshops, where you can get maps and guide books (mainly in Spanish, but there are a few English books too). There are also plenty of local shops to wander around. Remember to look up while shopping to see some beautiful façades, many of which have been reformed and rebuilt.

An El Corte Inglés store was built on Alameda de San Anton in 2005 and is one of the largest, including a large cafe and restaurant. There's ample free parking.

For your big shopping mall fix there's Mandarache Centre and Parque Mediterraneo, both have multi-screen cinemas and all the usual outlets and food malls.

Activities

Around Cartagena there are many forts, castles, batteries, walls and fortresses. The website: www.fortalezasdecartagena.com has a list of them all, along with photos and maps.

For a spot of sailing or yacht-spotting there's the sports port www.cartagenamarina.es 968 121213 with moorings available for boats of 12 to 65 metres, and special moorings for 'mega-yachts'. This is a very busy port and a great place to while away a few hours watching the huge cruise ships come in or the mega-yachts go out. The club can be found at www.clubregatascartagena.es and they are very inviting to non-members. It's a great place to enjoy a drink (or two) and watch Cartagena settle down for the evening. They have a sailing school and one of our favourite dive schools right here by the club.

There's also a tourist boat from the port that takes you on a round trip out of the port mouth and along the shoreline to view some of the historic naval batteries and forts. You can have a round trip of about 1 hour for €5.50 or have a round trip and a stop off at Fuerte Navidad for €8 (you could find our geocache whilst you're there!)

Diving from Cartagena is highly recommended, it's calm even in mid-summer and there's usually somewhere to park. I (Debs) make no apologies for mentioning diving so often in this book (though some people have criticised the frequency) – Murcia has some amazing dives. I've dived around the world at plenty of famous places, and still some of my favourite dives are here.

Adjoining Cartagena harbour is the small fishing port of Santa Lucía where you can see the auction and sale of fish which takes place in La Lonja where fishermen display their best catches to the dealers, suppliers and the curious.

Location Report: Romans, Dining, Geocaching & Diving

Being the second largest city in the region of Murcia you would think Cartagena would still have the big metropolitan feel of Murcia, but it's a refreshingly wide open and low slung place with a beautiful and busy port area. We had ice cream at the leisure port, overlooking the natural harbour formed by the mountains, which is full of bars and restaurants (which serve as cafes by day and clubs by night). We also visited the city's air raid shelter (it was a key strategic town during Spain's civil war) and museum, which was fascinating.

Cartagena has a long history of Roman occupation and battles. The reason the Romans wanted Cartagena was because they were amazed at how quickly Carthage, its North African rival, managed to pay off punitive damages imposed by Rome after the First Punic War. There was enormous mineral wealth in the hills surrounding the natural harbour which the Carthaginians discovered and swiftly colonised it (hence its name, from the Latin for New Carthage). The remnants of the mining works can be seen all around (and under the water!)

We also placed a multi-part geocache in Cartagena during a trip with our nephews. If you're not sure about geocaching take a look here: www.native-spain.com/murcia-region/geocaching-fun-for-kids-big-kids-and-gadget-freaks/ for some more information. This geocache is an excellent way to get to know the city and see some of the highlights. If you want to have a look at this cache, go to www.geocaching.com and search for fuertenavidad from user marcusj, I promise you it will be a fun day out with your family.

As you'll have noticed by now, if we're visiting a place near the sea, we'll probably be diving there. And Cartagena was no different. We dived with a lovely club called Hespérides. Our first dive included two sunken boats and a Harrier Jump Jet fuselage. We also dived around the Island of Escombreras.

And of course no trip is complete without some food. Now I hesitate to tell you about Techos Bajos because some restaurants I like to keep to myself! But I would feel bad if I didn't let you in on the best restaurant in Cartagena. It's rough and ready, with fast turnover and quick food. The prices are great, the menú del día is super value, and the ambience is fun! One word of warning, it's a fish restaurant, they sell fish, shellfish and more fish! You can of course order fried egg and chips! Go on a weekday and get the menú del día you won't regret it. Techos Bajos, Paseo del Muelle, 968 505020, it's out of the city in the small town of Santa Lucía.

Walking, around Cartagena you can find loads of trails. The GR92, PR1, PR2, PR4, PR7 PR9, PR12 and PR15 all describe routes covering places such as Portús, Los Belones, Calblanque, Cartagena city and Portman. Walking in the city is pleasant and easy as there are many pedestrianised streets. If you don't feel like walking around the city then try a Segway, for €57 for 2 hours you can whizz around the city, https://ensegway.es/en/segway-cartagena. A really good web site about walks in Spain, including several around the Cartagena area in particular is www.andarines.com. It has not been updates in some considerable time but the information on there is generally still fine.

There are a few horse riding clubs in the area, try Club Hípico Maipe, in La Palma, www.clubhipicomaipe.com, 679 572 690.

The Campo de Cartagena has many beaches, listed separately in the town guides. However, Cartagena itself has a superb beach, Cala Cortina, a calm sandy beach with toilets and showers and a life guard service. It's a very isolated beach (near Escombreras), considering how close it is to Cartagena. There's an excellent restaurant right down by the water. Some local dive clubs use this beach for try-dives as it has easy access for divers.

Fiestas and Festivals

Of course, Cartagena enjoys Holy week, Semana Santa, and its celebrations are probably some of the best in the whole region. Declared to have National Tourist Interest in 1968 due to the rich costumes and embroidery of its penitents, its remarkable religious images, the special colour of its regiment of Jews and grenadiers, the military stamp of the participation of the armed forces in the processions, the thousands of lighthearted child penitents, acts such as Pilate's Maundy, or The Encounter, the float of St. Peter starting at the Military Naval Dockyard or of Jesus of Nazareth at the Fish Market, and the very popular end of the Virgin parades with the home-coming of the thrones to the church.

And you can't think of Cartagena without thinking of the Carthaginians and Romans fiesta. This festival is based on the second Punic War and on characters such as Hannibal and his winning rival, Cornelius Scipio. Celebrations begin with the foundation of Qart-Hadast by Asdrubal in 223 BC and end with the Roman victory in 209 BC. For ten days, all the heroic deeds which took place during the years of the Carthaginian rule, as well as the defeat and invasion by the Roman Empire, are performed and lived in an unparalleled atmosphere by natives and foreigners alike. Troops and legions represent the scenes of events based on the city's history and perform grand parades in the costumes and armaments one would only expect to find in film production. In the second fortnight of September Cartagena and its people get inside history and revive it for ten magnificent days in which the heroic deeds of Carthage and Rome are remembered. The scenes are usually staged at the very place in which the event took place in ancient times.

You can eat and drink with Scipio himself, share a wedding cake with Hannibal, witness the kidnap of a beautiful damsel or the invasion of enemy tents by Carthaginian and Roman warriors. The Carthaginians and Romans Festival typifies the way of thinking and acting of a city which has managed to blend present and past. http://cartaginesesyromanos.es/

And finally, there's Carnaval in February. The Carnaval season has traditionally enjoyed strong popular support in Cartagena especially in the second half of the 19th century, though it was cut short when celebrating Carnaval was banned at the end of the Spanish Civil War. Secular celebrations were recovered from 1981 after democracy was re-established, and they are currently among the most important events of local festivals. Celebrations include parades, dances, fancy dress contests and chirigotas (satirical song competition) with an increasingly higher number of participants each year, locals and foreigners alike. www.carnavalcartagena.com

The festival scene in Cartagena keeps improving, music, theatre and folklore festivities can be found every month. Here's just a selection of some of the best.

The Mar de Música, held in July (unfortunately when the San Javier Jazz festival is on, too much of a good thing!) at the Auditorio Parque Torres (and other venues in the town), from where you can see the port, the Teatro Romano and the city whilst enjoying some super concerts and world class performers. Past years have seen Youssou N'Dour, Patti Smith, Marianne Faithfull and Madeleine Peyroux. You can buy an abono, which gives you a great price for all the gigs, or just turn up on the night and pay. www.lamardemusicas.com

During the same month they also have the Mar de Arte, Mar de Cine and Mar de Letras festivals covering arts, film and writing. Each year the 'Mar de…' is dedicated to a different country.

The Festival de Jazz de Cartagena is held during November and since 1980 Cartagena has hosted some of the most prestigious figures in Jazz. Alongside the concerts are live performances in different cafes in the city as well as exhibitions. Past performers include, Manhattan Transfer, Eli 'Paperboy' Reed, Macy Gray, Cassandra Wilson and the Ron Carter Trio. Again you can buy great value abono tickets, or just turn up on the night. www.jazzcartagena.com

Finally, take a look at the website www.muchomasmayo.com for information on events around the city celebrating the young artists from the area. Mucho Mas Mayo is a celebration in May that lasts about one week. Each year they hold a Noche de las Museos night during the May event where at least 13 of the museums open their doors for free during the night time hours (between 9pm and 2am).

Location Report: Cartagena

I had family on holiday with me in May, a couple in their late 70s, who love to explore but like limited walking. First of all I drove straight to the port area and parked in the underground car park which is open 24 hours and has security personnel. It is in my opinion reasonably priced for the 4 or 5 hours I spent there.

Walking up from the car park you arrive on quite a long promenade. The port has got a commercial shipping area, a marina for leisure craft and a large Naval Base. On the day that I chose to go and purely by co-incidence the P&O cruise ship called Ventura was in port for the day, so it was quite busy with tourists. Having never been on a cruise ship myself, I was staggered by the enormous size of the Ventura; it is a massive floating hotel.

Walking along the promenade there were some sculpture displays for all to have a look at. There appears to be open space for artists to exhibit their products. And further along you can catch sight of the Naval ships anchored. You cannot get that close to them though.

On the promenade itself there are a number of eateries and bars, including a McDonald's and something to cater for all tastes and pockets.

After spending time exploring this area we crossed over the road, into the main Town Hall square. The façades of the buildings here are quite magnificent, well worth a look at, along with a variety of monuments and statues that depict the Naval history of Cartagena. There is a tourist information office just at the entrance of this square.

We had a walk through the square and along the narrow road called Calle Mayor de Casco Antiguo (the main road of the old quarter). Again there are some interesting buildings to look at and shops to browse around plus many bars and restaurants. On this main road we stopped off at a large church the Iglesia de Santo Domingo and had a good look around inside; this is a very nicely decorated church, like many others that you see around Spain. One thing I will mention though is that there were a handful of beggars around the church, not pestering people but hoping to obtain money from tourists.

Having wandered around for about an hour it was time to eat and back to the Town Hall square, where there are quite a range of restaurants on offer. We chose the restaurant of Teatro Romano, The Roman Theatre museum restaurant. They did a menú del día for €11 per person, which is quite good for a tourist location and the food and service was very good. This is located in the Plaza Ayuntamiento.

After lunch, we drove to the Castillo de Concepción (Conception Castle). It is a place easy to get to by walking from the Town Hall square, but slightly strenuous for people with limited mobility. I parked for free by the old disused Plaza de Toros and University and did the short walk to the glass lift that takes you up to the castle grounds. The fee for the panoramic glass lift is €1 return per person.

The castle grounds are free to walk around and the views across the city are spectacular. Have a look for the peacocks that roam around the park area. At the time that we went the castle was closed so we did not wait around to go inside.

In my opinion this was just enough of a taster to look at the history and sights of this small part of the city. Obviously there is much more to do around Cartagena including a city tour on an open top bus and I would encourage anyone to spend at least a whole day exploring.

David & Desiree Billington

Services

Tourist Office, Plaza de Ayuntamiento, opens on weekdays and Saturdays except for siestas and in the morning on Sundays and holidays, 968 128955. www.cartagenaturismo.es, lots of information in quite good English.

www.cartagenapuertodeculturas.com where you can buy advanced tickets for attractions and tours.

Ayuntamiento, Calle Armendariz, 6, 968 128800, www.cartagena.es

Train Stations, Plaza de México, trains running to Murcia and Plaza de Bastarreche, local trains to Los Nietos on the Mar Menor, www.renfe.es, 902 240202.

Bus station, Calle Trovero Marín. You can download a detailed bus timetable and city map from www.cartagenaturismo.es, 968 505656.

Taxis, 968 531313, 968 311515.

The Port Authority, www.apc.es, 968 325800. Click on the "Cruises" link to see what cruise ships are due into port.

Beaches

Cartagena holds the distinction of being the Spanish town with the most beaches (12) certified 'Q for Quality' by the ICTE (Instituto para la Calidad Turística Española). These beaches are: Cala Cortina, Islas Menores, Playa Honda beach, Mar de Cristal, Cala del Pino, Cavanna beach, Barco Perdido beach, El Galúa beach, Levante beach, Playa San Ginés, Playa Paraíso and La Gola beach. This list may change each year, but you can bet Cartagena will still be near the top. In addition, Cala Cortina, San Ginés, Levante, Isla Plana and El Cuartel were awarded Blue Flag status too.

For details of each beach go to the appropriate town section.

Baterías

The dictionary of the Spanish Royal Academy defines the term battery as 'artillery pieces set ready to fire'. The origin of the term refers to the verb beat (fight) and it is not uncommon to read ancient texts using the word battery when they mean to attack something with a flourish.

A batería is a fortification to hold the guns ready to fight. There are many types of batteries around the entrance of the ports, ensuring effective control of maritime traffic. You can see one of the largest and most complete displays of coastal batteries in Cartagena.

Here's a list of the remaining batteries in the area: Batería 47 Baja, Batería de Castillitos, Batería de la Chapa, Batería de Cenizas, Batería del Jorel, Batería de Negrete, Batería de San Juan de la Podadera, Batería de Santa Ana Complementaria, Batería de Santa Ana Acasamatada, Batería de Trincabotijas Alta, Batería de Trincabotijas Baja, Cuartel Defensivo y Baterías General Fajardo, Batería de Roldán, Batería de San Isidoro y Santa Florentina, Batería de San Leandro, Batería del Atalayón, Batería de Loma Larga.

Some great photographs, old and new, of baterías can be found at the following websites: https://bateriascostacartagena.blogspot.com/ http://www.aforca.org/bateriasf.htm

These really are great places to visit. The views are tremendous and the buildings are often intact, open and free! If you only have time to visit one then try Batería del Jorel near La Azohía which gives a great view over Cabo Tiñoso. Be brave when driving up there, you may see road markings suggesting you cannot go further, just follow the other cars and you'll find plenty of Spanish people enjoying themselves in the military restricted zones!

Debbie Jenkins, Russ Pearce

Location Report: The Guns Of Cabo Tiñoso

The guns of Cabo Tiñoso are a fascinating place to visit. It doesn't matter if you are ex-military, reliving childhood dreams of soldiering, or just an admirer of architecture and landscapes, you are bound to enjoy a trip to this spot located halfway between Cartagena and Mazarrón. The narrow RM-E23 road winds its way up from the E-22 through spectacular scenery. Take care though, as vehicles descending may not go as slowly as you may wish them to!

The sinuous road ends abruptly just before a fence restricts vehicular access to the Castillitos Battery. There's plenty of parking space with extra room down a track leading to an abandoned water cistern. The official car park is pristine because it's impossible to get a vehicle onto the track leading up to it! From the cistern you get a great view across the bay to Cartagena, and a good look at the Batteries you are about to visit. Many of the buildings were restored in 2016 but there are still crumbling remains hiding behind the Greek-inspired facades.

Many people only make it as far as the Castillitos Battery. That's not surprising as it's an easy walk down from the car park. Take a torch to explore the dark tunnels, or just admire the facades of this castle-like structure. Make sure you climb up to where the big guns are located. Many people have decided they make a great location for selfies! It's interesting to explore the old buildings though. A guide for their lookouts was painted on some of the walls so you can see the outline of British, French and American warships from around the time of the Spanish Civil War.

Venture further along Cabo Tiñoso and you'll reach the Jorel Battery. According to the official information boards, this was constructed in 1912, although other sources suggest it is perhaps at least ten years younger. It continued to be actively used until 1993. The guns here were symbolically fired for one last time on 10 March 1992. The buildings have a beautiful Greek facade and there are plenty of nooks and crannies to explore. Needless to say, the views are fabulous in all directions.

High above the car park stands the Atalayón Battery, accessible by a steep track. Few visitors brave the climb to the place which once housed four anti-aircraft cannons. Construction began in April 1930 and took a full 18 months to complete.

Russ Pearce

Castles

The strategic role of the Cartagena Bay has created a network of military facilities that today make up the military heritage of the city. Some, like the Military Arsenal maintain their use, while others have changed their role within the armed forces, such as the Parque de Artillería.

The fortifications can be classified according to the century they were built:

- Reyes Católicos (Catholic Kings): Castillo de la Concepción.
- Sixteenth century, Carlos I: Muralla del Deán.
- Sixteenth century, Felipe II: Muralla de Antonelli, Casas del Rey or de Munición.
- Seventeenth and Eighteenth centuries: Trincabotijas (Felipe IV).
- Eighteenth century, Carlos III: Arsenal Militar, Muralla del Recinto, Parque de Artillería, Capitanía General de la Armada, Castillo de los Moros, Hospital Militar, Cuartel de Antigones, Cuartel de Guardíamarinas, Castillo de Galeras and Castillo del Atalaya.

And especially noteworthy are the castles located in the hills surrounding the city. For more information on the castles take a look at www.cartagenaturismo.es

The Surrounding Area of Cartagena

There are a number of districts that are in the area of Cartagena, the whole valley is referred to as Campo de Cartagena, which is a huge plain running some 50km north–south and 50km east–west. Its metropolitan area includes the municipalities of La Unión, Fuente Álamo de Murcia (see its own section), Los Alcázares (see its own section), San Javier (see its own section), Torre Pacheco (see its own section) and San Pedro del Pinatar (see its own section).

The districts include: El Albujón, Alumbres, Beal, Campo Nubla, Canteras, El Algar, El Plan, Escombreras, Hondón, La Aljorra, La Magdalena, La Palma, Lentiscar, Los Médicos, Los Puertos, Miranda, Perín, Pozo Estrecho, Rincón de San Ginés, San Antonion Abad, San Félix, Santa Ana and Santa Lucía.

El Albujón

El Albujón is 14km north of Cartagena and home of the famous drink, the Asiático, created in Bar Pedrín. The asiático is made from coffee, condensed milk, Spanish brandy, a liqueur called Licor 43, a pair of coffee beans, (optional) sugar and a sprinkle of cinnamon powder. El Albujón has little else of interest for the visitor. Its main economy is based around agriculture, in particular growing in greenhouses broccoli, celery, cauliflower, courgettes, cucumbers, tomatoes and beans.

Beal

Includes the towns of Beal, Llanos de Beal, Estrecho de San Ginés, and San Ginés de la Jara. The local mines are one of the most important features of this area (see La Unión for more details of the mining operations), with **Las Matildes** well worth a visit.

There's also a beautiful monastery, which you can see as you drive along the RM-12 motorway. The **Monasterio de San Ginés de la Jara** is a monastic enclave built in the seventeenth century, although its architectural identity is set in the mid eighteenth century. Sadly it's marked by the gradual abandonment and destruction and currently it's not possible to visit inside until restoration has been completed.

Las Ermitas del Monte Miral are on a hill nearby the monastery, Ermita de los Ángeles is the most famous. Also take a look at Cueva Victoria.

The two entrances of the cave are artificial, made long ago by miners. It's a large cave, formed by six large rooms and numerous galleries spread over different levels, occupying a length of two to three kilometres.

Beal celebrates its fiesta on June 29th in honour of San Pedro.

Canteras

Canteras is a coastal town with its most notable destination the anti-aircraft battery located in the mountains, Batería De Roldán. You gain access by Estación Naval de la Algameca, which is in very bad condition. However there are plenty of trails for walkers starting at Tentegorra.

The Batería De Roldán anti-aircraft battery was set up to strengthen the naval base in Cartagena, emanating from the 1926 Defense Plan. It had a very active role during the Civil War (1936-39) and was finally deactivated in 1965. Currently within the grounds of the Ministry of Defence and is in total state of disrepair. It was declared a Cultural Heritage site.

Location Report: Batería De Roldán

On a beautiful May morning we decided to take our dogs and our friend who was visiting on a bracing walk up a mountain. We drove down to Cartagena and through to the Tentegorra area (with the two large, almost Bauhaus, blocks of flats) and along the tree lined avenue to the parking place.

We passed the Hospital General Básico de la Defensa de Cartagena and watched very fit men and women running along the paved avenue under the blossoming trees with new shoots of spring.

The walk started off gentle and relaxing up a slight incline, the dogs frolicked; we chatted and looked to the climb ahead. Idyllic!

Then bam! Bang, bang, bang! The sound of gunshots from all around us, we ducked, the dogs came running back with tails between their legs! Were we under attack? Had we trespassed? What should we do?

We paused and looked at the map noticing blocked out areas nearby and surmised that we were walking alongside some sort of shooting range. Possibly heavy artillery! It took us a few minutes to be sure we weren't going to get shot and to get used to the bangs and wallops, but a couple of kilometres later it was just a distant memory and we carried on up to the saddle to enjoy the view.

The walk is on marked pathways, quite stony, through wooded areas, across open plains and along the cliff. Solid shoes are recommended and a walking stick if you prefer. Take plenty of water and some food; there are no bars up here.

The views from the summit are beautiful, you can see along the coast to other batteries and defence points such as Castillo San Julian, inland to the Castillo Atalaya and Castillo de Galeras, and out to sea to the Isla Paloma.

Roldán Batería is perched on the summit of Mount Roldán, at 485 meters above sea level. Hardly a mountain, but a good strenuous walk all the same. The battery was built to defend the city of Cartagena, the port and military shipyard from attacks by sea and air. This battery was built in 1933 (Plan Primo de Rivera) and has been out of service since 1965. It had four anti-aircraft Vickers guns.

We had a thoroughly enjoyable day out, but were quite cautious on our return to avoid the shooting, but it had all stopped, perhaps they were having a siesta!

Escombreras

The name Escombreras derives from *scomber* the Latin word for mackerel, a fish prized by the ancient Romans to make the sauce garum, a commodity food manufactured in Cartagena. From the fifteenth century it became an industrial area initially with factories devoted to mineral extraction.

In the 1940s the major petrochemical companies were established, with a major decline during the oil crisis. Today, oil, gas and chemical companies dominate the area. Fuel companies include, Repsol, Gas Natural, Enagas and Abengoa. The port gets the raw material, crude oil and the factories transform it into its main energy derivatives, gasoline, diesel, butane, propane etc. Making fertilisers or other chemicals are Fertiberia, Holcím, Ercros and Cemex.

Petroleum giants Repsol do have a visitor centre where you can learn about the industry. https://bglaudiovisual.com/en/references/museums/museums/repsol-visitors-centre-cartagena

There are a total of 24 companies that contribute to the continued growth of the industrial fabric of Cartagena as well as successive enlargements of the docking port and dock to accommodate large ships carrying raw materials. There's also a desalination plant.

It's well worth a drive around the area, follow the signs, and then your nose. The scale of the factories is huge, with abandoned pipes, broken buildings and new factories in every direction. There's a bar in the port used by sailors, so not the best for a relaxing (or nice!) coffee, but they do a good trade in currency. You can take a walk up to the top of the hill (if you can find the path out of the town) and get great views, really superb.

Isla de Escombreras sits at the entrance to the Bay of Cartagena. It has 4 acres of steep and rocky surface, a small pier, a beach and some old buildings. It is rich in archaeological finds including the remains of a Greek temple in honour of Hercules (often known at the time as the Isle of Hercules). They also found remains of salt fish production and industrial activity from the Roman era. Phoenician remains were also found and a Roman necropolis. It has been declared a Protected Natural Area.

Location Report: Diving Around Isla De Escombreras

Whilst diving around an island just off the port where oil, gas and chemical companies have their base probably doesn't sound like your idea of fun, you'd be amazed at the underwater wildlife and vegetation.

We left the port at Cartagena on a summer morning with 16 other hopeful divers and sailed for just 15 minutes out and to the East. All along the coast you can see the refineries and works, hear the noise of machinery and smell the chemicals. We weren't expecting much when the boat stopped and dropped anchor in the midst of all this.

It was a wall dive along the southern side of the island. Down to about 30m if you wanted to, with good visibility and plenty of moray eels to wave at. As we curved alongside the island we came to the slip between the land. Huge square manmade boulders had been used to fortify the bank and create a narrow inlet. We were to meet the boat inside this stream and needed to swim through. An up and over strong swimthrough brought us out into a tranquil 'swimming pool', protected area, with just 12 meters of depth. We used up our air looking for little critters and the fabled seahorses!

On a second dive to this area the current had changed and we were dropped off in the tranquil pool, made our way to the slip and found ourselves being whooshed through the opening and out the other side. Quite a ride. Fortunately the boat was meeting us out there as I'm sure I couldn't have made my way back against the current.

It's a surprisingly enjoyable dive site, with at least two dives suitable for new divers. Let me know if you spot the sea horses.

Lentiscar

Lentiscar is one of the largest councils in Cartagena, its geographic location means it covers the flat fields leading to Cartagena and the Mar Menor coast with Punta Brava, El Carmolí, Los Beatos and La Puebla.

The interior fields are dedicated to growing potatoes, artichokes, lettuce, broccoli and melons, while peppers are grown in greenhouses.

The village of **La Puebla** celebrates its fiesta in honour of the Sacred Heart of Jesus, between 8th and 9th of June. El Carmolí, with its various beaches such as Punta Brava, celebrate a special feast of St. James on July 25th, with bonfires on the beach with grilled fish, sausages and of course music. On August 15th the Feast of the Assumption (Asunción) is celebrated with karaoke and performances, children's activities, traditional games and paella for all attendees.

Los Puertos

Los Puertos de Santa Bárbara is located on the western edge of Cartagena, near the coastal town of Mazarrón with which it shares part of its coastline.

The landscape and natural beauty of this area is not to be missed. Drive along the N332 and enjoy the mountain views or down to Isla Plana, the thriving seaside town, and take advantage of the numerous caves used for caving and hiking.

Los Puertos has the Peñas Blancas, whose highest peak reaches 627 meters, and is especially popular among fans of trekking and climbing. It is the highest mountain in Cartagena and consists of a limestone wall (Carrascas Lomas) a mile long and a minimum height of 80 meters. From here you can see the geography of Cabo Cope, La Azohía and the mountains of Almería, and on a clear day the coast of Orán, the Sierra de María, Cabo de Gata and the Sierra Nevada.

It gets its name from its whitish appearance, the white layers are due to lichen cover, a microscopic algae, a fungus living on the surface of the rocks. This surface becomes slippery when wet so the climbers know the difficulty of climbing on the rock wall.

Among the fauna include the golden eagle, eagle owl and peregrine falcon, all protected birds.

It's an agricultural area, very focused on the intensive cultivation of tomatoes; you'll see evidence of the greenhouses in every direction.

Four kilometres from Cuesta Blanca, towards Mazarrón, there's a shrine called **De Los Puertos de Santa Bárbara**. The chapel was constructed in 1745 and is a single nave building with a pitched roof in keeping with the Baroque period.

Los Puertos de Santa Bárbara de Abajo celebrate their festivals in honour of Santa Bárbara during the last weeks of August, with special emphasis on the gastronomic festivities. During almost all the holidays you can enjoy the typical cuisine of the region, often based on contests of migas making, with prizes for the best. They start off with Vermouth, slaughter a pig or a bull and make michirones, and of course there's the hot chocolate with little doughnuts (chocolate con bollos).

The **Ethnographic Museum** in Los Puertos de Santa Bárbara offers an interesting and comprehensive display of all types of furniture, clothing, tools and even traditional vehicles of this area of Cartagena. Many residents of the council contributed with generous donations.

Perín

Fifteen miles from Cartagena, between Las Lomas, Las Carrascas and the Sierra de la Muela, is one of the largest provinces in Cartagena, Perín. Towns in this province include La Azohía, Peñas Blancas, Galifa, Portús and Cabo Tiñoso. There's a mixture of interior mountainous landscape and coastal marine areas.

Each of the local towns has their own customs, festivals and associations that promote all kinds of events throughout the year. There's a variety of economies, from agriculture to tourism.

There are lovely beaches in this area, try the beach at El Portús and keep your eyes open for the nudists!

Gone are the days of mining in Cartagena, though some old abandoned mine entrances survive. This area is also rich in baterías: Batería de Castillitos, Batería del Atalayón, Batería del Jorel and Batería de Loma Larga, see the baterías section for more information.

A great day out can be found by driving up through Campillo de Adentro (near La Azohía) right to the Batería de Castillitos. There are gun emplacements for you to sit on, fortress walls to walk around, numerous hidey holes for a picnic, old machinery in the underground buildings and towers to climb.

There are two towers: Torre de la Azohía and Torre del Moro. The Torre de la Azohía, which also appears in ancient documents named as Santa Elena and Santa Catalina, is located in the coastal town of La Azohía. The tower, along with the former tower of Puerto de Mazarrón, monitored maritime traffic in the wide bay. The Torre del Moro is near the village of Cuesta Blanca and located on private property. Dated around the 16th or 17th century, designed to protect the area from the Berber pirates, the fort is built of stones welded together with lime mortar.

Location Report: La Azohía

La Torre de La Azohía is a great place for a picnic. It's an easy walk up from the village, there's plenty of space and the tower is open to be viewed.

To reach the tower start from the centre of town, near the pier and the church, find a dirt track, in a relatively poor state, which leads to the foot of the tower, it's in the back streets, just keep looking up.

This fortification was built in the late sixteenth century to prevent the arrival of Berber pirates. It was restored some years ago, so, despite some attacks, it's in a good state of conservation. La Azohía tower is classified as a Site of Cultural Interest.

We've spent many hours here watching the fisherman sail by, following the antics of free divers as they search (unsuccessfully!) for something to catch for their dinner, and once we spotted a Loggerhead Sea Turtle who was also watching the freedivers (and probably laughing!)

It's also a great starting point for many of the scuba dives along this part of the coast.

We dive with www.rivemar.com, 968 150063, right on the corner in La Azohía. Parking can be a challenge in summer, but the location is fabulous. They have their own bar where you can relax after a dive and fill in your log book. They play loud music most nights! They also have a base at Cabo de Palos; another great diving location (though for more experienced divers).

The guys at Rivemar are recreational and tech divers and have been diving from here for the last 30-odd years, through three generations of the family (admittedly the youngest one is only a few years old!) Rivemar boasts the lowest accident rate in underwater activities throughout Murcia and is classed 'Compromiso de Calidad Turística' (a promise of high quality from the Murcia government).

There are dives for all levels of experience along this stretch of the coast. Try Cala Cerrada if you're a new diver, a lovely secluded bay with a maximum of 18m depth, a great place for a try dive. Or pop along to El Arco at a maximum of 37m, where you dive though an arch. For the more adventurous (and experienced) there are some cave dives around here too.

Pozo Estrecho

North of Cartagena is Pozo Estrecho, which in addition to the main town includes La Rambla, Los Roses, Los Sánchez and Las Lomas. The origin of the council dates from the Middle Ages when they created a crossroads next to which stood a well to water the cattle, which was known as La Corte del Campo.

Agriculture and intensive cultivation of seeds are the economic foundations of the area. Pozo Estrecho cultivates broccoli, celery, lettuce, melons, cotton and citrus fruits. There's a beautiful ruined house, La Casona de Pozo Estrecho, which can be seen as you drive around.

Rincón de San Ginés

Rincón de San Ginés is located 30km east of the city of Cartagena; there have been human settlements on the Mar Menor and Cartagena coast since prehistoric times. The Mar Menor was also used in the Middle Ages to develop different fishing equipment and techniques.

Rincón de San Ginés includes the following towns: Los Belones, Los Nietos, Cabo de Palos, Atamaría, Las Barracas, Cala Reona, Cobaticas, Islas Menores, La Manga, Mar de Cristal, Playa Honda, El Sabinar and Playa Paraíso. Many of these towns have their own section in the book, so go there for more details.

In this region there are many places of natural beauty that are protected, including: Calblanque Regional Park, Pico del Águila, Monte de las Cenizas, el Mar Menor, las Salinas de Marchamalo and some islands and islets in the Mediterranean.

San Antonio Abad

San Antonio Abad is located 1km northeast of the city of Cartagena and has a large number of inhabitants. The land ranges from the fields surrounding Barrio Peral, to the Monte de Galeras and part of Roman coast, where they found remains of humans 30,000 years ago.

A great place to visit is **Fuerte de Navidad, Christmas Fort**, which is very important for its strategic location within the defense system of the Cartagena Bay. It is located southwest close to sea level to easily monitor the entrance to the port. The port is bordered by two mountain ranges, San Julián, to the east and Galeras to the west, with these characteristic 'points' of Trincabotijas and Santa Ana to the east, and Podadera and Navidad to the west. The islet of Escombreras seals the circle to any hint of exposure to southerly winds.

The fortress was built in the 1860s to defend the inner harbour of Cartagena. It was designed by Spanish military engineers in a sober neoclassical style with solid construction lines that emphasize its image of power.

Getting to the fortress is easy by foot or car: head from the streets of Cartagena Real, towards the village of Concepción, take the road to La Algameca and the Navantia yards (ship-builders).

There's an interpretation centre which is open every day from 10:30 to 14:00 and 15:30 to 20:00 in the summer, and Saturdays and Sundays from 10:00 to 17:30 in the winter. www.cartagenapuertodeculturas.com

Another fort, **Fuerte de Galeras**, is situated on the summit of Mount Galeras, that marks the west bay of Cartagena. From there the castle dominates the city perfectly. Today the fort is still in a military security zone so that your visit and access have to be explicitly allowed. Take the road to La Algameca, which runs parallel to the eighteenth century wall and diverted the course of the Rambla de Benipila. Turn left, towards the entrance of the shipbuilding company Navantia. Take the road to the right, then turn right again, through the no entry warnings barrier. There is a paved path climbing up to Galeras.

Or visit **La Algameca and La Algameca Chica**, where the Combat Divers, Navy Diving Center and Special Operations Marine Brigade have their base. La Algameca Chica is a beautiful little port town, difficult to get to but well worth the effort. In the 18th century it was a pirate stronghold, it's now on land belonging to the Ministry of Defence. Neither the Ministry nor the city of Cartagena is responsible for these illegal houses that lack basic needs. They have electricity for just a few hours per day and water has to be brought in.

The tiny houses are built from whatever material came to hand and have been added to over the years, with a plank of wood here, a block of concrete there. All along the inlet small fishing boats are moored. Most have seen better days.

Location Report: Diving Around La Algameca

Cartagena offers one of the most unique places for scuba diving with 100 miles of coastline divided into three main areas: Cabo de Palos, Cartagena and Cabo Tiñoso-La Azohía, with 53 dive sites. With an average temperature of 14.5 degrees in winter and 25 in summer you can dive throughout the year. Though it gets a little too cold for me!

You take a zodiac to the Algameca river outlet, which is ten minutes away, where there's a buoy to indicate the attachment point to a sunken boat at 15m below the surface. The keel of the boat is at around 20-22 meters, stranded on a sandy slope. The old tug is covered by vegetation and numerous species of underwater creatures inhabit this manmade terrain. Moving on there's the wreckage of a small airplane. You can see the two seats, pilot and co-pilot, some electrical wires are still visible. The more adventurous divers get into to the seats, though the aluminium frame is sharp and dangerous.

These sunken artefacts are used by Navy divers to perform experiments and tests. Their base is just a couple of minutes away in Algameca, you can see them having fun off their jetty.

There are plenty of other dive sites along this coastline. There's a couple at Isla Paloma, the small island we could see when visiting the battery at Roldán (Location Report, Batería de Roldán for more information).

When you've finished diving for the day enjoy a snack and a beer or two at the bar in the Club de Regatas de Cartagena, they have outdoor comfy chairs and you can watch the yachtees playing with their big boats.

San Félix

San Félix includes La Asomada, Lo Baturno, La Piqueta, La Vereda and the industrial enclave of Los Camachos.

One of the most interesting sites in this area is **Villa Versailles** or Calamari, built around 1900. The villa was commissioned by the architect Victor Belchí Calamari. The main façade has a portico with arches resting on Tuscan columns. Marble was used to build the base and the porch, with brick and artificial stone for the rest of the walls.

The first owner of the land, a mining entrepreneur called Heller, turned it into a large botanical garden. The second owner, the Italian businessman Calamari, ordered the building of the present villa in the late nineteenth century. It's built in an eclectic style, classical-oriented. Some rooms have been preserved. After the war the villa was acquired by another mining entrepreneur, Celdran, who was in charge of restoring the large garden. His family continued to own the house until recently.

Santa Lucía

Santa Lucía is located southeast of the city of Cartagena, adjacent to the historic district, on the coast. Several archaeological excavations reveal that 2,000 years ago the Romans ruled the land. This small fishing port of Santa Lucía was at that time the residential district of the great Roman families.

The Valarino family arrived in the late eighteenth century and in 1834 opened the famous Glass Factory. After bringing employment to the residents of Santa Lucía for many years the factory closed in 1955.

In 1850 it was decided to close the port of Cartagena with its two breakwaters and later dredge the bottom of the bay. Most of the flora and fauna of the port died in that operation: mussels, crustaceans, and algae disappeared from the seabed. One of these two breakwaters led later to the San Pedro pier, known as The Curra.

Santa Lucía is a strategic defender of the bay of Cartagena, with a number of forts. The **San Leandro Battery** was built in the mid eighteenth century to defend the entrance to the port of Cartagena. Santa Florentina Battery is the union of two forts, San Isidoro and Santa Florentina. Again built in the eighteenth century and renovated in 1860 within the improvement plan. Santa Ana Battery was built in the first decades of the eighteenth century and provided ground fire for the port. It was reformed in the improvement plans in 1860 and 1956.

Santa Lucía was a fishing village for more than 2000 years and in the late nineteenth and early twentieth century the fishing fleet of Santa Lucía was one of the largest in the Spanish Mediterranean. The fishermen created the Fishermen's Association of Santa Lucía.

Fiestas Patronales de Santa Lucía are in honour of Santiago Apóstol and held around the 25th of July and usually last for two weeks.

Going Native: Writer, Poet, Shrimper!

We decided to move to Spain seventeen years go for a variety of reasons: health, financial and in the hope that my son would grow up bilingual. I have written more than twenty books. I was brought up in London before moving to Hastings. I now live with my son and husband and nine feral cats in Cartagena. I spent 4 years on the Orihuela Costa before that. I think moving into an urbanisation is a really bad idea. I have had such bad experiences I would never live on one again. I regret not moving to a wholly Spanish area when I first arrived

My problem with the urbanisation scene was in part the rules. The urbanisation we moved to was mainly British with an Irish ex-prison officer in charge as president. Basically, he treated people like his prisoners and the more rules he could inflict the better. It all turned exceptionally nasty when we complained about the son of one of his friends stoning our cat. After that a group of British pensioners effectively chased us off with constant vandalism to our car and shit at the door etc. And yes, we had to sell the house at a loss eventually.

He wasn't the only bad president around, I heard other stories too. In many cases the job of president of an urbanisation appeals to sad, fascist bastards who are retired and have nothing better to do than make people's lives hell. If I had done more advance research by going on forums and talking to people on the spot, I would not have gone near one. Even urbanisations that start out okay could elect the wrong president and turn nasty. I have heard many more stories.

At the time I bought I thought the idea of paying a community charge in order to share a pool etc. was a good one. In practice it was money not well spent. Where I am now there are no community charges, I swim in the sea or pay a couple of Euros if I want to use the pool in winter. And nobody tells me what to do.

There were a few helpful, nice people on the expat scene but too many that weren't. The scene was very nasty for those with either kids or cats. We saw others moved on also. I have to say it was mostly retired people doing all the malevolent stuff. I am not keen on the expat scene altogether and now have more Spanish friends than otherwise. The Spanish seem more relaxed in their attitude.

Now that I've found a great place to live in a Spanish city, I would like to stay here for the rest of my life. We have a wonderful beach for snorkelling nearby, lots of free concerts, good food, good enough weather to lead a very sporty lifestyle. And Cartagena has a fantastic mix of architecture from different periods, more than I have encountered in any other city in my travels, Punic, Roman, Mediaeval, Baroque, Eighteenth century, Modernist, all within the space of a few miles.

I got involved with local politics and conservation. I go on demonstrations now and have made friends with a number of locals who have concerns about the restoration of historic properties in the city. It's very important to be able to speak Spanish to get involved in this way.

The only thing I miss from the UK is shrimping!

Brexit has brought more problems. We intend to stay in Spain. Both I and my son will be naturalising. That way we get our lost voting rights back as well as freedom of movement and European citizenship. I would advise anyone staying to do the same. I am currently trying to become more multicultural as an antidote to the inward-looking British scene. I already do some translating and copywriting for European firms. I am learning other languages. Most of what I write for my own pleasure or to publish in books or magazines relates to my life in Spain.

Fiona Pitt-Kethley, www.fionapitt-kethley.com

http://www.amazon.com/Fiona-Pitt-Kethley/e/B001K7VT4S

https://www.patreon.com/user?u=5900448

Sleeping

The new kid on the block is the chain B&B Hotels whot have taken over the Hotel Cartagonova, Calle Marcos Redondo, 3, www.hotelcartagonova.com, 968 504200. From €53 per night. It is comfortable enough and very well located. Think of it as similar to a good Premier Inn.

Another chain, NH Hotels, www.nh-hotels.com, have two options in Cartagena. On Plaza Héroes de Cavite is NH Cartagena, 968 120908, with rooms available from €80. This is right next to the Ayuntamiento with great views of the port. They have their own restaurant, but just on the opposite corner is a lovely bar, with excellent prices, the Pico Esquina. Slightly away from the centre is NH Campo Cartagena, 968 504431 with rooms from €54.

For more hotels also take a look at: Hotel Los Habaneros, Calle San Diego, 60. Quite an elegant place for the price at €50 per night. Pricey restaurant. www.hotelhabaneroscartagena.com 968 502250.

Sercotel Hotel Alfonso XIII, Paseo de Alfonso XIII, 40, from €70 per night. www.hotelalfonsoxiii.com 968 520000. Slightly cheaper and just one street away on Calle Carlos III, 49, is Sercotel Carlos III from €50 per night. www.carlosiiihotel.com 968 520032.

Hotel Manolo, Calle Juan Carlos I, 7. Slightly out of town, from €55 per night. 968 330060.

For price conscious visitors or if you want a more rural experience then take a look at the towns around Cartagena, for example, in El Portús there's the naturist resort: www.elportus.com, where you can stay in the campsite from €26 per night or in their mobile homes from €50 per night. There's a gym and spa on site. Remember it's a naturist site!

Near Perín there's Casa Rural Batalla, Torre de Nicolas Perez 14, www.casaruralbatalla.net, 968 163399. It's quite modern, with a pool and weekly prices from €720 to sleep five people.

Also near Perín is www.lanietadelgasero.com, 630 078131. Which is a group of four houses which can sleep up to 20 people. You could also try Las Casas del Nene, www.lascasasdelnene.com, 630078131.

Eating

There are three main tapas areas in Cartagena, Calle Major, La Plaza del Rey and the fishing port towards Santa Lucía. Due to the fishing activity in the region octopus, squid and fish are good bets. Read the location reports on the tapas trails of Cartagena, which are usually in February, and remember many of the tapas bars also do a lunchtime menú del día and full evening meals.

One we regularly visit is the Pico Esquina near the ayuntamiento, 968 089881. They have a good selection of tapas, a nice outside eating area and usually excellent service. It's nothing special, just a nice place to eat and watch the world go by.

If you like your seafood then try either Techos Bajos, Paseo del Muelle in Santa Lucía, www.techosbajos.com 968 505020 or nearby Restaurante Veradero, Paseo de Alfonso XII, 968 505848. Both have excellent seafood, do menú del día and have carparking.

Recommended restaurants on Calle Mayor are Bar Columbus and El Tranvía. On Calle Jara look for Zócalo Caseta de Feria, La Bodeguilla and Bodega La Fuente. Closer to Plaza de España on Calle Carmen are Bodega Nicolás and Taberna La Satisfecha.

Also try:

- Bar La Paz, Alfonso X El Sabio, 16. A great location for breakfast with good tapas.
- Casa Del Pescador, Paseo del Muelle near the bus station, in the region of Santa Lucía for tapas and seafood.
- CBC, Paseo Alfonso XIII, 58, great variety of tapas.
- There is a clutch of bar restaurants at Calle Jorge Juan, 12-18 including Tapería La Esquinica and Mesón El Galgo. Mesón Espadas has possibly the largest variety of tapas in the city. Specialties include meat skewers, scrambled eggs and plenty of local meat, including horse, ostrich and red deer.
- Mesón Sacromonte, Monte Peñas Blancas, 32, www.restaurantesacromonte.es. Excellent food including fish, tapas and barbecued meat.
- Plaza San Francisco has a variety of tapas bars at a good price. Among them are Refugio de El Telar, Malavita and Rincon del Perlita
- La Tartana, Puertas de Murcia. Huge variety of tapas. It's also a restaurant.
- Tasca Del Tío Andrés, Alfonso XIII, 46, www.tascatioandres.es/. Good for seafood and octopus.
- Los Habeneros in the hotel of the same name, San Diego, 60, great for romantic occasions.

Location Report: Cartagena Tapas Trail 1

Every year Cartagena puts on a Tapa Trail, wher you pick up a form and head around the participating resteaurants collecting stamps. When you have visited all the restaurants you can hand your form in for the chance to win prizes, and you can vote for your favourite. I do the trail most years, here are my own thoughts on the best and worst places found on the tapas trail.

La Tasca del Tío Andres, Paseo Alfonso XIII 44 (This is on the main road that the AP7 joins in the city, 968 524444.) Their salmon and scorpion fish in pastry in an almond sauce was a truly gourmet tapa. We liked the look of the other tapas there plus the restaurant also. It has won awards and many Spanish eat there. Eventually we went back there for a meal. We had the same tapas for a starter for €3 each, salad and some melt-in-the-mouth steak. They have another restaurant in La Manga and a snack bar for workers in Escombreras.

D'Almansa (Calle Jabonerías 53) is in the Michelin guide. They produced a very delicate lasagne with prawns, scrambled egg and leek for the tapas trail. It's more of a regular restaurant than a tapas place. We ate dinner there on a subsequent occasion and it was good. It's at the more expensive end by Cartagena standards. We shared a lobster salad followed by stuffed lamb for myself, angler fish for my husband, oxtail for my son. He said the latter was exquisite. He was (as usual) the only one of us who could manage a dessert as well, a hot chocolate madeleine and ice cream.

We also spotted another Michelin Guide restaurant in the same street, El Barrio de San Roque. This street is quite near the military arsenal buildings and Teatro Circo (Map: A2). It can also be accessed by taking a stroll up Calle Mayor and staying with the left hand branch when the road divides. We subsequently went back there for birthday lunches and dinners. It is probably the best restaurant we have sampled in Cartagena. One of the pricier restaurants, but definitely worth it. Their duck and suckling pig are particularly good.

La Taberna Gallega (Calle La Palma 23, 968 527074) is a bistro-style small restaurant specialising in Galician dishes. Pleasant decor in the way of peasant tools, scallop shells, nets, etc. Their tapas was scrambled egg, kale and chorizo. Best chorizo we have had. They served some delicious Galician rye bread alongside. The fish and shellfish dishes that others were eating looked superb. They had chunky pottery dishes with paintings of fruit on them. It's tucked away in a small street near Plaza España.

Alameda Tapas (Alameda de San Antón 40) is a good tapas bar on the road between El Corte Inglés and Plaza España. They provided a very tasty thick ham tapas on baked potato covered with rich gravy and a basket of freshly-baked bread drizzled with olive oil. The other tapas looked good too, stuffed tomatoes, baked cheesy aubergines, etc.

This is very close to a more ordinary-looking tapas bar, Bar Saray. They had a vegetarian tapas option, leek pudding with onions and other vegetables alongside. It was very tasty and filling. Nice unpretentious place for a cheap lunch.

Meson Las Viñas (Calle Carlos III 49). This small restaurant is next to the Carlos III hotel. They produced an unusual tapas that was my son's favourite, a triangular pancake filled with flaky rich ham and deep fried (tasted much better than it sounds) with a garnish of lamb's lettuce. They gave us free olives while we waited for it to be cooked. Everything looks freshly prepared. Again, this would be a nice place for a cheap meal. They also have local Campo de Cartagena wine which is quite hard to get as not much is produced.

We particularly liked La Vagoneta in Alameda San Anton with its mining related decor. They did a simple but good tapa of deep-fried cheese cubes with a sweet roast pepper sauce. We were also impressed by the Musola Gallega, dogfish in a cumin sauce from Rincón Gallego. They boast of being in the octopus business for five generations!

The tapa in La Tartana (Puertas de Murcia 16 at the top of Calle Mayor) wasn't in our personal top few, though we did have a nice meal there on another occasion. The tapa was a caramelized foie gras.

Cervecería Principal (Plaza Vergara 2, just off Calle Mayor). I give this recommendation with some reservations. The first time we tried their advertised tapas it was pure bliss and a clear winner, a large piece of steak sitting on bread covered with cream cheese with caramelised peppers, toast and other vegetables alongside. We went back for seconds another day and it was much more ordinary, less steak and the vegetables more steamed than caramelised. Seems like you might have a brilliant meal or an ordinary one in this restaurant depending which cook is working!

La Patacha (Muelle Alfonso XII) tapa was a generous portion of fish in a sweet and sour tomato sauce. It's a converted boat on the port. There's a fish tank full of ugly bastards to watch while you eat and some unusual crabs and other crustaceans in another tank by the tables. Well-thought out decor throughout the boat and it's easy to find, right at the end of the main marina. They sometimes do a menú del día on weekdays for €11.90 at other times a buffet. In the evening it's at the expensive end by Cartagena standards. International cuisine with good fresh fish dishes.

The tapas featured at El Corte Inglés wasn't particularly good but it might be a nice spot for a drink and a salad at a table outside in the summer as the cafeteria is on the top floor and has a good view of mountains in the direction of Mazarrón. They also do a special Ancient Roman menu when the Carthaginians and Romans festival is on.

Fiona Pitt-Kethley, www.fionapitt-kethley.com

Night Life

Head for the area of Alameda de San Antón, not far from Corte Inglés, where you'll find clubs such as Gas and Goa. There are a number of bars in the area.

Another area to visit is the streets around Calle Mayor, especially Calle Aire and Calle Villamartin. There are plenty of tapas bars around and a fair few music bars too.

Plaza San Francisco has several options to choose from too. Bar Shooter, www.beershooter.com, is a great place to sample the growing range of craft beers on offer.

Location Report: Cartagena Tapas Trail Revisited

After Fiona's great expeditions we thought we should try and hit the tapas trails too. Whilst we tried hard to meet Fiona's target of twenty-seven tapas tastes, we only managed a measly eight bars, though all in one night! Remember, each year different restaurants particiapte and they change their tapas, so these are just examples of what are available.

We started with Pastelería Kuss on Calle Carmen, 8. It was supposed to be a surprise of chicken with orange sauce and crunchy sesame, the surprise was it wasn't crunchy nor orangey! The cakes looked nice though. We'd certainly go back to try a cake and a coffee.

On to Bodega Nicolás on Calle Carmen, 70. We've eaten here plenty of times as it's close to the theatre and their tapas is usually great, so our expectations were high. However, the beans with chorizo and morcilla were nothing special, though it had a hint of fenugreek or something similar and the red wine was awful.

Next we had a very messy tapas at Mesón del Descanso del Ícue, Calle Sagasta, 9. Toast with ham and a minty tomatoey sauce was spilled all down my shirt. It was well worth the mess though!

La Trola Tapas on Plaza Juan XXIII is a good place to bring kids. They have an extensive burger, chips and pizza type menu and are in a lovely location and the prices are good. All the tapas out on the bar looked tasty, however, the pork sarnie wasn't anything to write home about.

On to Plaza Alcolea and the Restaurante la Marquesita for a cod pastry. Well this was more like it, crunchy pastry, fishy fish, great service, nice decor and a menu that looks reassuringly expensive. We'll be coming back here!

Over past the Sexy Shop to Restaurante D'Almansa on Calle Jabonerías, 53. As Fiona noted it's not really much of a tapas bar, more a restaurant, though when we visited the decor could have done with a bit of an overhaul. They tried hard with their tapas, but it didn't really come off. A small measure of wine in a dirty glass didn't really come up to standard.

We bravely ventured out of the main shopping area and over towards the El Corte Inglés side of town for our final two choices. Restaurante Pincho de Castilla on Calle Jimenez de la Espada, 53 offered a cod in sauce tapas, which was excellent. In fact all the tapas on display looked excellent, and quite unusual, with puff pastry concoctions and filo pastry surprises. It's mainly frequented by locals who know a good bar when they see one. We'll be back here in a hurry.

Finally, down a backstreet, to a bar you would never have spotted if you didn't know it was there. And you really should know about this one. La Racleta on Calle San Martín de Porres is a trendy, busy bar, with glass windows and a restaurant out the back. Their little Spanish tower with cheese sauce and spicy salsa was delicious. All the tapas looked great. Another one well worth a second visit. They even poured the wine from a bottle!

Cehegín

Population: 15,200

Map Reference: 1.79°W, 38.09°N
Going due west of Murcia, just before you reach Caravaca and Moratalla, you'll reach the hilltop town of Cehegín. As with several of its neighbours, Cehegín is a medieval town comprising narrow streets and sand coloured buildings. The town is crowned by the Ermita Purísima Concepción, a 16th century creation. From here you get good views of the town and out towards the valley of the river Argos.

Cehegín has an **Urban Tourist Route** in the old part of the city, allowing you to wander around the narrow streets following a marked trail. Pop into the tourist information office and get yourself some route guides. They have marked the streets with signs found on the ground, some bronze plates and arrows that will lead you in the right direction.

The route takes you to the **Plaza del Alpargatero** where you'll see the bronze statue dedicated to the shoe factory workers who came from Cataluña, on to **La Casa de Doña Blanca,** a baroque building situated in the Cuesta del Parador, belonging to Marquesa Villar de Felices. This is a grand mansion with a large interior patio, a central skylight tower and a lookout tower, all three of which have different styles. The main façade is carved in sandstone and framed by the shields of the noble families, Carreño and Ruiz López.

Then along to the **Ermita de la Purísima Concepción**. The chapel was consecrated by the Bishop of Modrusia on 9th January, 1556. It is a Renaissance style building with three naves and a high choir. It houses a Mudéjar (Muslim) ceiling of great artistic interest, a wooden octagonal cross vault and painted inscriptions.

Come back down the steps and walk up La Calle Mayor where you'll see **La Casa de Las Boticarias** in front of The Casino of Cehegín a 17th century Baroque style building. Then take a look at El Palacio de Los Fajardo, an 18th century Baroque building with two floors and an attic, incorporated into The Archaeological Museum.

The **Archaeological Museum** can be found in three buildings, Casa del Concejo, Palace de los Fajardo and an annexe building on Calle Mayor. It's open Monday to Sunday: 10:00-13:30, 968 742525

Begastri, The Lost City, is an archaeological site on the hill Cabecico Roenas 3km away from the centre of Cehegín. Excavations and reconstructions are taking place in parts of the walls and other areas of the old city of Begastri. Begastri is one of the most important late-Roman sites in Spain.

There is a visitor centre costing €2 and visitors are welcome on Saturday and Sunday from 10am to 2pm.

The cross of Cehegín or Begastri (Archaeological Site where it was found) is a monogramatic style and made of bronze. It is from the beginning of the 6th century and it is similar to the crosses of Burguillos, Santa Elena de Jaén and the one in Cortijo de Iscar from Baena. These types of crosses were hung from the ceiling above the altar and they were compulsory. The cross is 39.5cm high and 31.8cm wide.

If churches are your thing then try **Iglesia Mayor de Santa María Magdalena**, a Renaissance style building, a prototype of the Santiaguista Temple in the Kingdom of Murcia, with 3 naves and a high choir covered with cross vaults, where the cross of the Knight of Santiago is stored. €2 for a 20 minute guided tour. Or **Santuario de la Santísima Virgen de las Maravillas**, www.virgendelasmaravillas.es, from the 16th Century.

Cehegín is on a green route, well marked and signed, that takes you on a pilgrimage from Caravaca de la Cruz through Cehegín, Bullas, Mula, the sanctuary of El Niño and to the thermal Baths at Baños de Mula, along the disused railway lines. The route is 48km long and should take about 10 hours walking.

There are two fiestas in Cehegín (apart from the usual Easter celebrations) the first being the Muestra de Comercio de Artesanía which is at the end of August and in September the main town fiesta of La Virgen de Las Maravillas is between the 8th and 14th, where the Recinto Ferial (the fair-ground/exhibition site) hosts over 150 clubs and barracas (private tent-like stalls for groups of friends) and festive groups.

The **Mesoncico Artisan Market** is held in the Plaza del Castillo in the heart of Old Cehegín. Held on the last Sunday of each month with more than forty stalls you can find traditional products such as sausages, salted meats, pickles, honey, artisan bread, homemade sweets, cheeses and liqueurs. There are also craftsmen who restore furniture, carvers and turners, jewellery, crystal carvings, etc.

Wine

Cehegín is also a great place for trying out some of the local wines from the Bullas DOC, in fact there are a couple of Bodegas (wineries) in town: Bodegas Carreño Peñalver F, Calle Jinés de Paco y Gea, 22 and A. Garcia Noguerola, Carretera de Murcia, 102.

Services

Turismo, Calle Begastri, 5, 968 723550, www.turismocehegin.es

Ayuntamiento on Calle Lopez Chicheri, 5, 968 740400, www.cehegin.com

The bus station is on Plaza de España, and taxis from, 619 443890 or 617 454839.

Sleeping

Hospedería Rural Molino de Sahajosa, on the Cehegín to Calasparra road, is a rural tourism destination, with large rooms and a swimming pool. A double room is around €50 per night including breakfast, 968 720170.

A handful of other rural options can be found at www.escapadarural.com/casas-rurales?l=cehegin.

The simple Hostal España in the town centre can be booked at www.hostal-espana-cehegin.com.es for around €45.

Eating

With its clearly inland location Cehegín is a good place for game and lamb. Try La Almazara on Calle Los Naranjos, 46. They do roast joints of meat, rices and other regional dishes, under €15 per head. www.restaurantelaalmazara.com

- Gastrobar El Sol on Calle Major, 17, has nice views over the town. www.restaurantesol.com
- Next door to the Hostal España is Marisquería Miami for seafood.

Night Life

The nightlife is rather more relaxed with more of a café society feel, you could try Ibiza on Calle Convento or El Molino on Calle Braille. Those with more energy might want to try the disco Sólido which is in Plaza de las Fuerzas Armadas.

Ceutí

Population: 11,500

Map Reference: 1.27°W, 38.08°N

Ceutí belongs to the region of the Vega Media del Segura, bordered on the north by the municipality of Archena and Villanueva del Río Segura and east by Lorquí. They are separated by the river Segura.

Ceutí's economy has traditionally been agriculture with an increase in business diversification leading to an upturn in cultural tourism.

This small town has two of the most important museums in the region. El Museo Antonio Campillo, the sculptor and adopted son of the city and the Museum of Modern Art (La Conserva Centro de Arte Contemporáneo).

El Museo Antonio Campillo jealously guards the largest collection of works by the great sculptor. In 2003 Antonio Campillo made a donation of his work to City of Ceutí. An old restored nineteenth century mansion hosts the show with a sculpture of a naked woman at the front of the museum, designed by Antonio Campillo, called **Walking Tall (Pisando Fuerte)** on Calle Clavijo, 968 692540.

Take a look at **La Ermita de San Roque**, patron of Ceutí, which was built in 1979 with a circular design. It is located at the exit of the highway to Mula and is one of the architectural emblems identifying Ceutí. The hermitage guards the entrance to the Natural Park of San Roque. The park has tables and BBQ areas.

La Chimenea de la Fábrica de Tomás Colañas is one of the oldest in the village. Built from bricks, slightly thicker that the other preserved chimneys, towards the end of last century it was damaged in an earthquake and lost its crown. Built in the 1930s development in the area at that time was mainly due to the growth of the vegetable canning industry. There are seven chimneys in the town, almost all inactive.

There's the **Museo 7 Chimeneas**. The building housing the museum dates from the late nineteenth century and was owned by D. Francisco García Lorente, the vegetable cannery owner. After painstaking restoration keeping as much as possible of the original building they installed the museum to show the history of the town through vegetable canning.

Calle D. Eloy, call 968 690151 to arrange a visit.

Over the last few years Ceutí has also developed an interest in street art, there are pieces around the urbanised zones, in public buildings (ayuntamiento, public library and the culture centre), near the Torrao and near the motorway. So as you're visiting keep your eyes open for some fabulous original pieces of art, sculpture and murals. There are 29 pieces spread around the town, www.ceutituristico.es. To look for a map, click on Museo el Aire Libre, 968 692540.

Alone at the base of a small hill is the wheel of **The Torrao**, also known as the wheel of the Apothecary (la **Noria del Boticario**).

The Arab Wall (**Muralla Árabe**), discovered in early 2002, is an Islamic adobe wall that was part of the farm access a thousand years ago. In 2003 the site was declared of historical interest. Head to El Alto, next to Plaza Vieja.

For the first three weeks of August (yes, three weeks!) Ceutí celebrates in honour of San Roque and Santa María Magdalena with an ambitious musical and cultural programme, processions, a night procession (4 hours) and of course food, drink and fireworks.

Services

Turismo, www.ceutituristico.es

Ayuntamiento, www.ceuti.es

Sleeping

There's a modern hotel (and restaurant) on the industrial estate (polígono industrial) in town, the Villa Ceutí, www.hotelvillaceuti.com, 968 693881.

If you're looking for something more interesting try nearby Lorquí, Archena or Molina de Segura.

Eating

Ceutí, along with many of the Murcian towns has in recent years added a tapas route to their calendar. For a couple of Euros participating bars will provide their speciality tapas and a drink. Ceutí usually hold their tapas trail in April or November; keep an eye on their website for more info: www.ceuti.es

The hotel Villa Ceutí has a nice restaurant if you like hotel restaurants.

There's the El Albero Restaurante in the centre of town, Calle de Mallorca, 10 that's worth a visit and was a winner in the 2009 tapas route. www.restauranteelalbero.net

Restaurante El Pavo on Calle Salvador Dali has a menú del día for just €8, one of the cheapest around and is a large celebrations type venue (though they welcome smaller groups too).

Another tapas route winner is the San Antonio Restaurante on Carretera Alguazas, www.restaurantesanantonio.es. And if you like rice try Bar Restaurante Domingo on Calle Isaac Peral, 2.

Cieza

Population: 35,000

Map Reference: 1.43°W, 38.24°N

Belonging to the district of Vega Alta del Segura, Cieza is bordered on the north by Jumilla, northwest by Albacete, the east by Abarán, south by Ricote and Mula, and west by Calasparra. The landscape is structured around the River Segura, with beautiful mountains such as Cañón de Almadenes. It is often overlooked on the tourist trail and also by people moving to the area.

Now if you like caves (and of course cave paintings) then come and visit Cieza. There's **La Cueva de Jorge**, with some of the most important Palaeolithic cave art paintings in the region. It was discovered by the caver Constantino López González in 1993 (member of Espeolología 'The Almadenes'). It is about 5 meters in length and one meter wide, its vertical section is oval. It is located in the Sierra de la Palera in the area of Los Almadenes, near the reservoir Alfonso XIII. It's dated between 15000 and 14500 BC.

The cave paintings of **Cueva del Laberinto** belong to the schematic style and were discovered in the course of the excavations made in the archaeological site near Cueva de la Serreta. The cave is located in the vicinity of major rock art sites, as is the archaeological site of La Serreta or Las Enredaderas. Access is not easy; after you've found them they are all protected with fences (they are declared a World Heritage Site).

Cueva De La Serreta is a cave-pit situated in the hamlet of Almadenes, on the left bank of the River Segura. The cave has an opening from which you can see part of the canyon that forms the river. The Serreta cave is important because, in addition to remains of cave paintings, there's a unique Roman site in its interior. The cave is reached by the road to Parra; it is easily accessible and well signposted.

And if you still haven't had enough of caves there's **La Cueva de los Cuchillos** (Cave of the Knives), on the slopes of Cerro de la Atalaya near the Santuario de Nuestra Señora del Buen Suceso, in front of Castle Siyâsa. Or La Cueva de las Cabras (Goat Cave) or La Cueva de los Pucheros (Cave of the pots).

The desert of Siyâsa (**Yacimiento de Siyâsa**), located on the Castle hill, is one of the most interesting archaeological sites of Western Islam. It was excavated during the 1980s under the direction of Julio Navarro, recovering a block of 19 houses and an impressive collection of objects, including ceramics, glass and architectural elements in gypsum, which are displayed at the Museum of Siyâsa.

El Museo de Siyâsa houses archaeological and ethnographic heritage of the town, including prehistoric rock art and remains from the 11th, 12th and 13th centuries, the Andalusian period. Calle San Sebastian, 17, 968 773153.

El Museo del Molino de Teodoro is housed in a flour mill from the 15th century, fully restored by the Municipality of Cieza between 1998 and 1999 to convert it into a museum. There's an interesting collection of machinery and equipment used in the mills of the time to undertake the cleaning process, grinding and sifting the wheat for flour. Paraje del Estrecho, 968 453500.

The **Auditorium Gabriel Celaya** is designed as an outdoor amphitheatre and is a great place to enjoy some of the cultural offerings of the city. It is located in Medina Park Siyâsa and during the summer months hosts numerous social and cultural events. The best example of these events occurs in the month of August with the Theatre Festival **'Ciudad de Cieza'**, ranked as one of the largest in the Region of Murcia. Calle Parque, 968 456259.

Perhaps one of the best reasons to visit the area is to enjoy the **Cañón de los Almadenes**. Northwest of the Murcia region, halfway between the towns of Calasparra and Cieza, in the upper reaches of the river Segura is an area of 116 hectares protected since 1992. The Canyon of Almadenes is an unusual landscape in the foothills of the mountains of the Molino, the Palera and Almorchón. The Segura River has carved this deep gash over millions of years, taking advantage of tectonic features resulting in a gorge four miles in length, with vertical walls in some places reaching over one hundred meters.

There are plenty of walking routes through the area. The GR7, PR1, PR2, PR3 and PR4 all come through here.

Cieza enjoys fiestas all year round including: Holy Week, declared of tourist interest, Fiesta de la Cruz de Mayo, with the rise of the image of Santo Cristo del Consuelo to his hermitage, Peach Festival, Film Festival Mágika, International Folklore Festival del Segura, Romería de la Virgen del Buen Suceso; Christmas and the Craft Market. It celebrates its patron saint fiesta in honour of St. Bartholomew in August, between 24th and 31st.

A hamlet of Cieza, **Ascoy**, is located 3 kilometres to the north and 40 miles northwest of the city of Murcia. It's worth visiting due to the cave paintings found in several caves in the **Barranco de los Grajos** (Rooks Ravine). There are traces of settlements from the Roman era. On the 14th and 15th of May, Ascoy celebrates their festivities in honour of San Isidro Labrador.

Services

Turismo, www.ciezaturistica.es, for what's happening locally.

Ayuntamiento, www.cieza.es

Sleeping

On the Pantano del Quípar road at km2.5 there's a casa rural and restaurant called El Ginete, www.ventaginete.com, 696 942174. There are two small houses for rent, rustic and traditionally restored for €150 per night.

Hospederia San Sebastian, Calle San Sebastian, 868 961868, www.sansebastianhospederia.com, has doubles from €70.

Eating

The restaurant Maripinar on Calle Maripinar, 24, is a large restaurant on the outskirts of town. 968 7611182, www.asadormaripinar.com.

There's also the restaurant at the casa rural El Ginete, www.ventaginete.com, they serve traditional local food in this small restaurant, where they also make their own wine.

Costa Cálida

With 250km of coastline, the Costa Cálida (Warm Coast) is one of Spain's little known holiday hotspots. Along with the Mar Menor the coast of the

Costa Cálida is home to water sports, fishing, scuba diving, sun bathing and nature reserves.

The Costa Cálida covers the area from the top of the Mar Menor right along to Águilas. Though the Mar Menor attracts the most visitors, the whole coast has lots to offer. West of Cartagena on the Golfo de Mazarrón the coast is very quiet with many unspoilt beaches and few high rise developments. See Puerto Mazarrón, Bolnuevo and Águilas for a few highlights.

Public transport to these less built up coasts is limited, you'll need your own wheels.

Fortuna

Population: 10,050

Map Reference: 1.13°W, 38.18°N

The town is dominated by the spa (Balneario), Roman ruins, the crypt reached through a 200metre tunnel at Manantial Church (at the Spa), a small palace (Palacio Atalaya) and casino. It's also just 2km from the centre of town to the Black Caves (Cueva Negra).

Iglesia Parroquial de la Purísima Concepción, in the central Plaza de Juan XXIII, this church is part of the Baroque Murcia. The date of construction of the temple is between 1728 and 1744.

Ermita de San Roque, located at the end of the avenue of San Roque and dated to the early seventeenth century, is the first church in Fortuna. Next to this building is the typical narrow street of San Pedro, which was for a long time the main street.

The newest building in the town is **Ermita de San Antón** and holds the image of San Antón throughout the year. It has a key role in the processions during Easter celebrations.

Santuario Romano de la Cueva Negra is one of the most important archaeological sites on an international level. The Black Cave is located at Sierra del Baño, about 3km from Fortuna. This is a set of three rock shelters facing the sun and a water fountain. This site is directly related to the other major Roman site of the town, the balneario.

There are a few interesting fiestas in Fortuna, including, Kalendas Aprili, which takes place the weekend after Easter. Its purpose is to remember old Roman traditions. Members of different groups rise in pilgrimage to the black cave, where they spend the day and then travel down to Fortuna at 7pm accompanied by a charanga (band).

However, the most important festival in the town is Sodales and Romans held in honour of San Roque 10th to 17th August, which commemorates the presence of the Roman people in the population for over two millennia. The highlights are the Íbero, Romano parade, declared of Regional Tourist Interest and the selection of the Nymphs. Various festivals and concerts, among other acts, complete the festive program.

Fiesta de San Isidro Labrador happens the weekend after 15th May. Many events are held; a pilgrimage, a tasting of typical dishes, dances and a procession.

Going Native:
Angela, Mick and Two Black Labradors

We retired here, from Yorkshire in March 2019, after a couple of visits and a lot of reasearch. Thankfully we got a good lawyer who is Spanish and knows the law, but speaks English well and worked on our behalf. We wanted to be away from the beach so we can have day trips, and get more house for our money, and near a typical Spanish town, so we can learn the culture and language. We also wanted a certain amount of privacy, in a multicultural urbanisation, where help is there if needed. We found all of that, and now live in a detached villa in El Reloj, Fortuna.

We made a 38 hour to drive from Yorkshire, with two Labradors in a minibus, via ferry at Calais through France avoiding the tolls! If we did it again I'd travel with more stops, make the moving day into a mini holiday. I really wish we had seen more of France and northern Spain.

We spent the first ten months occasionally grieving for our family and friends. We've visited the UK twice already and family have been here too, and we've got lots of trips in the planning stage. Don't under estimate the grief you will feel missing the people you love, make plans to visit and be visited, keep in touch as many ways as possible, WhatsApp, Instagram whatever you need. Don't let it spoil your joy of being here though, cheap flights are available all year round if you look.

We've had some challenges, the weather being one of them! We experienced our first *gota fria* three weeks after arriving, with 7 inches of clean water in our underbuild (little apartment underneath the house). Then another *gota fria* in September 2019, flooded our underbuild with canal water. The apartment was totally destroyed, the garden wall wiped out. The clean up and rebuild was demoralising at times, nothing moves quickly in Spain especially when your Spanish is zilch.

Speaking of the language, make an effort! It's necessary, especially if you're not in an expat area where everyone speaks English. The best thing about Murcia are the Murcianos, we love the people (except when they are behind the wheel of a car), they are very kind and helpful. We're looking forward to learning the language, and having more conversations with Spaniards in Spanish.

We are fortunate to be near the Thermal Baths at in Fortuna which we can visit all year round. They have a great menu del dia, an option for massage, so we can spend a whole day chilling out, eating, drinking and chatting. We also love a coffee at the local ice cream parlour. Our favourite beach is at Guardamar del Segura, it's long and has plenty of space. We love the various archaeological areas and exploring Murcia city, so much to see and do, walk along the river, eat tapas, visit the markets etc.

Would we go back? NEVER!

There are some lovely small towns in the Fortuna area, including: Peña Zafra de Arriba, Peña Zafra de Abajo, Fuente Blanca, La Garapacha, Hoya Hermosa, Capres, Las Casicas, Los Baños (with the Leana Balneario, see section below), La Matanza, El Reloj, La Gineta and Periquitos (which has a good clay pigeon shooting club at the bar of the same name, www.hotellosperiquitos.com).

Leana Balneario

Three kilometres outside the town of Fortuna on the Yecla–Pinoso Road is the Balneario, one of only a few hot springs in the Murcia region, just (22km) to the North East of Murcia city. The water quality is amongst the best in Europe for easing rheumatism and arthritis, originally used by the Arabs and the Romans. The spring has waters deep underground, surfacing at temperatures of 53°C, transported straight to the treatment rooms.

The thermal pools are open all day between 10am and 9pm; treatments are available throughout the day. The 3 hotels on site cater for the more expensive end of the market and they are suitably grand. The Balneario even has its own range of cosmetics and health treatments, which you can buy onsite or through their website: www.leana.es (968 685011). To enjoy the baths (two swimming pools) costs €12 for adults (€16 at weekends and holidays) and €6 for children. There are lots of treatments and special offers available.

Almazara Ramón Pérez

The olive oil sold at the Almazara Ramón Pérez is mouth-wateringly delicious. www.almazararamonperez.com, 968 685380. They collect olives from the region and all the way down to the Alicante coast and during the autumn press and filter them for oil. It's worth calling in for a tasting session on weekdays 09:00 - 14:00 and 16:00 to 19:00. You won't regret it, especially if they allow you to try their new lemon infused olive oil which began commercial production towards the end of 2019. Inside the show room and shop you can go downstairs into their bodega to buy some lesser known local wines. There are also plans to launch a range of craft beer.

Location Report: Embalse De Santomera

There are many places for walking in the Murcia region. An easy option with spectacular views is the reservoir known as the *Embalse de Santomera*, a few miles to the North East of Murcia city. The walk can easily be extended or shortened depending on your physical ability and your time requirements, and getting out into the natural environment is good for everyone. A trip here can also be combined with some other places of interest just a short drive away, such as picturesque Fortuna (or if you're crazy, Ikea).

The Embalse de Santomera is located just a couple of miles from the A7 motorway not far from Murcia city. Look for the Fortuna junction and follow the RM-423 until you see the signposts for the reservoir. Don't worry if you accidentally stray into the grounds of the Water Authority's *Casa del Agua*. This curious building can be visited by prior arrangement if you wish to learn more about how water resources are managed. There are some interesting sculptures and information boards in the grounds too, as well as some great views of the water.

A small car park can be found close to the old hostel which still has its colourful mosaic detailing various aspects of the local environment. A map is handily displayed of the PR-MU82 walking route. Taking a photograph of it is a good idea so that you can keep track of where you are. It clearly illustrates the 6.5km round walk and also shows some other tracks which you can explore.

The walk begins with a small climb up to the reservoir's dam. You could just take a stroll straight down and do a bit of birdwatching, but we followed the yellow and white waymarkers over the dam and into the hills. Along the there were beautiful views of the water and the countryside. If it's getting a little bit hot in the afternoons a morning stroll is probably better in the summer, and remember to take sensible shoes, a hat, sunscreen and plenty of water with you.

The path is easy to follow and the uphill sections were not too steep or strenuous. Rather than follow the entire length of the route, we turned onto a track marked by a purple spot just after the TV mast. This cut about 20 minutes off the walk, but it wasn't the easiest descent in places. Just remember to turn right when you rejoin the main path, even though your instincts tell you to go left!

You can take a picnic with you and eat it with a view of the reservoir if you wish. That does add extra weight though, and rather than eat at the side of the car park, it may be better to continue a little further along the road where a large open area complete with picnic tables and barbecues awaits. Take a beach umbrella for some shade though as there isn't a lot of shelter from the sun.

Alternatively, make your way back to the main road and continue into the town of Fortuna. There we can highly recommend the Panaderia La Purisma with incredible cakes and pastries which, having just finished a strenuous walk, you can easily justify sampling!

Russ Pearce

Services

Ayuntamiento, Calle Purísima, 7, 968 685103, www.aytofortuna.es

Tourist office, Avenida Juan Carlos I, 968 685586, www.aytofortuna.es

Taxis, Calle Vicente Medina, 626 515148

Sleeping

The Casas Rurales de las Señoritas in El Ajauque, 696 895838, www.casaruralfortuna.com, is a group of four restored rural houses, sharing a swimming pool, garden and bbq area. Accommodating up to six guests, the houses are priced from €120 per night.

El Viejo Establo is a group of seven casas, 968 687066, www.elviejo-establo.com which share a swimming pool, padel tennis court and gardens. The pool can be covered making it usable all year round. It's 5km outside Fortuna in La Matanza. Prices start at €130 for a small cabin accommodating two during low season but longer stays are much better value.

At the Balneario there are a number of hotels, www.leana.es, including: Hotel Balneario with 58 rooms, Hotel España and Hotel Victoria, 968 685011. Rooms start at €48 per person, but packages are also available including use of the facilities of the Balneario and some treatments, and represent better value than paying for use of the baths separate from your room costs.

Just outside of town there's the four star Hotel Los Periquitos at kilometre 9 on the Fortuna road, 968 685240, www.hotelspamurcia.es. There's also a spa, restaurant, swimming pool and treatment rooms. The prices are very reasonable for the facilities and the hotels, starting at €40. This hotel complex is right next to the clay pigeon shooting range, which is great fun, but might produce a little noise during the busy weekends.

Hotel Costas on the Abanilla road has 47 rooms, www.hotelcostas.net, 968 686493 with double rooms at €60. It's quite modern with a restaurant on site.

Hotel La Fuente and Camping La Fuente are on the same site on Camino De La Bocamina, 968 685125, www.campingfuente.com. This is a small hotel with 7 double rooms from €60, 6 bungalows and a campsite with some plots with individual bathrooms. There's a swimming pool and restaurant on site too.

Camping Las Palmeras in Los Baños, 968 686095, www.campinglaspalmeras.eu has plenty of space for touring vans.

You can stay in a cave house at El Solins in nearby Las Casicas, 630 886997. Reservations can be made through www.booking.com.

Eating

Los Periquitos has two restaurants and a café/bar, www.hotelspamurcia.es

Panaderia La Purisma, on Av Juan Carlos I, 968 68 52 09, has a lovely outdoor terrace and serves all manner of delicious pastries and cakes.

Bodega El Solins, in Las Casicas, 630 88 69 97, is a restored cave house that provides a lovely location for a meal. They specialise in suckling pig (when it's in season) cooked on a wood fire.

There are plenty of places to eat in town and at the Balneario, though prices are a little inflated.

Fuente Álamo

Population: 16,200

Map Reference: 1.17°W, 37.72°N

Going into Fuente Álamo is rather like visiting Croydon. Shut your eyes and listen to the plethora of English accents. The town has more than 18% non-Spanish residents, one of the highest in Murcia. We wouldn't like to mislead you into believing that Fuente Álamo is a worthwhile tourist destination; however it does serve a number of useful purposes, including an excellent selection of banks, a Post Office (where you can hire a post office box, apartado de correo) and a passable selection of DIY shops.

The area was originally used for transhumance by the shepherds and goat herders from La Mancha. There's a village and area named La Manchica (little La Mancha) to the south of Fuente Álamo.

Take a look at the recently restored **Iglesia de San Agustín, Plaza de la Constitución**, started in 1545 and finally consecrated in 1582 in honour of Saint Agustín. The tower was completed in 1621 and restored in 1845. Next to the chapel of the Virgen del Rosario was chosen as a burial place for the most influential townspeople.

Fuente Álamo has a golf complex to the North West, attracting even more Brits to the area, **Hacienda del Álamo.**

The museum, **Museo de Fuente Álamo**, covers three floors, with a permanent paintings collection of local painters on the top floor, an exhibition of works of forging, weaving, carpentry, ceramics, esparto or agriculture based on the Campo de Cartagena, and in the basement a workspace for training and the temporary exhibitions. The museum is open Tuesday to Saturday from 10:00 to 14:00, Mondays to Fridays 17:00 to 21:00, www.museofuentealamo.es

Close to Mercadona in town you can also find the open air water museum. With an old *aljibe* water tank and a metal water wheel to see, you can learn about the history of water management in the region.

A good market on a Saturday morning to the north of town (over the bridge) will give you your fix of churros, fruit, vegetables and dodgy CDs.

The local fiesta, San Agustín, is in August (18th to 28th), when the town resembles a sprawling fun fair. Also the first weekend in June sees the countryside exhibition, **Fería de Ganados**, held in the rambla by the bridge.

On the outskirts of town there's a technology park, www.ptfuentealamo.com, with a growing number of international companies, including Siemens.

There's the motorbike circuit of Fuente Álamo to take a look at too, **Circuito de Fuente Álamo**, Avenida Hacienda del Álamo, 623 183083. This is right near the Hacienda del Álamo golf resort, a side road off the island near the main golf resort entrance takes you to the circuit. A new longer circuit has opened recently.

In May every year the Fuente Álamo triathlon is held, attracting national and international competitors.

Frequently (at least a couple of times per year) the circus comes to town, by the bridge near Mercadona. Nowadays no animals are involved.

Ayuntamiento, Plaza Constitución, 1, www.ayto–fuentealamo.es, 968 597001.

Taxis, 968 597135

The municipal area of Fuente Álamo includes the following towns: Balsapintada, Cuevas de Reyllo, El Escobar, Los Almagros, Los Paganes, El Estrecho, La Pinilla, Las Palas and Los Cánovas.

These towns are interesting to visit too, with shooting ranges, motor circuits and their own fiestas. They also have large populations of foreign residents, including British people.

Balsapintada

Marked by a water reservoir which was built by the Romans and used by the Arabs, Balsapintada literally means 'painted reservoir', as the walls of the reservoir were painted red. It was a place to rest, el descansadero. The reservoir has now gone, but is remembered in the plaza.

Two major rivers crossed this area, Rambla de la Murta and Rambla del Albujón, which are now dry river beds and a great place to take a hike. This area was important in Roman times, statuettes of the god Hermes, water pipes made of lead, vases and coins from the time of the Emperor Caesar Augustus to Gallienus have all been found near here.

There's a shrine dedicated to Santiago Apostol, celebrations are held in late July, with cultural activities and horse/carriage related (camioneros) events such as dressage competition and a rociero. It's also a very loud and firework-led fiesta! Known as the Dia del Camiones, or truck drivers' day, many major truck companies now take part.

The town is known for its ham production and has a good agriculture basis, with an excellent road network.

Cuevas de Reyllo

Cuevas de Reyllo was named after an influential family in the area, the Reyllos, one of whom, Gregorio Reyllo Hemández, was the first mayor of Fuente Álamo in 1700.

There are some Roman archaeological sites in the Cueva Pagan and in the vicinity of Los Muñoces.

Today it is an important place for industrial development and livestock. The town is well known for their work with immigrants, teaching and training them, providing internet access and computer facilities.

The church was built in honour of Señora del Rosario in the early 20th century and recently restored. The fiestas for Cuevas de Reyllo are celebrated for the Virgen del Rosario on 7th of October.

El Escobar, Los Almagros and Los Paganes

Situated in the foothills of the Carrascoy mountains, the names of these towns come from the founders, the people who originally settled here. The towns had an abundance of firewood, water, esparto (which they use to make baskets) and food, along with a good strategic location and local ore mines, making them an excellent place to settle. Near the end of the 20th century these towns were almost de-populated when people moved to the cities.

The ermitas (hermitages) of Los Almagros and El Escobar were built in the 18th century. The patron of El Escobar is San Juan Bautista; the fiesta takes place in June. Los Almagros has the Virgen de la Luz, with festivities in September, and Los Paganes joins them.

El Estrecho

El Estrecho is a great place to start a hike from. The Rio Seco, the Ribera and Molino de Agua de los Celdranes were all created by the rivers crossing through here, leaving natural walkways (now that the rivers are mostly dry). El Estrecho means The Straits.

It's an agricultural area, not much else to see. El Estrecho celebrates its fiesta in honour of Santa Cruz around May 3rd.

La Pinilla

It's a beautiful village to mooch around, there are old houses painted in ochre, blues and yellows, stone walls, farmhouses with coats of arms, entrance arches to huge courtyards and narrow alleyways. So park the car and have a stroll.

The name comes from the Arabic, Ben-iella, which means 'son of the covenant'. It used to belong to Lorca, but now is probably the prettiest village in the Fuente Álamo area.

La Pinilla lies in the foothills of the Sierra del Algarrobo and is great for walking and hiking. Some of the oldest marine fossils have been found around Cabezos de la Fuente. There are a few Roman and Arabic remains around too, especially in the antiguo barrio del Fortín.

On 8th September they have their fiesta in honour of Nuestra Señora de la Luz. There's also the Romería del Los Cabecicos, where they take an image of the Virgin Mary up to the shrine at Los Cabecicos. The shrine is worth a visit as you get a great view of the campo de Cartagena.

The #DisasterFarm, where I (Debs) live now, lies just between La Pinilla and Las Palas, at the foothills of the Algarrobo mountain.

Las Palas

Take a look at Campo Nubla, La Manchica, Finca Almendros, Cabezo de la Cebolla, Fuentes del Mingrano, and Rambla de la Orilla for Roman, Arabic or Iberian archaeological sites. Flour mills were common, and you'll probably see the odd windmill or waterwheel as you drive around the town and countryside.

It has a public swimming pool, exhibition centre, football team and a neighbourhood association which actively contributes to organising all kinds of events. It's a hub for Brits too, with English-speaking restaurant owners and shops.

Their fiesta is held in honour of San Pedro Apóstol, around the 29th of June.

Los Cánovas

Originally considered as just a street in Cuevas de Reyllo, not much is known about the history of Los Canovas. In the 60s and 70s there was a massive population decline as residents went to France and Germany to find work. In the 80s wine growing was the main method of economic growth and currently pig, sheep and goat rearing, along with some industrial animal food equipment manufacture is the main industry.

There's a small church, an esparto specialist who will show you baskets, a car and figures (including Christ) made from esparto (strong grass) and one of the oldest restored flour mills in the area.

Los Cánovas celebrates its fiesta on the 4th of October in honour of San Francisco de Asís.

Sleeping

There are plenty of casas rurales around the Fuente Álamo area, www.casasrurales.net. Casa Pachera is just on the edge of town and sleeps up to 7 people. In Cuevas de Reyllo there's Casa de la Cuesta, 625 380356, www.casadelacuesta.es, which also has a pool.

Finca Liarte, Paraje de la Atalaya in El Mingrano, Las Palas, 699 089061, www.fincaliarte.com, is a group of four casas rurales located at the farmhouse. They have a covered swimming pool, Jacuzzi, children's play area, animals, football area, bikes for hire and a traditional Moorish wood stove.

If you're looking for a hotel then you could try Venta El Campo, at km23 on the Cartagena-Alhama, road (exit 21 towards Cuevas de Reyllo), 968 151414, www.ventaelcampo.es.

Eating

There are the usual collection of bars and restaurants found in a town this size; quite a few of them retain their Spanish feel despite the influx of Brits into the town.

For foodies then you must go to Restaurant and Heladería El Buen Yantar, Plaza Constitución, 6, 968 597073. They do a menú del día, but you don't get a choice, just one plate for each course, so best if you're quite happy eating anything. At the weekends they do a full menu and the mornings they have their own homemade croissants. They make their own ice cream too!

There's also the Oso Blanco on Gran Vía for something a little more upmarket, www.oso-blanco.es, 642 93 64 14.

In the outskirts there are a few ventas (see the location report), including the one mentioned above in the hotels section. Plus there's Venta Garceran, www.restaurantegarceran.com, Autovía A30 exit 172 near Balsapintada, 968 160549. They have a menú del día on Saturdays too.

At Hacienda del Álamo golf course there's the expensive Restaurante La Hacienda, 868 800107.

Location Report: Eating At The Motorway Ventas

As you drive around Murcia you'll notice roadside Ventas or bars. They're a bit like the roadside cafes in the UK, but with good food at reasonable prices! Some are chains and best to be avoided, some are family run and may be numbered (I, II, III etc) for convenience.

You'll find that most have a minimarket for general provisions like tinned foods and biscuits, many make their own bread or certainly get it locally and often they have a great butchery department where you can buy local meats and sausages. They're always good value even though they are in prime locations, so they're well worth a visit if you've forgotten something on a Sunday afternoon.

They're here for the motorist, coach parties and the long distance lorry driver. They have huge car parks, allowing the lorry drivers to sleep over after their lunch. These places can get very busy when a bus or a coach turns up, hundreds of elderly people will descend and take over the bar.

They usually have a bar where you can eat the never ending supply of fresh tapas and a comedor (dining room) for a menú del día or Sunday lunch. If you're ever looking for a good value menú del día on a Saturday then try a venta, you'll almost always be pleased.

Sometimes they can look a bit scary! But be brave, venture inside and enjoy good food and a great price.

Jumilla

Population: 25,700

Map Reference: 1.33°W, 38.48°N

Far off in the north east of the region, as you approach Jumilla you will find the endless acres of vineyards that are hard to miss! This gives the theme to the whole town, the wine of Jumilla DOC. Overlooking Jumilla is the 15th century castle, recently restored, which is best seen from the west of the town.

The **Castle** dates back to the Bronze age; the Iberians and then the Romans took control. There are remains of Roman pottery from the 1st century AD. Then for five centuries the Arabs move in and began building an Arab fortress on the remains of the Roman castle. After a few battles between Aragon, Castillia La Mancha and Murcia, where the castle changed hands a number of times, in 1461 the Marqués de Villena took control and built pretty much what we see today.

Opening only at weekends, times depend upon the time of year, but usually include Saturdays and Sundays between 10:00 and 14:00 with afternoon hours in the warmer months too. Admission is free. You need a permit from the tourist office to drive your car up to the castle; however there is a free bus service between 10:30 and 13:30, leaving from the castle gates. Otherwise it's quite a long walk up! www.jumilla.org/castillo 968 782020.

Many towns have a street named after Dr Fleming and there is a statue of him outside the Las Ventas bullring in Madrid. His discovery has saved many lives in Spain but especially those of the bullfighters.

Take a wander through the narrow streets of the old town for an insight into its fascinating history, being occupied by the Iberians, Romans and Arabs before the Spanish king

Alfonso X re-conquered what was then known as Xumilla for the Kingdom of Castile in 1241.

The magnificent **Museo Jesús Nazareno in Plaza Arriba** is a private museum, facing the Archaeological Museum. It is open on Saturdays and Sundays 11:00 to 14:00 and also on Saturdays 18:00 to 20:30. It's well worth going inside to see some of the splendid costumes and statues from Semana Santa, however even if it is closed the impressive building itself merits a photo! http://www.museojesusnazareno.es/

Remember to look round the **Archaeological Museum** too, as it has some fascinating exhibits, plus the information is in English as well as Spanish.

Other sites worth visiting in Jumilla include: the **Teatro Vico** a 19th century horseshoe shaped theatre, the neo-gothic **Casa Modernista**, the 15th century **Iglesia de Santiago** which was declared a national monument because of its Gothic, Renaissance and Baroque architecture and **El Cason**, one of the best preserved late Roman burial vaults in the country.

Just outside the town there are several good walks for those more active, especially in the **Sierra de El Carche and Sierra de Santa Ana**. In the Sierra de Santa Ana pay a visit to the Monasterio de Santa Ana and its fascinating museum. The monastery has been occupied by Franciscan monks since 1573.

The **Museum of Santa Ana** shows religious art and includes unique artefacts and memorabilia brought by the Franciscans in their missionary journeys throughout the world. There's a Salzillo statue of Christ and a number of mostly Baroque paintings. There are also ethnological objects such as instruments of carnage(!) and typical objects of everyday life of the convent. It has an important monastic library. Open throughout the year, mornings from 10:00 to 13:00. Winter evenings, from 16:00 to 17:30. Sundays and holidays 10:00 to 11:30 Closed Monday. 968 780136.

Other tourist attractions are the botanical garden in the farming town of Estacada, home to more than 150 species; the Jumillita in the mines of Celia (volcanic cones and rocks), of Roman origin and global geological interest; the paintings in the Ravine Good Air (Barranco del Buen Aire); the fossil footprints at the Hoya de la Sima; paleontological sites from the Miocene era (5.6 to 7 million years), with trace fossils of hyperion, sabre tooth tiger, bear, antelope and camel.

Tuesday is market day in Jumilla and the one day that you are likely to hear other English voices as you wander around the large, colourful market.

The local fiesta, **Vendimia**, has a strong wine theme too (what a surprise!) where the catch phrase is Bebes o Te Mojo, literally translated as drink or I'll soak you. The red wine flows abundantly from the fountain, as well as being drunk and thrown over the revellers on the final Saturday (don't wear your best clothes and pack some aspirin!) www.fiestadelavendimia.com

Jumilla's Moors and Christians festivities, the Fiesta of La Virgen de la Asunción (Jumilla's patron saint) and the National Folklore Festival of Jumilla also take place during August.

In 2011 the festival of Semana Santa celebrated its 600th anniversary: Semana Santa in Jumilla is the oldest in the region and considered to be of National tourist interest. www.semanasanta-jumilla.org

There's always something going on in town, take a look at www.jumilla.org for up to date information.

Services

Tourist Office, Plaza del Rollo, 1, 968 780237, Monday, Friday: 09:00 to 14:00 and 17:00 to 19:00, Festivals, Saturdays and Sundays: 10:30 to 14:00

Ayuntamiento, Calle Canovas Del Castillo, 35, 968 782020, www.jumilla.org

Buses, Avenida de la Libertad, 968 756308, www.sietediasjumilla.es/horarios-de-autobuses/

Taxis, Plaza de la Glorieta, 968 780654

Jumilla has a number of smaller towns in its vicinity: Fuente del Pino, La Alquería, La Estacada (with the botanical gardens), El Carche, Las Encebras, Torre del Rico and Cañada del Trigo.

Jumilla Wine and Bodegas

There are many Bodegas and wine shops, there is a strong wine tourist theme. Jumilla is the primary wine-growing region of the whole of Murcia and perhaps the best-known exported wine from the region. Red and rosé wines are particular favourites.

For more information in English about all the bodegas in the area have a look at www.vinosdejumilla.org

The Jumilla Wine Tour (Ruta del Vino) is certified as a Spanish Wine Tour, and together with Montilla, Mancha-Valdepeñas, Utiel-Requena, Rías Baixas and Penedés, it represents the only tours that have so far obtained this distinction, which is synonymous with quality wine tourism. The tour includes visits to the wineries, guided wine tastings, wine tasting courses, local food and produce and meetings with the producers. In more recent years they've added a musical theme for the summer, with a bodega visit followed by music. www.rutadelvinojumilla.com

Many of the bodegas will arrange a tour followed by a wine tasting for you, get in touch to book. With advance notice you can even book a tour in English. If you go to the Ruta del Vino website and click on Partners List, you will find the main bodegas, wine shops, hotels and restaurants listed there with relevant links.

You can also buy the wines online from their websites, the shops in Jumilla main town or in larger supermarkets in the Murcia region.

Carchelo Winery, located in Carche Valley near Jumilla since 1990, owns more than two hundred hectares of vineyard, mainly with plantations of Monastrell (Mourvèdre) and Syrah. The rest is split between Cabernet Sauvignon and Tempranillo. The vineyards are irrigated by night with water coming directly from the mountains or rainwater when possible. The bodega also owns 500 wine casks made of French oak. Look for the brands Carchelo, Altico, Canalizo and Vedré. 656 314526, www.carchelo.com

Casa de la Ermita, based about 11km outside of Jumilla in the Carche valley, is well worth a visit. They'll show you around the vines, the winery and the storage areas. You can have a tasting session and buy the wines directly at great prices. Almost all of their wines can be found in the larger supermarkets saving you a trip to the winery (are you crazy!)

Their main grape is the Monastrell. They grow two varieties of French grape, Petit Verdot and Viognier, which are adapting with extraordinary ease to the climate of Jumilla. Petit Verdot is one of the most prestigious varieties of the A.O.C. Margaux, in France. There is also an experimental area where they are trying out other grape varieties including Caladoc and Gewurztraminer.

This is my favourite bodega and if you ever come visiting bring me a bottle of their Petit Verdot and I'll be your friend forever. 968 975942, www.casadelaermita.com

Silvano García has been around since 1925, they produce Macabeo, Monastrell, Tempranillo, Syrah, Cabernet Sauvignon, Muscatel and Merlot grapes. Look out for the Viñahonda and Silvano García labels in supermarkets.

Since 2002 they've also been selling their wine jams and ecological olive oils. They are next to the Mercadona, so very easy to access. 968 780767, www.silvanogarcia.es

Hacienda del Carche in the Carche valley is a young bodega which opened in 2006 and produces Tempranillo, Syrah, Cabernet Sauvignon and Grenache grapes along with the native Monastrell for the development of red wines, and Macabeo and Sauvignon Blanc for whites. They also sell olive oil, balsamic vinegar and red wine jam. 600 479005, www.haciendadelcarche.com

Bodegas Juan Gil has been in operation since 1916 in the hands of the Gil family. Covering 120 hectares, they produce Monastrell, Cabernet Sauvignon, Shyrah, Merlot and Petit Verdot grapes. www.bodegasjuangil.com

Bodegas Lúzon has some of the most unusual and striking labels, for which they've won awards. In over 600 hectares they grow Monastrell, Tempranillo, Syrah, Cabernet Sauvignon and Merlot grapes. 968 784135, www.bodegasluzon.com

Sleeping

Hotel Monreal on Calle Doctor Fleming, 6, is a modern central hotel, around €55 per night for a double room, with a restaurant too, 968 781816, www.hotelmonreal.net

Another modern hotel is the Hotel Pío XII on Calle Ortega y Gasset, 12, 968 780132, www.hotelpioxii.com. They have a sister restaurant on the Santa Ana road, www.salonpioxii.com, El Salón Pío XII, which is huge and has enviable views, 968 783372.

If you prefer a casa rural then try Casa Consuelo, Parcela Los Alberciales, 673 971049, which has a swimming pool and two double rooms for rental. www.casaruraljumilla.com

Bar and Pensión Pipa on Calle Cánovas del Castillo, 150, is great value, 968 780086.

Location Report: Tapear In Jumilla

Here, in no particular order, are some of the best bars in Jumilla, from our correspondent Sue Walker, if you fancy going out for some tapas.

Cafetería de Estación de Autobuses, Avenida de la Libertad has the best sepia y champiñones ever.

Nuestro Bar, Los Milanos has incredible food at incredible prices: if we only lived closer to Nuestro Bar it would be our regular haunt. Faustino had a well-deserved excellent write-up on www.TripAdvisor.com after two American visitors had eaten there a couple of times. Whenever we are near Nuestro Bar we pop in for coffee or wine and tapas and always receive a warm welcome and very good service.

Bar Canarias, Calle Jesús Sánchez Carrillo, 4, is in our neighbourhood and near the local market. Bar Canarias is one of our favourites. The owner speaks good English, though we always try to speak to him in Spanish. Depending on his mood he will greet us in English, Spanish or a mixture of both! We took friends here for wine and tapas after going to a carol concert and they were impressed by both the food and the prices.

Bar La Tapa Rincon de Pedro, Calle Marchante, 8, is a typical Spanish bar: small, always busy, usually noisy and with a good selection of tapas as befits its name. It used to be a regular haunt when we first moved here and were renting a flat in the centre of Jumilla.

Bar Chaparral, Avenida de Yecla, 75, is a good place to go to with friends when you are very hungry but don't want to spend a fortune: its tapas is excellent and unbelievably cheap, so you can afford to buy loads. Our best Christmas party ever was upstairs in Bar Chaparral, which the Adult Education Centre had booked for its students. The amount of dishes they produced was amazing and all of them were delicious.

Cafetería Los Angeles, Plaza Pablo Picasso is great for a glass of wine in the evening. I don't think I have ever seen local people have an alcoholic drink without something to nibble on, which is a healthy habit we have adopted.

Of course these aren't the only places in Jumilla where you can find tasty tapas and the following bars and restaurants are also good places to visit on your tapas trail: Restaurante San Agustín, Restaurante Reyes Católicos, Bar Paraíso, Restaurante Monasterio, Duque de Lerma, Meson Jumillano, Cervecería Levante, Bar las Delicias. Plus many, many more! Or just pop into any bar that takes your fancy and enjoy!

Eating

There are quite a few tapas opportunities towards the centre of town, some of which appear in our location report above. Wander the streets and you'll find many more.

Gazpacho is a common staple of the town, however when ordering it check whether you are getting the familiar Gazpacho Andaluz, which is a popular dish in summer, or the local Gazpacho which usually contains both meat and snails and would therefore be a bad choice for a vegetarian!

Casa Sebastien, Avenida de Levante, this restaurant in the main market is known for its high quality local specialities, where you can eat for less than €15. Closed in the evenings. www.restaurantecasasebastian.com

San Agustín, Avenida de la Asunción, 64, renowned as a fish restaurant though its meat dishes are equally good, for less than €15 per person.

Menú del día €11. www.facebook.com/restaurantesanagustin

Loreto, Calle de las Canalejas, 73, this restaurant is in a beautiful old building with interior courtyard. Traditional cooking with modern touches and menus from €20 (lunchtime only) to €30. www.restaurantedeloreto.com

Michelangelo, Avenida Reyes Católicos, this is Jumilla's main Italian restaurant, though there are several pizzerias in town.

Also try:

- Meson Jumillano, Avenida de Murcia, 49, menú del día €10.
- Casa Molowny, Calle Barón del Solar, 66, less than €15.
- London, Avenida Levante, 36, bargain menú del día for €7.50
- Monasterio, Avenida Asunción, 40, menú del día at €9
- Reyes Católicos, Avenida Reyes Católicos, 33
- Duque de Lerma, Calle de Albano Martínez, 34
- Pueblo Nuevo, La Estacada (Pueblo Nuevo)
- Campo Nuevo, Carretera De Murcia, km57
- Los Badenes, Carretera Jumilla–Yecla, km79, www.hostalrestaurantelosbadenes.com
- Media Luna, Carretera Yecla, km75 (La Alquería) www.salonesmedialuna.com

Night Life

To start the evening you can try having your first drink at Sarao Café, Keltoi 'Irish pub' (though don't expect to find Guinness there!) or Chaplin. Later on you could try Tabú, El Buscón de Quevedo, or Hypnos which tends to be for the younger crowd.

La Manga del Mar Menor

Map Reference: 0.72°W, 37.66°N

Most Brits who know anything about this region will have heard about La Manga (the sleeve), due to its enormous golf course and housing estate of the same name and the infamy of British footballers. However La Manga club is somewhat a misnomer as it's actually south of the true La Manga.

The true La Manga is the geographical feature that separates the Mar Menor from the Mediterranean. This heavily developed strip, which is some 24km long and in places only 100m wide, can be seen for tens of kilometres inland. La Manga has a number of pleasant beaches and is in places home to the jet set with a few stunning marinas.

The hotels along La Manga are popular with Spaniards and this really was the first area of tourist development in the region, when it was discovered in the 60s. It's now overrun with Brits and Germans.

La Manga can only be reached by car from the south (Cartagena end) and the spine of La Manga is a busy service road providing access to the hundreds of hotels and holiday flats. Some of the designs would be equally at home in the tasteful (yeah right!) American city of Las Vegas, employing sandcastles and boats for their architectural inspiration.

You may walk from La Manga out to the island Isla del Ciervo, where you can get some reasonable views of the other islands on the Mar Menor.

As it's located between two seas La Manga is also an ideal place to practice nautical sports. Sailing and water-skiing schools with regular courses, windsurfing and catamarans, kitesurfing, whatever whets your appetite. And of course there are some great places for scuba diving, such as Cabo de Palos (see the Cabo de Palos section for more information) and the rocky depths next to Isla Grosa.

Courses in windsurfing, sailboats etc. www.mangasurf.com, 968 145331, Isla del Ciervo, Exit 23.

Kayaking, sailing and windsurfing run by a young English couple, www.aqua-adicta.co.uk, 659 434811, Calle Pintor Rosales 28, Mar de Cristal.

Kite surfing, at Kite Centre La Manga, Gran Vía km 2, Isla del Ciervo, www.kitecenter.es, 616 678001.

Scuba diving from Scuba Murcia, Gran Via de La Manga, Edif Babilonia 11a y 7b, www.scubamurcia.com

Scuba and Sailing with La Manga Surf, 968 145331, www.mangasurf.com

Hire bikes and quads from La Manga Bikes & Quads, Gran Via, km6.7 Urbanisation Mangalan, 968 14 0265.

Of course, you can't have a section on La Manga without a little more detail on La Manga Club, www.lamangaclub.com It's had an interesting history: building started in 1970 with a 9-hole golf course and a small residential area, sold in 1981 to European Ferries, adding tennis facilities and a four star hotel, taken over by P&O Ferries and a new hotel built in the 90s, increase to three golf courses, creation of four football pitches and the attraction of international teams for winter training, sold to the Medgroup in 2005 and the opening of a spa. Now you can get married there, play golf, cricket or tennis, have a relaxing massage, go scuba diving, or just laze around in five star luxury.

Services

Tourist Office, Gran Via, 968 146136, www.murciaturistica.es

Other useful websites, www.lamanga.net

Location Report: La Manga Strip

There are in fact two La Mangas in Murcia, La Manga del Mar Menor and La Manga Club. The former is the one most people usually explore first and this is a long narrow piece of land that more or less divides the Mar Menor Sea from the Mediterranean Sea. Its name translated from Spanish means, 'the sleeve' and from an aerial perspective it does look like a long arm jutting out protectively around the Mar Menor sea. It was formed when sand and sediment built up on underwater mountains eventually forming this nineteen kilometre column of sand and dunes. In the 1960s La Manga del Mar Menor, commonly called La Manga Strip, was discovered as a tourist resort and today it is covered in apartments and villas, the majority designed with the holiday maker in mind.

Many people drive down the Strip, only to return with a confused look, questioning why it is so popular. Close up the La Manga Strip can be less impressive with some sixties style apartment blocks, hotels themed as castles and, in summer months, fairly heavy traffic. However it is incredibly popular with tourists from within Spain and abroad for a number of very good reasons.

For beach lovers it really has everything. On one side you have the calm, shallow waters of the Mar Menor, the beaches are gently slopping and it is ideal for small children or the less confident bather. Then you can simply cross the road and enjoy kilometres of golden beaches and rolling breakers on the Mediterranean side.

Water sport enthusiasts of all types also flock to La Manga Strip and there are numerous water sports centres to visit. Half way down the strip, by the side of the Hotel Cavanna is water sports centre where the locals recommend you should head to if you would like to try out wind or kite surfing. If scuba diving is your thing then continue on further down the strip and visit the Deep Impact Diving Centre where they offer training for novices and visits to dive sites for the experienced divers. For sailors there are a number of marinas and sailing schools on the strip and you can either take to the water on the Mar Menor or the Mediterranean. However access to the Mediterranean from the Mar Menor is through a canal with a drawbridge so you must check the opening times to ascertain when you can pass if you have a tall mast.

Golfers have not been forgotten and towards the end of La Manga Strip is Veneziola Golf, a nine hole pitch and putt course. The breeze straight off the sea can be a challenge and there is a pleasant club house with a bar and coffee shop where you can drink in views of the Mediterranean.

Of course it wouldn't be a proper Spanish holiday resort without places to eat and drink and La Manga Strip offers both of these in abundance. Popular areas to try are the Plaza Cavanna, Plaza Bohemia and Tomas Maestre marina. They all have a choice of bars and restaurants and a good atmosphere. There are also many other restaurants on either side of the strip waiting for you to discover. A recent and very popular addition is the Restaurante El Parador which is an old finca with a palm tree garden and stunning views of the Mar Menor.

If you are looking for some heady Spanish nightlife then the area called El Zoco on the strip is the place to go. It has a mixture of bars, restaurants and clubs and all are open well into the early hours of the morning.

La Manga del Mar Menor is a seasonal resort. Visit in the winter and the strip will be extremely quiet and many businesses, bars and restaurants will be closed. Visit in the summer months and you'll enjoy wonderful beaches, good food, fun and relaxation.

Martine Cherry, www.rhumhor.com

Beaches

There are plenty of beaches along the strip, some to note are:

Marchamalo, La Manga, typical beach of the La Manga stretch, sandy and pleasant with calm waters. Very crowded during peak times.

Banco del Tabal, La Manga, Fine sandy former blue flag beach, situated between Playa de Marchamalo and Playa Pedrucho on the Mediterranean side.

Cala de Pino, an urban blue flag beach, which can get very busy. Golden sands and calm water.

La Cala, La Manga Club, private, secluded beach for the La Manga club.

Ports

Puerto Deportivo Tomás Maestre, www.puertomaestre.com

Club Náutico Dos Mares, www.club-Náuticodosmares.com

Club Náutico Las Isleta, 968 145339, www.clubNáuticolaisleta.es

Sleeping

There are hundreds of rooms for rent, apartments, villas and hotels in this area.

Hotel Entre Mares, www.entremares.es, 968 56 41 23, is a hotel and spa on the La Manga strip. They have lots of offers on their website, worth a look.

Hotelania lists two hotels, www.hotelania.com, Los Delfines and Las Gaviotas, both frontline La Manga strip.

On a little spit on the strip the Sol Galúa, 968 563200, https://www.servigroup.com/en/hotels-in-la-manga-del-mar-menor/servigroup-galua-hotel/ offers a tremendous seafront view.

Hotel Poseidon La Manga is an adult only hotel which can be found at kilometre 6.5 on Gran Via, www.hotelposeidonlamanga.com, 968 337000. They have 142 rooms and feature offers on their website.

Hotel La Manga Club Principe Felipe, is possibly the most expensive hotel in Murcia, this is 5 star luxury. 968 331234, www.lamangaclub.com

If you prefer your own villa then Villas La Manga on Gran Vía, km3, 968 1452222, www.villaslamanga.es can oblige. They have 60 villas with shared pool. Or if you want to stay at La Manga Club then there are the Las Lomas Villas, www.lamangaclub.com or they can help you hire one of the villas on site which will include access to the facilities.

If you have a smaller budget (!) then you might like to camp, www.campinglamanga.es, offers bungalows, caravan and tent pitches with shared facilities, supermarket, pool and laundry, at kilometre 11 on the strip. 968 563014/19.

Eating

There are lots (literally hundreds) of places to eat along the whole strip of the Mar Menor, on the Med side or on the Mar Menor side. Many places close in the winter though, and you may have to hunt a little.

Restaurante El Parador, In El Vivero, Los Alemanes beach, is on the front line Mar Menor. An old house nicely rebuilt with a palm tree garden, beach club and bar. A friendly and warm place in winter, it's one of the La Manga restaurants in fashion and therefore expensive. www.paradordelmarmenor.com.

Restaurante Isla Cristina, Casa Martín, in Puerto Bello, has reasonably priced food. Nice place particularly when there is good weather and the outside terrace is open.

You will also find plenty of Chinese restaurants of varying quality, pizza places, bars and a few Spanish restaurants! If you have the budget there are great restaurants at La Manga Club too.

La Unión

Population: 19,800

Map Reference: 0.88°W, 37.62°N

The history of La Unión is inextricably linked to the development of mining in the coastal Sierra de Cartagena and La Unión. The oldest settlement of the area is in the village of Portmán, a name of Catalan origin, Port Many, which derives from the Latin Portus Magnus, the name of the town during the Roman rule. See the Portmán section for more information.

Mining in the surrounding hillsides have unearthed archaeological sites that attest to the operation of the mines from time immemorial. From the port of Portmán, the Roman mines of Carthago Nova exported ingots of silver, lead, iron, zinc and other minerals throughout the empire.

The Fundación Sierra Minera (FSM) is a non-profit organisation, which brings together the people of the Sierra Minera de Cartagena, La Unión. Their website includes details of all the mines in the area, their state of activity and the Foundation's aims, which are to recover their cultural heritage and provide environmental training for the population at risk of exclusion (the so-called 'third sector').

www.fundacionsierraminera.org

You can visit the interpretation centre at the **Mina de Matilde**, which tracks more than 2000 years of the history of mining and how it has changed the landscape, heritage and environment of the Sierra Minera. www.fundacionsierraminera.es/mina-matildes/

In the village of Roche there's another innovative project from the FSM, called **Huerto Pío**. Based on a farm that belonged to one of the most important mine owners of the mining history, Pío Wandossell. One of his descendants gave the Fundación Sierra Minera this farm of 4.05 hectares for carrying out this ambitious project to restore the local heritage of the area, promoting ecotourism through creation of a public park and indigenous agro-forestry species. Throughout the year there are open days, look out on the website: www.fundacionsierraminera.es/huerto-pio/

El Parque Minero is an excellent opportunity to see the whole process of the old underground mining industry of the nineteenth century and to experience unforgettable travel in more than 4,000m2 of galleries of a mine open to the public. Adults: €11, visit during Summer: Tuesday to Saturday at 10:00 and 12:00. and also at 18:00, Sunday: 10:00 and 12:00 and Winter: Tuesday to Sunday at 10:00 and 12:00. Closed Mondays. The visit lasts two hours and includes not only the visit to the mine but a train trip through the park.

www.parqueminerodelaunion.es, 968 002140.

Walking through La Unión you can see some unique modernist buildings declared of cultural interest, such as La Casa del Piñón on Calle Major, currently the home of the Ayuntamiento, www.ayto-launion.com. On the upper floor be sure to visit the **Mining Museum**, surely the best museum in Spain dedicated to this subject. The museum is going to be moving back to its original site in the Antiguo Liceo de Obreras in a couple of years. Next door is the **Museo del Cante de las Mineras** where you can get an interactive look at the history of the town's flamenco festival.

During the first fortnight of August (since 1961) you can hear the flamenco songs of La Unión in the most important flamenco festival in the world. This takes place in the impressive Antiguo Mercado Público. During the **Fundación del Cante de las Minas**, declared of International Tourist Interest, there's a wide range of activities arranged to teach, share or delve into the world of singing, dancing and guitar. www.festivalcantedelasminas.org.

There's the Old Public Market, **Antiguo Mercado Público**, which also houses the **Catedral del Cante** for concerts (see Fundación del Cante de las Minas above), which you can't miss. It's huge, built from iron and glass in a modernist style, on Calle de la Noria. Built by Catalan architect based in Cartagena, Victor Beltrí, this market, along with the Grand Hotel in Cartagena are the most outstanding works of modernism in the Region of Murcia.

The **Ethnological Museum** located in the village of Roche in a new building, shows the customs and traditions of the local area. Avenida M. Cano Vicedo, 968 541614, call to make an appointment for a visit.

The Roman Archaeological Museum is found in the village of Portmán in the building of the Old Charity Hospital. It has the largest Roman mosaic in the region belonging to the Roman villa called Huerta del Paturro, 968 548144.

Services

Tourist Office and Ayuntamiento, Calle Mayor, 55 (in Casa del Piñón), 968 541614, Monday to Friday 9:00 to 14:00, www.ayto-launion.org

Sleeping

There's the Hotel Sierra Mar on Calle Real, www.hotelmania.net/hotel/la-union/hotel-sierra-mar/, 968 560825, which has 53 hotel rooms, plus five apartments.

Or the excellently priced Encarna Vargas, Calle Tetuán, 31, in the centre of town, www.hospedajeconencanto-encarnavargas.es, 609 620064, a very pretty, modern hotel.

Eating

El Vinagrero on Calle Bailén, 8, www.elvinagrero.com, 968 541084, has been feeding the people of La Unión for the last 100 years. The beautifully appointed, cosy restaurant is well worth a visit.

Nearby in El Algar is Hotel Campomar, http://www.hotelcampomar-cartagena.es/, which also boasts an excellent restaurant.

Lo Pagán

Population: 3,000

Map Reference: 0.79°W, 37.82°N

Lo Pagán is a seaside town at the northern most cusp of the Mar Menor, with therapeutic mud baths and a long sandy beach, with calm waters which shelve gently. This is the eastern most town on the Murcian coast, on the tip of the Mar Menor.

The appeal of this area (coupled with San Pedro del Pinatar) revolves around the salt marshes and man-made 'pans' where salt is harvested, now a protected Nature Park. Migrating birds use the marshes as a stop-over and bird-watching is popular. The mineral content of the mud makes it a sought-after remedy or conditioner, especially for the skin, and there are several therapy spas. The towns and beaches themselves combine to form the most popular Mar Menor resort, offering a wide variety of bars and restaurants, plus a good little marina.

On the seafront there is a commercial fish market in the Parque del Mar Juán Carlos I. On Explanada de Lo Pagán, near the Casa del Mar restaurant there's the daily fish auction, at around 10am weekdays and Saturdays.

On the third Sunday of the month from 10am to 2pm there's the artisan market on the Explanada. Every Thursday morning there's the weekly market on Avenida Salzillo.

Nearby is the regional park of Las Salinas, which is home to a variety of protected birds and wild life. On the salt flats you'll find flamingos and herons in particular, and if you're very lucky a flock will fly overhead while you're bathing on the long sandy beaches.

At the northern end of the town (just as it turns into the one way system, near the recently restored windmill, called **Molino de Quitín**) you can take fantastic walks across the Mar Menor. The path creates a dyke, where on the left hand side there are mud baths and on the right the Mar Menor. If you have the stamina you can walk the length of it (several miles) across to the La Manga side, where you'll find another windmill, called **Molino de Calceteras** (at Punto de Algas). You can't actually cross to La Manga though, but the views are worth the effort.

The windmill at Punto de Algas is where, if you're lucky, you'll be able to see traditional fishing techniques. You'll also be able to see flamingos on your bracing walk! It's a good spot for a photo.

There's a marina, www.clubnauticolopagan.es or 968 186969 with 424 moorings.

There's a summer outdoor cinema (cine de verano), Cine Acapulco on Calle Queipo de Llano. http://salacinedeverano.blogspot.com

The most important festival is the procession of the Virgen del Carmen, on the 16th of July.

Beaches

The most popular beach is La Curva. You can sunbathe, swim, snorkel, scuba dive, sail, go fishing or canoeing. At night it is the centre for the bars and clubs. Each year there are beach football championships, sandcastle building contests and a graffiti contest! www.lopagan.info

Services

Tourist information, Lo Pagán comes under the municipality of San Pedro del Pinatar, www.sanpedrodelpinatar.es

Sleeping

Hotel Lodomar on Calle Río Bidasoa, 1, 968 186802, www.lodomar.com/ has apartments and rooms for rental in this four star spa hotel.

Another four star hotel, the Hotel Traiña on Avenida del Generalísimo, 84, 968 335022, www.hoteltraina.com is a large modern place, with a Michelin mentioned restaurant, the Véronica. Look on their website for special offers.

More reasonably priced the Hotel El Neptuno on Avenida del Generalísimo, 19, is still quite plush and is right on the seafront. 968 181911, www.hotelneptuno.net

Or try the smaller, Hotel Paloma on Calle Río Eresma, 47, 968 183461, www.anecu.com/hotel-paloma-review/

Eating

Being a seaside town you can expect the ubiquitous fare of pizza, hamburgers and ice cream as well as traditional food such as paella and fish. There are no shortages of restaurants, though in the winter months some will be closed. As with many of the seaside towns caldero (fish and rice stew) will probably feature on the menu of the Spanish restaurants.

El Rubio 360, Explanada Reyes Católicos, serves fresh in season fish, caldero, rice and homemade desserts with incredible views, www.elrubio360restaurante.com, 968 181032.

Restaurante Venezuela on the main Paseo Marítimo has been in business since 1961, www.restaurantevenezuela.com, and has won a number of awards. 968 181515.

Restaurante La Panocha, on a back street, Calle Castilla, is a reasonably priced place for a menú del día. www.lapanocha.es 968 182201.

In the summer, try www.santamariabar.com

Night Life

This is a young town in summer, with lots of bars and drinking till the early hours. The nightlife district of Lo Pagán is called The Curve (La Curva) and is located opposite the beach of the same name. Tambalillo, Valgáme Rock Bar, and D'Lounge are bars to have a drink at before going to the clubs. The nightclubs are all together, and have a terrace on the roof, giving a great view of the Mar Menor. Clubs worth mentioning are Idolo, Tela Beach, and Santa Maria.

This area is also renowned for its live concerts in the open air.

Lorca

Population: 92,300

Map Reference: 1.69°W, 37.68°N

In 2011 a massive earthquake hit the town of Lorca destroying many buildings and damaging thousands of others. Assistance has helped those people in urgent need of re-housing but work will continue for many years to rebuild the town. Many places are open and functioning but recovery is a long process. The businesses in Lorca still need your patronage!

Lorca is a genteel city just off the main Águilas - Murcia motorway. The town's most interesting architecture is from the 16th century onwards.

The region around Lorca was already inhabited by the Iberians during the Bronze age (El Argar culture). Lorca was probably called Eliocroca by the Romans and Lurka by the Arabs. The old part of the town, made up of narrow streets and alleyways, achieved its present shape under Islamic rule.

During the Reconquista, Lorca was a dangerous border town, caught between the Spanish kingdom of Castile and the Moorish kingdom of Granada. The square tower of homage of the city fortress can be seen from many points of the town. It was named **Torre Alfonsina** after King Alfonso X of Castile.

Lorca is the largest town in Spain by area, stretching across an entire valley and with a municipal township that reaches the coast with a population that was last counted at 89,600. It has mountains to a height of 1500m to the North West and an 8km of coastline. The surrounding area is covered with vineyards, almond and olive trees. The attraction of Lorca lies in its history and archaeology, present in the character of its streets.

The town blends its historical heritage with modern life. Lorca is also an important commercial centre and to this end has a well designed network of roads, railway and communications. All connected with a coach station, a railway station and the main N-340 (A-7/E-15) motorway, making this area easily accessible and also relatively central to a wide selection of some of the most beautiful countryside in the south east of Spain including the Sierra Espuña, the Sierra Los Vélez and the Levante Almeriense.

Its **Castle** (Map: B2) is prominently visible from far off and Lorca forms another portal to the Sierra Espuña. The castle started out as an Islamic fortress between the 8th and 13th centuries and the oldest parts of the castle, the essential water systems, still remain. Today the castle is used for many town activities including fiestas and civic functions and is called the **Fortress of the Sun**. Entrance costs €6 with lots of local history exhibits to view. Opening times depend on the season but are generally Monday to Sunday 10:30 to 19:30 plenty of other activities including meals and guides for a little extra cash. 968 959646.

Palacio Guevara is a Baroque building belonging to the Guevara family built between 1689 and 1705. There is a beautiful courtyard and wonderful period interior rooms, including a great collection of paintings. The palace is open to the public and one of the main features worth seeing is the **Sala Chemist**, located in one of the outbuildings. The display is a complete chemist shop, intact as it was in 1896, complete with carved oak furniture and fittings and shelves lined with original medicines and ointments, many made by the local chemist before the days of the large laboratories. It's on Calle Lope Gisbert, call 968 477999 for opening hours and rates.

Possibly the most outstanding church in Lorca is **La Colegiata de San Patricio** (Map: D2), which was built between the 16th and 18th centuries and towers over the central part of town. The **Iglesia de San Mateo** which was built principally in the 18th and 19th century has a stunning vaulted interior. Telephone 968 46 99 66.

The town has a number of museums including the **Museo de Arqueológico Municipal** (Map: E1), which is on Plaza de Juan Moreno (968 406267), open Tuesday to Saturday (closed for siesta) and Sunday mornings. The building housing the museum is worth a look too, it's the restored **Casa de los Salazar**, also known as the Moreno, built in the 17th century following Italian models, with naked female torsos flanking the doors. Entrance is free. www.museoarqueologicodelorca.com

There is also an embroidery museum based on the top floor of the **Casa Museo De Bordados Paso Azul.** Popularly known as the Casa de las Cariátides, built in the 19th century, this is a great example of eclectic architectural style. www.museoazul.com 968 472077.

The Ayuntamiento (17th and 18th century) is actually worth a look inside since it contains enormous canvasses depicting past battles around Lorca. It also has a collection of contemporary paintings by local artists. www.lorca.es/, 968 47 97 00.

One central landmark is the **Columna Milenaria** which is a Roman milepost from 10 BC from the time of emperor Augustus on which a sculpture of San Vincente was placed in the 15th century.

The **Centro para la Artesanía de Lorca** (Center for Craft) is located in a building between the Palacio de Guevara and the Iglesia de San Mateo on Calle Lope Gisbert. There's an open space with an indoor exhibition and sale of craft products, temporary exhibition gallery and space for live demonstrations of crafts. 968 463912, www.murciaartesana.com. Open Monday to Friday from 10:00 to 14:00 and 17:00 to 20:30 Saturday: 11:00 to 13:30. Closed on Sundays.

Lorca is host to the **FERAMUR** convention every September, placing it in the centre of artisan and craftsmanship in the region. The fair lasts three days, during the main Lorca Fería and includes crafts and food from local artists, cooks and sculptors. This is an excellent place to come for an afternoon of browsing, or to by those gifts for people back home. Or of course to enjoy the handmade chocolates! www.feramur.es, 968 477313.

In October Lorca hosts the **FERICAB Pure Bred (PRE) Spanish Horse Fair**, placing it as one of the top five International PRE horse fairs in Spain. If you're into horses then this is a great opportunity to see hundreds of beautiful Spanish horses in one place. 968 468978 www.fericab.lorca.es Or come and visit me at the #DisasterFarm to meet Rocco, a dirty grey PRE.

El Grupo Espeleológico de Lorca (www.espeleomurcia.es) will help you find cavities and caves to explore, by hiking, canoeing or mountaineering. At the weekend visit the Cueva de Agua de Ugéjar in the Paraje del Talayón mountains at 881 metres.

For a list of local routes take a look here: www.lorcaturismo.es/enelmediorural/enelmediorural.asp, you can download a route map and details and make your own way. If you prefer a tour of the city then take a look at local guides: www.

lorcatallerdeltiempo.com or look at what the Tourist Office has to offer at www.lorcaturismo.es/.

The **Regional Park Del Lomo de Bas** offers rocky vegetation, mulberry trees, palms and figs, numerous species of reptiles such as the protected tortoise and toad. Gulls, white egrets, eagles and peregrine falcons fly overhead.

Lorca is a very unusual shape for a municipality, a blob with two legs, one of which reaches down to the sea, the other straddles Puerto Lumbreras and Águilas. There are almost forty towns in the municipality with Lorca being the third largest region in Murcia (Murcia and Cartagena taking the first two spots). The towns: Aguaderas, Almendricos, Avilés, Barranco Hondo (Lorca), Béjar, Campillo, Carrasquilla, Cazalla, Coy, Culebrina, Doña Inés, Escucha, Fontanares, Garrobillo, Hinojar, La Hoya, Humbría, Jarales, La Paca, La Tova, Marchena, Morata, Nogalte, Ortillo, Parrilla, Río, Sutullena, Torrecilla, Tercia, Tiata, Torrealvilla, Pulgara, Purias, Puntarrón, Ramonete, Pozo Higuera, Zarzadilla de Totana, Zarcilla de Ramos and Zarzalico.

Lorca's Easter celebrations are probably the most splendid in Murcia (depending upon whom you talk to!) When it comes to fiestas and traditions, Lorca has its fair share and some of the important dates in the celebration calendar include the 23rd November when San Clemente is honoured.

On the 8th September the Virgen de las Huertas, patron saint of Lorca is honoured in a tradition that began in 1244. The Grand Fería of Lorca takes place sometime during the month of September (the third week of September usually), lasting 10 days and includes all the usual events such as horses, paella, loud music and drinking. Lorca also boasts one of the largest fairs at their fiesta.

Services

Tourist Office, Calle Lope Guisbert, 12, open weekdays apart from siestas and in summer it opens in the afternoons during the weekends. There are good guides in English available. The website has a good 'callejero' so you can get acquainted with where everything is before you visit. 968 441914, www.lorcaturismo.es

Ayuntamiento, Plaza De España, 968 407000, www.lorca.es

Trains on the Murcia to Águilas line, on the outskirts of town towards the motorway junction.

Bus Station next to the train station, not only to Murcia but also Granada, www.buslorca.com, 968 441 107

Taxi ranks at Plaza de Calderón, Plaza Ortega Melgares, Calle Glorieta de San Vicente and Plaza Óvalo. You can call a cab on 968 471110.

Beaches

Surprisingly, Lorca also has some wonderful beaches. There's Calnegre, 1,200m long and 20m wide, the most important, which has all mod cons, including showers, lifeguard etc. Close to this beach are Playa Larga 550m in length and Los Hierros. The coves of Siscar, Junquera, Baño de las Mujeres, San Pedro and Cala Honda hide among the cliffs.

- Playa Calnegre: 200m, a protected area in the Regional Park of Lomo de Bas, isolated, average occupancy, golden sand and calm water, parking, bus, cleaning, Club Náutico de Mazarrón and Águilas 16km.
- Playa Larga: 600m, a protected area in the Regional Park of Lomo de Bas, isolated, low occupancy, golden sand and gravel and moderate waves, parking, bus, Club Náutico de Águilas 12.5km.
- Playa de Los Hierro: 400m, a protected area in the Regional Park of Lomo de Bas, isolated, golden sand and gravel, moderate waves, parking, bus, Club Náutico de Águilas to 12.5km.
- Playa de Siscar: 180m, isolated, family, average occupancy, golden sand-gravel, parking, bus, Club Náutico de Águilas and Mazarrón.
- Cala de Junquera: 40m, a protected area in the Regional Park of Lomo de Bas, isolated, low occupancy, gravel, moderate waves, parking, bus, Club Náutico de Águilas 13.5km.
- Cala del Baño de las Mujeres: 40m, isolated, average occupancy, family, golden sand-gravel, calm waters, parking, bus, toilet, Club Náutico de Águilas.
- Cala de San Pedro: 25m, in a protected area of the Regional Park of Lomo de Bas, isolated, dark sand, moderate waves, parking, bus, Club Náutico de Águilas and Mazarrón 15.5km.
- Cala Honda: 100m, in a protected area, low occupancy, isolated, bus, Restaurante La Cava, near the bus station, Club Náutico de Águilas 15km.

Sleeping

Hotel Amaltea on Carretera de Granada is a large modern hotel on the outskirts of town with large gardens, three lakes joined by small cascades and an impressive pool with a Jacuzzi. There's a restaurant and bar on site. 968 406565, www.amalteahotel.com

For a little luxury try Hacienda Real Los Olivos, Camino Altobordo, Diputación de Purias, 968 959100 www.haciendareallosolivos.com. Built in 2006 it has all services you can expect, swimming pool, restaurant and bars.

A little more economical is Jardines de Lorca on Alameda Rafael Méndez,

968 470599, www.hotelesdemurcia.com

For some rural tourism try Hotel Los Sibileys, Nogalte 84, 968439024 www.spanishcountryhotel.com, set in 60 acres of olive farm right on the border of Murcia. They offer horse riding nearby, off road biking, yoga classes, cookery courses, swimming pool, terraces and restaurant.

Two different casas rurales around the Lorca area can be found on this website: www.turismorurallanoria.com, 696 961486.

For those on a budget you could try the Albergues de Lorca, www.alberguesdelorca.com, 646 775737, these are like youth hostels and offer low cost accommodation often in dormitories, with plenty of activities available to keep you busy. The site lists three different locations in the Lorca area.

Eating

As you would expect for a large town (and district) there are all sorts of places to eat. Of course you'll find the Chinese restaurants, Burger King and McDonalds and pizza places, and fortunately a wealth of great small family run Spanish bars and restaurants, and a few top class ones too.

For something out of the ordinary try the castellated Restaurante Hiroshima, Camino Viejo del Puerto km3, www.restaurantehiroshima.com. This is one you won't be able to drive past and not notice! A popular place for weddings and communions, it's worth a visit at Christmas or Easter too (book at popular times). One of the few places that have a children's play park. 968 465451.

Restaurante La Cava, near the bus station, Alameda Constitución, 3, is situated in a 200 year old reformed house, with three floors and a terrace. Great for families and romantic meals. They have a menu de degustación for €50, where you get to try lots of different dishes. www.restaurante-lacava.es/

Also try:

- Casa Roberto, Calle Musso Valiente, 5, modern restaurant with reasonable priced fixed menu.
- Rincón de los Valientes, Rincón de los Valientes, 13, traditional, local food at a good price at the west end of town.
- Bar El Gato on Camino del Gato for a cheap and cheerful lunch.
- Jardines de Lorca, Alameda Rafael Méndez.

Los Alcázares

Population: 15,400

Map Reference: 0.85°W, 37.74°N

Central on the west side of the Mar Menor, its name comes from the Arab Al–kazar. Los Alcázares is pronounced Los Al-Katha-Res. The Romans and then later the Arabs used this town as an ideal location for thermal baths. You can still enjoy the benefits of the spas in the hotel La Encarnación.

Visit the **Aeronautical Museum** on Avenida de la Libertad, 37, 968 582107, www.murciaturistica.es/es/museo/museo-aeronautico-municipal-54/. See the history of Spanish military aircraft, with displays of models of different planes, aerial photographs, helmets, weapons, aircraft propellers, guard posts, antiaircraft guns, etc. Wednesday to Sunday from 10:00 to 14:00 Groups by appointment.

From the port you can get excursions to the **Isla Perdiguera** which is inside the Mar Menor. If you have plenty of energy then rent a bicycle and enjoy the many kilometres of flat cycle paths that are starting to join up the towns of the Mar Menor. Some ideas for routes can be found at www.bikemap.net/en/l/2514868/.

The near Mercadona has over a dozen food outlets including an excellent Thai/Vietnamese/Cantonese and a good Indian. There is also the Post Room for internet use and postal service to the UK, various beauty salons and cycle hire. Nearby on the north side of the Avenida de la Libertad is El Patio II (www.restauranteelpatio.es/el-patio-2-los-alcazares) which is a large Spanish restaurant specialising in meat dishes cooked on a huge open grill (veggies beware).

A short distance along the Avenida de la Libertad is the **Oasis Centre** which has a mixture of more eating establishments including some that cater for the all–day breakfast brigade. For those who are home–sick there is the Big Breakfast Butchers which can provide British cuts, barbecue meats and home–made sausages.

Los Alcázares was used as a location for the movie re-make of Ernest Hemingway's Garden of Eden, starring Jack Huston, Richard E. Grant and Mena Suvari and the dis-used military airbase at the southern end of the town was also used for the movie, The Green Zone featuring Matt Damon, Greg Kinnear and Jason Isaacs.

The old town of Los Alcázares is very Spanish with a maze of narrow interesting streets. Parking seems to be easy apart from July–August when the Spanish arrive on holiday.

All around town there are a series of murals. This urban art has turned some of the streets into open-air galleries. Find out more in our blog: www.nativespain.com/activities/the-murals-of-los-alcazares/

The annual July fiestas at Las Lomas del Rame features a procession, dancing, activities for children, outdoor disco and live music plus fireworks and a giant paella.

In August (usually the 13th to 22nd) they have their local fiesta, Semana de la Huerta, when groups representing market garden areas throughout Spain and other European countries gather to display their folklore, handicrafts and prepare gastronomic feasts from their local produce. You'll find loads of peñas (temporary party rooms) in the rambla in the town centre.

Fiestas are popular here; there's a week–long fiesta in mid October when on the 12th October caldero is the highlight of the fiesta named after it, El Día de Caldero. People gather on the beach to prepare it in the time honoured way, cooked over driftwood.

Services

Ayuntamiento, Avenida de la Libertad, 50, 968 575047, www.losalcazares.ces

Los Narejos

It's worth mentioning Los Narejos in this section as it joins closely to Los Alcázares and often you'll end up accidentally here when you're looking for somewhere in Los Alcázares!

Los Narejos is situated practically on the beach and has been a traditional Spanish resort for many years and as such the gastronomy features high on the list of things to do. You can try the most famous dish of the Mar Menor, the caldero. It's similar to paella, but stronger in flavour with lots of fish; the stock comes from boiled fish heads. The locals eat it with alioli (garlic mayonnaise) and needless to say it has to be washed down with plenty of red wine.

The Patron Saint of Los Narejos is La Virgen de la Purísima and fiestas in her honour are held during the first week of December.

The main shopping centre is called Las Velas, which has all you need. This includes a cinema which shows up-to-date films in English on Saturdays and Tuesdays, www.cinelasvelas.es/original-version-english/.

Services

Tourist Office, Avenida Rio Nalón, 17, 968 582119.

Beaches

Many local beaches have been awarded the highest grade possible for water quality and have EEC Blue Flag status over the years. The town was the first in the region to achieve the coveted Q Certification for quality of beaches and the town's Tourist Information facilities have also earned a Q Certificate. In 2011 none received the award, however, all beaches are of excellent quality with extensive services.

- Playa de Manzanares: 400m, urban, high occupancy, calm waters, dark

- sand, SOS, rescue, Red Cross, local police, parking, bus, toilet, showers, umbrellas / deckchairs, anchorage area, disabled access, the Yacht Club Alcázares 500km.
- Playa de Las Salinas: 1,000m, in the La Hita Protected area, semi-urban, average occupancy, dark sand, moderate waves, anchoring area, SOS, Red Cross, local police, parking, bus, toilet, showers, umbrellas / deckchairs, anchoring area, Club Náutico de Los Alcázares 3km.
- Playa Los Narejos: 1,000m, urban, high occupancy, calm waters, dark sand, SOS, rescue, Red Cross, local police, parking, bus, toilet, showers, umbrellas / deckchairs, anchoring area, disabled access, Puerto Deportivo Tomás Maestre 2km.
- Playa del Espejo: 800m, urban, high occupancy, calm waters, dark sand, SOS, rescue, Red Cross, local police, parking, bus, toilet, showers, umbrellas / deckchairs, anchoring area, disabled access, Club Náutico of Alcázares 1km.
- Playa de las Palmeras: 1100m, urban, high occupancy, calm waters, dark sand, SOS, rescue, Red Cross, local police, parking, bus, toilet, showers, cleaning, bins, parasols / sunbeds, anchoring area, disabled access, the Alcázares Yacht Club 1km.
- Playa Carrión: 200 m, urban, high occupancy, calm waters, dark sand, SOS, rescue, Red Cross, local police, parking, bus, toilet, showers, umbrellas / hammocks, anchoring area, disabled access, next to the Yacht Club Alcázares.
- Playa de la Concha: 200m, urban, high occupancy, calm waters, dark sand, SOS, rescue, Red Cross, local police, parking, bus, toilet, showers, umbrellas / hammocks, anchoring area, disabled access, next to the Yacht Club Alcázares.

Sleeping

There are some campsites locally nearby in San Javier or Los Urrutias.

Hotel 525 on Calle Río Borines, www.525.es, 968 574760, is just a few minutes from the beach. It's large, with five floors and over 100 rooms. They have a spa and a top class restaurant and free underground parking for guests. They also run a children's club!

Senator Mar Menor Golf on Calle Infanta Cristina, www.senatormarmenorspahotel.com, 968 583060, has 174 tourist apartments right on the Serena Golf 18 hole resort (www.laserenagolf.es/). There's a spa, fitness centre and heated swimming pool. Also there's a restaurant on site.

Hotel Costa Narejos, Calle Río Dobra, 2, in Los Narejos is a popular choice, www.hotelcostanarejos.

com, 968 583980. It's quite large with good size rooms and some larger family rooms, right next to the beach. There's a cafe and restaurant, a spa and swimming pools. They frequently have special offers on their website.

Hotel Cristina on Calle La Base, 2, 968 171110, www.cristinahotel.net is in the more economical bracket.

Location Report: Enjoying Los Alcázares

There is much to do around Los Alcázares and these are a few of the things that we feel you should experience during your stay.

El Patio II, is a very typical Spanish restaurant specialising in meat cooked over the embers of olive trees. It embodies everything about Spanish restaurants. You can't judge a book by its cover, from the outside it is not particularly inviting, inside is a different matter. If you really want to experience Spanish life book a table in the rear salon for Sunday lunch from 2pm onwards and join generations of Spanish families celebrating birthdays, communions or just a meal together. Carretera San Javier, 968 575959.

Cocina Asiatica Run Restaurant is a great favourite of ours and everyone else who has tried it. Go for the set RUN box menu which includes: salad, dimsum, crispy rolls and a box with a Thai red curry, crispy duck, king prawns and rice. You need a good appetite for one each or order one set Box meal and add to it a few extra dishes. Elegant surroundings, great food at a great price. Calle Rio Nalon 31, 968 582887.

The Complejo Polideportivo Municipal is the restaurant at the sports centre. Don't be put off by the sports centre bit, it is a delightful little restaurant and offers the best tapas in town bar none. Avenida Joaquín Blume, 968 171773.

The Sports 525 is still one of our favourite bars. It is of a higher quality than those around it and being Spanish run the measures are larger and the price very reasonable. It would make a perfect venue for cocktails before dinner at Rosalind's. It's in the Mercadona Plaza.

Rosalind's Roof Garden Restaurante is a terrace restaurant above Mercadona. It is certainly the most elegant restaurant in Los Alcázares and is perfect for a special occasion or a farewell dinner. It serves superior Mediterranean cuisine, although slightly higher priced than other nearby venues it is still only about the cost of a good pub restaurant in the UK. Avenida Rio Nalon, 968 574111.

The El Chato, just past the rambla where the market is held, is a delightful and atmospheric wine bar and restaurant. It is much larger than it appears from the outside and offers an excellent menu including tapas. Well worth a try for a pleasant relaxed evening of above average Spanish cuisine. Avenida De La Libertad, 968 170161.

The Hindustani Roti was the first Indian Restaurant to open in Los Alcázares and in my opinion still the best. It suffers a bit as it is situated halfway down the Plaza just round a corner on the left. This would still be my first choice for an Indian meal. Calle Rio Aranguin 29, 968 583156.

Be sure to visit Cartagena and Cabo de Palos, especially for lunch at the harbour side restaurants, and the trip through Calblanque Regional Park using the track just outside the La Manga Club. Bathe in the Mar Menor and try the new Municipal Punta Calera Spa in Los Narejos (Calle Pintor Francisco Bayo, 968 583616). Turn left at the Euromarina building and at the first roundabout take the first exit, straight over the second and continue on until you see the tennis courts and Olympic sized outdoor pool on your left. Every type of water feature is available, a steam room and flotation tanks, absolutely superb at €10 for around an hour.

David Buse

Eating

There are lots of places to eat including plenty of pizza restaurants and British run bars. We've included a wealth of information on bars and restaurants for this town, as we had plenty of contributors who live near here. If you want to contribute your favourite bars and restaurants for future editions then get in touch at www.NativeSpain.com

Roblemar at El Oasis is possibly the most exclusive restaurant in Los Alcázares. Great Tapas, seafood and meat dishes.

Restaurante Tropical is in the centre of town, just off the Real de Feria parade of shops behind the Town Hall. The Tropical does great tapas and has both indoor and outdoor seating. It's also only 50 yards from the promenade, so you can walk off your meal afterwards with a gentle stroll!

El Chato, Avenida de la Libertad,72 does great tapas in a traditional

Spanish style. Very popular with the locals so you may need to book (even in the quiet season at weekends).

The Hotel Balneario, an old spa hotels right on the promenade, next to the marina, is the oldest hotel in Los Alcázares. Decorated in a quirky colonial style with wicker chairs, ceiling fans and brass bar fittings, dining here is like stepping back in time to 1930's Cuba. The food and service here is of a high quality, but quite pricey.

Italian, Angela's Pizzeria, just at the bottom of the Balneario Plaza opposite the Hotel Costa Narejos, for great value pizza & pasta.

There are 3 or 4 excellent Chinese Restaurants in Los Alcázares which provide reasonable prices. These include El Chino in Edificio Europa and Cocina Asiatica in the Balneario Plaza, and the Hong Kong, just past the El Arbol supermarket.

For English fare, The Pasty Shack and the Penny Farthing are next door to each other in the Balneario Plaza, the former being great for sandwiches, savoury pastries and cakes and the latter having a good selection of British favourites, including chicken & mushroom pie, fish & chips and a variety of roast Sunday lunches as well as a great range of sticky sweets and puddings.

Location Report: Eating In Los Alcázares

Los Alcázares is often described as being split into a new and old town. Los Alcázares, New Town Dining: Most visitors in Los Alcázares start by visiting the 'new town' which has been the focal point for new property development over recent years. Here there are now many apartments and villas favoured by foreign tourists and the majority of these visitors head towards the Balneario plaza by Mercadona supermarket when they are looking for refreshment. In this square, and the avenue leading off towards the beach, you will find a very good choice of bars and restaurants. You can eat Italian, Spanish, Asian, Indian, Chinese, Mediterranean, American and English meals. If you are just out for a drink then there is selection of popular bars with Irish, Scottish, Spanish, Italian and sports themes.

When we have family and friends staying we have a few favourite restaurants that we all like to visit: El Patio, a large Spanish restaurant opposite Mercadona that is known for its signature dish, Carne a la Piedra (meat on the stone). An extremely hot stone is placed on your table together with a plate full of strips of raw meat and a dish of sea salt. You spread the salt on the stone and then cook the individual pieces of meat to taste, even more enjoyable when eaten with their garlic potatoes. In summer months you can sit out in their lovely garden area, although it gets very busy and I would recommend booking a table. Carretera San Javier, 968 575959.

Cocina Asiatica Run Restaurant, despite our guests initial concern at the name of this restaurant it is probably the one we visit most often in this area of Los Alcázares. It offers superb Asian food in an elegant setting and the staff are really friendly. The set menu is extremely good value and is highly recommended if you are feeling hungry. Calle Rio Nalon 31, 968 582887.

La Diva, this is a great little restaurant to try if your party likes different types of food. It offers an international menu so there is always something on the menu to suit every taste. They have created a really intimate cosy feel and when the nights are cooler it is a good place to head for if you are looking for warmth and cheer. Avenida Rio Nalon, 29, 968 171029.

Los Alcázares, Old Town Dining: The 'old town' in Los Alcázares is a maze of little streets with a central shopping area that is full of Spanish tourists during the months of July and August. I think some of the best Los Alcázares restaurants are located in this area and it is the place to head for if you really want to immerse yourself in everything Spanish. These are our favourite restaurants:

La Encarnación, for a meal with a truly authentic oldy worldy Spanish feel, you must try this restaurant on the seafront in Los Alcázares old town. On warm evenings you can sit outside overlooking the sea. However to fully appreciate the wonderful old Spanish décor you have to eat inside, it is truly like stepping back in time. The food is beautifully presented and the service top class, the perfect place to go for a special celebration. If you go through the restaurant you will find a lovely internal courtyard that is a hidden gem. It is full of hanging ferns and flowers and it is the ideal place to have a coffee and relax. You can get married here too. Calle Condesa, 2, 968 575048.

Ramóns, this is the place we return to time and time again for an evening meal. Not only do they serve some of the best tapas in town but they have the most wonderfully attentive bar staff. They speak very little English but if you don't speak Spanish they will provide a tapas menu in English or of course you can point at the dishes behind the counter and those of other diners. We especially love their bacalao (cod with caramelised onions), pulpo (octopus with oil and pepper) and solomillo troceado (steak chopped into small pieces served with fries and peppers). In fact a Friday night with a few beers and a plate of pulpo is our idea of a perfect night out. There is a sit down restaurant if you do not fancy tapas and it has an extensive menu. Ramón's is well known for its scrumptious deserts, so always leave space for one! www.restauranteramon.com, Avenida Libertad 50, 968 574173.

San Antonio Restaurant, is an unusual restaurant as it is actually situated on stilts over the Mar Menor in an old Balneario (bathing hut). You walk through the entrance out onto a wooden deck which has lovely views across the water and back across to the promenade of Los Alcázares. In the day-time it is a great place to enjoy the sun and at night-time the twinkling lights across the water are magical. It offers a good choice of tapas, fish and paellas.

Cervecería La Ponderosa, is a small bar and old brewery that is located just 50m from the sea front in Los Alcázares. We like to go for a drink after a meal however you can also eat here. Inside you find the bar made up of wooden barrels and continuing the brewery theme are large beer stills acting as a screen. It's small and cosy inside with an outside terrace for the warmer days and nights. Calle Fuensanta 18, 968 575172.

Martine Cherry - www.rhumhor.com

Mar Menor

This is a closed sea which maintains a warm sea temperature in whatever stage of the year (except December and January when only the most hardy Brits will brave the waters!), with an average of 18 degrees centigrade. The Romans and the Arabs built thermal baths around the coast and to this day people visit the area for the therapeutic properties of the bathing.

It has 170km2 of area (42,000 acres) and 73km of coast. The Mar Menor is the largest salt lagoon in Europe. Its waters are rich in iodine and never get deeper than 7 metres. It belongs to four municipalities: Los Alcázares, San Pedro del Pinatar, San Javier and Cartagena.

Special Report:
Serious problems in the Mar Menor

Its extensive terrestrial and marine biodiversity and clear salt water mean that, until recently, it has been a small corner of paradise right here in Europe. However, scientists have issued repeated warnings that the area is in serious decline. Reasons include over-exploitation of farmland and ground water, and the dereliction of duty on the part of the authorities who failed to do anything about the steady decline of the area until 2017.

"More than 1,000 desalination plants were in operation, and their discharge meant nitrates in the Mar Menor, a practice tolerated by the authorities until 2017," says the report by WWF and ANSE.

Efforts to restore the Mar Menor have been patchy, and not much progress has been made.

In 2019, thousands of dead fish were washed up on the banks of the Mar Menor owing to a lack of oxygen, showing that the lagoon is once again in the worst possible condition. Experts blame intensive farming for contaminating the soil and the groundwater with nitrates from fertilizers. This causes eutrophication, when an excessive amount of nutrients are in the water, provoking the growth of phytoplankton which reduces the amount of oxygen.

There have been many demonstrations and protests. Join the Facebook group Salvemos el Mar Menor (in Spanish) to find out more: www.facebook.com/groups/1811344692427805

There are considerable salt works in the area which coincide with important ecological reserves for birds, plants and other wildlife.

Langoustines are one of the delicacies pulled out of the Mar Menor along with the caviar.

To get a good view of the Mar Menor, take a walk up the hill Cabezo de la Fuente from Los Belones village (near La Manga golf complex).

Beaches

Some notable beaches (also see Los Alcázares, San Pedro del Pinatar, Lo Pagán, Santiago de la Ribera) include:

- Los Urrutias is a relatively new resort with almost a mile of golden beach with good facilities, enhanced by an unusual offshore marina in a hexagonal shape. Behind the beach is a modern, spaciously laid out town with an attractive promenade and public spaces. The coast either side is protected land, preserving the quality of the environment.

- Los Nietos is divided into an old town just off the coast and a newer resort area with a very good beach. Los Nietos is another Mar Menor town with a popular marina. A great place to eat in Los Nietos is Pescador Ros only open in summer months, a bit scruffy looking, but good food and not too expensive. Big enough to have a life all year round, it is popular with buyers seeking a place to live, as well as holidaymakers. Linked to the city of Cartagena by rail, it is especially suitable for those who prefer to travel by public transport.
- Mar de Cristal is separated from Los Nietos by a small river. It's a compact and friendly little resort with three good beach areas and a new, pretty promenade with bars and restaurants. A good sized marina adds to the charm.
- Playa Honda & Playa Paraiso are at the very southern end of the Mar Menor, these two beach areas have seen quite a bit of expansion in the last few years and have evolved into fully–fledged resorts. They are nestled in the hills of the Calblanque Nature Park behind, the protected Marchamalo salt flats to the side and the whole length of the Mar Menor in front. This is also a good spot to enjoy the mud!

Mazarrón

Population: 31,000

Map Reference: 1.31°W, 37.60°N

Mazarrón is the municipality that includes the towns of Mazarrón, Puerto de Mazarrón, Cañadas del Romero, Gañuelas, La Majada, El Saladillo, El Mingrano, La Atalaya, Leiva, Pastrana, Cañada de Gallego, Las Moreras, Bolnuevo, Balsicas and El Alamillo.

The main town of Mazarrón is a functional market town that has sprung up out of the old mining industry in the area. The region used to mine the mountain ranges which were rich in lead, zinc, silver, iron and alum. The remnants of the mining industry can be seen throughout the region.

This mining landscape boasts an incredible array of colour to satisfy any photographer. It's easy to get to but you must remember this – you visit at your own risk. There are hidden mine shafts underground and they have not been mapped, but there are plenty of well worn paths which hopefully mitigate the danger. Remember to wear sensible shoes and take water, sunscreen and insect repellent - and be careful! For more information and tempting photos, see https://nativespain.com/activities/multicoloured-mines-of-mazarron/

This is the central shopping area for a number of satellite housing estates, such as Camposol. There are many useful DIY (bricolage) shops just out of town towards Puerto de Mazarrón and the outskirts.

A new museum has just opened in Mazarrón housing a collection of old motorbikes alongside a history of the region's mining industry. https://museoparedes.es/

When people say they're going to Mazarrón they usually mean Puerto de Mazarrón 10 kilometres away, which is a much more interesting tourist destination (see the later section). Here's some information about the other towns in the municipality. **For Bolnuevo and Puerto de Mazarrón see their own sections.**

Cañada del Romero

Twenty kilometres away from Mazarrón, this town is named after the herb that grows abundantly here (and all around the region), Rosemary. Originally this was a farming town, where the miners employed nearer to the coast would live to avoid attacks from the Berbers. There's a shrine (ermita) dedicated to San Juan on a hill, and they celebrate him on the 24th June, with the usual processions, eating and drinking.

Cañada has around 200 inhabitants, many of them immigrants.

Gañuelas

Gañuelas can be found in the Sierra de la Almenara, with white washed cave houses on one side and traditional Spanish houses on the other. Along with the Sierra de las Moreras this area has been declared of national importance (L.I.C, Lugar de Interés Comunitario) due to the presence of tortoises, Golden Eagles, owls, Peregrine Falcons and Trumpeter Finches.

The local festival is held in honour of San Bartolomé on 24th August. It's usually a busy weekend with several events, including dances, contests, paella and chocolate tasting. There's a procession around the town and the festivities end with a firework display.

La Majada

Around 9km from Mazarrón lies the small town of La Majada, the Flock, a place where shepherds would rest their flock before continuing on their Vía Pecuaría (livestock routes).

There's a semi-ruined flour mill, an ermita and plenty of wildlife to be seen. Just to the south is the Sierra de las Moreras, Mulberry Sierra, and you'll see plenty of bee-eaters and jackdaws making their nests in the clay banks of rivers.

On the 8th September there's the fiesta for Santa Maria (Saint Mary's Day), with verbenas (open-air celebrations), musical performances, election of the festival Queens, sporting, cultural activities and chocolatada (chocolate celebrations).

Going Native: Jennifer & Graham Devote Themselves to FAST (First Responders on Camposol)

We are Jennifer and Graham Salt and are a retired couple in our 70s. We arrived in Spain in December 2014 from France where we lived previously. We chose the Costa Calida and Murcia area with its beautiful coastline as it's not too commercialised.

We could not have had a more different lifestyle from France where we came from a small country village to live on a large urbanisation called Camposol near Mazarrón. We love living here and came here to Camposol because we had heard of the organisation FAST (First Aid Support Team). FAST provide First Responders who attend to a call before the arrival of an ambulance. Well, what a surprise, husband Graham joined and trained to be a First Responder and also took another course and passed out as a Trainer. Myself, I took on the post of Secretary, and have been in that position since 2015. We are both devoted to FAST and it gives us both a lot of satisfaction to think we are helping the residents of this urbanisation.

We love to drive into El Puerto de Mazarrón where there are a wide choice of restaurants and, nothing we like better, is to sit and enjoy a menu del dia and look out at the beautiful coastline that surrounds the Port. One of our favourite restaurants is Viggos in the Port, a very bustling restaurant but a lovely choice of menu. It's great to be able to enjoy a menu del dia for approx. 10 euros including starter, main course and dessert etc.

We also enjoy visiting the beautiful city of Cartagena with its magnificent architecture, Roman amphitheatre, and bustling streets. We enjoy waking up to blue skies and sunshine most days so what is not to like?

I am learning Spanish so the only downside to living in Camposol is that there are hardly any Spanish people living here to talk to and practice with.

So maybe if we had our time again we would probably have chosen to buy a property in the Port where there are a lot of Spanish.

Do we have any regrets about moving here from France, no not at all. We take each day as it comes and make the most of it and enjoy the beautiful climate.

Graham and Jennifer Salt

FAST - EMERGENCY FIRST RESPONDERS: www.fast2016.org: 968 970 626: FAST is a fast response medical emergencies team operated by trained volunteers on Camposol.

El Saladillo

You'll spot El Saladillo if you head to Camposol. Golf courses and urbanizations have now shaped this landscape. It's a very flat area, dry and with little agricultural production these days. It's a great place for hiking through the dried riverbeds and on to the mountains close by. The Camino de los Pasos runs through here.

There's an ermita dedicated to San Antonio, and on 19th March there's the fiesta for San José.

You can't mention Saladillo without mentioning Camposol, the large urbanisation that now dominates this area. The best place to get accurate information about the area is from the Camposol Resident's Association, www.camposolresidents.es. Their website has photos and a forum for getting in touch with other residents. Over 3000 Brits have homes there, with a further 2000 having holiday homes. There are also plenty of other nationalities around, but Brits far outweigh the rest. Sector D is the newest part and is really quite a hike from the two shopping and commercial areas.

El Mingrano

Originally a farming and livestock town, goats and sheep have passed through here on the transhumance way for thousands of years. From the 1st century AD there has been documented archaeological evidence of ceramic production in the area.

There's a small chapel dedicated to the virgin and next to it a mill, now declared of national interest.

La Atalaya

Originally a mining town (lead, silver, iron), agricultural production played an important role in the later years. You'll see ruined flour mills around. La Atalaya means 'the watchtower'.

They celebrate the Fiesta del Corpus with verbenas (open-air celebrations) and food tastings.

Leiva

A great place for countryside walks, Leiva has fewer than 300 inhabitants. Take a look at the Molino de Leiva, a flour mill in disrepair.

Leiva is near a forest road crossing the Coto de Fortuna, one of the most prominent places in this area, which was exploited by the Romans for mining. Coto de Fortuna is where you'll see well-irrigated citrus and almond trees. Follow the route on foot or by bicycle, starting at the 9km point on the road from Morata, between the villages of Leiva and La Atalaya. Climb the Sierra de Herrera and leave behind one of the most representative old mines, San Juan. From the top you can see the surrounding villages and the neighbouring districts of Lorca.

Pastrana

Another mining town, now changed to production of melons, lettuces and peppers. The landscape is marked by the tomato growing greenhouses, which in recent years has improved the wealth for the inhabitants of the village and changed the social landscape with the massive influx of immigrants, mostly North Africans, working in these greenhouses.

There's a castle, Castillo de Pastrana, where they've found remains of Moorish farmhouse walls of numerous residential structures and bones which indicate the presence of a medieval cemetery. There are traces of the route of a mining railway, carrying the ore from the mine to the coast at La Positiva.

The closest natural areas are the Sierra de la Almenara and Sierra de las Moreras, declared LIC, Site of Community Importance and SPA, Special Protection Area for Birds. You'll find a tortoise reserve, Golden Eagles, eagle owls and Peregrine Falcons.

On the 25th July they celebrate Santiago de Apóstol (Apostle of Saint James) with verbenas (open-air celebrations) and sporting and cultural activities.

Cañada de Gallego

Cañada de Gallego is 11km away from Mazarrón and is one of the most populated districts with a population of around 1,500. Situated between the coast and the Sierra de las Moreras the first known human settlements were from the Middle and Upper Palaeolithic eras. From the Neolithic period (between 6000 and 3000 BC) is the site of the Cueva de los Percheles.

Archaeological evidence of the settlement in this area are located on the beach Percheles. There is the site of a Roman villa, of which there are no visible structures, which would have been devoted to farming, fishing and the production of purple dye. This dye extracted from shellfish, was very popular in Roman times.

Recently the area has experienced tremendous economic and social growth, mainly due to the tomato growing activities, which are evidenced by the huge population of plastic greenhouses!

Part of the 35km of coast belonging to the Mazarrón region the beach, Playa Percheles, is well worth a visit.

On the 13th June they celebrate San Antonio (Saint Anthony's Day).

Las Moreras

Las Moreras includes the most urbanised tourist beaches: Bahía, Playa Grande, Bolnuevo and Playasol. The village of Las Moreras is located just two miles from the town of Mazarrón, on the road that connects it with the Port of Mazarrón and Bolnuevo.

In its surroundings is the archaeological site of Cabezo del Plomo ('the lead head', sounds like a band!), which is a major Neolithic settlement. It is a fortified village situated on a hill in the foothills of the Sierra de Las Moreras. There are walls and circular huts and the remains of a burial ground. The site is declared of Cultural Interest.

During the Middle Ages there were turbulent times in these border areas, people moved inland and based their economy on agriculture and mining. In the eighteenth century fishing was popular, and mitigated the effects of piracy. The mining fever had its heyday in the 40s.

In the mid-twentieth century Mazarrón economy was transformed by the new techniques of irrigation and cultivation using greenhouses, that's what you'll see all along the coast.

Balsicas

Balsicas is located 7 miles southeast of the town of Mazarrón and dates back to Roman times its territory being used as farmland. Mainly an agricultural town, the increase in beach tourism and the creation of new developments in the area near El Alamillo, has in recent years produced strong population growth. Recent industry involves the production of animal feed and growing of fruit and vegetables.

One of the most curious festivities throughout the Region of Murcia happens on the 28th December, the braying contest, rebuznos, a celebration that began more than 220 years ago. It's for Santos Inocentes (April's Fools day) when there are also typical dances and songs called pujadas, food tasting and mass for the Patron Saint.

El Alamillo

The Roman settlement of El Alamillo covers a wide expanse of land between the foothills of the Sierra del Algarrobo and the beach of the same name. The road linking the towns of Puerto de Mazarrón and Cartagena passes this important complex, which includes several remnants: an establishment from the Republican period, a pool of water, the remains of an aqueduct and a Roman-imperial villa.

At present most of the structures excavated in the late eighties in this site are protected and covered to prevent damage. The Villa del Alamillo is one of the most important Roman complexes excavated in the Region of Murcia.

Location Report: 5 Top Night Spots In Puerto De Mazarron

Hartley Hartley performs as the inimitable Magenta Slipperz. We asked him (and her) to give us 5 top night spot tips in the Puerto de Mazarron area.

Bar Salud. Urbanisation Camposol. Sector B: Cool lighting, chilled ambience and great hosts. This boutique bar has excellent entertainment throughout the year with discos, quizzes, live singers and the ever popular rock 'n' roll bingo. A fantastic beer, wine, spirits and cocktail selection with all the usual soft drinks too. https://www.facebook.com/BarSaludCamposol/

Cat's & Tel's Bars. Urbanisation Camposol. Sector A: Hey, two bars I know, but in the summer they merge their hospitality and bring us an amazing array of entertainment outside on their joint terrace. Every Saturday and every Wednesday through those warm Costa Calida evenings you'll find a wonderful line-up of quality entertainment including solo singers and bands. You can reserve a seat for a small donation to charity. You won't be disappointed. Check out dates and the lineup here: www.facebook.com/catsbarcamposol

La Perra Chica. Puerto de Mazarron: Located on the most beautiful beach, right on the Paseo, you'll find this little Spanish gem. Wonderful views, top class food, drinks and service. The menu is varied, from tapas to a la carte. You decide, no rush, no pressure. Just great times. www.facebook.com/LaPerraChicaPtoMazarron/

Oasis de las Palmeras: Next to the iconic sand erosions at Bolnuevo, less than 10 metres from this famous golden sand beach, with views right along this beautiful coastline. This restaurant and bar is cool, chilled and has that 'Ibiza Vibe'. Lots of seating, some quirky, pallet-like made chairs and tables, cosy, relaxed but always comfortable. Every other Wednesday during the summer they host flamenco nights. Every Friday all year round you'll find a live act with a large dance floor. Booking or early arrival is recommended for these popular nights. www.facebook.com/oasisdelaspalmeras/

Sully's Sports Bar. El Alamillo Plaza. Puerto de Mazarron: The famous Sully's Sports Bar, right on the front at El Alamillo. Excellent outside terrace, all major sporting events on numerous televisions throughout including on the terrace. Pool table, great drinks and bar meals. Music nights at the weekends with quality acts from all along the Costas. www.facebook.com/pages/Sullys-Sports-Bar-Grill/195779614555168

As ever, always check with the venue, particularly if making a long journey, to ensure events are as planned. Enjoy this wonderful area of the Murcia region, The Costa Calida. Hartley

Services

The Tourist Office is in Puerto Mazarrón, Plaza Toneleros, 968 594426, www.visitamazarron.com.

The ayuntamiento on Plaza Ayuntamiento (strangely!) in Mazarrón itself, 968 590012, www.mazarron.es

Taxis at 968 590676 for Mazarrón, 968 595122 for Puerto Mazarrón

Bus Station, Avenida Doctor Meca, there are 3 buses per day to nearby Cartagena, 968 153480.

Sleeping

On Camposol you can stay at Sensol Golf Villas, www.sensolgolfvillarentals.com, 968 970614.

In Las Moreras there's plenty to choose from including the Hotel Atrium on Avenida Antonio Segado Del Olmo, 20, www.atriumhotel.es, 968 158383. This is a small boutique hotel, with a solarium and Jacuzzi, and the restaurant Manduca. Or the Hotel Playa Sol, Calle Velero, www.hotelplayasol.es, 968 156503, again quite small, with their own restaurant, the Amapola.

In El Alamillo you can rent an apartment from Montemar Vacacciones. www.bellavistaproperties.es.

For more rural tourism try one of the houses from www.ventaseca.com, they have six casas rurales to sleep between 4 and 6 people, in the Cañada del Romero area.

In Mazarrón itself there's the Hotel Guillermo II, Calle Carmen, 7 www.hotelguillermo2.es, 968 590436, a little shabbier than the seaside hotels, but reasonably priced and the restaurant is ok too.

For accommodation in Puerto Mazarrón and Bolnuevo see their own sections.

Eating

Many of the hotels mentioned above have their own restaurants which are worth trying. In Mazarrón there are plenty of Spanish bars, pizza places and a few Chinese restaurants.

For restaurants in Puerto Mazarrón and Bolnuevo see their own sections.

Molina De Segura

Population: 70,400

Map Reference: 1.21°W, 38.05°N

Molina de Segura is marked by its privileged position at a crossroads on the banks of the Segura River, very near the regional capital. Traces of the Palaeolithic and Bronze culture as well as the Iberian, Carthaginian and Roman cultures establish that the territory was a place of pilgrimage for ancient civilizations. With the arrival of the Arabs, Molina de Segura became strong, taking the name of Mulinat as-Sikka and experiencing a period of glory during the reign of King Lobo.

In modern times Molina de Segura suffered serious crisis and was struck by the plague. Development and modernisation helped Molina de Segura flourish with an agricultural economy, thanks to booming canneries.

Despite its long history there are no ancient monuments left standing from before the 18th century. The oldest area of interest is the Arabic walls on the castle hill which date from the 11th to 13th centuries.

The ancient fortress and walls of **Molina de Segura on Castle Hill (Barrio del Castillo)** are freely accessible. The origins of the fort date back at least to the Islamic period. These walls and towers were built around the twelfth century as an important strategic location to monitor and control this significant crossroads between the east coast and southern Spain. The wall of Molina de Segura is declared of Cultural Interest.

Dating from 1835 to 1850, **La Ermita San Roque** is worth a visit. Also, **La Iglesia Parroquial de Nuestra Señora de la Asunción** is located in the centre of town. Although its history goes back centuries it was inaugurated on November 30th 1765 and declared a historic artistic monument of national character on March 2nd 1983.

Both buildings have religious statues and engravings by Berrnabé Gil Riquelme (1910 - 1976), demonstrating a deep knowledge of anatomy and ability to express the deepest emotions of the human soul.

In the early hours of Christmas Eve, 1858 the largest meteorite ever found in Spain fell in Molina de Segura. The meteorite, which weighed 112.5 pounds, was described as, "a rectangular stone, black in colour and of an extraordinary weight compared to its volume, it was ten stone and fifteen pounds," according to the report commissioned by Rafael Martinez Fortún whose farm the meteorite landed in. Small pieces of the meteorite have found their way to museums around the world for study.

For nature lovers, in the north are the more mountainous areas of the municipality with the riverbed and banks of the River Segura irrigating crops in the centre, with the dry and flat landscape crossed by numerous ravines and gullies giving it a desert-like appearance.

The town has two large protected areas whose boundaries are, in part, within the municipal territory of Molina de Segura. They are the **Parque Regional de la Sierra de la Pila** (north of town) and the **Paisaje Protegido Humedal de Ajauque y Rambla Salada** (Wetland Protected Landscape in the west of town). Other interesting natural areas located in the municipality are the Cañada de las Salinas, a rambla and a large wetland with abundant vegetation, the Vereda de la Rambla del Carrizalejo, in the hamlet of Comala and the Rambla de las Canteras, which is in El Chorrito.

In the first half of September Molina de Segura adorns streets and balconies to receive the arrival of their patron saint, La Virgen de la Consolación. Following a tradition that goes back to the eighteenth century on the Saturday before the first Monday in September (did you get that?) they move their patron from the chapel to the Church of the Assumption. This pilgrimage is the starting point of the festivity of Molina de Segura, which extends into the third Monday of the month, when the Virgin is returned to the hermitage.

Molina de Segura has a number of towns in the municipality: Campotéjar Alta, Campotéjar Baja, Comala, El Llano de Molina, EL Rellano, EL Romeral, Fenazar, La Albarda, La Espada, La Hornera, La Hurona, Ribera de Molina, Torrealta and Los Valientes.

In El Llano de Molina is the old Noria del Llano, a water wheel, a short walk from the former home of Don Carlos Soriano, now the **Molina Ethnographic Museum**. It is a power wheel, similar to many others in the region, made of iron and wood. The water is collected through some containers or buckets installed in the wheel itself that drives water flow. When the wheel reaches its highest point the buckets pour water in the canals from which water is distributed to the channels of the orchards. The entire system from the wheel to the water distribution pipes is in excellent condition.

The Carlos Soriano Ethnographic Museum is located in the house of the molinense lawyer, Carlos Soriano. The Ethnographic Museum began in 1999 and houses archaeological collections found in the town of Molina de Segura, huertanos exhibitions of traditional costumes, household items and original furniture from the house of Carlos Soriano and old machinery. Plaza De La Ermita in El Llano de Molina, 968 388519.

If you want an adrenaline burst try your hand at paintballing with www.paintballlimitemurcia.com, 968 672240. If you really love your paintballing you can even stay in one of the casas rurales!

For horse riding fans then the Complejo Aros riding school, www.clubaros.es/en/, 968 292942, is not to be missed. They have regular high-level events of show jumping and dressage, plus offer riding lessons and hacks. They are near the Altorreal urbanisation on Carretera Cruce Altorreal-La Alcayna.

Services

Tourist office, 968 388500.

Ayuntamiento, www.molinadesegura.es

Sleeping

For excellent value (and for larger groups) the Albergue Municipal El Rellano in Pedanía de El Rellano on Parque Ecológico Vicente Blanes, www.albergueelrellano.es, is a youth hostel with a swimming pool that can provide full board or just beds.

Again in the El Rellano area there's the casa rural La Cañá, Calle Los Alonsos, www.casasrurales.net/casas-rurales/casa-la-cana--c3799, great value.

In Altorreal is the 18 hole golf urbanisation (www.golfaltorreal.es), with apartments via 609 646993.

If you want a casa rural with its own paintball area take a look at the three houses available here, www.miscasasrurales.com/casas-rurales/la-casa-colora/7744. Each house can take between 8 and 14 people.

In Los Valientes there's Casa Los Arcos, 636 827531, www.casadelosarcos.es which sleeps 8 people.

In the centre of town try Hotel Villasegura, Calle Avenida de Madrid, 129, 968 610019, www.hotelvillasegura.es, a modern hotel with 43 rooms and not much else worth mentioning!

Eating

You'll find the usual selection of restaurants in a town this size, Spanish bars, pizza places, Chinese restaurants and a few fast food chains.

You could try the Casa Herminio on Carretera Fortuna-Molina km7.9, www.casaherminio.com, 968 619816. They have a 12 metre long barbecue area where they cook meat and paella dishes. They cater for large groups and couples or families. If you want paella call ahead and book.

Another great restaurant in the centre of town is Tasca La Parranda on Paseo de lo Rosales, 18, 616 117728. They have an outdoor terrace and indoor salon, serve locally grown homemade food and make their own bread.

To while away an hour try Bar Stop, 968 610013, right in the centre of town, Calle Mayor, 189, this is a traditional small bar where you're invited to chill, try the tapas and enjoy a beer or two.

Moratalla

Population: 8,100

Map Reference: 1.89°W, 38.19°N

As you approach Moratalla from the east you will be greeted with a magnificent skyline with the castle, church and sprawling mosaic of rooftops spilling down the mountainside. Being an ancient town of Arab origin the old quarter is a warren of narrow streets and whitewashed houses with balconies that almost touch, overflowing with flowers. The farola (Map: C4), the three pronged street lamp in the centre of town is a great meeting place.

The town is capped by a castle with excellent views to the surrounding countryside and forest. It makes a great base for walking, climbing and cycling. In the centre of town on Calle Constitución there's a 16th - 18th century convent, **Convento de San Francisco**, with an exhibit room. There is also a theatre and sports centre.

It is the most mountainous zone in the Murcia region with 20 peaks that exceed 1400metres, with the highest of 2027m to the tip of the **Revolcadores**. There is snow on the mountains (and sometimes in the town itself) in the wintertime and the weather is warm but a welcome few degrees cooler than the coast in summer. The Alharabe and Benamor rivers pass through the area, making it a very popular spot for fishing.

The Trieta de Moratalla (Map: C5) theatre shows most of the cultural acts for the town. It was built at the beginning of the 20th century and restored some 80 years later, like many of the theatres in Spain. The **Trieta Theatre** is one of the more representative examples of civil architecture in Moratalla. The Parque Inglés (where the theatre can be found) was constructed in 1917 and replaced the bullring, 968 730258.

The theatre has also doubled as the local cinema from the 1920s and now shows modern releases.

Well you can't really miss the **castle** (Map: B2) when you're heading in to town, it's that great big thing that dominates the view! Though once you're in the labyrinthine streets you can sometimes lose it!

The castle was started in the 9th century as a defense system of al-Andalus, the Moors. The Order of Santiago reconstructed it with emphasis on the 9-sided Tower of the Tribute in gothic style at 22 meters high. On the door there's the grate in which was hung the body of the Commander Alfonso de Vozmedíano in 1465. Five towers completed the enclosure: La Magdalena, La Redonda, La Blanca, Los Limones or Quebrada and the Cuatro Vientos.

Sadly the castle is very rarely open to the public but it is beautifully restored and lit up at night! Watch out in town and on the ayuntamiento website for special opening hours.

The **Church of Santa Maria of Asuncion** (Map: C2) has had a small building on this site from as early as 1468. Later it was extended and a gothic window and three arches were built. The tower was built between 1930 and 1932, after the old one went to ruin at the end of the 19th century. After the Civil War restoration works began.

The Church is a great meeting place. It has a large square outside with seating, a fountain and panoramic views of the town and the mountains. It's great to while away a few hours looking down on the rooftops of Moratalla, watching the town at work, or simply reading a book. This square is also the launch site for fireworks during fiestas.

Underneath the patio there is a modern restaurant, which is in my opinion, a little overpriced and the service can be poor. However, for the views it can't be beaten!

Ermita de Santa Ana (Map:C3), built in 1607 was ruined during the Civil War and all the inner decoration destroyed. It was repaired when the war was over but damp took its toll deteriorating the temple and forcing the Ermita to be closed in 1988. In October of 1994 restoration began with these new works trying to adapt the temple to the directives of the Vatican. During restoration the workers found a spring in the subsoil which is the origin of the damp!

The **Convento De San Francisco** (Map: C4) and **Ermita of San Sebastián** were constructed in the 15th century. In the 16th century the Council of the Franciscans took over. In 1833 there was a great fire. The exterior is in baroque style with colonial influence with its geometric designs and red, black and grey colouring of the images of San Sebastián and San Francisco.

The Roman Bridges, **Puente De Jesucristo and Puente De Hellín**, are still in use. The first was constructed on the Boulevard of Aludio in 1562 and called the Bridge of White Juan, but soon changed to Bridge of Jesus Christ. It is made of stone and, unfortunately, the parapets have been repaired numerous times without considering the original design.

The second bridge of Roman origin was constructed in 1548 on the Alhárabe River in the neighbouring locality of Hellín to facilitate commercial relationships between the two towns. At the moment the bridge is in good condition and continues to be used by the agriculturists, mainly to get to their orchards. Recently restoration works have been undertaken.

The mountain above Moratalla is called **Cerro de San Jorge** and is 848m. The highest mountain in Murcia region (Los Obispos, 2027m) is within the Moratalla district of Inazares and the district has dozens more peaks at over 1000m. Wide portions of the municipality are protected in ZEPAs (Special Protection Areas) or LICs (Site of Community Importance areas).

There's a basic 4.5km walk from the top of town following paths around Cerro de San Jorge which should take between 2-3 hours.

There are longer walks along Benamor river too, either heading southwest towards Benamor de Abajo or northeast towards where the river Moratalla and Benamor join at Molino Traviesa. This walk is a good 7 hours' round-trip in either direction so take plenty of provisions. You should also take boots that can handle getting wet. When you're dog-tired after a long day's walk you don't even have to cook since there's plenty of tapas bars and restaurants a few minutes' stroll away in town.

A good book to buy is Excursiones por Moratalla from Natursport; ISBN 84-932242-2-7. It lists twenty-six walks varying from a few hours' 'easy' walks to several days' walks and ones that require serious fitness. www.natursport.com

You can also find the remains of the earliest settlements in the district dating back to the Neolithic era. If you like history then be sure to visit the **Dolmen at Bagil in the Cerro de Las Víboras or Los Castillicos** and the cave paintings at **Cañaíca del Calar or La Risca**.

There are a few riding schools around Moratalla one to note is Picadero Pascual situated 2km away. It has 25 stables and an outdoor and indoor school. Classes are available onsite and also there are excursions which offer beautiful scenery and good riding. The excursions are through the mountainous forested areas or in the lower areas amongst the olive groves. Excursions last from one hour to whatever duration you want. Riders are accompanied by at least one guide depending on the size of the group and the minimum age to participate is eight. Many different levels and styles of dressage activities are also available. www.facebook.com/Centro-ecuestre-Picadero-Pascual-968192196596658/

Moratalla has a large number of traditional bakeries and you can smell the fresh loaves and wood smoke for most of the day. Most bake twice a day: at the crack of dawn and again around suppertime. Go for a stroll at these times of day and follow your nose. Some of the bakeries use traditional wood-fired ovens and these are easy to locate thanks to the giveaway large pile of logs outside.

There's a great market on Saturday (Map: D4), sprawling right down through the lower part of town, food at the top and clothes and 'stuff' further down.

Location Report: Around Moratalla

If you like noise then come and see the Moratalla Tamboristas at Easter. Well, what can we say about Moratalla's Easter celebrations? They're loud! Allegedly (and I'm hoping someone with more knowledge will correct me if I'm wrong) Jesus was a drummer. So in Moratalla they celebrate by banging drums, big ones, everyone, children, grandparents, big kids and even adults.

The only day they stop banging the drums is on the Saturday before Easter Sunday, because, I suppose, Jesus couldn't drum when he was dead. The rest of the time leading up to Easter they drum, from morning till night and through to morning again.

We read in La Verdad (Murcia's main regional newspaper) that there were 1,500 drummers in the streets one year. And an additional 7,000 visitors during Easter.

The drums themselves are works of art. There are only a few masterful craftsmen who have the skills and knowledge to make them. Each drum has a characteristic sound (loud!) and is the result of several months' effort to obtain the perfect note from the goat or ewe skins (never plastic).

All Tamboristas dress in colourful tunics. The main concentration of Tamboristas is down in the 'lamppost' square. Sometimes the drummers drum together in unison, more often they compete to bring other drummers into their beat. It really is loud.

The 19th April is día del patrón de Moratalla, Jesucristo Aparecido, the day Jesus Christ appeared (apparently), who is the patron of Moratalla. This is a more solemn procession. Followed by parties!

15th June is día del Santísimo Cristo del Rayo, the day in 1621 when a ray of light came down in the image of Jesus on the Crucifixion. It's now celebrated with a Huertano parade (peasant dresses and processions) and floral offerings, along with the obligatory solemn procession. Followed by parties! And then…

11th to 17th July (and some extra days) for the main fiesta (postponed every year from June to allow the apricot harvest to be picked!), this is when the bulls run, the music plays and the beer flows even longer. This really is the main fiesta of the year and again includes: huertanos, the election and coronation of the King and Queen and the ladies of honour, a literary contest, fireworks and lots of music (and beer!) though the main activity is the running of the bulls through the streets most days of the fiesta. It's recommended for new visitors to stay behind the barriers that spring up around the narrow streets for all the days of the fiesta, as you never know when a bull might appear! www.encierrosdemoratalla.es

29th & 30th September & 1st October for día de San Miguel, San Miguel day (isn't that the name of a beer? that must explain the drinking and general merriment!) which is actually the 29th and celebrates the medieval period, with a medieval market, games and celebrations.

Bodega Tercia de Ulea is a winery located in Moratalla. It is an old farmhouse in the countryside, restored in the traditional way. It is one of the youngest in the D.O. Bullas wineries. www.terciadeulea.com 968 433313.

Moratalla has a number of satellite towns, Benizar (La Tercia, Mazuza, Otos), San Bartolomé (El Sabinar, Calar de la Santa), Campo de San Juan (Casicas de San Juan, Zaén de Arriba, Zaén de Abajo, Casas de Aledo, La

Ribera), Cañada de la Cruz (and Los Odres), Roble, Arenal, Béjar, Inazares, Cobatillas, Río Segura and La Rogativa.

Benizar (La Tercia, Mazuza, Otos)

Benizar is 30km north from Moratalla with fewer than 1000 inhabitants. It is surrounded by El Calar and the sierra de La Muela. There are traces of a Moorish castle dating from the 12th century on a rock overlooking the hamlet.

Under its cliffs and caves prehistoric man found a place to shelter from danger and to demonstrate their artistic skills, leaving the walls of the **Los Abrigos de Benizar** an interesting legacy of paintings belonging to the Levantine and Schematic styles. Head for **Rincón de las Cuevas** to see the caves. It's also noted for its many water springs.

Moorish Benizar, with twisted and steep streets, whitewashed houses dripping with cheerful pots of geraniums and a 12th century castle perched on a hill, are some of the attractions that have dramatically boosted rural tourism in recent years.

Benizar Castle can be seen on an enormous rocky crag that dominates the valley. It dates from Islamic times, specifically the 12th century, and was a strategically important defence. In 17th century the Council gave it to the Hermitage of Santa Barbara and more recently it was sold privately.

They celebrate their fiesta between the 3rd and 8th December, in honour of Santa Bárbara, where they have an encierro (bull running).

Tourist office, C/ Barrio Nuevo, 968 730208.

San Bartolomé (El Sabinar, Calar de la Santa)

A drive (!) up to almost the top of the **Revolcadores** is possible, the road is not paved, but it's not too bad. You ascend by car to over 1,800 meters. The view from the summit is marvellous.

At **El Calar de la Santa** in El Sabinar you can find even more rock paintings. El Sabinar is oriented in an easterly direction and about 1300 meters above sea level. A three metre high mouth opens to the cave and inside there are two zones of paintings: one on the left, where you can see only faint traces of paint and one on the right which has the best paintings. You can clearly see a cruciform motif, which is a typical representation of Schematic Art. El Calar de la Santa, along with other rock art finds, have made the Northwest region an important area nationally within the post-Palaeolithic rock art.

Campo de San Juan (Casicas de San Juan, Zaén de Arriba, Zaén de Abajo, Casas de Aledo, La Ribera)

Campo de San Juan & **Casa de Cristo**, The Hermitage, is located 6km outside of Moratalla on the San Juan road. Look for signs off to the right when about 5km outside of the town. It was constructed in the 17th century in the popular baroque style. In 1811 the Napoleonic Troops who had arrived in Moratalla set the Monastery alight and in 1829 the friars returned to the recovered Convent.

The origin of the ermita is related to the story of the appearance of Christ to the Rui shepherd Sanchez, on the 19th of April 1493. Originally the hermitage comprised of the **Mercedario Convent** which was confiscated in the 19th century. Throughout the 19th century diverse works of repair and restoration were made, with the new tabernacle constructed by the local cabinetmaker Valentin Lozano Sanchez.

There is also a **Centro Regional de Interpretación del Arte Rupestre** (Center of Interpretation of Rock Art) and an excellent (and very popular) restaurant. Even if you're not keen on visiting the hermitage, the views from up here are superb! Well worth the short drive from town. www.turismoruralmurcia.es/events/centro-de-arte-rupestre-de-moratalla

Cañada de la Cruz (and Los Odres)

Cañada de la Cruz (also popularly known as La Cañada) is situated at the western end of Moratalla, four kilometres from the border with the province of Granada and five from the province of Albacete. This is the westernmost town of the Region of Murcia at the foot of Revolcadores.

Their fiesta is in honour of the Immaculate Conception, during the second week of August, including dances, concerts and the obligatory encierro, the release of cows/bulls into the streets.

It is an area rich in game, especially wild white pigs, hunting is allowed from November to March.

An unusual project, Aldea de Los Odres, was initiated to rejuvenate the small hamlet of Los Odres which was in disrepair. It was a long-term plan taking into account the requirements of the few local inhabitants that remain. You can stay in one of the restored houses or in a wooden cabin. www.miscasasrurales.com/casas-rurales/aldea-los-odres/10

La Rogativa

La Rogativa Ermita is impressive not only for its construction but also by its geographic surroundings near the tip of Revolcadores (ceiling of the Region of Murcia) at 2027m. The legend goes that in May 1535 a young man saw a white dove that dropped a stone on the ground where it was transformed into the Virgin with a bleeding wound on her forehead. So they made a wooden sanctuary for her. This was later destroyed by fire and during the 16th and 17th centuries rebuilt. Santuario De La Rogativa on the road from El Sabinar, 968 738005.

Services

Tourist Office, www.conocemoratalla.es, www.turismomoratalla.info

The Moratalla tourist board have made some superb videos, take a look: www.youtube.com/user/turismomoratalla

Ayuntamiento, Calle de la Constitución, 968 730001.

Bus Station, Carretera de Caravaca, daily buses to Caravaca de la Cruz.

Taxis, El Calara, 968 730055, 677 572996, 677 574341, Francisco Javier García, 968 730010, 606 505385.

Sleeping

Moratalla is the heart of rural tourism in Murcia. Of course the best place to stay if you are a couple (or only have one youngster) is at our little house right in the medieval town centre. We love staying here, especially around fiesta time, as it's close enough to walk easily (2 minutes) to all the madness, but far enough away so that you get a great night's sleep! It's a completely renovated lower floor of a 200 year old house (we haven't finished the upper 2 floors yet). Well to be honest, it used to be the donkey house, but all traces of donkey poo have been removed, all that remains is the ring he was tied to. Have a look at (Map: B2) www.moratallatownhouses.com or get in touch with me at debs@nativespain.com and tell me you read the book to get a discount.

If you fancy camping then try Camping La Puerta, out of town at the village of La Puerta, 7km up the valley to the north west, 968 730008. It has a restaurant and swimming pool and offers parking for caravans, camping plots and also some cabins. www.campinglapuerta.com

There are plenty of rural tourism possibilities. For example there is Hospedería Rural la Tejera on the road to La Puerta at kilometre 2. There's also the four houses at Casas Rurales Luis, www.casasruralesluis.com, 968 738 038 or the two houses at Casa Rural La Risca in the Campo de San Juan, www.casarurallarisca.com, 968 700 280. You really are spoilt for choice in Moratalla.

Los Odres is owned by a friend of ours and is an odd (interestingly odd) development in the town of Los Odres, www.miscasasrurales.com/casas-rurales/aldea-los-odres/10. Basically a whole village has been bought, renovated and turned into a tourist site. There are all types of houses from typical Murcian village houses to wooden houses built specifically for tourism. If you are part of a big group and fancy taking over your own village this is the place to come.

If you'd prefer a hotel then take a look at Hotel La Tejera on the road to Camping La Puerta, www.hotel-rural-la-tejera-moratalla.vivehotels.com/en/, 968 706261. It's a cross between a motel and hotel, with a swimming pool, restaurant and accommodation for more than 50 guests.

Eating

For such a large tourist town it is wonderfully unspoilt by chains, there isn't a Burger King nor McDonalds! There aren't any Chinese nor Indian restaurants. This is real Spain, with excellent local bars and restaurants, small coffee shops that sell homemade bread and cakes, pizza bars that make their own pizzas and are run by Italians and a homemade ice cream parlour (which unfortunately has sporadic opening times!)

Moratalla is a great town for exploring and trying out different food. For tapas walk along Calle Major to find various bars to choose from, then down towards Camping La Puerta if you're still hungry. If you want a good lunch then the San Juan road has what you need.

One of our favourites is Monte Benamor, Carretera San Juan, 67, 968 706464. They have a great menú del día, wonderful evening meals, yummy tapas and all for great prices. There's a good wine list too, with some local wines to try.

A restaurant everyone seems to recommend is El Olivar. We've tried this one twice and were disappointed both times. The ambience is poor, the prices stupid and the food average. www.restauranteelolivar.es

In the centre of town there's the La Plaza on the Plaza de Iglesia, 968 706565, which can be expensive, but has excellent views across old town.

You could also try Taska La Esencia, www.facebook.com/taskalaesenciaa/, 690 603966

Night Life

Night life mainly happens in the summer out on the Carretera de Caravaca where there are a number of café pubs. At weekends you can also find a lot of more lively entertainment along Carretera de Campo de San Juan. During fiesta times then nightlife goes on from midday to the early hours of the morning, each day of the fiesta, so choose your accommodation carefully.

Mula

Population: 16,700

Map Reference: 1.49°W, 38.04°N

Mula is on the river Mula, and is another hillside town topped with a castle (like Moratalla). Many of the streets appear to be pedestrianised and you'll be surprised to find a car in the most unlikely of places! Mula is also the epicentre for a geological fault line and has experienced a number of minor earthquakes over the years.

The first thing that you notice as you get close to Mula is the castle. **Castillo de los Vélez** (the castle on top of the hill) is 16th century and can be reached by footpaths which meander up from the top of town.

The castle is of Renaissance architecture, is defensive in nature and made of simple shapes, situated on a cliff. Of the two entrances, one of them is accessed through the top of the wall and the towers of the ancient Muslim palace and a drawbridge. A visit to the castle is a vital stop for the visitor. It is unfortunate that currently the City of Mula is in dispute over the ownership of the castle.

At the centre of town you'll find the small park of La Glorieta Juan Carlos I, and around the park is the convent and church of San Francisco.

In the Plaza del Ayuntamiento is the **Parroquía de San Miguel** (16th century), a tower and a clock tower standing next to each other. The church has a Latin cross with shrines to the Marques de los Vélez and San Felipe. There's a museum of paintings donated by Doña Pilar de la Canal. Among the most important painters are Ribera, Mengs and Juanquin Campos.

Other religious monuments include the Real Monasterio de la Encarnación, Parroquía de Santo Domingo de Guzmán (16th century), the Ermita de Nuestra Señora del Carmen (18th century), and la Iglesia de la Purísima Concepción, part of the Convento de San Francisco.

There's a museum, **Museo del Cigarralejo**, open Tuesdays to Sundays in the mornings. This is an archaeological site of the Iberian culture (5th century BC) that includes the remains of a settlement, a necropolis and a sanctuary. The museum displays remains of pottery and utensils found in the excavations. Calle del Marqués, 1, 968 661422, entry is free.

The **Casa Pintada** (Painted House) is a museum located in a Renaissance palace and collects many of the works of Christopher Gabarrón (painter, sculptor and responsible for the excavation of the Cigarralejo).

The National Fast Painting Contest is held the second Sunday of November each year, coinciding with the craft market called Las Cuatro Plazas. Painters from around the country compete to complete a painting during the day, whilst being watched by the general public. It began in 2007 with 114 painters and has gained national interest, the winner gets €1,500 and there are plenty of runner up prizes. Visit www.facebook.com/pages/category/Artist/Pintura-En-Mula-904221262950192/ and take a look at some of the recent years' entries.

There's Spanish Film Week and the National Short Film Competition organised by the Second Cineclub Chomón, www.semanacinemula.es/.

The Easter celebrations are particularly vibrant in Mula due to the drumming! Easter and Tamborada have been declared of **National Tourist Interest** in Mula. The processions begin on Good Friday from the Parish of San Miguel with the Via Crucis, and continue with the procession of Palm Sunday Morning from Santo Domingo to meet Jesus Triumphant in the Plaza del Ayuntamiento. The Tamborada has its origins in a popular revolt to the edict of the centennial Brotherhood of Carmen (1606) to prohibit drumming processions outside. Peak day is on Easter Tuesday, where thousands of drummers wait in the Plaza with sticks in the air for the sound of the bugle, at 12pm, which gives way to a thunderous burst of drums throughout the city.

They also celebrate Fiestas de San Isidro on the second Saturday of May, in honour of San Isidro Labrador, patron of the garden and countryside. There are processions with the saint from the parish of Santo Domingo in the morning, accompanied by choirs and dance groups and locals dressed in traditional costumes, to the roundabout where Las Cuatro Plazas market can be found. In the afternoon you'll see the Bando Huertano procession with floats towed by farm machinery, each with their own sound system! The floats are designed to emulate local farming activities with sausages and bread (and some alcohol!) being freely distributed. At night there's a concert in Parque de la Feria, where the parade ends.

The Theatre and Crafts Fair takes place from 19th to 25th September and each day also sees a different religious festival being honoured.

On the second Sunday of each month the **Las Cuatro Plazas market** is held at Plaza del Ayuntamiento, except during the summer months. The craftsmen of the region gather with a wide range of traditional products including esparto items, objects of wood, clay pots and bowls, chairs made of bulrush, wool carpets and rugs, the fragrant sausages of the region, bread and homemade sweets, wine, oil, etc. At each market there are craft demonstrations, tastings of typical products, activities and events.

There are a number of satellite towns: Yéchar, Los Baños de Mula, El Niño de Mula, La Puebla de Mula, Fuente Librilla, Casas Nuevas and Los Ojos.

Yéchar

Lying seven kilometres from the town of Mula in the foothills of the Sierra de la Muela is Yéchar, in a beautiful landscape, surrounded by apricot trees. People visit to enjoy the outdoor life, in particular walking around **Fuente Caputa (Roman remains), the Embalse del Mayés or the Embalse de la Cierva.** They celebrate their fiesta in August.

Los Baños de Mula

In the satellite town of Los Baños de Mula you'll find restored bath houses all along the main street, including: Los Baños Generales, www.losbañosdemula.es; El Delfín, www.bmeldelfin.es/; El Intendente, www.bañostermalesdemula.com, and Los Baños del Pozo, www.balnearioelpozo.es. These are in simple buildings of one or two stories with balconies of wrought iron railings outside. Some are beautiful with patios and flowers, inner courtyards, small barred windows, huge wooden doors, flagstones and curving staircases. Have a wander around this pretty little hamlet.

Los Baños de Mula is situated in the basin of the river Mula, the Rio Pliego, and streams that flow into them. However, only the river Mula has a permanent flow throughout the year, which disappears only during temporary episodes of prolonged drought.

The **Cerro de la Almagra** has been declared of archaeological cultural interest. You can see the remnants of the Roman city, surrounded by walls and towers for defense. They have found the remains of furniture, as well as fine ceramics (Hispanic and African), a number of early Christian sarcophagi and fragments of decorated stone slabs dated from the sixth and seventh centuries, as well as finding a string of beads made of different materials.

They celebrate their fiesta around the 12th October, with the usual parties, a huertana day (local traditional farmers' dress) and religious processions.

El Niño de Mula

Just 3.5km from Mula lies El Niño de Mula, which was known as Campo de Albalat or Balate until the seventeenth century when it changed its name.

El Santuario Del Niño Jesús De Balate was built in the eighteenth century in Baroque style. It has a Latin cross with a central nave covered with a barrel vault. There are two towers for the choir.

Economic activity of El Niño de Mula is linked to its traditional role of catering for travellers on the journey from Murcia to Caravaca de la Cruz. This has led to the proliferation of good restaurants and rural accommodation.

They have their fiesta in the middle of September.

La Puebla de Mula

La Puebla de Mula is 5km away from Mula town. You'll notice the **Castillo (or Fortaleza) de Alcalá,** like a finger pointing to the sky on the hill near Mula town. It's 120 metres above ground and gives you a view for many kilometres all around. Handy for a fortress! To reach the fortress take a detour on the existing road connecting Mula and Baños de Mula, heading towards Librilla. At the foot of the hill, on the eastern side you can begin the ascent on foot. It was an important strategic stronghold for many centuries and has been declared of Cultural and Historical interest. Visit the door and the wells of this Muslim castle that supplied water to the city. This area has been inhabited since prehistoric times.

The Tower of Puebla de Mula has its origins around the late fourteenth century. Its walls are made from recycled materials of Roman origin and from the nearby site of the **Cerro de la Almagra**. It's in a passable condition and has been declared of Cultural Interest. You can find the tower at the top of the town on Calle de Arriba, where it opens out at the end. You can't go inside as it is a private property.

They celebrate their fiesta around the 7th October.

Fuente Librilla

Fuente Librilla is located in the foothills of the Sierra Espuña. It has archaeological sites that indicate first settlements go back to Argaric time. There's a proliferation of Roman villas due to the natural waters (Fuentes) creating excellent agricultural resources and of course wealth.

At first sight it's a barren landscape, but its beauty lies mainly in the winter months, when the almond blossom invades the fields, then this area is one of the most beautiful sights in the region of Mula.

They share their fiesta with La Puebla de Mula around the 7th of October.

Services

Tourist Office, Casa-Horno/Casa del Artesano, Calle Páez, 968 661501, www.mula.es/turismo

Ayuntamiento, Plaza Del Ayuntamiento, 968 637510, www.mula.es

Bus Station, Senda de la Moreira, has buses to Murcia and Caravaca, 968 292211.

Sleeping

Hotel Entresierras on Autovía E15, km642 in Librilla is one of the best places to stay in the area; it has a Portmeirion feel to it. 968 657676, www.hotelentresierras.es

Hospedería Rural Casas Nuevas, on the road between Pliego and Lorca at km14, 968 431820, www.Hospederíacasasnuevas.com. It can sleep up to 24 people for around €60 per 2 people per night. Excellent for walking in the Sierra Espuña. They also have a small restaurant offering locally produced food.

Hospedería Rural Molino de Filipe, out of town in the Rivera de los Molinos, 321, 968 662013, www.hotelruralmula.com/, has the restored remains of a 16th century mill. They still sell their own hand crafted flour. It's a very rustic place, with a tower room and apartments for rental. There's a swimming pool, gym and games area. Great value in an excellent location.

If you want to stay in a casa rural and also enjoy the thermal baths of Mula they you could try Baños de Mula El Delfín, Calle de los Baños, www.bmeldelfin.es, 968 661227. At the weekends they offer treatments using the special waters!

Eating

For tapas the best spot is off the park of Glorieta Juan Carlos I where you'll find many restaurants and bars to try. There are also various places to eat, mostly out of town towards Baños de Mula or Niño de Mula.

- El Churrasco, Calle Fray Pedro Botía, 4, specialises in churrasco and paella.
- Restaurante El Hogar, Calle Hospital, 968 63 75 51, for traditional fare.
- Restaurante Cervantes, Calle Don Juan Fernández Castillo, 53, 968 660800, in nearby Yéchar for good rice and rabbit.

Murcia and Surrounds

Population: 443,300

Map Reference: 1.13°W, 37.98°N

The city of Murcia is set in the heart of a rich fertile plain at just 43 metres above sea level. Unlike the rest of the region, where the terrain is dry and rugged, the soil here is irrigated by the River Segura and the land has been widely and fruitfully cultivated.

In the city itself the old quarter is made up of a maze of narrow streets huddled together around the Cathedral. This labyrinth is only broken by the main roads crossing through it such as the Gran Vía Escultor Salzillo.

The most pleasant parts of the city, indeed the most typically Murcian, are to be found around the gardens on the banks of the River Segura. A considerable part of the population of Murcia do not in fact live in the city itself, rather they live in houses and farmsteads scattered around it. A wide variety of fruits and vegetables are grown not only for the Spanish domestic market but also for export to the rest of Europe. For this reason Murcia is often referred to as La Huerta de Europa: The Market Garden of Europe.

What is there to do in Murcia City?

A good website to look at before leaving the UK is: www.turismodemurcia.es/en

For a monthly updated guide take a look on www.laguiago.com. Their small printed booklets can be picked up for free at the tourist information centres and some bars.

Murcia is an ancient, Mediterranean and hospitable city which was founded and fortified in 825 AD by Abderraman II with the name Mursiya, in the fertile planes of the Segura.

Murcia, paradise of light and the orange blossom, is a happy and extroverted city, highlighted by: the Cathedral, Catedral de Santa María, the Church of Our Father Jesus (home to the museum of the celebrated sculptor Salzillo), the Episcopal Palace, the Convent of Santa Ana (Map:D2), the Church of San Miguel, the Monastery of Santa Clara la Real, El Almudi, the Sanctuary of Fuensanta, the Gardens of Malecón and the Casino.

PLAZA CARDINAL BELLUGA: Nothing could be more relaxing than making the short drive into the city on a Sunday morning, and sitting in the Plaza Cardinal Belluga with your newspaper (La Verdad or El Semanal) and a coffee and tostadas, watching the world go by. On many occasions we've been entertained by marching bands, balloon sellers or by watching cars magically appear out of buildings.

The Cathedral (Map: D4) was built between the 14th and 18th centuries, with some parts being rebuilt in 1735 after flood damage. You can get great views, almost 100 metres up, in the tower which dates from the 18th century. An admission fee is now charged for visits but at €5 it isn't too high a price, but add on a further €5 to go up the tower and it starts to get expensive. www.catedralmurcia.com/visit/

The building was constructed on the land occupied by the old Arabic mosque. In 1385 the foundations were laid, in 1388 the first stone was laid and in 1394 the new building was under way and finished in

October 1467. The passing of the centuries have brought together different styles: Gothic, Renaissance and Baroque, which, with their own features, have turned the cathedral into an eclectic work.

The bell tower (1521-1791) is 90 metres high (95 with the weathervane) with each of the five parts which make it up measuring a different width. Francisco and Jacobo Florentino were the masterminds behind the first part, which is square and in the Renaissance style, with Hispanic Plateresque ornamentation. The second part, completed by Jerónimo Quijano, proceeds from a more purist phase of the same style. The third part is in the Baroque style, the body of the bell tower is Rococo and the final domed part has a neo-classical touch and was designed by Ventura Rodriguez. In the fourth part, the conjuratorios, from which the storms were invoked with the Lignum Crucis, stand out.

The bells, with the exception of the Mora (14th century), which is kept in the museum of Bellas Artes, are from the 17th and 18th centuries. They all have a name: la de los Conjuros, la Catalana, la de la Oración, la Fuensanta, la Concepción, la Segundilla, etc. The most important of these being the largest, **Ageda Martillo**. The 25 bells have served to warn the Murcians of the terrible floods and wars, but also to remind them of celebrations, happiness and holidays.

The interior is mainly Gothic, with a layout of three naves, an apse surrounded by a nave and chapels. These chapels are dedicated to the patron saints of the different guilds, and tombs of the bishops and nobles who collaborated or promoted their construction. Of the 23 chapels, the **Chapel of Girola**, known as Los Vélez is particularly noteworthy. It is built in the Flamígero Gothic style and has an impressive dome forming a ten-pointed star. The chapel of **Junterones**, one of the largest Spanish Renaissance works, and the baroque chapel of **La Inmaculada** also stand out. In the main altar the heart and entrails of Alfonso X are kept, according to his will as proof of his love of Murcia and gratitude for the loyalty shown to him by the city.

The door of the Apostles (**Puerta de los Apóstoles**) was built in 1488 by Diego Sánchez de Almazán in a Gothic style; its name comes from the sculptures of the four apostles on the door jambs. There is a shield in honour of Queen Isabel the Catholic.

The chapel of the **Marqués de los Vélez** is outstanding. In the shape of a polygon, it is adorned by the coat of arms of the Chacones and the Fajardos, held by two wild men. The stone chain, which runs around the chapel, is also remarkable.

The Door of the Chains (**Puerta de las Cadenas**) is made of two parts, the lower part from the 16th century and the upper part from the 18th century. In the Renaissance façade, there are three reliefs of the brothers San Leandro, San Isidro and San Fulgencio.

The main façade is an exceptionally beautiful jewel of the international baroque style, it is like the front of an altarpiece, bringing together originality and synthesis of the typical baroque concepts. Unique in its genre, it was raised with the initiative of the cathedral council, the help of Cardinal Belluga (Cardinal in Rome and a great benefactor of the city) and the intervention of the crown and it was carried out by Jaime Bort in the Baroque-Rococo style. www.diocesisdecartagena.org (Spanish only)

The **Episcopal Palace** in Cardenal Belluga square rises up next to the majestic frontage of the cathedral. It is said that bishop Mateo decided he wanted a residence from which he could contemplate the newly finished façade of the cathedral, leading to the construction of his square palace.

It is made up of two joined buildings: the so called Martillo (hammer) of the palace (the bishop's viewpoint) is a part of the building which towers above the rest, built before the construction of the main building had begun, to provide a viewpoint over the river Segura and el Paseo del Arenal, or Glorieta. And the main body or palace: clearly influenced by recent Italian Manierism, it is therefore related to Roman palaces.

The balcony doors of the façade have their origin in those conceived by Michelangelo for the Farnese Palace, Rome, in 1546. The wall treatments, which consist of ornamental frescos, are another characteristic of Roman and Neapolitan palaces. The pinkish hue attracts attention from across the Plaza.

Inside the imperial staircase is of great interest and it follows the ideas of the Roman Baroque style. It consists of the patio, organised in three Dorian arcades and an upper, more compact part and the small, circular bishop's chapel.

The shield, which presides over the main balcony of the palace, commemorates Bishop Roja under whose term of office the work was finished in 1786.

Across from the Cathedral is a striking modern building which is part of the Ayuntamiento complex, which surprisingly complements the Baroque cathedral facing it across the square at Plaza Cardenal Belluga. This building was designed by Rafael Moneo.

The **Casino** was designed and built by Francisco Bolarín El Joven, the younger, to distinguish him from his father, who was also an architect. The façade is the work of the architect Pedro Cerdán Martínez. The style is eclectic, with decorative classical and modernist elements.

The Moorish patio is built on two levels and finished off by a great iron and glass dome. Highly decorative, it is inspired by the Royal Halls of La Alhambra and El Alcázar in Seville. The Gallery is an enormous covered passage, a bit like a private street. It is used to access the different areas of the casino as well as being a meeting place. El Congresillo, the interior hall, was the meeting place of the influential characters in the economic and social life of Murcia.

El Patio Pompeiano is decorated with a beautiful statue by the sculptor Jose Planes and has fourteen columns. The Dance Hall was witness to the social life in Murcia for more than a century, it was built by the famous architect José Ramón Berenguer in the neo-Baroque style. The valuable paintings which adorn the room, four matrons in the clouds, represent the music, the sculptures, the paintings and the architecture. Four medallions represent the illustrious sons of Murcia: Romea, Salzillo, Floridablanca and Villacís.

The Ladies Powder Room has a beautiful ceiling fresco. The work of the painter Marín Baldo, it shows an allegory of the night represented by the goddess Selene. The eyes of the winged woman falling in flames appear to be following you around the room.

There's also the library, the billiards room and two tearooms with enormous windows looking out onto Calle Trapería.

The Casino is on Calle Trapería, 22. It's certainly worth a special visit for the fantastic stained glass and Arabic tiles, combined with colonial feel and good coffee. Entry costs €5. www.realcasinomurcia.com

The Jardin Floridablanca (Map:D5) is a great place to escape the heat of summer under the shade of its well-established rubber trees. It was built in 1848 by Carlos III and was the first public garden to be built in Murcia. It lies within the traditional neighbourhood of del Carmen, on the right bank of the River Segura.

Other points of interest are the **Museo de la Ciudad** in the 16th century house of the Lopez-Ferrer, displaying the history of the city, Plaza Agustin, 7, 968 274390 and the **Hydraulic Museum**, showing the water mills of the Segura river along with temporary art displays, Calle Molinos, 968 358600.

La Huerta (agricultural countryside)

It has been said that in order to know Murcia it is necessary to know the Huerta, as it is difficult to understand one without the other. Spreading throughout the Vega Medía area of the river Segura, it occupies the plain between two parallel mountain ranges through which the river Segura runs on its way to the sea.

The Arabs came up with a complete system of irrigation using these fertile plains. The Contraparada weir, started by the Romans and perfected by the Moors, is the starting point of a clever system which takes advantage of the water. It allows the water to enter the Vega so that via the many irrigation channels which branch out it can reach the furthest point of both sides of the river, encouraging the cultivation of fruit trees, especially citrus fruits, and vegetables.

The so-called living waters which come from the river are separated by a dyke or azud (known as **Contraparada** since the 18th century). Situated in the middle of the riverbed it causes the water level to rise so that water can be channelled and distributed through two major irrigation channels, Alquibla and Aljufia, which run through both of the Segura river banks.

From there the stream moves to smaller irrigation channels, which in turn, provide other channels with water until they reach the watering points and it flows directly into the land where it is used. The Contraparada is the first stop for those who wish to know La Huerta.

This irrigation system is complemented by the collection of surplus water through special doors or escorredores which run into collection channels or azarbetas which in turn run into the azarbe or collection/irrigation channel, so that the water can be reused.

Very close to the Contraparada is **The Wheel of La Ñora**, a hydraulic invention powered by the current in order to elevate the water for irrigation. This wheel is similar to the Wheel of Alcantarilla, also very close to Murcia, which was built in the 14th century (www.museodelahuerta.es/). Right next to it is the museum of **La Huerta** situated in an orchard of lemon trees. There, you can get to know **La Barraca**, the traditional house of the Huerta and centre of the family and working life for the huertanos, at first hand. Dozens of barracas are put up in the city during the spring fiestas. This ingenious yet curious irrigation system is deservedly famous, so much so that in many foreign guides it is described as the most typical and important aspect of this region. It is true that in a way the history of Murcia is that of its irrigation. Its conservation and use is guaranteed by the Town Hall and the Committee of Landowners through the regulation established in the Huerta bylaws.

From the **Castle of Monteagudo** or the **Sanctuary of La Fuensanta** the fertile huerta offers an extraordinarily beautiful view in every shade of green. However, it is also worth seeing the huerta from inside, in the valley.

The Silk

Silk has its own special chapter in Murcia's history. Of ancient origin, it is believed that Justiniano introduced it to Spain, although it was not until the arrival of the Moors, with the plantation of white mulberry trees, that it boomed and a silk was produced which became renowned throughout the East.

The 16th century was a time of expansion for Murcian silk. It was so great that its production was directly linked to the general state of the economy, as the silk industry in the 17th century and early 18th century was the trigger for the process of industrialisation in Murcia. The dominant position which Murcia held in silk production and commerce was contributed to by the fact that the mulberry tree was virtually the only tree grown, as the huerta provided optimum conditions. Other factors which influenced the rise of this industry were the good conditions provided by the valley of the river Segura for the breeding of the worm and the excellent quality of the silk produced.

The Murcian Council built the **Contraste building in Santa Catalina Square** at the beginning of the 17th century and it was from here that silk production was controlled, turning Murcia into the centre of silk activity in the region. The city benefited greatly from the taxes collected for silk in El Contraste. The irrigation channels were repaired, the **Malecón**, a containment wall against floods, was reinforced, and the bridge of Los Peligros was built.

This activity also influenced the communication routes as all of the interior routes had to pass through the capital, and therefore the Contraste building. As for exterior routes, thanks to the volume of Murcian silk exported via Toledo, the old Castille Road, now known as the Silk Road, re-emerged at the same time as the Andalucía-Levante route.

Finally, factories were built. The first of these was the Piamontesa silk spinning factory in 1770. Among others were La Grande and La Pequeña and you can still see a chimney in the Seda Park. In 1892 the Estación Serícola was built in La Alberca and today it is occupied by the **Centre for Agricultural Research and Development**.

Particularly significant was the guild of silk spinners (torcedores) and weavers, which was rich and powerful and had its own procession, that of The Betrayal. The procession no longer exists but the paso or Easter sculpture is now paraded on Easter

Monday by the brotherhood of Christ the forgiver (Cristo del Perdón).

On the morning of Good Friday a large branch of silk cocoons is placed at the feet of Our Father Jesus of Nazareth. When spring arrives the huertano group (peña) The Silk, who keep up the commendable tradition of silk worm breeding as a symbol of what it represented, goes to the Santa Catalina convent during the pilgrimage in order to bless the crops. In spring it's not unusual to see children coming out of school holding boxes containing silk worms and mulberry leaves, as a reminder of what silk meant to the region.

Museums, Exhibition Centres & Theatres

Santa Clara Museum houses archaeological and religious artefacts in a 13th century monastery. Gran Vía Alfonso X El Sabio, 1. Open Tuesday to Saturday from 10:00 to 13:00 and from 16:00 to 19:30, Sunday and holidays from 10:00 to 13:00. Access to the museum is always as part of a guided visit. Reservations at the museum or call 699 396544 or 968 272398. www.museosdemurcia.com/santaclara

Salzillo Museum (Map: A3) holds the most important processional religious images by the world-famous wood carver, Francisco Salzillo. Original sketches and 550 Christmas figures, and also the famous platforms bearing groups of life-size Biblical figures carried down the streets on the shoulders of the faithful in Holy Week. Plaza de San Agustín, 1, 968 291893. Open Monday to Saturday, from 10:00 to 14:00. Sundays and holidays from 11:00 to 14:00. 15 June – 15 September: from Monday to Friday from 10:00 to 14:00. Closed Saturday and Sunday. www.museosalzillo.es Entrance €5.

Fine Arts Museum (Museo de Bella Artes), has Spanish paintings from the 16th to the 20th century, prestigious artists both from this and other regions. Obispo Frutos, 12, 968 239346. Open Tuesday to Friday from 10:00 to 14:00 and 17:00 to 20:00. Saturday, Sunday and holidays from 11:00 to 14:00. Mondays closed. https://www.museosregiondemurcia.es/museo-de-bellas-artes-de-murcia

Archaeological Museum has a permanent and temporary exhibition space with an archaeological theme. Gran Vía Alfonso X El Sabio, 7, 968 234602. Free entry. Open Tuesday to Friday 10:00 to 14:00 and 17:00 to 20:00. Saturday 11:00 to 14:00 and 17:00 to 20:00. Sundays and holidays 11:00 a 14:00. Closed Mondays. https://www.museosregiondemurcia.es/museo-arqueologico-de-murcia

Cathedral Museum on Plaza Hernández Amores, 1, 968 219713.

This is inside the Cathedral. Walk on glass floors and observe the original walls below. Open Tuesday to Saturday from 10:00 to 17:00. Sunday and Mondays closed. This also comes with an audio guide and costs €5. You may also visit the tower (if it's neither too windy, nor raining and the guide can be bothered!) for an additional €5. www.catedralmurcia.com/visit/

Ramón Gaya Museum is set in a beautiful mansion, the Palarea house and holds the works of one of the best contemporary Murcian artists: Ramon Gaya. Sketches, posters, writings and an anthological selection of both Gaya's and other artists' work. This is well worth a visit; take in the beauty of the house whilst you're wandering around. The wife of our vet works here, Victoria, so say hello to her from us! Plaza Santa Catalina, 968 221099. Open Tuesday to Saturday from 10:00 to 14:00 and 17:00 to 20:00. Closed on Sundays and holidays. Also closed on Saturdays during the summer! The square is also a great place to eat a little tapas, buy some yummy pastries and enjoy people watching. www.museoramongaya.es

Science and Water Museum (Map: C5), with water as its main theme, also has a children's planetarium, science square, temporary and thematic exhibitions. Plaza de la Ciencia, 1, 968 211998. Open Tuesday to Saturday from 10:00 to 14:00 and 17:00 to 20:00. Sundays and holidays from 11:00 to 14:00 outside of the summer months. During the summer the museum is also closed on Saturdays. www.cienciayagua.org

Bullfighting Museum of Murcia was founded in 1919, it contains posters, bullfighter's costumes and utensils. It also has a specialist library and video collection. You can just pop in for a beer or coffee in the bar and enjoy the many photos around the walls. Francisco Rabal, 3, 968 285976. Open Tuesday to Sunday, from 10:00 to 20:00. www.clubtaurinomurcia.es

Santa Eulalia Visitors Centre has different rooms where daily life in medieval Murcia is virtually recreated. You can see the original structure of the city's walls and learn a little about their construction. Plaza Santa Eulalia, 968 221612. Open Tuesday to Saturday from 10:00 a 14:00 and from 17:00 to 20:00. Sunday from 10:00 to 14:00. Closed Mondays and holidays. www.murciaturistica.es/en/interpretation_centre/centro-de-visitantes-muralla-de-santa-eulalia-402/

Almudi Palace Arts Centre, housed in an 18th century building originally the city's corn store, the local Arts centre has two exhibition halls. The town's historical archives are to be found there too. On the façade, you can see a medallion relief of the Matron of Murcia or The Bread Store (Pósito del Pan), by Hernando de Torquemada. It shows a matron holding aside her own child to feed another, the symbol of the Murcian hospitality. A pelican, the symbol of abundance, crowns the relief. Look out for regularly changing exhibitions. Plano de San Francisco, 8, 968 358600. Open Monday to Saturday from 11:00 to 14:00 and from 18:00 to 21:00. Sundays and holidays from 11:00 to 14:00. www.murciaturistica.es/en/monument/palacio-del-almudi-328/

Teatro Romea was built by Manuel Molina in 1862, where the Convent of Santo Domingo had been before. It was inaugurated by Isabel II and rebuilt by Justo Millán after two fires in 1877 and 1899. It has paintings by Medina Vera, A. Latorre and A. Meseguer. Its name honours the Murcian actor Julián Romea. Plaza Romea, 968 355390, tickets 968 3551701. www.teatroromea.es/

Auditorium and Congress Center, where many big name concerts, ballets and operas are held. Avenida 1º de Mayo, 968 341060, www.auditoriomurcia.org

The Aquarium at the University of Murcia is open to the public. It includes some of the most interesting and striking species of the world's marine life. See reefs with corals and real fish from the Indian Ocean, the Pacific Ocean, the Red Sea, the Caribbean Sea and of course, a vast representation from the Mediterranean and the Mar Menor.

Besides sharks, complex associations are shown between different marine animals (symbiosis between clown fishes and anemones for example) and even examples of adaptation to diverse environments, as it is the case of the stone fish (one of the most poisonous animals of the world). Acuario de la Universidad de Murcia, Antiguo Cuartel de Artillería, Calle Cartagena, 968 398563, www.aquarium.um.es

Opening hours vary according to the time of year. April to October - Tuesday to Saturday from 10:00 to 13:30 and from 5:00 to 8:30. Sunday from 11:00 to 2:00. November to March – Tuesday to Friday from 10:00 to 5:00. Saturdays 10:00 to 1:30 and 5:00 to 7:00. Sundays 11:00 to 2:00. It costs just €1 but groups of 6 can book a guided tour for €3 per person.

Terra Natura Murcia. Just outside the city there's the wildlife park with over 300 animals. It closes for only 2 days per year, Christmas day and New Year's day, with the water park open June to September. Check on their website for closing times. There are restaurants, picnic areas and bars. €18 for adults and €14 for children. 968 36 82 00, http://murcia.terranatura.com/, located to the north-west of the town of Espinardo. Access is via the A-7 motorway. The park lies right next to the Murcia University Campus in Espinardo. The address is Calle Regidor Cayetano Gago, Espinardo.

Walking Around The City

El Paseo del Malecón is the best known Murcian esplanade built to fight against floods from the river Segura that cuts through the city. El Malecón is a wall built in the 15th century and despite being the object of various repairs by the 18th century it had deteriorated considerably because of the rain, the wind, horses and the continuous traffic of the city. It was rebuilt in 1736 by the Mayor of the city, D. Francisco de Luján y Arce. Nowadays, it is an exceptional esplanade three metres above the ground. It stretches more than 15,000 metres into the agricultural countryside like a stone tongue around the Western Side of the city, running between the Botanical gardens and those of the old Convent of San Francisco. Particularly noteworthy is the Arch dedicated to María, the statue of the Murcian philanthropist D. José María Muñoz and the old façades of the huertos and the houses that were beside the Malecón.

On the left side are the Maristas School and Murcia Parque. On the right side you can find the Botanical Garden, which is the largest park in Murcia.

A Stroll Around the Squares and Main Streets. A few meters from the Cathedral and Plaza de Belluga, near the River Segura, is La Glorieta, which has traditionally been the centre of the city. Built in the eighteenth century it is a garden square with the 14th century town hall.

It is still possible to see the old medieval urban fabric of the Andalusian period as you walk along beautiful pedestrianised streets, such as La Platería and La Trapería, which connects the Plaza de la Cruz (just behind the Cathedral) with famous Plaza de Santo Domingo, one of the most popular meeting points in Murcia. The La Platería and La Trapería form a cross in the centre of the old town. The small streets off these main streets are well worth investigating.

On La Trapería you can see the beautiful eclectic façade of the Casino (established 1847), with a sumptuous interior that combines different styles, from the Moorish patio inspired by the actual rooms of the Alhambra and the Alcazar of Seville, to a Roman-Pompeian courtyard, a wonderful English library with over 20,000 volumes and a beautiful neo-baroque ballroom.

At the top of La Trapería you'll find Plaza de Santo Domingo, a square with huge trees including a centenary ficus planted in 1893, and then head to the right under an archway to find the Teatro Romea. Of the many squares there are two with a special charm: that of Plaza de Flores, which has the oldest bakery in the city, loads of bars and restaurants and of course flower stalls and Santa Catalina with the Iglesia de Santa Catalina which is one of the oldest temples in the city of Murcia, apparently built on the structure of an Islamic mosque.

Fiestas

Murcia also benefits from a diverse programme of festivities: carnivals (February), Easter (March/April), the Spring Festivals (March/April), the Fair of Murcia (September) and Christmas (December), which, together with cinema, theatre and music festivals, conferences and art exhibitions mark out the animated cultural life in the city. Many of these events take place in the Teatro Romea and Centro de Congresos.

Easter is a perfect time to visit Murcia to see a traditional Spanish fiesta, Semana Santa, the ornate wooden sculptures of the city's famous artist, Salzillo, are paraded throughout the city. Just after Semana Santa the Spring Festival (Fiestas de Primavera) is a week–long party that includes the outstanding Bando de la Huerta and the Entierro de la Sardina (burying of the sardine).

Murcia Three Cultures Festival is held during the month of May when there are plenty of concerts, plays, cinema, exhibitions, shows and artistic activities to choose from, all closely related to the Islamic, Jewish and Christian cultures.

El Bando de la Huerta is the Murcian Fiesta par excellence. It is always celebrated on the first Tuesday after Easter and it opens the Spring Fiestas. In the most important squares and parks during the days before the parade the groups or peñas of huertanos (people from the Huerta) mount their famous barracas where you can find traditional Murcian dishes. You also have the opportunity to enjoy folklore performances and see the old houses and customs of the huerta, recreated by the peñas. The peñas huertanas play a major part in the proceedings and take significant names such as La Seda (The Silk), El Tablacho (dam gate), La Esparteña (typical huertano shoe), El Zaragüel (typical huertano trousers), El Azahar (orange blossom), etc.

Tens of thousands of people of all ages go to the streets in their regional costumes: for men the zaragüelles, waistcoats and monteras (huertano cap) and for women, the beautiful refajos (skirts), aprons and shawls.

The parade began in the 19th century when a group of huertanos, led by their Mayor, went to the city to protest about shortages. They paraded in a large group made up of carts and horses ridden by young men offering home-grown products. The passing of time has turned it into the coming together of the huertanos and the city dwellers, in order to pay homage to the huerta.

The day begins early with a floral offering to the Virgin of the Fuensanta, patron of the city, left in front of the Baroque façade of the Cathedral. After this people walk through the streets and squares and visit the barracas in order to enjoy the typical huertano products. In the afternoon, the parade sets off from the Infante Don Juan Manuel neighbourhood and moves through the centre of the city, handing out food, toys and gifts. www.turismodemurcia.es/en/Fiestas_in

El Entierro de la Sardina is a unique and original fiesta which takes place on the Saturday after Easter Sunday. Together with the Bando de la Huerta it is the big Murcian fiesta. The Entierro is the victory of Don Carnal over Doña Lent. A pagan festival with its origins in mythology and fire, it is a magical, unmissable night for any visitor to the city.

There's a giant sardine permanently in the river so take some photographs! (Map:C4)

The origin of the Entierro de la Sardina goes back to the mid 19th century when a group of students from Madrid who used to get together in the storeroom of the San Anton pharmacy decided to form a funeral procession presided over by a sardine. The sardine symbolises fasting and abstinence, as they wanted to revive the carnavalesque festival held in Madrid on Ash Wednesday.

The festival is organised by the Grupos Sardineros, who stir the city into excitement with their parades in the days leading up to the event. This is particularly true of Saturday morning in the boulevard Alfonso X el Sabio, where a widely attended and informal parade takes place.

The night before the parade Doña Sardina, represented by a woman, usually a journalist chosen by the Sardineros, reads the Last Will and Testament of the Sardine from the balcony of the town hall, making humorous references to public events and characters.

The parade is made up of two different parts: The start has brass bands, dancers, all kinds of groups to liven up the party, a Chinese style dragon, people on stilts, or giants and people wearing huge heads (cabezudos). The second part is made up of floats adorned with Greek motifs and dedicated to the Olympian Gods, which accompany the Sardine until it is burned next to the Town Hall. Thousands of toys of all shapes and sizes are given out from the floats, the most notable being the overused whistle!

Fireworks, music, brass bands, dancers, floats, toys, carnival groups, hachoneros (people who guard the floats), a concert of whistles... All of these come together in a night of madness and magic, when everybody without exception, fights for a toy. www.turismodemurcia.es/en/Fiestas_in

Christmas Holidays, begin with the Cuadrillas de Ánimas and Campanas de Auroros, pious brotherhoods who walk the paths of the huerta on Christmas Eve, under the protection of the Virgen del Rosario de la Aurora, announcing the birth of Jesus.

On Twelfth Night there are the Mystery plays, ancient religious dramas represented by the neighbours of some nearby towns, especially Churra and Patiño.

Christmas time also brings craftwork exhibitions and musical concerts. The squares and churches of Murcia fill up with Belenes, the traditional nativity scene in Murcia, which is internationally recognised. Markets are set up and the traditional Three Wise Men parade also takes place, together with other Christmas activities.

In the Cathedral Square (Plaza Cardenal Belluga) for around five nights over the Christmas period a festival of lights and opera is held. Usually three performances per night at 7pm, 8pm and 9pm, this extravaganza is free for all comers. www.turismodemurcia.es/en/Fiestas_in and is worth a special visit to the city.

September Fair is celebrated in the first fortnight of September, was granted by King Alfonso X the Wise and takes in a wide range of celebrations. For example, a fun fair, bullfighting, the cattle fair, the **Moors and Christians fiesta**, the **Tunas festival**, the **International Mediterranean Folklore Festival** and the **Great Romería** (pilgrimage) to accompany the patron Virgin on her way to her mountain sanctuary.

The Moorish and Christian camps are set up and they parade through the city with their army to commemorate the founding of Murcia by the Moors and the conquest of the city by Alfonso X the Wise. Their eye-catching clothing together with the gun powder and the music add a touch of historical colour to the September Fair.

The Tunas Festival has been celebrated since 1988 and Tunas (music bands) come from all over Spain and even outside to compete. Performances, parades, serenades, etc, give the city a student atmosphere.

The Mediterranean Folklore Festival includes processions and performances in the streets and cultural centres.

Debbie Jenkins, Russ Pearce

Location Report: Bando De La Huerta

On the first Tuesday after Easter this one day in particular stands out, Bando De La Huerta ('proclamation of the countryside'). If there's one fiesta that you should go to all year in Murcia (apart from your local village's, of course), this is it. Simply eschewing shorts and tee shirts will not be enough to prevent you from standing out as the extranjero (foreigner) in this fiesta. About 90% of the people at the festival wear national dress, so take a camera! There are lots of stalls (barracas) where you might be lucky to get a sample of traditional local food and drink, alternatively, all the restaurants and bars will be open. The processions and entertainment start in mid afternoon and go on all night, have a good siesta beforehand and enjoy!

Practicalities: You'll need to get hold of some national dress (lots of adverts for places selling it in the local Murcia press during the weeks leading up to the festival, plus all the large supermarkets offer cut price versions). Try and get a copy of the local newspaper (e.g. La Verdad) on the Monday before to get the running schedule for the day. We parked out on the East side of town (near the river) and walked the couple of kilometres into town, you don't want to even try to get closer than this with your car. Also be very careful when leaving by car, you may be under the alcohol limit, but not many others will be! If you drive in about 3pm you'll find that the roads coming into town are eerily deserted, everybody's getting some rest before the real partying.

The Romerías (pilgrimage) to the Virgin of the Fuensanta deserve special mention. Twice a year, in spring and September, the Virgin comes to the city from her mountain sanctuary and is accompanied on her journey back from the Cathedral. The September Romería is extremely well attended, as well as historical. It commemorates the solemn coronation of the Virgin. More information at www.turismodemurcia.es/en/Fiestas_in

Hospital: The region's main hospital is to the south west of the city off the Murcia to Caravaca highway, called Arrixaca, between el Palmar and Alcantarilla. There are four other hospitals in the city.

Shopping

El Cortes Inglés (Map: C2) is probably the most famous Spanish department store, along the lines of Debenhams or John Lewis. There are two in the city one on Avenida de la Libertad and the other Gran Vía Escultor Francisco Salzillo. Out of town at El Tirol (near Ikea) a new El Corte Inglés and Hipercor have been built, with free car parking.

There are lots of shops along Gran Vía and its side streets. Also in the streets between Calle el Escultor Salzillo to the west and Calle Saavedra Fajardo. Excellent shoe and clothes shopping as you'd expect in a main modern Spanish city.

Books can be bought at Diego Marín, Merced, 25. Lots of local maps and the Natursport guides (you just need to find them, there appears to be no logic in the shop's layout!). 968 24 28 29, www.diegomarin.com

Maps from La Casa del Mapa, Palacio de las Balsas, Plaza Balzas, 1. Upstairs on the first floor of this local government building you'll enter a mapping paradise, as long as your world revolves around Spain. The map stocks are exhaustive, including all the 1:25,000 topographical / military maps. The only problem with this shop is the opening hours, 9:00 to 14:00 Monday to Friday, only. 968 98 92 46, www.cnig.es

There is a crafts centre at el Centro de Artesania on Calle Francisco Rabal, 8. Excellent furniture and homeware shops at interesting prices surround these narrow streets. www.carm.es

On Barrio del Carmen (near Floridablanca) you can find Armaría Del Carmen (with another outlet in Cartagena near the train station) which sells guns, fishing tackle and scuba gear. There are lots of other good shops in this area too, and it's a great place for a bit of people watching on a Saturday morning.

Around the city there are several branches of Carrefour. There's also Makro to the south. Of course, there are the shopping malls at Thader and Nueva Condomina, the latter containing an Eroski supermarket: see the shopping section for more details. There's also Ikea just on the outskirts of Murcia, exit 763A on the A7 road to Alicante, just north of Murcia city. It's a big one! Check for opening times on their website www.ikea.com

Here's a list of the shopping malls in the Murcia region, listed alphabetically by town.

Centro Comercial Y De Ocio Águilas Plaza, Avenida del Hornillo, Águilas

Centro Comercial Y De Ocio Espacio Mediterráneo, Calle Londres, Polígono Industrial Cabezo Beaza, Cartagena

El Corte Inglés, Alameda San Antón, Cartagena

Parque Comercial Y De Ocio Mandarache, Avenida Ronda Ciudad de La Union, 30, Cartagena

Parque Comercial Y De Ocio Almenara, Camino de en Medio, Campillo, Lorca

Centro Comercial Y De Ocio Las Velas, Calle Catamarán, 1, Los Narejos, Los Alcázares

Centro Comercial Vega Plaza, Avenida de Granada, Molina De Segura

El Corte Inglés, Centro De Liquidación La Serreta, Carretera de Madrid, Cartagena, km377, Molina De Segura

Centro Comercial Atalayas, Calle Molina de Segura, Murcia

Centro De Ocio Zigzag, Avenida Juan Carlos I, Murcia

El Corte Inglés, Avenida. Libertad, 1, Murcia

El Corte Inglés, Gran Vía Escultor Francisco Salzillo, Murcia, www.elcorteingles.es

Parque Comercial La Noria (Outlet), Centro Comercial La Noria Outlet Shopping, km5, La Ñora, Murcia

Parque Comercial Nueva Condomina, Carretera Nacional A-7 Salida D. Juan de Borbón, Churra, Murcia

Parque Comercial Thader, Avenida Juan de Borbón, Churra, Murcia

Centro Comercial Dos Mares, Carretera Nacional 332, Cruce El Mirador, San Javier

There's a large Polígono, good for furniture and building materials to the south west, just off the main road to Caravaca.

Buying cameras and other photo equipment in Murcia isn't cheap compared to on–line places elsewhere in Europe, although at least you will be able to take it back when it goes wrong. Try El Corte Inglés in Murcia for a good selection.

For a huge selection of household electrical, computers, software, DVDs and music you could visit Mediamarkt, Ronda Sur Zona Infante and at Thader. Or for more specialist electronics and electrical bits and pieces (like power supplies for a wireless router) try Electronica RAYTE right opposite the RENFE train station (which is good for parking for Barrio del Carmen and Floridablanca!) at Plaza Industria.

Markets

The main Markets in Murcia are Saavedra Fajardo, Verónicas, La Alberca, Vistabella, El Carmen, San Andrés, Espinardo and Cabezo de Torres.

Close to the Plano de San Francisco, near the old Convento de Verónicas and very close to the Palacio del Almudí, the Paseo del Malecón and the river Segura is the wonderful Verónicas Market.

In the fifteenth century the market was held in the Arenal area, now known as the Plano de San Francisco where at the door of the Customs House taxes were charged on goods arriving and leaving the city. In 1799 there was a fish and supplies market under the columned portico of the Palace of Almudí. In 1850 Juan José Belmonte, in an eclectic style, built a market place which was renovated in 1864 by Jerome Ros. It was demolished in the early twentieth century.

The current building, in sober modernist style, was designed by architect Pedro Cerdan and built between 1912 and 1916. As well as being known as Verónicas market, it is also known as Mercado del Oeste (Western Market) and the Mercado de la Verdura (Vegetable Market).

An important action taken by the architect Daniel Ruiz Carbonell in 1975 allowed the creation of a mezzanine floor, which gave the market a greater number of units and stalls. Subsequently, the building has suffered other reforms designed to adapt to new business needs

The building is a large rectangular hall with a gabled roof. The original façade, Art Nouveau, has remained until today. The two main entrances are made from brick and white stone, with flat disks, diamond points and columns. The side walls have windows for optimum ventilation inside, framed by large arches alternating with red brick pillars.

The mezzanine is built on a reinforced concrete frame independent from the rest of the structure, which allows better use of space. Downstairs there are 116 stalls with another 120 upstairs. The market is always busy, providing a great mixture of fresh produce, fish, meat, seafood, vegetables and fruit. There are bars inside to rest your weary legs. It's open every day in the mornings.

Services

Concejalía de Turismo y Congresos, Calle Los Molinos, Edificio Museo Hidráulico, 968 358600.

There is another at Plaza Cardenal Belluga, 968 358600. There is also a kiosk at Plaza San Francisco, 968 216801. https://turismodemurcia.es/en

The Ayuntamiento on Glorieta de España, 1, 968 358600, www.murcia.es is in an enviable Neo-Classical building, the Casa Consistorial de Murcia (Map: D4).

The main bus station is to the west of centre on Calle Sierra de la Pila, 1 in Barrio San Andrés, 968 292211, wwww.estaciondeautobusesdemurcia.com, Buses go to all Spanish cities and around Europe.

Taxis are by the train and bus stations and at various other places around the city such as Plaza Martinez Tornel, Avenida de la Libertaz and Calle Alfonso X. You can also call for a taxi on 968 248800 or 968 297700.

RENFE Murcia train station, El Carmen, Estación de Ferrocarril de Murcia, 968 252572, www.renfe.es, with trains to Barcelona, Madrid, Alicante and Valencia.

The city is now served by Murcia International Airport, also known locally as Corvera, 25km away. See the airports section for more details.

Sleeping

There's a whole world of hotels, motels, pensions and apartments for rental in the city. We've listed a few that we've tried ourselves or that friends or family have tried. Remember that you have the right to view a room before making a booking and it's often worth the extra few minutes!

At the expensive end of the spectrum there are plenty of four star hotels right in the city.

AC Hotels www.espanol.marriott.com has the splendid and large AC Hotel Murcia on Avenida Juan Carlos I, 39, with a gym, restaurant and swimming pool, in a central location.

NH Hotels has three to choose from for between €40 and €70 per person per night (if you can get a deal, otherwise the prices are really quite high). Hotel Rincón de Pepé on Calle Apóstoles, 34 is right above the Rincón del Pepé Restaurant and the walls of the city bar. The Hesperia Murcia on Calle de la Madre de Dios, 4, is the cheapest of the three. Finally in the business district in the north of the city is NH Amistad Murcia, on Condestable, 1, near El Corte Inglés. 968 282929, www.nh-hotels.com

Hotel Occidental Siete Coronas, Ronda de Garay, 5, right by the river with a great view and good parking, www.barcelo.com, is another chain hotel. You can get some deals from their website.

From €55 per night (if you can get a deal), there's the Hotel Arco de San Juan, Plaza Ceballos, 10, 968 210455, www.arcosanjuan.com. Again very centrally located, with a good restaurant, La Plaza, below.

Hotel Cetino (formerly Hotel Hispano), Calle Radio Murcia, 3, 968 216152, www.hotelcetina.com/ has always been good value and the rooms are more than adequate. It's very close to the cathedral. The lovely Hispano restaurant is directly opposite too.

Hotel Nelva, Avenida Primero de Mayo, 9, 968 060200 www.hotelnelva.es has 250 rooms from €60 per night. It's a large corporate hotel, with a gym, swimming pool, gardens and terrace, right on the main road.

A little more economical would be a pensión or hostal, and again there are plenty to choose from. Pensión Segura on Plaza de Camachos, 19, www.pensionsegura.es, 968 211281, is in a superb location very near the cathedral. Or try Pensión Campoy in Barrio del Carmen on Calle Diego Hernandez, 32, 968 254591.

Outside of the city you can find more rural accommodation along with hotels and pensions. Have a look for Pilar on www.booking.com for comfortable rooms and a garden with a swimming pool for just €50 a night. It's just a short walk from the centre along the Malecón.

In Valladolises there's Casa Veraneo Paraje Cabecicos del Rey 146, 968 060190, www.casa-veraneo.com. A two bedroomed house with a swimming pool, which is very close to the airport.

In La Alberca (6km out of the city) there's a youth hostel, http://reaj.com/albergues/el-valle/, 968 840620, which has a large swimming pool and beds for up to 50 people.

On the motorway between Murcia and Cartagena (campo de Cartagena side of the mountain) there's a great venta, (where we've spent many nights whilst waiting for our house to be finished) called Venta el Puerto in Baños y Mendigo, www.hotelventaelpuerto.com, 968 383061, with excellent value for money rooms and a really good bar and restaurant.

In Monteagudo Pensión Puerto Rico, Calle Rafael Alberti, 2, www.pensionpuertorico.com, 968 850022, offers excellent value rooms right on the main street.

If you need to stay in El Palmar (where the main hospital is located) then try Arrixaca Apartamentos, Calle del General Mola, 968 889065, www.arrixaca.net.

Eating

In Murcia, there are a great number of bars and squares where you can enjoy a delicious appetiser in the open air. The most well-known Murcian tapas include: pisto, zarangollo and la ensalada murciana, all of which are prepared with vegetables from the rich Murcian markets. Some of the most popular bars are El Palomo and Los Toneles, both situated on Calle Cánovas del Castillo, the Pepico del Tío Ginés on Calle Ruipérez, Los Zagales in Calle Polo de Medina, El Patio in Calle Paco and La Parranda situated in Plaza San Juan.

At weekends, the bars serving tapas in Plaza del las Flores, la Plaza Mayor and Alfonso X el Sabio are much frequented. If you want a formal meal there are restaurants in every part of the city where you can find great quality at a fair price.

Location Report: Eating And Drinking

Murcia has a plethora of excellent eateries. If you want a snack, some tapas or a full a la carte menu there's always somewhere great to go. Here are some of our favourites from the last few years.

The lovely El Rincón de Pepe, Apóstoles, 34, www.restauranterincondepepe.com/, does a superb menú de degustación for around €50 per person (wine extra.) Start off in the bar La Muralla in the 8th century Moorish walls below and then head on up to the stylish restaurant, relax and enjoy the seven course menu. Or go a la carte and choose from steaks, fish and traditional Murcian cuisine.

For a good pizza in a beautiful square try Pizzería La Tarantalla, Plaza San Juan. It's unusual to find a good thin crust pizza base outside of Italy, but Tarantalla have a great chef. Their salads are good too, lots of dressing!

If you fancy a bit of a drive before dinner then see if you can find El Cañal Los Almillas, Camino Viejo Gilandario 9, Aljucer near Murcia, http://losalmillas.com/ Whilst it is difficult to find it's worth the effort. It's near a canal that provides water to the huerta. It has a garden area for kids and has excellent food, with the speciality being meat on a hot plate that you cook yourself. They have a good wine cellar too!

If you enjoy your cakes and tarts then try one of the Maite shops, www.confiteriamaite.com littered around the town. There are eight locations in the city where this forty year old coffee shop offers delicious tarts, pastries, chocolate creations and puddings to eat in or take away.

Squeeze in at the counter of Pasteleria Zaher, Riquelme 13, http://pasteleriazaher.es/, a hugely popular pastelería (bakery) and enjoy a Murciano pastel de carne (meat pie) with a glass of cider or red wine. The pies are swooshed along the counter direct from the huge kitchens and sliced in front of you while you jostle for elbow space. The service can be brusque, the décor leaves much to be desired, but the taste of this delicious meat pie will stay with you forever. If you want your pie with a little more panache then try Bonache, www.pasteleriabonache.com, around the corner on Plaza Flores, who have been making pies since 1828.

If you're looking for somewhere to try a good rum and coke, whiskey or gin and tonic then two places spring to mind. There's the rum bar La Roneria, www.la-roneria-y-la-gintoneria.com, on Calle Canovas de Castillo, right near El Rincón de Pepe. Or the Gin Bar right next door to La Tarantalla on Plaza de San Juan. Both bars have a great selection of alcohol from around the world.

After a night listening to jazz, enjoying cocktails in underground bars (La Muralla) and snacking on tapas, stop off for an energy boost at Churros y Chocolate, Plano San Francisco (near the botanical gardens), a great little churros kiosk in Murcia city and a firm favourite amongst revelling Murcianos. Churros are long, thin doughnuts dipped in hot chocolate and are available from midnight to keep you going into the early hours.

A great site at www.atapear.com is devoted to tapas all over Spain. In Murcia city, the best tapas can be found around Plaza de las Flores and Arco de San Juan. Cafés are centred along Gran Vía Alfonso X and Plaza de Santa Domingo.

- Arco, Arco de Santo Domingo, 1, Lots of good specialities, try anchovies with pimientos and potatoes.
- Casino, Calle de la Trapería, 3 course set menu.
- Churra, Marqués de los Vélez, 12. Roast potatoes with garlic, zarangollo (see above) and great puddings.
- Fénix, Plaza de Santa Catalina, 1, Octopus cooked in the oven and caballitos (not the literal translation of little horses, but prawn tails).
- Restaurante Hispano, Calle Radio Murcia 4, opposite Hotel Cetina, http://www.restaurantehispano.es/, really good set menus.
- Mesón de Pepe, Calle Arquitecto Emilio Pérez Piñero, https://www.mesondepepe.es/. Oven cooked lamb.
- Paco Pepe, Madre de Dios, 14. One of the best restaurants in Murcia.
- La Parranda, Plaza de San Juán, http://www.laparranda.es/ Typical Murcian tapas. Local cheese, potatoes with garlic mayonnaise and salads.
- Pepe el Torrao, Ronda Norte, 6. Caballitos (prawn tails), octopus, shellfish Galician style, red prawns from Santa Pola.
- Perela, Calle Ruipérez, 5, Great tapas in a good atmosphere.
- Pepico del Tío Ginés, Calle Ruipérez, 4, http://pepicodeltiogines.es/ good wine from

Jumilla to go with your blayeres, which are rolls stuffed with things.

- Rincón de Pepe, Apóstoles, 34, www.restauranterincondepepe.com/. Excellent quality tapas, including mojama (cured tuna) and other local specialities. Widely reported to be one of the best restaurants in Murcia.
- Taberna de las Mulas, Calle Ruipérez, 7, specialising in goat dishes.
- La Tapa, Plaza de las Flores, 13, Great variety of tortillas and an impressive quantity of tapas.
- Toneles, Canovas del Castillo, 7, mainly vegetarian options, with local produce.

Vegetarian Restaurants in Murcia

El Girasol, Calle San José, 22, 968 217235.

Night Life

Murcia boasts authentic Spanish nightlife centred on the area between Calle Saavedra Fajardo and Museo de Bellas Artes. Late night bars are found around the north end of Gran Vía Alfonso X and its side streets.

A disco bar worth trying is El Perro Azul on Calle Simón García. There's also Fitzpatrick's Irish theme pub on Plaza Cetina. It's also worth trying the Woodstock Rock Bar at Calle Santa Rosalía 2. Look out for live events at https://www.guiadelocio.com/murcia

Jazz can be found at Jazzazza out in Aljezares, http://www.jazzazza.com/ and sometimes at La Muralla del Rincón de Pepe on Calle Cánovas del Castillo.

Around Murcia

The city of Murcia has 443,300 inhabitants (INE 2018), the seventh Spanish municipality by population. However, due to the large extension of the area (881.86km²), population density (488 inhabitants/km²) is far from the highest in Spain. Of the total municipal population around 42% of the people reside in the district capital, with the remainder divided among the 54 districts. Most of these districts have several towns with a total far exceeding 100.

Within the two major areas that divide the city, Campo de Murcia and Huerta de Murcia, it is in the latter where the vast majority of districts (45) and population (93.57% if you include the urban population) reside, with much denser settlements in the Campo de Murcia.

The districts are: La Albatalía, La Alberca, Algezares, Aljucer, Alquerías, La Arboleja, Baños y Mendigo, Barqueros, Beniaján, Cabezo de Torres, Cañada Hermosa, Cañadas de San Pedro, Carrascoy-La Murta, Casillas, Churra, Cobatillas, Corvera, Los Dolores, Era Alta, El Esparragal, Garres y Lages, Gea y Truyols, Guadalupe, Javalí Nuevo, Javalí Viejo, Jerónimo y Avileses, Llano de Brujas, Lobosillo, Los Martínez del Puerto, Monteagudo, Nonduermas, La Ñora, El Palmar, Puebla de Soto, Puente Tocinos, El Puntal, El Raal, Los Ramos, La Raya, Rincón de Beniscornia, Rincón de Seca, San Benito, San Ginés, San José de la Vega, Sangonera la Seca, Sangonera la Verde, Santa Cruz, Santiago y Zaraiche, Santo Ángel, Sucina, Torreagüera, Valladolises y Lo Jurado, Zarandona and Zeneta.

La Alberca, Santo Ángel and Algezares

There are plenty of reasons to visit La Alberca, Santo Ángel and Algezares, especially if you love mountains, climbing, walking, historic buildings, good food and easy access from the city. These three districts sit right next to each other, touching the centre of Murcia, and are accessed to the south of the city.

Castillo De Santa Catalina Del Monte or Verdolay, this fortress is located in a strategic location overlooking the Huerta de Murcia, in the northern foothills of the **Cresta del Gallo**, controlling, therefore, much of the Vega Baja del Segura. It is accessible from the town of Murcia (about 6kms south) towards the famous Sanctuary of Our Lady of the Fuensanta (**Santuario de la Virgen de la Fuensanta**), but taking the road to the hermitage of La Luz. Nearby there's also an interpretive centre for you to find out more about the cultural and natural environment.

Ermita De San Antonio El Pobre, located on the edge of a ravine, with excellent views, there's a small church, the remains of a room and a hermit's cave. The church was built in the eighteenth century as a square plan with chamfered corners, with an outer octagonal. The shrine is attributed to the architect D. Jose Lopez and was built around 1735. Its origins date back to the existence of a hermit named John the Poor, who had great devotion to San Antonio, being closely related to the founding of the Convento de Santa Catalina del Monte.

The chapel was used for a long tradition in Murcia: the blessing of the silkworm. Year after year the hermit carried the seed of the worm to the hermitage of San Antonio to be blessed. The procession and ceremony were held on the first Friday of March.

On the subject of silk, there's a silk museum. **La Exposición Permanente de la Seda** (Permanent Exhibition of the Silk Road) is in an orchard cabin (traditional shack) located at the headquarters of the Peña Huertana la Seda. The exhibition offers visitors the opportunity to see the old ways of life in La Alberca and the traditions and customs of the Huerta del Segura. There are tools, machinery and materials in connection with the rearing of silkworms and its production. Carril De La Villa, La Alberca, 968 847606.

If you fancy a drive through the countryside and up the mountain (there are a few stomach churning turns) try this itinerary. From La Alberca follow the road up to El Valle, then: **La Balsa de El Valle**, recreational area named after the circular pond whose water is used to irrigate the Jardín Botánico de El Arboretum.

The Arboretum, this botanical garden offers the opportunity to view a selection of trees from Spain and around the world. It also has an information point to answer questions regarding this environment. The **Centro de Visitantes de El Valle**, is a mainstay in the management and conservation of the Park and offers a broad perspective on natural and environmental issues.

At **Rambla de El Valle**, see the whole ecosystem, including myrtle, reeds, hackberry and elm. It is also the habitat of species such as the natterjack toad. **Los Viveros Forestales** (Forest Nurseries) is a nursery aimed at the cultivation of plants for reforestation with the main species produced stone pine, Aleppo pine and cypress.

Las Antiguas Canteras (The Old Quarry), Located in the Sierra de la Cresta del Gallo, is a former restored quarry. The **Centro de Recuperación de la Fauna Silvestre** (Wildlife Recovery Center) is managed by the Department of Protection and Conservation of Natural Environment Directorate with the purpose of providing adequate care and treatment for all species of wild animals.

Ermita de San Antonio el Pobre is a Franciscan Property currently restored, built in the eighteenth century, Baroque style. (See earlier for more details). The Convento de Santa Catalina was founded by John Merchant for the Franciscan Friars in the fifteenth century. (See earlier for more details).

Santuario Nuestra Señora De La Fuensanta is the patron saint of Murcia and a shrine is dedicated to her, 6km to the south of the city. From here visitors can enjoy splendid views over the huerta. Leave yourself a good hour to enjoy wandering around up here, as there are actually three buildings to see including the Fuensanta. **Monasterio de las Monjas Benedictinas** was restored in 1950, has a beautiful façade and more rustic walls. La Casa del Cabildo is accessed by a ramp as you come through from the car park, this is in neo-Arabic style, with arches, yellow and red stone work, buttresses and a gabled roof. There's also a bar!

Continuing on, you arrive at **El Valle Natural Park**, areas of which have an almost lunar like appearance. The park is of great geological importance. From the panoramic view point, the **Cresta del Gallo** (The Cock's Crest), which is set at the foot of the peak from which it gets its name, you can enjoy impressive scenery. Continuing along the road you arrive at another vantage viewpoint Columbares which is south facing. The total distance of the excursion is approximately 32km.

The drive is in the Carrascoy Regional Park and El Valle. These mountains aren't actually that high (on this side of the motorway), the highest point is the Pico Columbares at 649 meters. However, the terrain is steep and the hills of the park are crossed by ravines and gullies (Barranco del Sordo, the Rambla del Valle and the Rambla de los Serranos) that create a lunar landscape to the west-east. Large areas of the park have been declared Special Protection Area for Birds (SPA) and Site of Community Importance (SCI), both forms of protection at European level.

The views from up here are stunning. It's worth coming at night too to see the city twinkling below. In the day time you can peek into some large gardens, see tennis courts and swimming pools, luxury houses and Murcians out and about. Bring some binoculars for excellent peeping!

Carrascoy-La Murta

While much of Carrascoy was vacant in the early divisions of land during the 13th century, the name of La Murta, derived from the shrub of the same name (also known as myrtle), can be found in documents from that period referring to the tower of La Murta. Perhaps they were referring to a lookout tower? Taking into account the abundance of small fortresses and watchtowers built in Islamic times this could be the case. Though so far we haven't found the tower ourselves!

After many hundreds of years of ownership changes, in 1969 the population of Carrascoy was at its highest, with a total of 401 inhabitants. But the reality of a large area of dry land, surrounded by rugged geography, dedicated only to crops or a livestock industry that disappeared over the years, has only the single core Carrascoy village, La Murta, with just over a hundred people.

La Murta has one of two astronomical observatories that exist in the Region of Murcia. The observatory is managed by the city of Murcia and the **Astronomical Society of the Region of Murcia**. This building, with a dome diameter of five meters manufactured in the United States, contains a Meade telescope, a 16-inch Schmidt Cassegrain. This is one of the most technologically advanced telescopes used in many international observatories and ready to give great results, not just for academics but also in scientific research.

You get to the observatory by following the road out of Corvera towards La Murta, and then about ½ kilometre outside the village you'll see signs to the right, follow the dirt road up! At the moment it seems that visits are hard to come by but who knows what the future holds. Perhaps they will begin again.

La Murta is in the Carrascoy natural park. The predominant tree species are conifers, with numerous specimens of pine, Aleppo pine and some oak. Along with the trees there are a wide range of shrubs such as juniper, saw palmetto, broom, pigeon pea and black hawthorn. Around La Murta there are almonds, carob and olive trees. In the Rambla you'll also find oleander, tamarisk and baladre. The scrubland has a variety of plants such as rosemary, thyme, esparto, horehound, cat's claw, white rock rose, broom and reeds.

SWEET SMELL OF SUCCESS: Every few months the Spanish army use the Carrascoy Mountains as their base for training camps. They bring the young, enthusiastic men and women up and dump them in the mountains and expect them to find their way back to base camp (whilst the trainers enjoy a pie in the village). The new recruits often end up near our house, wandering down our road in ones and twos, looking cold, lost and hungry. If we're walking the dogs we can usually spot them minutes before they notice us. The smell of their Paco Raban, Hugo Boss and Glo by JLo precede them by a mile.

The continuous mountain landscape provides nests and breeding grounds for a variety of birds and animals. Most common are blackbird, wood pigeon, dove and robin. More unusual are the bee-eaters, nightingales, partridges, woodpeckers, goldfinches, kestrels, thrushes, little owls and birds of prey such as eagle, peregrine falcon, golden eagle and owl.

Reptiles include long-tailed lizards or Iberian ocellated lizards, frogs, Montpellier snakes and horseshoe snakes (the cats bring these home now and then for us to have a closer look).

Among mammals there are foxes, wild boars, rabbits, hares, hedgehogs, badgers, martens and weasels.

The fiesta is in honour of Santa Cruz, the Holy Cross and is celebrated around the 3rd of May. Usually the weekend before the 3rd of May they begin partying, leading up to the holy day. The always have a rociero and a giant paella. Local food is typical of the area, rice and vegetable based, with plenty of meat.

They also excel in making michirones. Desserts are special too, flores (flower shaped deep fried pastry) and nueces (dough balls dripping in syrup). La Murta has three bakeries (yes, three for 100 people!) that export their bread to many restaurants in the region. You'll often find the local police making a middle of the night visit to try the just baked bread (for quality control of course).

If you want to try out some of the La Murta recipes and learn Spanish at the same time get: Spanish Village Cooking – *Recetas Del Campo*. It is written in Spanish and English, with more than 80 photographs, 150 traditional Murcian dishes from 35 local cooks. These recipes have been handed down through generations, grandmother to mother to daughter, making use of local, homegrown ingredients and traditional cooking methods.

Buy your copy, or gift it: www.Native-Spain.com or Amazon.

Corvera

Sheltered by the Sierra de Carrascoy and 20 kilometres from the capital of Murcia is the village of Corvera, one of the locations that are known as Campo de Murcia. Corvera is probably more famous for its recently opened new international airport.

Corvera celebrates in honour of the Virgen del Rosario at the beginning of October, when residents recover the old traditions of the massacres of pigs, sausage making and eating migas. And more importantly having fun together!

Corvera Golf and Country Club can be found here, http://corveragolfandcountryclub.com/, with its 18 hole course.

Sunday morning is market day and Corvera can get busy. The market is in the main square and has all the usual tat as well as good food stalls.

There are plenty of restaurats to choose from. For an excellent menú del día with plenty of choice and large portions then El Perillas on the main street is your best bet. A favourite is Las Palmeras, right by the fountain in the town square. They're open every day except Tuesday and this family run business offers excellent traditional tapas, menú del día and Sunday lunches. For a drink try the garden at El Portón. There's an English-run bar at the top end of town, near the petrol station, 62 Corvera. They have live music, quiz nights and fish and chips! www.62corvera.com

Guadalupe and La Ñora

Along with the hamlet of La Ñora, Guadalupe is home to the monastery of Jeronimos (Monasterio de San Jerónimo), sometimes called the Escorial of Murcia. It's a large building with a polygonal dome and sturdy exterior columns at the corners. The interior is richly decorated with carvings and stained glass. It was built between 1705 and 1738, in the Baroque style. Carretera de Guadalupe, 135.

Interestingly the paprika pepper was introduced into Spain from the New World by Christopher Columbus in 1493 and offered up to the Catholic Kings in the Monastery of Guadalupe. It was probably the monks of the Jeronimos Monastery which spread the crop to each of their convents. This is why the name for the dried red peppers is La Ñora.

One reason to visit La Ñora is to go shopping in the discount factory outlet. They have a Nike shop, sunglasses, Desigual, Zara and many other brand name outlets at factory prices. When you come off the motorway you'll see the shopping area, just follow the signs.

Javalí Viejo

One of the most interesting things about Javalí Viejo is the gunpowder factory. Even though it's an industrial facility it is a beautiful building, with stone pillars and columns and crowned with the royal arms of Isabel II. To the right of the factory is the chapel of Santa Bárbara, patroness of the artillery corps.

The **Fábrica Nacional de Pólvora Santa Bárbara** (gunpowder factory) was installed by Royal Order on July 1st 1747. The long life of the plant has not been without serious accidents that claimed the lives of many workers and military personnel. Before the Civil War, between 1916 and 1931, the workshop was expanded and they began the production of nitrocellulose and nitro-glycerine powder.

Monteagudo

The town of Monteagudo is located 4km northeast of Murcia city. The most distinguishing thing about Monteagudo is the hill, an unmistakable landmark on the landscape that you'll see if you drive in from Alicante airport.

Ancient civilizations chose the slopes of the hill as a place of pilgrimage or settlement. King Lobo (King Wolf) structured a series of forts to protect the city of Murcia, the **Castillo de Monteagudo,** Castillejo and Larache, in the 12th century.

The strategic **Cerro de Monteagudo** with its splendid view of the Vega Baja del Segura and its proximity to the capital city explains the continuous settlement here since the Neolithic period. The slopes of Cerro de Monteagudo have revealed evidence of Argaric, Iberian and Roman times. In the last century the **Monument of the Sacred Heart of Jesus** (Jesus with arms stretched, which can be seen for miles) was built on top of the hill, completing this unmistakable landmark.

Monteagudo Castle fits the land on which it stands and takes advantage of the defensive elements of the hill. It is divided into two distinct areas, one around the bottom of the peak which has 12 towers, square or rectangular, and the other is the castle itself, without the keep or courtyard, of which 5 towers are preserved. The castle is characterised by its reddish colour from the mud with which it was built. The mud gets harder with the passage of time, like cement.

It is not possible to climb up to the statue today as it is unsafe to do so and the access routes are fenced off. Instead, you can visit the Monteagudo Visitor Centre alongside the San Cayetano church at the foot of the hill. This has been built to allow you to explore the history of the hill, its prehistoric roots and Islamic foundations. Closed on Mondays, it welcomes visitors Tuesday to Saturday 09:30 – 14:00 and 17:00 – 19:30, and Sundays 10:00 – 14:00.

Fiestas in honour of San Cayetano Monteagudo are held between the last days of July and first week of August. The fiesta program is a mix of religious and civic events including a solemn procession with the image of the Virgin of Antigua and San Cayetano in the streets of the town and a fun parade of floats, in which Monteagudeños take to the streets with many different costumes. www.monteagudo.info/

El Palmar

El Palmar is located 5km from the city. In the Puerto de la Cadena (the motorway that goes over the mountain, N301), the natural route of transportation between the Vega del Segura and Cartagena, traces of various civilizations have been found. El Palmar is a natural epicentre of trade for Murcia.

Talking about the motorway over the mountain, as you reach the highest point you may have noticed a fortress. This is the **Castillo de la Asomada** located in a strategic place at 532m above sea level. It looks a little like the hill from the film Close Encounters from a distance.

The construction of the fortress was directly connected to the control of this route. Current access to the castle is made at kilometre 407 on the N301; follow the country road for about two kilometres, then detour to the right for 700 meters to get to the bottom of Cabeza del Puerto. Then walk to the summit, where incidentally you'll find a geocache placed by us (see geocaching section).

The building has its origins in the Islamic period, probably around the twelfth century. Its construction clearly reflects the control of space and communications between the coast and the interior kingdom. On the other side of the motorway you'll see another fortress, el Portazgo.

The city of El Palmar has some pretty buildings, but the traffic and poor parking make it difficult to enjoy. In the early twentieth century the Bernal family, the most wealthy family in El Palmar, built on Calle Major an elegant Art Nouveau mansion that today serves as the cultural centre of the town. In 1910, the Bernal family also built the theatre, Teatro Bernal, www.teatrobernal.com, on Calle Lorca, 63, 968 882329, that has an interesting program of events throughout the year.

El Palmar is a service town for the city of Murcia and has the Hospital Psiquiátrico Román Alberca (Psychiatric hospital) and the Ciudad Sanitaria Virgen de la Arrixaca (A&E and major teaching hospital). www.murciasalud.es

Ojós

Population: 500

Map Reference: 1.34°W, 38.15°N

The name comes from the Arabic word Oxox which means ambrosia of the gardens. Gradually the population of the town is reducing. The landscape is characterised by the citrus orchards, fruit trees and large palm trees that rise and stand above the horizon in an environment surrounded by mountains. The Segura River cuts through here, leaving the town in a deep valley with steep sides.

Among the interesting buildings is the parish church, Moorish style, and dedicated to St. Augustine, dating from 1505. It contains treasures of the Eucharist, Salzillo inspired imagery, including: the crucified Lord, The Nazarene, The Sorrow and the Golden Goblet.

On the Ojós and Mula road is the **Embalse del Mayés** (a dam) suitable for camping and fishing for catfish. In the gorge El Solvente is a dam that channels water from the

Tagus-Segura to be distributed by irrigation canals.

El Salto de la Novia is another area of great beauty that is part of the municipality, which has built a small tunnel on the highway through town. Near the village there are two bridges over the river, next to one of them there is an artificial geyser, the Paseo de las Palmeras.

The town's economy was based on agriculture, the cultivation of citrus fruits such as orange or lemon, although in recent years, is encouraging rural tourism with the addition of new accommodation.

Sleeping

There are a few casas rurales around, notably, the houses belonging to El Valle De Ricote, 650 504920, www.elvalledericote.com who have four houses in the area.

Pliego

Population: 3,900

Map Reference: 1.51°W, 37.99°N

Pliego is in the valley of Mula, between the sierras of Ricote and the Espuña, with five miles of riverbanks and springs.

There are two castles, **Castillo de las Paleras and Castillo de Pliego**, both built in the 12th century. The remains of the Castillo de las Paleras are located on a small hill on the right bank called Barranco de La Mota. You can get there easily from the centre of the town, but you cannot access the inside of the enclosure or the top of the hill. All that remains are the ramparts and some parts of the walls of this Islamic origin castle. The view over the valley is worth the trip.

The Castillo de Pliego is a little more castle like, there's a tower and walls visible. Again access is through the old part of town.

The fourteenth century **Torre del Reloj** stands on the corner of Federico Servet and Calle del Reloj, a tall clock tower crowned with a single bell. A little further on there's **Los Caños**, a sundial, probably used to keep track of the water irrigation usage.

Visit the village of **Mudejar** embedded in the old town, which includes Islamic rural farmsteads. Also in the old town you can enjoy sights such as St. James Church built in 1667 and declared a National Monument, Casa de la Tercia, La Casa del Poeta Federico Balart and the Ermita de la Virgen de los Remedios.

Pliego is superb for mountain sports such as hiking, climbing, mountain biking and caving. There are at least 3 mountains over 500m, Alto de la Muela (504m), Cairel (601m) and Alto de Almoloya (561m). Pliego also has the extensive forest areas in the northern slopes of the Sierra Espuña Regional Park.

There's also an olive oil museum, **El Museo de la Almazara Santiaguista**. The word mill, almazara, comes from Arabic and means 'place where it is squeezed'. Well the place where it is squeezed is right in the centre of Pliego town, originally used to make oil it is now only a museum, showing the whole process. The Phoenicians and Muslims started the squeezing process and very little has changed since their invention.

Location Report:
Vías Pecuarias And The Transhumance Routes

Pliego, in the Sierra Espuña, lies on one of the transhumance routes, used until recently to move livestock from summer to winter pastures. These Vías Pecuarias are road networks of historical importance that serve the mass transfer of livestock around the Iberian Peninsula. Transhumance is the ancient custom of moving domestic animals from one grazing ground to another, from lowlands to highlands, with the changing of seasons; sheep, cattle and goats have all been involved in this annual domestic migration process

Moors introduced Merino sheep during the 8th century and their Berber shepherding methods allowed Spain to gain a monopoly on the fine quality wool, which, over the last six centuries has become one of its most important industries. Herds are moved early in the spring, both to take advantage of the fresh grass and to avoid the summer heat, but also because most farms do not have enough pasture for large flocks.

For centuries farmers have burned their fields after harvest to remove dead and depleted vegetation as well as to reduce the acidity of the soil. This custom promoted the regeneration of nutrient-rich grasslands for their animals, as well as fallow time for croplands to recover. Practices such as transhumance lessened the stress to the soil caused by overgrazing.

These drovers' roads in the region of Murcia act as genuine ecological corridors that intertwine 15 natural areas and are of great strategic value in the exploitation of natural resources and regional planning. The region of Murcia has preserved a large number of them; you'll see large billboards announcing their presence as you drive around.

There's a Friday market with food stuffs along Avenida de Mula and Calle San Benito and clothes, household wares etc. on Calle Mayor and Juan de La Cierva. Throughout the year there's an artisanal market, look on the ayuntamiento website for dates (usually around Christmas, Easter and fiestas).

Pliego enjoys a few fiestas, La Candelaria on February 2nd, which is the feast of the Presentation of the Virgin in the Temple. All mothers who have had a child within that year come to the Parish Church to present the child to the Virgin.

Of course Easter is well and truly celebrated, with the highlight on Friday night with the procession of the Holy Burial, showing carvings by Sánchez Lozano.

Finally there's the festival of San Marcos, which takes place on April 25th with the recitation of thirty-three different faiths and a meal in the mountains.

Services

Ayuntamiento, www.pliego.org

Turismo, www.pliego.org/turismo.html, 968 666321.

Sleeping

Camping De Pliego on the Pliego to Alhama de Murcia road has space for caravans, tents and also a wooden house. Contact the ayuntamiento for more info.

There are plenty of casas rurales around, try Casa Huerta Pinada 1 and Pinada 2 on Paraje El Prado, 968 667288. These restored houses provide accommodation for up to 10 people. www.huertapinada.com. They have a large covered swimming pool and a smaller pool, a small cave-house area, lovely gardens including a play area for children and barbecue area.

Or Villa Arribaon Camino de la Hoya, www.villaarriba.com, 968 667220 a small reformed house with a swimming pool. Or Casa Verde, Camino Olivar, 679 900302, www.casaverdecocon.blogspot.com which can sleep up to 8 people and has a lovely swimming pool.

Eating

Restaurante Los Escudos on Calle Los Pasos seems to be a good choice. Specialises in seafood and homemade desserts!

Portmán

Population: 1,000

Map Reference: 0.85°W, 37.59°N

South of the municipality of La Unión at the foot of the mining area of the Sierra of Cartagena-La Union in a bay washed by the Mediterranean Sea lies the tiny town of Portmán.

It has a very rugged topography surrounded by mountains, in the north lies the hill of Sancti Spiritu at 434 meters, Fortuna and Lajas hills to the south, to the west El Pino (271 meters) and La Gallera (177m), whose slopes plunge into the Mediterranean Sea and to the east is the la peña del Águila (387m) and las Cenizas (307m) integrated in the regional park Calblanque.

The mountains offer brilliant walks and an abundance of wildlife. The PR4 (Murcia-Cartagena) cuts through here from Portmán to El Llano del Beal (Cartagena). It's 6.5km and takes 2 to 3 hours each way. It's an easy route but avoid getting too close to wells in mining area (be careful not to leave the trail).

Take a walk around the **Batería de la Chapa** on the mount of las Cenizas, near the Portmán lighthouse. This is just one of the many fortifications around the coastline, with the goal of protecting and defending the coast and the entrance to the bays of Portmán and Cartagena

Portmán became a strategic site in Roman times and there are numerous remains of Roman mining operations and industrial facilities for the smelting of mineral throughout the area. With the new mining boom in the middle of the nineteenth century a period of growth and prosperity ensued.

Huerto Del Paturro, northeast of the Portmán bay is a major archaeological site with a rich Roman villa. They've found mosaics, stucco, ceramics and black-glaze pottery.

For many years Portmán's economy relied on mining and fishing. Many job opportunities in the service and tourist sector were created along with La Manga Club.

Numerous events and festivities are celebrated throughout the year. The fiesta in honour of its patron Santiago Apóstol on 25th July, the traditional maritime procession of the Virgen del Carmen on July 16th Carnival and Easter.

Sadly what Portmán is most known for today is the pollution of its beautiful bay. Since the beginning of its operation in 1957 the French company Peñarroya-Spain produced huge amounts of mineral debris resulting from the extraction methods used to open pits as a way to cut costs. It's estimated that some 315 million tonnes of waste ore were created between 1957 and 1987, when the mines closed. At first this debris was deposited at the bottom of the quarry, forming large dumps and swamps, which have destroyed the original landscape of the Sierra. However, the biggest problem came from waste from the washing of rocks to obtain the minerals.

It has become something of a political minefield, with successive governments promising to clear up the mess and then not coming through. Whilst some work has been done, it stopped in late 2018 and shows no sign of starting again.

Despite this, it's a nice spot to linger by the beach. The fishing port is quite pretty if you can ignore the industrial clean-up area behind it. There are a couple of options for lunch or a drink too with El Cubano and Chiringuito El Lastre well attended on nice days.

Puerto Lumbreras

Population: 15,000

Map Reference: 1.81°W, 37.56°N

Continuing west from Lorca you reach the town of Puerto Lumbreras, the final town in Murcia. Puerto Lumbreras is a relatively new municipality in the Region of Murcia, created in 1958 after independence from Lorca. However, the foundation of the population goes back to prehistory. Its location between the Andalusía and Murcia border makes it an obligatory passing place for goods and visitors.

Despite the name Puerto Lumbreras is not by the sea and it isn't a sea port. It's around 25km from the sea. Originally the inhabitants of Puerto Lumbreras lived mainly in hill caves and there's plenty of evidence of this as you travel around.

The 18th century church, **Iglesia Parroquial de Nuestra Señora Del Rosario** is found on the main street through town surrounded by houses. It has a Latin cross with a nave and two aisles.

Castillo Nogalte can be found on a mountain ridge at the southern edge of the Sierra de la Torrecilla which overlooks the right bank of the spectacular Rambla Nogalte. This hill is also known as Castellar.

The fort and its surroundings have undergone a series of renovations designed to restore and rehabilitate the building and the cave houses which are under it. They have also improved access, so from town you can go by car to the foot of the castle.

This is an interesting fortress that has its origin in an undetermined point in the last centuries of Islamic rule, possibly the 12th century. The cavehouses are also interesting to see.

The **Visitor Center at Nogalte Castle** is located at the top of Cerro Castellar. The restoration of some of the cave houses at the foot of the Castle led to the creation of the visitor centre. If you like mooching about in cavehouses this is a great, intact example. www.turismopuertolumbreras.es/

This is a great area for outdoor pursuits. You can clearly differentiate two types of landscapes: the mountains, the highest mountain being Cabezo de la Jara (1,242 meters), the Sierra de Enmedio and Peñas de Bejar; and the valley, which includes the plains of Esparragal and between Cabezo de la Jara and the Sierra de Enmedio there's Puerto Adentro. The rambla Nogalte sits between them.

The Rambla Nogalte has not always been an ally of Puerto Lumbreras. The provision of drainage and runoff make it very prone to violent floods. The rambla was used for markets and festivals, but on October 19th 1973 it was the scene of a tragedy when a sudden flash flood swept away the neighbours gathered there. The death toll exceeded one hundred.

Today, the old roads have been transformed into the Mediterranean Highway E-15 and A-92 North. Whilst the bypass has reduced the number of visitors to the town the construction of this modern Mediterranean motorway brought the correction of the streams and the loss of the danger from the rambla.

Enjoy the landscape and take a hike. The website: www.turismopuertolumbreras.es has a downloadable walking guide with some interesting circular walks in the area. Click on 'Publicaciones' then find the "Excursiones".

You can go horse riding just a few miles down the road over in Almería at www.finca-cerro-caballero.com

Puerto Lumbreras has three other districts, El Esparragal, Puerto Adentro and Cabezo de la Jarra. The landscape is similar in each district.

In **Cabezo de la Jarra** you'll find the observatory. The **Astronomical Observatory of Cabezo de la Jara** opened on June 21st 2002 and is situated at a height of 800m on top of the hill of the same name. The Centre has an area of 80m2, consists of a nave with a vaulted dome and observation room where there is a MEADE Reflector Telescope LX 200. The dome is located at one end of the room forming the main body of the centre. The last Saturday of each month is an open day, but you must request a visit in advance. Cabeza de la Jara, 646096487.

Their fiesta patronale is held in the first weeks of October in honour of Nuestra Señora del Rosario. They have a very active agenda of music, culture, mass and parties.

Services

Ayuntamiento: www.puerto-lumbreras.com

Turismo: www.turismopuertolumbreras.es, 968 436153

Sleeping

If you never want to lose your hotel then stay at Sercotel Hotel Riscal, www.hotelriscal.com on the A7 exit 580, 968 402050. You'll spot this one from a few miles away with its brightly painted outside walls. Some call it the Lego Hotel and it's easy to see why. Don't let this put you off, it's good value and clean and modern.

If you prefer a youth hostel then try the Albergue on Cabezo de la Jara near the observatory on 646 775737.

There are no options in town as everything seems to have closed in recent years including the Parador.

Eating

There are plenty of bars and restaurants in town plus a few pizza places. Hotel Riscal has a restaurant, Restaurante Riscal, which is worth a look.

Puerto de Mazarrón

Population: 10,800 (2012)

Map Reference: 1.26°W, 37.59°N

Not to be confused with Mazarrón, this seaside town is the centre of much of the tourism on the south coast and Mediterranean. Puerto de Mazarrón is 70 kilometres from the regional capital and 6km from the town of Mazarrón. For more information on Mazarrón and other towns in this area see the Mazarrón section.

Middle Palaeolithic remains have been found in the vicinity of **Cabezo del Faro**, but it's the seabed which has the richest archaeological heritage. Buried a few miles from the coast, there were two Phoenician ships anchored in these waters during the seventh century.

The discovery and excavation of these ships, at Playa de las Isla, has seen a revolution in the understanding of prehistoric shipbuilding. The site was discovered in 1988 thanks to a survey made by the **National Research Center for Underwater Archaeology** who documented large amounts of ceramic material. Shortly afterwards they discovered a wooden structure and began to systematically excavate the area.

Although the site is not open to the public you can access the results of the excavations in the National Museum of Underwater Archaeology in Cartagena (see Cartagena section for details), which showcases a wide range of ceramic items found during the survey and excavations. The two ships are still in the process of extraction, consolidation, restoration and adaptation for exhibition at the museum.

You can also see artefacts at **Centro de Interpretación del Barco Fenicio**, including replicas of the Phoenician ship and old documents. The centre has 60 square meters, equipped with the latest techniques in sound, touch screens and panoramic video projection. Visiting hours 10:00 to 13:00 and 17:00 to 20:00, an hour later on summer evenings. It's closed on Mondays. Entrance is free.

Punta de Gavilanes is located between the beaches of Bahia and La Pava and is a fenced off area of archaeological interest. It has a stratigraphic sequence of vertical and horizontal walls ranging from the likely start in the first half of the fourth century. It was used as a burial place. Human occupation of this area goes back to the beginning of the second millennium.

Going Native:
Paul and Gill Clarke on 'A Place in the Sun'

Gill and I have had a very long-held ambition to live in Spain. We did lots of research to find somewhere with opportunity for walks, local attractions, and close to towns, cities and places of interest. We also wanted to be amongst Spanish residents and embrace their culture and cuisine.

After watching hundreds of episodes we wrote to *A Place in the Sun*. They invited us for a screen test which went well, and the next thing we were off to our chosen area, with Jonnie Irwin as presenter, hunting properties with our budget of £45,000.

The programme was an excellent experience. When we filmed in Puerto de Mazarrón, in the middle of a down pour, Gill told me this was where she wanted to be. Watching her expression to camera it was very clear she had found what she had been looking for, and so had I. We discussed it in more detail, and it was the sea in front of us, the long paseo, the marina, the light house, the people and the varied restaurants that captured us.

The final shoot with the offer on a property was from El Faro (the lighthouse) looking over the port, breathtaking views, with a drink in your hand and our paradise in front of you. Our offer was declined even though it was within five percent of the budget, but in hindsight it was for the best, we had got carried away in the excitement. The next day with an agent we looked at an apartment in Bahia and as Gill walked into the property (which needed a lot of updating) she wanted it and the rest is history.

We purchased in the June and then flew out in August for the first time and spent the whole fortnight painting - yes painting in the heat. The next time we flew out in the October Gill decided she would practice ordering the food in Spanish. I still get the giggles remembering fourteen tapas turning up, including octopus, which we'd never eaten before! We pretended we knew what we were doing, but I don't think the waiter was convinced.

Bahia Beach is perfect, with stunning views. It's so easy to travel around, the scenery is breathtaking, the people are welcoming and we've started to be known by the local residents. We have loads of opportunities to explore and eat really healthily. We frequently walk along the paseo or stop for a drink in El Faro and sit and watch the scenery and the people (never get bored of people watching). We've tried all the different restaurants. We often eat at Vigos as it's good food, nice staff and great to sit near the marina. Cartagena is wonderful to visit and steeped in history. You need to go a few times to explore it all and then go back for more. There are some lovely walks at the end of the beach at La Azohia with spectacular views.

I don't think we would do much differently, we knew where we wanted to be, our budget, what we didn't want and went for it. It was a gamble but nothing is straightforward, and the time was right, if we had left it we would have spent the money on something else and never seized the moment. If you sit down and have a coffee in any area of Mazarron someone will start a conversation and tell you not to tell anyone else how good this place is because they don't want it spoilt.

The only challenge we face is the language, which we are learning. We tried to learn too fast at first to integrate whilst on holiday which wasn't practical. When we had work men it was brilliant because they taught us and we taught them. Our advice for people looking at Spain is to do your research, have an idea beforehand of what works for you and what doesn't, spend time in different seasons and really immerse yourself. The Murcia region is vast and has so much to offer, beautiful landscapes, plenty of open space, opportunities to explore, great food and great people.

Next for us is to look to move permanently to Murcia, to explore our bit of paradise further, in more detail and with much more time to do so. Gill is going to start blogging when we move out to Murcia which will include where we have been and what we got up to. Gill is a natural in front of camera. Watch out for her work!

Under the iron factory in the central section is a large elongated room, bounded by straight walls erected by stone plinths stuck in mud, of which parts of some of the blocks have fallen to the floor.

Another museum, **Museo Arqueológico Factoría Romana de Salazones**, the old Roman Salting Factory, can be found near San Gines La Torre del Puerto. If you like fish then this fish factory will be of interest! As well as providing interesting historical and archaeological artefacts, this museum includes a large industrial complex from the 4th and 5th century for cleaning, cutting and salting fish. The rest of the factory runs under the present streets of the village, adjacent to the museum. The factory was discovered in 1976 whilst making the foundations of a building. Open 10:00 to 13:00 and 17:00 to 20:00, and an hour later on summer evenings. Closed on Mondays. Normal entry rate is €2.50.

The **Paseo Marítimo** is an attractive promenade providing pedestrian access to the beaches and has many shops, bars, restaurants and ice-cream parlours. Traffic access is strictly regulated and the Paseo is a pleasant area to stroll at any time of the day or night.

If you fancy a slightly more strenuous walk then **El Sagrado Corazón de Jesús del Puerto de Mazarrón** (The Sacred Heart of Puerto de Mazarrón) is located on the hill with El Faro at El Monte de Santa Catalina.

It was built through the initiative of a neighbourhood council, which raised the money needed for its construction, and was inaugurated in June 1948. These sculptures, Jesus with his arms outstretched, are found in most Catholic countries. The road leading up to the statue is the **Subida del Faro Manuel Acosta**, then Avenida de Maro Santo and ends at the lighthouse. From here it's an easy walk up to the statue where you can get great views and photo opportunities. There's even a very welcome heladería!

If you're into geocaching (see the geocaching section if you don't know what this means) then there's even a hidden treasure to find. Search for El Sagrado Corazón de Jesús on the geocaching.com website for details.

Talking about the lighthouse, **El Faro** is worth a visit in itself. It is located 60 meters above the water level on top of a promontory overlooking the entrance to the port and the bay.

The main economy of the region is fishing, agriculture and of course tourism. The most important crop is tomatoes and you'll see a sea of tomato greenhouses as you drive around the area. They also produce melons, lettuces, watermelons, cucumbers and peppers. Fishing in the area has increased and many fish farms have been opened, especially near el Alamillo. However it's the tourism section that mainly supports the economy.

Beaches

There are good beaches as you head out of town (North East) and all along the coast towards Águilas, in fact 35km of them (just a small part of the 250km of coastline in the Costa Cálida)! There are also loads of great dive schools based around here, and brilliant dive locations.

- Playa de Bolnuevo: 1600m, urban, high occupancy, golden sand, moderate waves, anchoring, parking, bus, SOS, rescue, Club Náutico de Mazarrón.
- Playa de Raya: 350m, isolated, low occupancy, vegetation, pebbles, waves, anchoring, parking, bus, toilet, showers, Club Náutico de Mazarrón.
- Playa de Bahía: 190m, urban, high occupancy, golden sand, calm waters, rescue, parking, bus, disabled access, toilets, showers, anchoring, next to Club Náutico de Mazarrón.
- Playa de Nacres: 400m, urban, high occupancy, golden sand, calm waters, parking, bus, toilet, showers, anchoring, next to Club Náutico de Mazarrón.
- Playa El Castellar: 1200m, urban, high occupancy, sand-gravel, moderate waves, parking, bus, toilet, showers, anchoring, next to Club Náutico de Mazarrón.
- Cala Amarillo: 110m, isolated, nudist protected area, vegetation, sand-banks, calm waters, anchoring, parking, bus, Club Náutico de Mazarrón.
- Playa de la Grúa: 85m, protected area, vegetation, unspoiled, isolated, nudist, anchoring, parking, bus, Puerto Deportivo de Mazarrón.
- Cala de Covaticas: 1,000m, isolated, low occupancy, moderate waves, anchoring, parking, bus, Club Náutico de Mazarrón.
- Playa del Ballenato: 200m, isolated, untouched, low occupancy, sand-gravel, moderate waves, near the Club Náutico de Mazarrón.
- Playa de Percheles: 300m, isolated, golden sand, moderate waves, anchoring, parking, bus, near Club Náutico de Mazarrón.
- Playa La Pava: 100m, urban, high occupancy, golden sand and moderate waves, parking, bus, toilet, showers, anchoring, Club Náutico de Mazarrón.
- Playa Junta de Dos Mares: 400m, urban, high occupancy, golden sand, calm waters, parking, bus,

toilet, showers, anchoring, disabled access, next to Club Náutico de Mazarrón.

Club Náutico de Mazarrón is on Calle Paseo de la Sal, 609360260.

Mazarrón Club De Regatas is a little further along the coast near Playa de Bahia, 968 594011.

If you fancy some time under the water try one of the many dive schools.

Buceo Mazarrón, Puerto de Mazarrón, PADI and BSAC, 968 154078, www.buceoenmazarron.es

Centro de buceo del Sureste, in the port at Playa de Bahia, www.buceosureste.com, 656 957270.

Buceo Hispania, 968 153828, www.buceohispania.com

Fiestas

They enjoy their fiestas down here in the port. On the evening of the 5th January there's Reyes Magos (the day of the three Wisemen) celebrated all around Spain. In Puerto de Mazarrón the Reyes Magos arrive by boat and parade through the main streets handing out toys to the children. The nativity play of the Reyes Magos is celebrated the following day.

Around 19th March there's San José (Saint Joseph). Celebrations start up to a week before with verbenas (open-air celebrations), sporting activities, fallas (giant statue) and giant satirical dolls representing the events of the last year.

From the start of July to the end of August there are sporting and cultural activities, and musical performances taking place almost daily.

Around 16th July they celebrate for the Virgen del Carmen. Dozens of boats decorated with multicoloured flags accompany the virgin during the procession. The 15th August is Asunción de la Virgen with the usual sporting and cultural activities.

17th November sees the Fiestas del Milagro (Miracle festivals) in Bolnuevo and Puerto de Mazarrón. The Sunday before the 17th they take the Patron Saint La Purísima from Bolnuevo to Mazarrón; the Sunday after they take her back to her hermitage in Bolnuevo. During this week acts such as the ofrenda floral (floral offering) to the virgin, processions and religious activities take place.

The Sunday of La Romería (the pilgrimage), Moor and Christian parades take place, commemorating the Moorish invasion of the coast when the virgin miraculously interceded, expelling the Algerians.

On 4th December the Santa Bárbara Procession goes to the mining area.

Services

Tourist Office, Plaza Toneleros, 968 594426, www.visitamazarron.com

Location Report: Bahía De Mazarrón

Mazarrón Bay covers the area between Cabo de Cope and Cabo Tiñoso and belongs to the municipalities of Cartagena, Mazarrón, Lorca and Águilas. It has an area of approximately 49 kilometres of coastline, 16 kilometres of which are urbanised, occupied by resorts like Bolnuevo, Puerto de Mazarrón, Isla Plana or San Ginés and old fishing ports such as La Azohía.

This coastline around Puerto de Mazarrón is one of the most significant natural areas of Europe and the largest expanse of undeveloped coastline of the Iberian Peninsula in the Mediterranean Sea. The park, along with the bordering areas of Almenara and the Sierra de las Herrerías is the habitat of vulnerable species and the perfect place for the reintroduction of endangered species like the Iberian lynx, the monk seal, the imperial eagle and vulture.

There are endangered species including the tortoise, eagle, Iberian skink, natterjack toad, marbled teal, the white-headed duck, curlew, the storm petrel, the big-eye mouse-eared bat and the Greater Horseshoe bat. Looking to the water, in the Mediterranean sea the following are also endangered: loggerhead turtle, common and bottlenose dolphins, sperm and fin whales.

The whole area south of the bay is covered by four interrelated natural areas, the area of Calnegre, Lomo de Bas, Marina de Cope and Cabo de Cope and protected under the guise of a regional park (in 2001 there began a plan to develop the area of Marina de Cope, currently in the hands of the Constitutional Court, see the Águilas section for more details). Inland it includes the Rambla Ramonete, the Llanos de Ifre, Sierra de las Herrerías, Rambla Villalba, Pastrana, Pinilla, and the hills of Percheles, Parazuelos, Ceperos, Loma Negra and La Pinilla, and finally the area formed by the mountains of Las Moreras and Bolnuevo.

North of Puerto de Mazarrón, you have the nature reserve of Sierra de la Muela, Cabo Tiñoso and Roldán.

This is a semi-arid Mediterranean ecosystem with a great variety of landscapes, with coastline and coves of alternating sand and gravel beaches, dune systems such as the beach coves at Calnegre and Percheles, cliffs, low-lying rocky shores, fossil dunes, islets and mouths of ramblas. The heights of the hills range up to 492 meters at Morrón Blanco (in Las Moreras), La Panadera at 102 meters (in Calnegre), Lomo de Bas peaks at 600 meters, Cabo Cope at 248 meters, La Atalaya (in Loma de Ceperos) at 188 meters, 134 meters at La Pinilla and 71 meters at Percheles. There are a series of gullies that traverse some of these hills; the most important are Pastrana, Pinilla and Garrobillo Villalba.

Sleeping

You are spoilt for choice for campsites, for example: Garoa, Playa de Mazarrón, on the road towards Bolnuevo, 968 150660, www.playamazarron.com. Camping Bellavista, Carretera de Vera Km, 3, 968 449151, www.campingbellavista.com. Camping Los Madriles, towards La Azohía, www.campinglosmadriles.com 968 152151.

There are lots of hotels in this area too, here's a selection.

Hostal La Línea on Calle Cartagena, 2, Diego and Encarna run this comfortable (though the rooms are small) hostal, with aircon and bathrooms and some of the best tapas in Murcia. 968 594549, www.pensionlalinea.com.

Hotel Playa Grande, Avenida Castellar, 19, upmarket hotel right on the beach, 45–75 Euros per night. The hotel has the restaurant La Meseguera with specialities of typical Murcian Food. 968 155715, www.hotel-playagrande.com.

A beachfront hotel with restaurant is the Hotel Bahía, Playa de la Reya, 968 594000, www.hotelbahia.net. They have special offers on their website so it's worth checking before you book.

Hotel La Cumbre, in the La Cumbre area of town (500 metres from the beaches), 968 594861, www.hotellacumbre.com has its own swimming pool and 121 rooms.

If you'd prefer an apartment then have a look at the Pueblo Salado Apartments, www.pueblosalado.com, on Avenida Tierno Galván, 968 594937. Or try Montemar Vacaciones, 968 153515, www.bellavistaproperties.es for plenty to choose from.

Eating

Puerto Mazarrón has many different dining options.

Bel de Mar, Avenida Costa Cálida, part fishmongers and part cafetería, for good, fresh fish, that you select yourself. Bel de Mar is very close to the Turismo office.

On the seafront there are many places to buy cheap platos combinados and do a little tourist shopping. Also, there are about a million (OK, a slight exaggeration) Chinese restaurants in Puerto Mazarrón. Our intolerance of MSG prevents us from trying them all, but, statistically, at least one of them must be good.

Our friends on Facebook have recommended the following restaurants: La Barraca, behind the Grand Mundo is worth a try. Viggos in the port is owned by Bocapizza and offers the usual Spanish food, the grilled fish platter is excellent and they also do American ribs, chicken wings and cheesy chips as a starter. Chez Zoe, at the end of the paseo has a great cook.

Unanimously, the The Old Market Tavern came out tops for Brits living in Puerto de Mazarrón. They serve English food including full breakfast, fish and chips, pie and chips and steak, have occasional music nights and a quiz every Monday. Look for them on www.facebook.com/TheOldMarketTavern/.

As the port area has been redeveloped, a more international flavour of restaurants has been introduced. There's an Italian and a German restaurant, but highly recommended comes the Moroccan fare of Restaurante Alhambra where you can sit ooutside in an Arabic tent and enjoy delightful kebabs and couscous.

Along the seafront you'll find plenty of disco–pubs which are open in the summer.

Ricote Valley

Map Reference: 1.35°W, 38.15°N

The Ricote Valley was the last stronghold of the Moors in Spain and is one of the most beautiful and undiscovered parts of Murcia, along the fertile plains of the river Segura. The region clings to its Arab heritage as shown by the numerous remains from this period, including the ingenious rural irrigation system.

Ricote maintains a rich and highly individual gastronomic tradition in which the local wine features strongly, how pleasant! After indulging in the delights of the local cuisine you may feel like enjoying a few days of healthy relaxation and pampering at the wonderful 19th century spa in Archena very close by.

Sporting activities such as river–rafting on the River Segura, mountain biking or horse riding along routes offered by various riding centres are the most popular activities.

The beautiful **Regional Park Sierra de la Pila** is situated between the towns of Jumilla, Abarán, Blanca, Molina de Segura and Fortuna, right here in the Ricote Valley. It has a total area of approximately 8,836 hectares. It has been proposed as an SCI (Site of Community Importance), and is also capable of being incorporated into the Natura 2000 network. Most of the park is designated as SPA (Special Protection Area for birds).

The park can be divided into two large sections separated by Barranco del Mulo: An eastern sector which has the highest peaks (1,264 m La

Pila with El Cenajo with 1,200 m) and the western sector dominated by the summit of Caramucel at 1,023m altitude.

The main towns in the Ricote Valley: Abarán, Albudeite, Villanueva, Ulea, Ojós (see own section), Ricote, Campos del Rio and Blanca.

A good source of information for all of the locations in the area is: www.valledericote.com

Abarán

Abarán belongs to the Vega Alta area. Bordered on the north by the municipality of Jumilla, the west by Cieza, south by Ricote and Blanca and east with Fortuna. As in the neighbouring municipalities of Valle de Ricote, the Segura River makes itself known, with beautiful spots like Jarrax, where there is a dam surrounded by lush vegetation.

The origins of human settlement in Abarán date from the Bronze Age, although the first documented information comes from the year 1244.

One of the most important buildings in the town is the **Iglesia de San Pablo** inside which there is an image of the Infant Jesus created by Salzillo. Other interesting buildings are the **Ermita de los Patronos Santos Médicos** located high in the town and forming part of a landscaped walkway that provides an excellent viewing point. The **Santuario de Nuestra Señora del Oro** located in the mountains of the same name, the Plaza de Toros and the recently restored Teatro Cervantes are all worth a visit.

The most important festivals of the town are the Feast of the Child, in which the image of the Infant Jesus is carried from house to house and Holy Week, with the procession of penitents. In September they celebrate the festivities in honour of Saints Cosmas and Damian.

There are three other towns in this region: San José Artesano, Hoya Del Campo and Venta de la Aurora. Hoya del Campo and Venta del Aurora are known for their first usage of a motor for lifting water, designed by Dr Jesús Templado Sánchez, which facilitated the irrigation of more areas of land and led to the creation of these populations. This was known as the Motor Resurreción del Campo.

The history of San José Artesano is very recent as this neighbourhood in Abarán originated in 1957 with the construction of a group of houses that are nowadays the oldest part of town. These homes were the result of the construction programs of the Franco regime. After the first 50 homes in 1957 the district was expanded.

If you fancy a walk try the **Ruta de Norias**. These water wheels, dating back to Arabic times are still used today for raising water to higher channels so they can irrigate more land. There are five water wheels to visit (four in working order): La Noria Grande dates from 1805 and is reputed to be the largest in Europe, is located in the Parque de las Norias (Avenida Constitución); just 600m away is the Noria De La Hoya De Don Garcia dating from 1812; cross the footbridge over the Seguro river and get to Noria De Candelon built in 1850; the smallest wheel is Noria De La Ñorica a little way down the path and finally Noria De Felix Cayetano is located on the left bank of the River Segura, (next to the MU-14).

The wheels are made from wrought iron and wood, and four of them are situated in the regional park with paths located on the left bank of the River Segura.

This park area is excellent for a stroll with well paved and marked paths. One of the routes is the **Eco Tourist** route that takes in Jarral, Soto Damián, Cañada de Hidalgo and Darrax. The full trail is just 1.9 kilometres and a pleasant 3 metres wide, with no traffic.

Tourist Office: Plaza de la Zarzuela, 14, 968 450808, open Monday to Friday mornings only. www.abaran.es

Albudeite

Albudeite is an Arabic term that means low water since the Mula River that passes there is of little volume. Located in the region of the Mula River, this small town is situated in a landscape of gullies and ravines that contrasts with the green oasis formed by the gardens cultivated by residents.

This location was most likely founded by Muslims who built a castle here which controlled much of the Mula River valley and the route between this region and the plain of the Segura. The remains of the fort are half hidden under the houses today, but you can still see some walls reused as foundations of new buildings that have been declared historical and artistic interest.

The parish church of **Nuestra Señora de los Remedios** was begun in the sixteenth century on the foundations of the old mosque. Inside the temple there's a carved wooden Madonna from the seventeenth century. Another attraction for tourists is the water wheel of **Maciaján** built entirely of metal. Its dimensions are remarkable, 10 meters in diameter with 64 buckets.

A peculiar party is held on Palm Sunday when they appoint two mayors: one for married people and one for singles. The day ends with the burning of an effigy representing the apostle Judas. There is a tradition that has remained among the people of Albudeite of planting a poplar tree in the square. There is evidence that since 1890 a poplar tree has been planted in the church square and replaced every sixty years, which is the lifespan of this species. www.portaldealbudeite.com

Blanca

Blanca is a city of about 6,200 people in the Comarca de la Vega Alta del Segura. Bordered on the north by the municipality of Abarán, South by the municipalities of Ulea and Ojós, to the east with those of Molina de Segura and Fortuna, and the West with the Ricote. It was originally called Negra because of the colour of the local rock. It's a really beautiful little town, great for some stunning photos.

The earliest archaeological remains are around the castle, from the 11th and 12th centuries. You can reach the castle from the town, just follow the path upwards.

Take a look at the **Ermita de San Roque** dating from the first half of the eighteenth century and the church of **San Juan Evangelista** built in the sixteenth century with a carving of Christ tied to a column. There are some beautiful frescos and cupolas too.

There's a recently (1998) renovated theatre in town, **Teatro Victoria**. The construction of this theatre dates back to 1937. It re-opened on April 24th 1999. The remodelling ensured the exterior was maintained, however the interior was adapted with all the latest technical equipment. Calle Teatro, 15, 968 778011.

One of the best Spanish artists recognised nationally and internationally is Pedro Cano (1944), who comes from Blanca. Also the inventor Antonio Molina Cano (1879-1953), who devoted his life to transforming hydraulic energy into electrical and mechanical energy, was born here.

The **Centro de Interpretación de la Luz y el Agua**, located in the former Factory of Light, along the Segura River, shows visitors how water is used as power. Open Tuesday to Saturday: 10:00 a 14:00, closed Sunday and Monday, 968 775093.

If you enjoy walking then the natural park, **Parque Regional Sierra de la Pila**, is worth a visit. On a clear day you can see across to Moratalla and down to the Mar Menor. There are over 50km of walkable paths.

If you're feeling more adventurous then try canoeing in the local rivers. Get in touch with Blanca Club de Piragüismo, Avenida Río Segura, 695 358956, www.blancaclubpiraguismo.com

Blanca celebrates their fiesta for San Roque. It's very unusual as it divides its celebrations into two times throughout the year. First with the Spring Festival in April (the week after Easter Sunday) then in August (16th). Both celebrations are large and raucous and in total take up four weeks. There are bulls running through the streets, sometimes a bullfight, large headed costumes, street parties, music and dancing. It's a great time to visit.

There are five other towns in the Blanca area: La Estación de Blanca (where there's a train station and is a great place for access to the Sierra de la Pila), Bayna, Tollos, Runes and Buyla.

Tourist Office, Avenida Rio Segura, Centro de Interpretación de la Luz y el Agua, 968 775001, www.blanca.es

Location Report: River Rafting / Kayaking

Some people might think that there's not a lot of water in the rivers of Murcia, but they'd be (a bit) wrong. The Segura river north of the city of Murcia is fairly full, flowing and surprisingly clean. We started off in the lovely town of Blanca, at the riverside, where we parked early on a Sunday morning in September and were shocked to find hundreds (really!) of people wandering around waiting to be taken to the departure point further up river. There are at least three centres that use Blanca to collect the wannabee kayakers and rafters, so make sure you know which group you're with.

Predictably the six large coaches (really!) were late in departing, but everyone was in great spirits, racing from coach to coach, swapping seats, quickly rushing back to their cars, changing their clothes (again), having another quick fag before being herded onto the coaches for departure. I've always loved the phrase "herding cats" and the images it brings to mind. The guys at MurciAventuraS are aces at herding Spanish Cats – an altogether more difficult proposition than herding the orderly British queuing cats. Finally we arrived near the quayside and the organiser warned us to stay together and not get mixed up with the other groups – I thought he was going to tell us to hold hands and walk in pairs.

After waiting for a few other groups to set off, we got our life jackets and helmets and were ushered into the kayaks. A few minutes later and our group of six rafts and 5 kayaks were off. Each raft has a captain who knows what he's doing, the rest of you just splash around a bit and get wet. It's not terribly energetic, the most energy used is in splashing the other rafts with as much force as you can muster, shouting and jeering. You do get very wet though, and stay wet the whole day. We were lucky with a wonderfully hot day. At about two-ish we pulled the rafts into the riverside for lunch. A tent had been set up and pans of paella were brought over from the local restaurant. There wasn't anywhere to sit, but there was cold beer and hot paella and a break from bouncing around on the rubber dinghy.

The most exciting points were two weirs – the first was quite small but still sent a huge ripple of excitement through the group. The second, just after lunch, was considerably larger and much more fun. Some people body surfed down the weir too.

It's very much a group thing – we were the only "pair", all others were in gangs, some quite large. There were some families taking part, with children as young as five. I think we were the oldest and the only foreigners! It's probably more sensible to do this in the summer months as you get wet! They put details on their facebook page, but it's best to send them an email with the size of your group and preferred dates. The starting point is the town of Blanca.

Follow them on facebook: www.facebook.com/murciaventuras or phone on +34 615 82 88 40

Campos del Rio

The main attractions of the town are the church of San Juan Bautista, which has a picture of Roque Lopez, a disciple of Salzillo; the Clock Tower and the Mirador del Castillo. Also notable is Calle del Rosario which consists almost entirely of stately homes of the early 20th century.

Campos del Río is comprised of a network of badlands or lunar landscape, which shows a strong contrast to the Mula River valley. The local economy is primarily agricultural. Currently the irrigated areas are continuously growing, with mainly peach, orange and apricot trees. There are also traditional almond and olive trees. The cultivated areas are a strong contrast with the badlands. The canning industry absorbs much of the workforce, although livestock is also an important sector, especially Murcian Goat rearing, with over 8,000 of these special breed in this area.

Their fiesta is celebrated for San Antón on the 17th January and in honour of San Juan on 24th June.

Ayuntamiento: 968 650135, www.camposdelrio.es

Ricote

The town of Ricote, with its domineering old fortress, which the Arabs called **Alarbona**, nestles between the orchard area (huertano) and limestone of the Sierra, where the vines grow that embody the famous and traditional wine.

The fortification is located on a high hill in the Sierra del Salitre (known as The Peñascales in medieval times) and is found immediately east of the town of Ricote, 150 meters above the village. It has total domination over the whole valley of Ricote and controls the Segura River passing through the area. Access is from near the sports hall (polideportivo). From there follow the path on a difficult walk to the fortification.

The **Castillo de Los Peñascales** are the ruins of a fortified complex of considerable size. Sadly it hasn't been preserved and is in ruins, nevertheless you can still get a good idea of its original size, and the views are worth the effort.

The history of Ricote is broken into two main eras: the Muslim population of the Middle Ages and the Order of Santiago in the thirteenth century, which lasted until the nineteenth century.

Worth a visit is the church **Iglesia San Sebastián De Ricote**, where notable works are stored. It's located in the centre of town on a small rise and is of the Baroque period. The construction of the temple began in the early eighteenth century, possibly on the land occupied by other Christian sites in turn built on an ancient Muslim mosque in medieval times. The church was built and financed at the expense of the Order of Santiago whose presence is evident in both the church and the iconography.

Also of great interest is the **Casa Grande**, pure Baroque Murcia with remarkable carved grilles.

There are a number of other towns in the Ricote Town area, including: Las Ventanas, La Cuerda, Collado Gil, Vite, Rambla de Charrara, Cuesta Alta, Cañada Gil, Las Lomas, Lichor, Ambrós, La Almarcha, La Bermeja, La Alcoba, Berrandino, Fuente del Cieno, Ainás and Patruena.

The oldest residential properties in these towns are houses with stables, low walls of masonry and upper chambers for grain. Typical nineteenth century homes, now renovated, whose original builders had to be the humble villagers, engaged in agricultural work in the dryland environment. There really isn't much to see here, but they're great, remote outposts with a true step back in history feel.

The biggest fiesta celebration is devoted to San Sebastián and takes place on 20, 21 and 22 January.

Ulea

Ulea was inhabited by Iberians, Romans and Arabs, as shown by remains found in the area. There is also evidence of a walled Roman settlement, which would date back to the third and fourth centuries.

The natural environment is determined by the river, leaving a trail of green, dotted with tall palm trees that tower over the rest of the trees. The pine forests in the mountains are also quite striking, with typical places like Las Lomas and Las Fuentecicas.

Historically, Ulea economy is based mainly in agriculture with orchards of oranges, lemons, apricots, pears and peaches.

Fiestas are held for San Bartolomé in August and the lignum crucis, parties in honour of the Holy Cross, whose main events are on May 1st.

Also of note in the Ulea area is the town of Venta Puñales. In the late nineteenth century, when being a bandit had become a way of life for famous criminals, Ricote Valley area was frequently visited by **El Periago** (or Vivillo, his second name). Since the Venta de Ulea was crowded with travellers and visitors, its owner took care of arming guests with daggers. When the Venta was visited by the bandit, it was met with surprise guests that faced him with knives. The bandit escaped and went to Molina de Segura, where he was killed in the cave where he hid. So the last assault of the Partía del Vivillo ended in this town which would later take the name of Venta Puñales (Wholesale Knives).

Ayuntamiento: 968 698211, www.ulea.info/

Villanueva

Villanueva is buried deep in the Valle de Ricote, on the right bank of the river Segura. It sits upon a hill that rises 50 meters above the river with an orchard of fruit trees and palms surrounding it.

Worth a visit is the church dedicated to **Our Lady of the Assumption**, patroness of the town, which was built during the 19th Century and represents a great example of the neoclassical style. Walk up to **El Corazón de Jesús** (The Heart of Jesus) sculpture located on top of the mountain, which gives one of the best views over the valley. There's also the **Golgo**, former power station, which is now used for fishing and refreshing baths in summer.

The most significant holidays are in honour to San Roque and Our Lady of the Assumption, celebrated in August.

Around the town of Villanueva del Segura, on the border with the neighbouring municipality of Archena, is the district of La Asunción in the popular area of La Morra. From these hills you can see one of the most picturesque landscapes of Murcia, the beginning of the Ricote Valley, where the banks of the River Segura surrounded by citrus orchards are interspersed with palm trees.

Ayuntamiento: 968 698186, www.villanuevadelsegura.es

Sleeping

There are lots of casas rurales in this area and it's a wonderful location for camping too.

For your own casa rural take a look at Las Casa de Ainás, www.casasdeainas.com, 649 010930, which is a small complex of two houses with shared swimming pool. Casa Rural La Centella in Ricote, on Calle Algezar, 669 330822, is a small reformed town house with bbq and terrace.

Three beautiful casas rurales complexes near Blanca can be found at www.casadelahiguera.com, 626 684908. There are several options including Swallow House and Fig Tree houses, fully restored ancient farm houses.

Eating

In each town there are excellent restaurants and bars serving local food. In addition it seems that the place to go is El Sordo, www.elsordo.es, which has been around since 1917 serving the people of the Ricote valley. They have their own bodega and offer a wonderful selection of homemade desserts, also try their menú de degustación. They can be found on Calle Alharbona in Ricote, 968 697150.

San Javier

Population: 31,700

Map Reference: 0.84°W, 37.85°N

Probably best known as the local name for the old Murcia airport (2 miles away), since 1998 San Javier has been the home of an increasingly popular jazz festival in late June. The **Festival de Jazz de San Javier** includes the International Jazz Festival (see location report), the International Festival of Theatre, Music and Dance, Music of the Soul; Pecata Minuta; Menorrock and the National Folk Festival.

San Javier itself is just off the coast, a well-established town with a long history illustrated in its museum. It has excellent shopping and leisure facilities, including an impressive sports centre.

A town just inland from the Mar Menor, its one way system is tortuous! However, once on foot you can visit some 17th century churches, including **La Ermita and the Iglesia de la Virgen del Rosario.**

The **Plaza de España** is the commercial hub of San Javier. In 2003 an ambitious project to link the two old squares created this central administrative block, with the courts, property registration, social security agencies, employment service, as well as banks and solicitors, and of course a few bars. There is an underground car park for easy parking in the centre.

The large square is also the centre of numerous cultural events and festivals throughout the year. The most important at Christmas, with their Belén de España which occupies an area of 1,600 m2.

In the **Plaza de España La Iglesia de San Francisco Javier** has a rich artistic heritage including sculptures (most of them gilded carved wood), altars and liturgical furnishings. There's also a pulpit made of carved wood. If you want to have a museum visit, take a look at **Museo Parroquial de San Javier**. The San Javier Parish Museum is located in the church of San Francisco Javier, behind the sanctuary. This church was founded as a chapel, in the seventeenth century and dedicated to the holy missionary. It's free to visit, and open Tuesday to Saturday from 10:30 to 13:30, 968 571085.

The **Museo de Historia Local de San Javier** also on Carretera de Cartagena, 968 192526, has an impressive display of archaeological, ethnographic and anthropological items. It also houses the Museo del Belén de San Javier. You can see over 500 figures and sculptures for the Bethlehem (Belén) displays. Entry is free.

Parque Almansa is the largest park in the municipality of San Javier. There's a beautiful walkway with arches and a long pergola. Inside the park there's the **Parque Almansa Municipal Auditorium,** which is the most important cultural forum in San Javier. This is a semicircle-shaped outdoor theatre reminiscent of the classic Roman amphitheatres, with an architecture that makes the acoustics and view from any seat excellent. This is where the annual International Festival of Theatre and Dance and the International Jazz Festival are held (see Location Report).

And if you think it might be a bit cold for events in the winter time then don't worry they put up a large tent with space heaters and of course a bar for the Soul Music festival in December (and other gigs!)

La Villa del Retiro, built in 1900, has been restored and is for private use. Built in the Colonial style it is one of the most unique houses in the area. Find it on Avenida Del Retiro.

La Finca del Recuerdo (The House of Remembrance), from the 19th Century in the vernacular style is now abandoned. It is a typical town house in the area, with a main house and an inner courtyard, behind there are outbuildings. This is on Los Girasoles.

The fiesta for San Francisco Javier is in December with a sound and light show, festivals, photo contests, exhibitions and sports competitions. And at Christmas there's the Belén when visitors from all over Spain are attracted by the fame of this temporary monument.

A shopping phenomenon is the Dos Mares complex, just off the motorway (Carretera Nacional 332), www.centrodosmares.com. It's open 365 days of the year with about 70 shops, 16 bars/restaurants, a cinema and bowling alley. Some stores do actually close on Christmas day and a few of the national holidays, but the vast majority remain open.

Location Report: San Javier Jazz

If you love Jazz buy an abono. This is like a season ticket and gets you into the vast majority of the gigs at a reduced price. You buy the abono and get seats assigned where you sit for each gig. There are usually a couple of gigs that cost extra.

The biggest benefit for queuing-obsessed Brits is that you get to jump the queue. You also don't have to fight for the best seats, which means you don't have to turn up 2 hours before the gig starts! Some people are incredibly organised, bringing cushions (the seats are a bit 'firm'), sarnies, binoculars and cameras. You don't need the sarnies because there are nice snacks available at an OK price from the bar. Oh, did I mention the bar? There's a bar. Enjoy.

You don't really need the binoculars either, unless you want to get a close up on those flaming fingers, as most seats get a good view (especially if you have an abono).

Order tickets by telephone 968 191588 and pick them up on the night. Tickets were still available for sale at the venue at 8pm on the night of most concerts. Prices range from €12 to €30, or buy the abono for €100 (plus extra for 2 concerts). www.jazz.sanjavier.es

The venue is great too, I'll be looking out for other interesting gigs here in San Javier at Auditorio Parque Almansa. There's a bar, park for the kids and plenty of parking. Let me know if you'll be going, we can have a drink!

There are nine towns in the San Javier area: Los Pinos, El Mirador, Los Sáez, La Grajuela, Lo Llerena, Pozo Aledo, La Calavera, Santiago de la Ribera (see the next section) and Roda.

In the main these satellite towns of San Javier (with the exceptions of Santiago de la Ribera and Roda which have become more tourist destinations) have a strong agriculture basis, with abandoned flour mills, waterwheels and wind farms around. There's an extensive network of irrigation systems, canals and greenhouses.

Roda is worth a mention as it has some beautiful architecture and of course the **Roda Golf and Country Club. Hacienda de Roda**, the main country estate, has a number of buildings built between 1610 and 1620. In 1997 during restoration works they found the old terrazzo floors dating from the first third of the eighteenth century. They also realised that the exterior walls facing the garden, about 70 inches thick on the ground floor are built upon another very old 15th century building which was basically a fortress.

Services

Ayuntamiento, Plaza de España, 3, 968 573700, www.sanjavier.es

Tourist Office, Calle Padre Juan (Centro Socio Cultural Príncipe de Asturias) in Santiago de la Ribera (close by), 968 571704.

The nearest train station is in Balsicas, 10km away.

Buses from Autobus Urbano, Autocares La Inmaculada.

Sleeping & Eating

As San Javier and Santiago de la Ribera merge into one it's easier to keep all the restaurants and hotels in just one section for these two towns. See the Santiago de la Ribera section for places to stay and where to eat. Also take a look at the Lo Pagán section.

Santiago De La Ribera

Population: 8,100 (2010)

Map Reference: 0.80°W, 37,80°N

Perhaps the most attractive of the Mar Menor resorts, Santiago de la Ribera sits on the shores of the Mar Menor directly in front of San Javier (and is in the municipality of San Javier) and the two are closely linked. Home to a superb marina area and some of the best restaurants in the region, it is no surprise that luxury villas and manicured gardens are the standard.

This town is on the coast of the Mar Menor and has 4 miles of beach. You can frequently enjoy a free display from the airforce training school from the nearby air base. This town is very popular with the townies from Murcia at the weekends, especially in the summer. Santiago is a great place to go and have seafood and enjoy the sunshine.

The original farm house, the **Finca Torre Mínguez**, is still standing and has a large and beautiful front garden. It was built by Antonio Lissón an alderman of the town and is considered the origin of Santiago de la Ribera. It's recognisable by its yellow walls and tower!

If you fancy a stroll then try the perhaps the most beautiful promenade on the coast of Mar Menor. It's about two miles, recently renovated century-old, tree-lined and mostly pedestrian. The wind whips across it so go for a calm day unless you want to be bent over! As you stroll, look out for Restaurante Lonja Mar Menor, which is open for lunch and evening meals all year round.

As you start your walk along the promenade take a look back at the beautiful summer houses from the late 19th and early 20th centuries that also enjoy the sea view: Chalet Barnuevo, Casa Conde Lisea, Villa San Francisco Javier, Torre Javiera and Villa la Pinada. Alongside these old buildings there are only a half a dozen high rises, giving Santiago de la Ribera a unique skyline in this area.

Along the promenade there are wooden walkways leading to raised platforms, some equipped with changing rooms, showers, shade and stairs leading down to the sea. These were originally private accesses but now are open for all.

The **Club Náutico (Yacht Club)** is a useful visual landmark on the walk as it's in the shape of a sailboat. They have regular regattas and there's a sailing club. www.rcrsr.es Paseo Cólon, 968 570250.

In the region there are some windmills, most of them in disrepair, no longer used since the middle of the 20th century. They are Mediterranean-style towers, with four pairs of arms, eight triangular sails and a rotating ceiling. Their origin dates back to the 17th and 18th centuries. In all there are 6 water mills, 1 flour mill and 2 salt mills.

There are at least four big fiestas in the area. The **Pilgrimage of San Blas** is held every February 3rd. This festival has its roots in the sixteenth century when the Trinitarian Monks brought the party and devotion to San Blas to these shores. However, the introduction of the pilgrimage is much later, only since 1980. This is the favourite party for Santiago de la Ribera residents and was declared of Regional Tourist Interest. There are paella making contests, and tastings!

Fiestas del Carmen held on July 16th or the following Sunday to avoid a clash with Lo Pagán, brings the Virgen del Carmen in procession to the Mar Menor sea. Lots of boaty and water oriented activities.

The Fiesta Patronales de Santiago Apóstol is held on July 25th and of course there's Carnival in February which in recent years has gained a lot of interest, http://www.carnavaldelaribera.com/

In January for the Reyes celebrations Santiago de la Ribera has the Cavalcade of Magic Kings who arrive by sea and parade on horseback accompanied by floats.

Beaches

Santiago de la Ribera has 4 miles of golden sands and calm waters, warm and shallow on the Mar Menor. This makes it a very attractive destination for visitors, especially those with children.

- Playa de Colón, this 1000m beach runs parallel to the Colón promenade. This sandy beach has small waves and is rocky in some areas due to the old ramblas and streams that would lead to the Mar Menor. The appearance of this beach changed dramatically in 1987 when clean sand was brought from the bottom of the sea.
- Playa Barnuevo, Located in the town centre, between the General Air Academy and former fishmonger, this beach is 400m long.
- Playa El Castillo, is 450m long and found between the Jardín del Atalayón and Lo Pagán.
- Playa El Pescador, situated in the urban population among the oldest fisheries and the marina, it's 280m long.
- Playa De La Hita, which is just past the old airport and the campsite, and perfect for bird watching. This beach is declared an SPA (Special Protected Area for birds) by the European Union.

For a trip out to La Perdiguera Island there are daily departures from the Pier Canoe Club. Daily from July 1 to September 15 at 9:30 and 10:30. Back to the 13:00 and 18:00.

Services

Tourist Office, Calle Padre Juan. Centro Cultural Príncipe de Asturias, 968 571704, www.turismo.sanjavier.es/

There is now a ferry service to take visitors over to La Manga, 649 201 610, http://www.marmenorferry.com/

Sleeping

Camping is available on the road towards Balsicas at Camping Pueblo San Javier, www.campingsanjavier.com, 968 191080. There are plots for caravans and tents, plus some bungalows available too. They have a swimming pool, bar, supermarket and all the usual amenities.

The Hotel Albohera, on Calle Marín, Esquina Bolarín in Santiago de la

Ribera offers good value rooms, www.hotelalbohera.com, 968 335910. Another good value hotel in Santiago is the aptly named Hotel Mar Menor, Avenida Del Mar Menor, 4, www.hotelmarmenor.eu/, 968 571901.

If you want somewhere to eat and also enjoy the local speciality of caldero then try the Hotel el Marino, Calle Muñoz, 2 in Santiago, www.elmarino.es, 968 572121. It's a pretty hotel with good access.

One of the few high rise (8 floors) hotels in the area is the Hotel Ribera, Explanada De Barnuevo, 10 in Santiago, www.hotelribera.es, 968 570200. It's good value with rooms from around €60 with a sea view.

Pensión La Obrera on Calle Zarandona, 7, 968 570042, www.laobrera.com, has 22 rooms and a restaurant downstairs. Or try Pensión Manida, Calle Muñoz, 11, 968 570170, www.hotelmanida.com

If you'd prefer to stay in an apartment at Roda Golf (or any of the other golf courses) then try any of the lettings agencies, for example: www.holidaylettings.co.uk, www.rentals-rodagolf.co.uk or www.ownersdirect.co.uk. Roda Golf is very near Los Alcázares, so look at that section for more information too.

Eating

One dish to try is the caldero, rice stew with fish and a secret ingredient, the peppers (small dried red peppers, las ñoras), oops, not a secret anymore.

In a seaside town like this you can be sure to find good local produce and seafood, plus the usual pizza and burger places and of course plenty of ice cream parlours.

Bar Restaurante Lonja Mar Menor on Paseo Colón, 968 570309, has excellent seafood with huge open freezers where you can select your fish, right on the seafront. It also has an excellent, though usually very busy, bar where you can have great seafood tapas.

If you're out shopping the Dos Mares complex has plenty of chain restaurants for you to try, Belros Dulce y Salado (cakes and savoury pastries), Bombon Bos (croissants and cakes), a Kebab place, Burger King, Fosters Hollywood, McDonalds and Telepizza, I can feel my arteries clogging up as I type! They also have Lizarrán where you can try tapas and pay for the number of cocktail sticks you end up with and Cervecería Gambrinus which serves meals made from real food.

San Pedro del Pinatar

Population: 24,900

Map Reference: 0.80°W, 37.81°N

Just south of Lo Pagán on the Mar Menor you'll find San Pedro del Pinatar. These two towns pretty much run into each other. It shares a border with the province of Alicante and is only 46km from Murcia city. San Pedro del Pinatar is located between the Mar Menor and the Mediterranean Sea. Included in the Comarca del Mar Menor and in the agricultural region of Campo de Cartagena its surrounding communities are San Javier and Pilar de la Horadada. It is one of the districts of the maritime province of Cartagena.

There are fourteen kilometres of coastline between the two seas (the Mediterranean and the Mar Menor). The beaches on the Mar Menor (see beaches section for more details) are Villananitos, La Puntica and La Mota. In the Mediterranean are the beaches of La Llana, which are the Playa de las Salinas, Barraca Quemada and Punta de Algas. Next to Las Salinas is the port. Across the harbour are the Playa de la Torre Derribada and El Mojón.

San Pedro, just like the rest of municipalities in the district of Mar Menor, shows traces of civilization from the Palaeolithic era, especially the Roman and Arabic. Underwater archaeology has revealed that the Phoenicians and Greeks traded along this coast, and the Romans were the pioneers in the exploitation of the salt, forming the basis of the salted fish industry. The Arabs created the system of fishing weirs.

Until the seventeenth century the town was called El Pinatar, but the construction of a chapel under the patronage of San Pedro the Apostle (and fisherman) completed the town's name. With the Reconquista San Pedro del Pinatar became one of the ports of the city of Murcia. Felipe II built a tower, which remained garrisoned until the eighteenth century, to ward off Barbary Pirate attacks.

In the nineteenth century San Pedro del Pinatar was transformed into a summer resort and became the home of many famous Spanish figures, including Emilio Castelar, the family of Servet-Spottorno and the baron of Benifayó. Today, San Pedro del Pinatar is one of the most prosperous municipalities in the Region of Murcia and one of the major tourist destinations in the Costa Cálida.

La Casa de San Sebastián was built as a place of recreation for the powerful and famous family Servet. It's known as the **La Casa Del Reloj**, was built in the late nineteenth century, and today is part of a complex dedicated to a restaurant that has adopted the same name. Very few houses of this type of construction exist on the Mediterranean coast, this was an example of a second home built by the rich.

The most important wetlands in the Region of Murcia are found here in San Pedro: the Parque Natural de Las Salinas y Arenales de San Pedro del Pinatar, with almost 900 hectares.

You'll see flamingos, gulls, albatrosses, herons and owls. There are dunes with sea lilies, sedges and reeds.

The visitor's centre for Las Salinas is on Avenida de las Salinas, 968 178139, www.murcianatural.carm.es/web/guest/arenales-y-salinas-de-san-pedro-del-pinatar

On the 16th of July they celebrate their fiesta patronal, Fiestas de la Virgen del Carmen. The people from San Pedro have deep links to the sea (sorry!), and they feel a strong devotion to the Virgin, known since medieval times as the Star of the Sea, who guides and protects the fishermen's long, hard days at sea.

The Fishermen's Guild is responsible for organising the Pilgrimage and Maritime Procession of the Virgin del Carmen, who on the morning of July 16th travels by boat on the Mar Menor, along with hundreds of decorated boats. This is also a time for remembering the fishermen and sailors who died and those who never arrived in port. Carnations are offered into the sea as tributes.

Ports

There's a main port with a couple of marinas in the Salinas area. There's the Club Náutico Villa de San Pedro on Avenida Puerto, www.clubNáuticovillasanpedro.com, 968 182678. It's got great facilities, a swimming pool and reasonable prices. For the bigger boats (and there are some very big ones over here!) there's the Marina de las Salinas, www.marinadelassalinas.es, 968 182880, right next door.

Location Report: The Salinas

The Sierra de Escalona along with Sierra de Carrascoy provides the backdrop to the salt plains. This is known as La Bella Durmiente, Sleeping Beauty, because it appears to be a woman lying down.

The reddish colour of water is produced by algae that live in very salty environments.

Making Salt In the Mar Menor: The water from the enclosed lagoon is pumped into the first pond, which acts as reservoir. The water is then transferred to other shallower ponds, known as heaters. Here the effect of evaporation from the sun and wind increases to saturation. Finally, water is transferred from the salt ponds or other ponds called crystallizers. When the sun has made the precipitation of salt crystals it's time to remove the salt plate. This operation is performed with care to avoid damaging the clay base. Finally, tractors load the goods onto trucks to take to the washing, packaging, storage and distribution sections.

The current salt plains are located on a former swamp formed in a coastal depression. It is a flat area with a shallow basin closed by a sand bar. The movement of water between the Mediterranean and the Mar Menor makes the extensive mud surfaces regularly exposed.

Beaches

- Playa Puntica: 500m, urban, high occupancy, calm waters, dark sand, SOS, rescue, Red Cross, local police, parking, bus, toilet, showers, umbrellas / deckchairs, anchoring area, disabled access, sailing, windsurfing, surfing, kitesurf, catamaran. Club Náutico de Lo Pagán 200 meters.
- Playa Villananitos: 700m, urban, high occupancy, calm waters, dark sand, SOS, rescue, Red Cross, local police, parking, bus, toilet, showers, parasols / sunbeds, anchorage area, disabled access, sailing, windsurfing, surfing, kitesurf, catamaran. Club Náutico de Lo Pagán 150 meters
- Playa Torrederribada: 2200m, isolated, average occupancy, moderate waves, golden sand, SOS, rescue, Red Cross, local police, parking, bus, toilet, anchorage area, sailing, wind-surf, surf, kitesurf, catamaran. Club Náutico de San Pedro del Pinatar 1km.
- Playa Playuela: in the protected area of the Regional Park of Las Salinas, 350m, semi-urban, average occupancy, dark sand, moderate waves, anchoring area, SOS, rescue, Red Cross, local police, parking, bus, toilet, showers, anchoring area, disabled access, next to the Yacht Club of San Pedro del Pinatar.
- Playa La Llana: in the protected area of the Regional Park of Las Salinas, where the Mediterranean and Mar Menor meet, 1,500m, isolated, high occupancy, golden sand, moderate waves, anchoring area, SOS, rescue, Red Cross, local police, parking, bus, WC, cleaning, paper, kiosk spa anchorage area, San Pedro Marina 1km.

There are seventeen administrative districts: Barrio de los Ángeles-Las Esperanzas-Barrio de San Juan, Barrio del Carmen-El Salero, Los Antolinos, Los Tárragas, Los Peñascos, Loma de Abajo-Molino Chirrete, Las Beatas, Los Sáez, Loma de Arriba, Los Veras, Los Plazas-Los Gómez, Los Imbernones,

Las Pachecas-Lo Romero, Lo Pagán (see own section), Los Cuarteros, Las Salinas and El Mojón.

It's certainly worth visiting Las Salinas. Exploited since Roman times, and probably earlier by the Carthaginians, salt was used in the salted fish industry. Muslims continued ploughing salt and in the eighteenth century a wharf was built on the Mediterranean Sea to facilitate production. From 1879, when the salt was no longer a state monopoly, the area was sold a number of times. An extension of the facilities saw the two most characteristic windmills in the area being built, Quintín and La Calcetera, which until the 70s decanted water from the Mar Menor and ground the salt.

Along with the salt production, fishing has been a major source of income for this area. They use the fishing system brought by the Arabs, that of the weirs. A maze of reeds, sticks and nets divert the fish from one part of the Mar Menor to another. Until 1960 the most abundant fish species in the Mar Menor were mullet and bream. Currently the catch is dominated by eel and mullet, although there are also anchovies, shrimp, sole and bream. East of the weirs large accumulations of seaweed have given name to the remotest spot of all: Punta Algae.

The salt ponds are home to flamingo, the black-necked grebe and common tern or farfet.

Location Report: The Spa

My personal experiences of the luxury of a spa visit have been few and far between and to be honest, a little scary. I had a weekend break at Ragdale Hall, where the food was sparse, the treatments were regimental and the alcohol was non-existent (except for the illegal stash we kept on the outside window ledge of our room). I had a massage in Turkey, where the scary, hairy woman tried to pry the flesh off my bones and drown me in soapsuds. And a massage in Thailand, where the tiny (yes even smaller than me!) masseuse was clearly more interested in massaging my husband than she was in me. Perhaps that's why she twisted my arms round my neck and ran repeatedly up and down my spine.

So, my expectations were low and my fear level was high when I booked for myself, my (ex-)mother-in-law (Helga) and my sister-in-law (Julie) to have a day at the spa.

I chose the Thalasso Centre next to the Thalasia hotel in San Pedro Del Pinatar. Their website www.thalasia.com really doesn't do justice to their location and facilities. They have 34°C seawater pools with different underwater massages, Jacuzzis, waterbeds, cascades, etc. You can enjoy the marine circuit with wet and dry saunas, bithermal showers, the ice cave or the relaxation pool. Or have a treatment in one of the 40 individual rooms for beauty, aesthetic and physiotherapy programmes.

You can download a brochure of therapies, which runs to 8 or so pages of closely typed weird sounding torture treatments. Some gems include: masaje drenante linfático, hidrocinesiterapia and sustrato vegetal.

Or for those of you with a larger budget and who like to wear your chocolate, rather than eat it, you can have a Chocolat Massage. Or why not try Extracto de Caviar or Ceremonia Gold (they really do use gold leaf!). And of course there's the Vinoterapia, where for the price of 20 good bottles of Casa de la Ermita, you can have a bath in wine. Me, I prefer drinking the stuff!

The best bet is to go for a package of treatments, a programa. This will save you money and reduce the difficulty of deciding which treatments to have. We chose Thalassoreumotológico, where for 3 hours and just 45 Euros each we got to play in the pools, have a limo corporal and a hidromasaje marino.

I suppose the limo is what most people associate with the spas of the Mar Menor, the mud! I was really looking forward to getting dirty and rolling around in the stuff but it's a much more civilised affair than I was expecting, unless of course you don't enjoy getting virtually naked in front of a person you've never met before, wearing paper knickers and then having hot mud plopped on your joints and finally being wrapped in a paper blanket.

Really it's much more fun than it sounds and the darkness in the room saves your blushes. The mud has no odour and is really fine and silty and makes great farty sounds when you move around!

The hidromasaje was lovely too. You get your own room, with a big waterbed (like the suspended animation capsules in the film Alien, but without a cat or alien), candles, soft music and a ½ hour of floating around in bubbles. At first I couldn't relax I was waiting for something exciting to happen, then I think I fell asleep.

In between treatments we sat on the terrace of the café and had some refreshing water (and a little wine!) and looked at the view. You're right in the natural park and can see the whole of the Mar Menor, salt plains and hundreds of birds. We didn't see any flamingos but I'm sure if you're lucky you will. Then after all of that pampering we met the men at Restaurante Ramón in Los Alcázares and enjoyed a superb lunch.

TIPS

1. Don't worry about what you look like in a bikini (bikinis aren't mandatory, well not for men anyway!), no one else is looking; everyone is too busy enjoying the bienestar (well being) of the place.

2. Take a robe or hire one. It's nice to wander around and enjoy the facilities without worrying about flashing your wobbly bits.

3. You must wear indoor pool shoes and a bathing cap. You can buy these at the spa for a reasonable price.

4. The changing area is mixed sex, there are cubicles but take care when wandering around you never know who you might bump into naked (probably my mother-in-law).

So overall, did I enjoy it? Yes, it was a super way to spend a Saturday morning with my family. The atmosphere is relaxed, the prices were good, the facilities are excellent and the staff friendly. All in all a good day out. I never did find where they stored the chocolate though!

El Mojón is the furthest point in the Murcia region and uniquely one half of this town is situated in Murcia and the other in the Alicante province (belonging to Pilar de Horadada, which is well worth a visit!) A quiet town in the winter, with a population explosion during the summer, like many of the towns along the coast.

Going Native: Cath Duhig Joins The Spanish Masters Athletics Squad

We were staying with friends in a rented place in Villamartin and rented bikes for a day. We got a bit lost, and… found our way to **El Mojón**. Originally from Norfolk, England I now live permanently in El Mojón, San Pedro del Pinatar, after 13 years of "commuting".

The best thing about living here is the climate, and the peaceful, laid-back quality of life. It's wonderful to have all the facilities available without feeling that anything is on top of us. "Our" beach is only about 3-5 mins stroll from our house. Not everyone is money-chasing, there are still lots of family businesses and customer care is good.

I particularly enjoy the active, outdoor lifestyle as a committed (some would say obsessive) competitive athlete. We have great beaches at El Mojón and Torre Derribada. The athletics training facilities at San Javier, Pilar de la Horadada, and Torrevieja are all great, and there are lots of local road races.

One of my biggest challenges is feeling secure with paperwork. We have had some medical issues and understanding the liaison between the public and private sectors has been interesting. We live on the border between two different autonomous regions and that has also been interesting. Advice: use a gestor or tax advisor or solicitor, as relevant. Don't listen to "Fred in the bar" or someone on Facebook. The Spanish expect you to *ask* if unsure, not wait until someone decides to enlighten you.

If I had to do it all again I would worry less, but get proper advice on what procedures are necessary to get the right paperwork rather than rely on well-intentioned "helpful" people.

We're looking forward to many more years of a relaxed and happy "retirement". We are both active, sporting people and like how that is an accepted part of Spanish life and accommodated as normal.

We want to live as "Spanish" a life as possible. We are joining in with as much of local life as we can, learning the language and customs, etc. I have just been accepted to compete for the Spanish Masters Athletics squad, renouncing my GB team status.

You can contact me on Facebook: https://www.facebook.com/cath.duhig

---

San Pedro del Pinatar is great for spas, with three good ones in the area. There's the Thalasia, as discussed in the location report, Avenida del Puerto, 327-329, www.thalasia.com, 968 182007. There's Aguas Salinas on Calle Crucero Baleares, 2, Lo Pagán, www.aguassalinas.com, 968 184136 and also Lodomar on Río Bidasoa, 1, www.lodomar.com, 968 186802. They all offer special packages and deals and have attached hotels, so keep an eye on their websites.

For diving there's Turkano, www.turkana.org, 617 355636, also based in the port, but a little further down. They offer a wide range of activities including scuba, learning to sail and kitesurfing. The diving is fine around here, but if you want something more adventurous head down to Cabo de Palos. Frequently these dive clubs will put on a trip down there, but it's a bit of a trek.

They have their weekly market on Monday mornings on Calle Víctor Pradera and Calle Libertad.

Services

Tourist Offices, Avenida de las Salinas (Edificio CIT), 55, www.sanpedrodelpinatar.es/turismo/, 968 182301.

Ayuntamiento, Plaza Luis Molina, 1 968 180600.

Bus Station, Alalde José María Tárraga, 968 182942.

Taxis, Calle Víctor Pradera, 968 181760, 968 180808 or 968 186996.

Nearest train station in Balsicas, 968 580052.

Sleeping

Take a look in the Lo Pagán section for more information as these towns merge into each other.

For a luxury experience try Hotel Thalasia, Avenida del Puerto, 327-329, www.thalasia.com, 968 182007. They frequently have offers on their website, a room plus different treatments from the Thalasso Spa next door. There are over 200 rooms of various sizes. There are also two restaurants, the Thalasia and La Sal.

Hotel Paloma on Calle Río Edesma 47, www.hotel-paloma.com, 968 183171 is more cost conscious. It has 25 rooms and a restaurant on site.

If you're interested in a more self-catering environment then the apartments at Aparthotel Bahia, Calle Mar Adriático, 4, www.aparthotelbahia.com, 968 178386, has 35 self-catering rooms plus the usual services of a hotel.

Eating

If you want somewhere a bit special then you could try the Casa del Reloj, www.restaurantelacasadelreloj.com, 968 182406, on the main road. You won't miss the distinctive building with its high peaked roof, vertical lines and bright paintwork. It's not terribly expensive, but you do get a sense of quality!

If you find yourself at the port there are several options for anything from a coffee to a full menu del dia. Try The Clipper Pub (www.theclipperpub.com/), Torombolo (www.torombolo.es/) or at the Club Nautico there's Porto Chico.

Sierra Espuña

Map Reference: 1.53°W, 37.80°N

The Sierra Espuña is a Parque Regional, which is right in the centre of the Murcia region, between the rivers Pliego and Guadalentín. It is actually an artificially planted forestry project which was started in 1891 to combat the deforestation which resulted in erosion and flash floods.

The park contains some of the higher peaks in Murcia, including the Espuña mountain (1585m), Pedro López (1566m) and Morrón Chico (1446m).

There are a couple of information centres in the park itself: Puerta Espuña and Las Alquerras. The park contains a number of different varieties of pine trees and many different types of wildlife including Montpellier snakes, butterflies and Barbary sheep.

It's usual to get to the park by car, from Alhama or Totana (the more adventurous can walk or go by bike from these towns). There are a vast variety of walks and cycle routes through the park which are best described in the book Descubrir Sierra Espuña (from Natursport, 609 623061, www.natursport.com, this book can also be bought from the main bookshops in Murcia, see Murcia section).

Other towns in this area are Aledo, Mula and Pliego. See their own sections for more details.

Walking and cycling in the vast park area is becoming increasingly popular. It's a good idea to let someone know where you're going and when to expect you back as it is easy to become enveloped in the pine trees and lose your way. Wear appropriate clothing, take some food and water, expect the weather to change and take a good map. For more information visit www.sierraespuna.com.

For a fun holiday in the Sierra Espuña try www.espuna-adventure.com Their activities include quad biking, 4 x 4 tours, walking, kayaking, mountain biking, parascending, golf, climbing, wine tours and music evenings. They have a hotel and apartments. Hotel la Mariposa, Gebas, Alhama De Murcia, 968 631008.

The Visitor Centre, **Centro de Visitantes Ricardo Codorníu**, 968 431430 is an old Ricardo Codorniú mansion located in the heart of the Espuña, where you can learn about the Regional Park. The Center has a reception area, an audiovisual room and Conference Training Room and Lab.

Ricardo Codorníu y Stárico was a forestry engineer and advocate of the cause of forestry. He carried out numerous projects among which the reforestation of the Sierra de Espuña was just one. A generous man, a pioneer in the conservation of trees and birds, Ricardo Codorníu, known as the Apostle of the Tree, devoted his life to the dissemination and teaching of the forest environment through conferences and publications. He was also one of those responsible for the introduction of Esperanto in Spain, a project to create a common language for all mankind, founding the Esperanto Society of Murcia in 1902.

Next to the Interpretation Centre is the area known as **Espuña Huerta**. This is one of the most historic places in the park, since it was the hub of the tasks of recruitment led by Ricardo Codorniú, here he performed the first experimental crops to study the viability of the plants in this environment, which subsequently he used for reforestation.

At the end of the sixteenth century the first wells to store snow, pozos de la nieve, were built. During 125 years 25 of these snow stores were built, which could store up to 25,000 metric tons of ice. Look out for these ice domes on your travels.

A great vantage point, **Mirador del Collado Bermejo**, offers one of the best panoramic views of the Sierra as it is situated at an altitude of 1,201m.

For a great view of the snow wells try **Mirador del Collado Mangueta**. Mirador del Collado Pilón gives views to the southwest of the Sierra, at a height of 1,065 meters.

The Gebas ravines are one of the most spectacular natural features in the area. This is a desert-like space, like a moonscape or bad-lands, which consists of gullies and canyons. With 2,271 hectares, it is divided between the municipalities of Alhama de Murcia and Librilla. To see this wonderful landscape descend on the eastern side of the mountain to the town of Gebas, where there is a viewpoint. Some useful websites www.espunaturistica.net and www.ecoespuna.com.

If you fancy a spot of potholing then Pliego is the place to go. There's the **Cueva Santa Bárbara** with a distance of 107 meters and a height of 15 meters; Sima del Lames with a distance of 150 meters and a drop of 25 meters and Sima de la Higuera, the most important cave in the municipality, 5,500 meters long and with a height of 154 meters this is the largest cave in the Region of Murcia. To enjoy the caves contact the Club Pliego Espuña who are responsible for regulating access, or the Murcia Potholing Federation, www.espeleomurcia.es/federacion/actualidad-ferm.

Debbie Jenkins, Russ Pearce

Location Report: Downhill Mountain Biking in the Sierra Espuña

The idea of cycling UP the Sierra Espuña never really appealed to my lazy bottom, however, freewheeling all the way down? That's a different matter. With food at the end? Great, count me in!

An early start at the lovely hotel in Gebas in the Sierra Espuña, the guys were loading the trailer with bikes and spare kit, everyone piled into the vehicles and 3/4 of an hour later we were at the summit, ready for the descent. Even in August it's cold at the top of the Sierra Espuña, I was shivering and ready to get started. We started the ride above the clouds, which cleared up pretty quickly as we descended.

The downhill sections were mainly on tarmacked road and off-road trails, which are clearly signed and well maintained. The road sections are a little hair-raising if you're a wuss like me. The roads twist and wind, with views far off into the valleys below. There is very little traffic up in the mountains, but take care, and of course wear a safety helmet. As you near lunchtime the track levels out and then you have to work a bit harder for your lunch, with the last half an hour on an uphill road ride back to the hotel.

It's a great activity for the whole family, as long as you're all quite confident cycling on roads. It's great value, and the lunch was welcome (as was the glass of wine).

We went with the guys from The Espuña Adventure, who run the Mariposa Hotel which is where lunch was served. You get a knowledgeable guide to make sure everyone is safe and doesn't get lost or left behind. I think I won the award for the slowest downhill bike ride ever! At regular points Mark Langton would meet up with us to make sure everyone was OK, and give people an opportunity to stop and go back to the hotel if they wanted to.

They put dates on their website, but get in touch to find out when the next one is planned. They also do kayaking, quad biking and walking tours. The Espuña Adventure – info@espuna-adventure.com – +34 968631008

Torre Pacheco

Population: 35,200

Map Reference: 0.95°W, 37.74°N

The landscape is characterised by the almost total absence of water channels and mountainous terrain, except the **Cabezo Gordo** which is the only mountain you'll see as you drive across the campo de Cartagena. Cabezo Gordo (Fat Head) is well on its way to becoming Cabezo Delgado (Skinny Head) as they slowly whittle away at it.

Torre Pacheco's history goes back to the Ice Age when they settled in Cabezo Gordo. The archaeological site of **Sima de las Palomas** in Cabezo Gordo is one of the most important Palaeolithic sites in the region. Originally a vertical mine shaft emptied by miners looking for magnetite in the area in the late nineteenth century, its 18 meters depth make it difficult to excavate. However, it has provided more than 120 hominid bones and teeth dated between 150,000 and 35,000 BC. These remains must belong to at least nine different individuals. They have also found the fossils of many prehistoric animals: elephants, hippos, aurochs, horse, wild ass, megacerino (giant deer), red deer, roe deer, Spanish goat, panther, lower carnivores (fox, lynx), hare, bats, insectivores, rodents, minor potential marine mammals, birds of different species and fragments of eggs, turtle (often burnt), smaller reptiles and inland marine molluscs (gastropods). Read more in the location report.

The cultural heritage of the town is dotted with beautiful houses, including **Caserón de Ros** (Balsicas), **Casa Fontes** and **Casa de Valderas** (Roldán), and imposing windmills and watermills, such as Pasico and Tío Pacorro.

El Molino del Pasico is located next to the **Ermita de Nuestra Señora del Pasico,** in the village of Hortichuela. Windmills were introduced into the area from the sixteenth century and flour mills from the eighteenth century to the mid-twentieth century. There are many examples of mills around the Campo de Cartagena, however, the mills in Torre Pacheco are worth a visit due to the restoration and conservation projects undertaken. This mill was restored in 1991.

While you're admiring the mill take a look at the Ermita too. The **Ermita del Pasico** is located a mile from Torre Pacheco. It is a rustic building inside which is a French alabaster stone located in the trunk of an almond tree. This has an image of La Piedad, known locally as the Virgin del Pasico. There have been many miraculous deeds attributed to the Virgin. Some devotees have dedicated plaques of appreciation for the assistance. The big day for the Virgen del Pasico is on Easter Monday when the locals spend the day with family.

Torre Pacheco's economy is based primarily on intensive agriculture, producing a large amount of fruits and vegetables, especially melons, aimed mostly for exportation. The services sector has gained importance in recent years, especially after the development of IFEPA which benefits from the location of the town being near Cartagena, Murcia and Corvera airport.

IFEPA is a showground for trade fairs and exhibitions, built around 25 years ago, and is now one of the most important business meeting arenas in the southeast of Spain. The **Institución Ferial Villa de Torre Pacheco**, in collaboration with different organisations and associations hosts a series of national events every year. Of particular note are the Turismur tourism show usually held in February, the horse show **Equimur** in April and **Entreculturas** in March. If you sign up on their website you get advance notice and discounts on tickets. Avenida Gerardo Molina, 45, 968 336383, www.ifepa.es

Torre Pacheco's fiesta patronale is in honour of Virgin Mary Our Lady of the Rosary held in the first fortnight of October. There are floats, parades, music and brass bands.

Also of importance is the Melon Festival in August as a tribute to one of the most important food products of the municipality. Between the 5th and 7th of June there's the Fiestas Trinitario Berberiscas with musicians and stilt walkers, falconry display, juggling, children's theatre, etc. The festivities are located on the esplanade next to the Performing Arts Center.

Late August marks the National Festival de Cante Flamenco de Lo Ferro, one of the flamenco song contests in Spain. www.loferroflamenco.com

Location Report:
Cabezo Gordo, The Murcian Mountain Of Secrets

It is hard to miss the imposing mountain called Cabezo Gordo. It rises up out of the plain which surrounds the Mar Menor and dominates the landscape. Translated into English its name is 'Fat Head' mountain and if you catch it from a certain angle it really does look like the profile of a head sticking up from the dry earth. Some people know it as the Marble Mountain as the north side of the mountain is being mined for marble. The mining is clearly visible if you are driving on the motorway.

Most days the view of the mountain is crystal clear but on the occasional day when bad weather is forecast it is a sure sign that the rain is on the way to the Mar Menor when El Cabezo Gordo disappears.

However the mountain is not just an unusual and rather beautiful landmark it is also a place that is extremely important to geologists and archaeologists as it has held long hidden secrets which shine light onto the history of the region and the humans and animals that once lived here.

Around one hundred years ago miners excavated large parts of the mountain, probably looking for iron ore or possibly access to water. They finished mining in 1917 and it wasn't until 1991 that a local ecologist who was exploring the caves left by the miners found a fossil in the back wall of a cave. This fossil turned out to be upper and lower jaws of a Neanderthal human.

The following year after examination of the miners' rubble excavation of the site began and continues to be undertaken today. Bones of at least eight or nine Neanderthal individuals have been found, from both adults and children. It is stated that these are the second oldest human remains on the Iberian Peninsula. Drills and hammers made from marble, quartz and rock crystal have been collected and dated from the Palaeolithic period. In addition some extremely interesting remains of fauna have been discovered including evidence of a panther or lion, hyena, hippo, elephant, rhinoceros, deer, wild horses, aurochs, Spanish goat, hare, rabbit and turtle.

Once a year, in the summer months, the site is opened and the University professor Michael J. Walker shows the latest discoveries to the public. It is really easy to miss this chance to find out more first-hand and it is always worth keeping an eye on the local press to see exactly when it will take place. Buses are usually arranged from Torre Pacheco centre to the site and it is a popular local event.

Even if you are not able to visit at that time it is interesting to take a drive over to the mountain and explore the exterior slopes. On the mountain's south side you will find a car park and although you cannot see any of the Neanderthal bones you can spot plants that are unique to this habitat and appreciate the many different types of rocks that have been scattered from the mining activity in the area. There are boards displaying information about the mountain and its hidden secrets, but you will need to understand Spanish. You will notice straight away various cave entrances on this side and there are more around the mountain.

Stout shoes are recommended and the area is not suitable for younger children as there is still a lot of loose mining debris which could be hazardous for small feet. Follow the path up the mountain to find the cave which is an entrance to the mine Sima de las Palomas and you will be around 100 meters above sea level. Here you will have a fantastic view of the Mar Menor across to the hills at Calblanque and La Manga Club.

Martine Cherry, www.rhumhor.com

For walkers then a trip up Cabezo Gordo is a must. There are a variety of different routes to take; some include a 200m tunnel originally used for mining iron ore, more recently used for growing mushrooms. There are natural caves, shrines and dried up riverbeds. And of course the archaeological site of Sima de las Palomas. Some of the routes are not well marked and require quite a bit of scrambling. If you're not super fit stick to the paths and enjoy the view.

Torre Pacheco also includes the following towns: Roldán, Balsicas, Dolores de Pacheco, El Jimenado, San Cayetano, Los Olmos-Hoyamorena, Hortichuela, Los Meroños, Los Camachos and Santa Rosalía.

Of note is Balsicas, one of the largest by population of the towns in the area. It owes its name to small ponds built in the sixteenth century in order to water animals. There are a number of beautiful houses built from the 15th century onwards for noble families from Torre Pacheco. There's the **Castillo de los Vizcondes de Ros** built for the writer, Antonio Ros de Olano, who had a great political and military career in the 19th century.

Roldán is also worth mentioning. The beautiful **Casa Valderas** looks more like a palace than a 19th century farmhouse. It belonged to the family Melgarejo and is now owned by the city. The neoclassical **Casa Valdez** is a rectangular three-storey building with stables, a mill and food storage rooms. The decorative motif in blue and white stands in contrast to the ochre colour of the house.

And of course there's the **La Torre golf resort**, www.latorregolfresort.com.

Services

Tourist Office, Plaza del Ayuntamiento, 1, 968 579937, www.torrepacheco.es/turismo,

Ayuntamiento, 968 577108, www.torrepacheco.es

Sleeping

You could stay on the La Torre Golf Resort, Calle Anchoa, 6, 900 983 177, www.latorregolfresort.com/hotel. As you would expect the quality is high, along with the prices. They have three restaurants on site too.

There are a few casas rurales around, two at Casa Rural Agapito, on Paraje El Albardinal, www.tuscasasrurales.com/casa-rural-agapitos-1-y-2-f14332.asp, 656 591356.

Eating

Many people head for the La Torre resort where there are a number of restaurants. The Ginkgo Club Asia Restaurante is a pricey Asian style restaurant and the Vinoteca Spanish restaurant is a little more economical. There's also the Limonero Arrocería, Acacia Trattoria (Italian), The Clover Irish Sports Bar and the Heladería Avellano on the site.

In San Cayetano there's the Restaurante Rincon de Joaquin, on Calle Enrique Garcia Alvarez, 968 580893 www.rincondejoaquin.com, which serves traditional Murcian food including homemade puddings!

Totana

Population: 21,400

Map Reference: 1.50°W, 37.78°N

The **Church of Santiago** was built during 1535 to 1567 due to the considerable increase in the population, which meant that the small church of La Concepción was insufficient to house the community in their religious ceremonies. The architecture of the church is, in general, Tuscan. Three scenes from the life of Christ are depicted on the inside, The Prayer of the Orchard (La Oración de la Huerta), the Holy Burial (El Santo Entierro) and the Fall (la Caída).

La Torre, The Tower was built as an annexe to the church between 1606 and 1608, again in Tuscan style. The body of the tower is made up of three levels and covered in brick. The interior light comes from three small windows. The last level where the bell is found has two arches on either side. The bell tower's aim was to alert the town to the presence of Muslims, to announce the delivery of water, to signal the start and end of the working day and to call the faithful to religious rituals.

The Ayuntamiento was possibly built in the 16th century, although it was restored in the current century (1939 - 1940). It's a typical brick construction of Totana from that era. The **Casa de las Contribuciones** (The

Contribution House) is built in an eclectic style and consists of three floors and a semi-basement towards the Plaza de la Constitución. It is listed as a grade 2 building of monumental interest.

Take a look at the **Fuente de la Plaza Mayor** which stands in front of the church of Santiago, in the Plaza Mayor. It's an enormous baroque style fountain built in 1753 by the sculptor Juan de Uzeta. This fountain was needed due to the considerable increase in the population of Totana, which meant the water supplied by the Frailes Fountain was insufficient, leaving the population almost on a daily basis without water.

La Cárcel, The Prison, was originally a church dedicated to the medicinal saints Cosme and Damián. It was designed by the architect of the Diocesis, Don Justo Millán Espinosa, who also built the Teatro Romea in Murcia, the Church of la Caridad in Cartagena and the cemetery in Totana. Today it houses the Town Cultural Centre and the Universidad Popular.

Ermita de San Roque is situated on the slope of a hill, surrounded on the South and East side by stone walls and the rest of the building by an inner courtyard which allows access to the three flights of steps leading to streets San Roque, Santa Eulalia and La Monja. It's a Tuscan style building with a rectangular floor and one nave, covered with a semi-circular dome supported by arches and semi-spherical cupolas on the transept; adorned with eighteenth century pictures of floral motifs of garlands or chains in blue and red tones.

There's an aqueduct, **Arco de las Ollerías**, built by D Pedro de Mora Cánovas from Totana in 1753, to transport water for irrigation. This is found on the access road to the Ermita de la Huerta.

One of the principal attractions of Totana is just outside town towards the Sierra Espuña. The **Santuario de la Santa** (Sanctuary of Santa Eulalia de Mérida) is nestled in a valley to the northwest of town, this 17th century monastery, decadent in striking pink stands out against the green of the pine forest. The origin of the sanctuary is placed at the second half of the first century; documentation exists from the 14th century where they already had news of the existence of a small sanctuary, built by the Order of Santiago. The present day sanctuary was built with alms from the followers in 1574.

A man named Alonso de Murcia took over the hermitage and he and his son gave wine for charity. Later it became the property of Ginés Arredo who decided against continuing the custom established by his predecessors. Consequently, the Town Hall fined him, obliging him to deliver wine to whoever should ask for it.

In the last third of the 16th century devotion to the Saint grew, people believed she had miraculous powers, curing the sick and the crippled who drank from the fountain situated opposite the Hermitage.

The church is built in Tuscan style formed by a central rectangular nave; the roof is a mixture of wood and crafted Mudejar. Inside the altarpiece of the main altar is the work of Jerónimo Caballo and is dated from 1717.

Saint Eulalia de Mérida (292 AC) was raised to the altar by Pope Urbano VIII in 1644. She was proclaimed Patron Saint of almost all of Christian Spain and nowadays is the only Spanish Saint from the first centuries. Her remains are preserved in Oviedo Cathedral. There is a traditional pilgrimage on the 7th January in honour of the Saint where the people from Totana and visitors come together to enjoy the religious ceremonies, music, food and dancing.

Santa Eulalia also gets celebrated on December 8, 9 and 10, where parties, religious ceremonies and migas eating are encouraged. Totana celebrates carnival in February/March each year and in July they have 'Velada de Habaneras y Canciones Populares' (Evening of Habaneras and Popular Songs).

Totana has one of the biggest and most varied concentrations of **craft workshops**; its production puts it in direct competition with Granada. The majority of the workshops are family owned where they make and sell their own creations.

Pottery is one of the main crafts. The pieces are crafted from clay made from fuller's earth and are extracted with pickaxes and hoes from the Canteras del Canvete. Many pieces are made for domestic use in the kitchen and for preserving food. Pieces such as the tinajas (large earthen jars) and orzas (glazed earthenware jar) for the preservation of liquids and food or the lebrillo (earthenware bowl) used for washing and the cántaro (pitcher) used to transport water, together with botijos (earthenware jugs).

In the middle of the 18th century the majority of pottery shops were found on the banks of the Rambla de la Santa, in the Triana district. In the 19th century some were already being found in the former district of Sevilla, today Paseo de las Ollerías. With the arrival of the new century pottery suffered waves in its production; however, the tinajas were very popular and became the potter's number one product. In the middle of the century there was a decline in this craft sector due to the fall in the use of the domestic utensils, like the lebrillo or the cántaro and they started to make pieces for the garden, like flower pots and window boxes. At the same time a great innovation of variety of forms and treatment of the clay took place, they started to glaze the pieces with transparent glass and worked white clay. Many items are exported around Europe, including to France, Belgium, Germany and Holland.

There is the **Centro Tecnológico del Barro** (Technological Centre of Clay) situated in an old oven on Paseo de las Ollerías, where the old clay pots were made. There are a couple of shops specialising in selling local pieces, including Bellón on Paseo Ollerías and Ibero Alfar on Calle Tinajerías. There are a number of other workshops out of town, between the N340 and the road to Mazarrón.

Walkers can enjoy a huge variety of routes, with a mixture of difficulties and distances. You can download route maps from the tourist website: www.turismo.totana.es, click on "rutas de senderismo".

Location Report: La Bastida De Totana

La Bastida de Totana is an archaeological site just outside the town of Totana. La Bastida de Totana was an Argaric Culture, which once numbered between 200 and 300 households and was inhabited between 1650 BC and 1100 BC approximately (the Bronze Age). It was discovered in 1869 and declared of Cultural Interest in 2005. With an area of 40,000m² various excavations at the site have found over 10,000 pieces of ceramics and metal, mainly urban habitat structures, more than a hundred graves, as well as numerous examples of their culture and urban planning.

El Cabezo de La Bastida, with an altitude of 448 meters, is located 6km from the city centre in the foothills of the Sierra de la Tercia in the Guadalentín Valley. Mountains around the site are the Espuña in the north (highest point 1577m), west of the Sierra de la Tercia lies the Sierra de la Almenara, at 600 m and to the east the Carrascoy Sierra (1065m).

The Society of La Bastida was characterised by its hierarchical social classes: high chiefs and warriors, middle free men, low serfs or slaves. The houses were built of adobe with flat roofs of straw and mud and with one or more rooms. There have been some reconstructions to show what it would have looked like. You can see more on the website: www.regmurcia.com

The burials were carried out under the house and could be single, double or triple burial sites. The types of burials were either in a cist (a box or chest) or urns and vases.

The main economic activities were agriculture, grain, sheep, goats and swine. Also production of pottery with ceramic clay or plaster cooked in small batches for the production of tools. In short, La Bastida de Totana is the most important Argaric site in the Region of Murcia and one of the most important legacies of this culture in Spain.

There's an Interpretation Centre and Museum of La Bastida de Totana (Centro de Interpretación y Museográfico de La Bastida) located within the Archaeological Park. La Bastida cannot be understood as an isolated nucleus due to linkages with other settlements, so the Interpretation Centre and Museum displays items that addresses issues such as environment, changes in territory and population and the funerary world to provide greater cultural relevance and tourism.

Towns in the area include: Paretón, Raiguero, Lebór, Viñas, Huerta, Ñorica, Sierra and Morti.

Services

Tourist Office, Plaza de la Balsa Vieja, 968 418153, www.turismo.totana.es/

Ayuntamiento, Plaza De La Constitución, 1, 968 418151, www.totana.es.

Bus Station, buses to Murcia, Mazarrón and Lorca. Train Station, Águilas, Murcia line. Estación Intermodal de Totana, 968 425427.

Sleeping

If you fancy a night under the stars try the campsite Camping Totana on the 340 motorway at junction 614, 968 424864, www.campingtotana.es/ There are spaces for tents and vans, plus a few bungalows.

The hotel Executive Sport on Calle El Granado, 1, 968 418209 www.executive-sport.com, has its own spa and mini golf course and caters for the sporty visitor. They often have offers on their website, many focusing on romantic breaks (and smothering yourself in chocolate!)

Hotel Totana Sur off the A7, km616, is just out of town towards Lorca, 968 421037. A useful stop off point on the motorway, it has a good restaurant too. From €50.

For a spot of luxury stay at the old Monasterio Santa Eulalia, on the road between Totana and Aledo, 968

487004, www.hoteljardinesdelasanta.com. This is one of the true four star hotels in the region and with only 35 rooms it is really quite intimate.

Eating

Tapas can be had on the Plaza de la Constitución. Also worth trying is Restaurante Santa Barbara on Calle Santa Barbara and Cairo on Calle la Fuente.

Yecla

Population: 34,100

Map Reference: 1.12°W, 38.62°N

The northern most town of Murcia is Yecla (96km north of Murcia). Yecla is one of the three wine producing regions with its own DOC in Murcia (the other two being Bullas and Jumilla). The name Yecla comes from the Arab word Yakka.

The first signs of settlement in the town of Yecla go back to the sixth millennium BC on Monte Arabí. **Monte Arabí** is an important archaeological site (a UNESCO World Heritage Site) along with all forms of rock art in the Mediterranean Iberian Peninsula. The three shelters (semi-caves) on the long hill, visible from the road near the Rambla del Arabí, contain cave paintings and rock art. You can reach the hill via the road connecting the towns of Yecla and Fuente Álamo. Access to shelters is difficult; you need to walk part of the journey on a poor condition track. All three caves are protected by fencing.

Up on the hill you'll find the **Santuario de la Purísima Concepcion**, which offers great views of the town and surrounding areas. The church is located in the Plaza de la Purisima. The church was built in two phases from 1775 by Joseph Lopez, who made the plans and in a second stage after a break, by Jerome Ross, who ended his construction 1868 and is responsible for the characteristic dome.

There are many churches in the town including **La Iglesia de la Asunción** on the Plaza de la Asunción built in gothic and renaissance style in the first half of the 16th century and the Iglesia de San Francisco in Baroque style. The old town is quite beautiful but rather short on interesting bars, restaurants and cafes.

There is also a castle, **Castillo de Yecla**, from the 14th century, 180m above the town. There's not much left of it, remains of the interior wall, exterior walls and a well.

The Roman villa **Torrejones** is in the hamlet 3km east of Yecla. It was one of the four large villas (along with those of Marisparza, Casa de la Ermita and El Pulpillo) around which the farm land was structured in the Yecla area in Roman times. It covers an area of more than 4 square kilometres, of which only a fraction has been excavated. The artefacts collected in the field are not limited to Roman times, but also extend from the Iberian period until well into the Middle Ages (thirteenth century) at the end of Islamic domination.

The **Municipal Archaeological Museum Cayetano de Mergelina** has three hundred square meters divided into seven rooms, where you can explore the prehistoric times, the Iberian world, the Romanization of the plateau and the Middle Ages in Yecla. Calle Spain, 37, 968 790901, museoarqueologicodeyecla.org.

The current theatre, **Teatro Concha Segura**, is located on land which was the old Granary House, Casa Panera del Pósito, and was built between 1886 and 1887. There's an active agenda including opera, theatre and dance. There are 558 seats and it can be found on Calle Alfareria 2, 968 751134.

The principal industry is the manufacture of furniture, with 40 furniture shops along one road alone.

The fiesta of San Isidro is in the middle of May and their Fiesta Patronales is in December.

On the 3rd February they celebrate San Blas, with pan bendito, blessing the bread, jams and greasy poles. San Antón is a popular festival dating from the end of the eighteenth century, held around the 17th February. Leading up to the spring festival is the Pilgrimage of San Marcos on 25th April, with songs, dances and traditional games.

Bodegas

Findings from archaeological excavations in the area have confirmed that grape growing and wine production has been practiced in this area for over two thousand years and was probably introduced by the ancient Romans. There was a period of expansion at the end of the 19th century when French wine merchants became involved in the region due to the effects of the phylloxera plague in France. Official DO status was acquired in 1975.

The vineyards are planted at an altitude of between 400 and 800 meters above sea level, in calcareous soils. Wine DO Yecla is divided into 2 major parts, Yecla Campo Arriba and Yecla Campo Abajo, which combined comprise 6,500 hectares of vineyard for red wine varieties Monastrell, Garnacha, Tempranillo, Merlot, Cabernet Sauvignon and Syrah. And for white wines Airen, Meseguera, Macabeo and Malvasia.

Bodegas La Purísima, Carretera Pinoso, 968 751257 www.bodegaslapurisima.com, has been producing wine since 1946. They produce a variety of wines including some bag in box table wines, Valcorso from 100% Merlot and organic wines. They have a shop on site, open from Monday to Friday all year round at the following times: mornings from 09:00 to 14:00, afternoons from 16:00 to 19:00.

Bodegas Castaño, Carretera Fuente Álamo, 3, 968 791115, www.bodegascastano.com. A family run and owned winery, started in 1950, with 450 hectares of grapes. They have their Dominio Espinal in white, rose and red and one of our favourites the Hécula. If you want to visit them they will organise a walk in the vineyard and tours in the winery showing the different stages in winemaking. You will also be able to taste the best wines produced in Bodegas Castaño and if you want you can also enjoy the typical home-made dishes in their dining room.

Bodegas Señorio De Barahonda, Carretera Pinoso km3 has visits Tuesday to Saturday 11:30 to 12:00 but is closed during August. Finca La Castañona, 968 718696, www.barahonda.com

Bodegas Y Viñedos Evine, Camino de Sax, km7 Paraje Las Cabezuelas, 639 209556, www.bodegasevine.com. They have 60 hectares of vines, mainly Monastrell.

Bodegas Y Viñedos La Casa De Las Especias, Carretera de Yecla Fuente Álamo, km14, 627 088572, www.casadelasespecias.com. It gets its name from the spice trade which was run from here and has been the home to generations of wine makers.

For more about the wines of Yecla take a tour at www.yeclavino.com

Services

Tourist office, 958 754104,

Ayuntamiento, Plaza Mayor, 968 754100, www.ayuntamientoyecla.com

Taxis, 968 791216

Sleeping

Good value is the Hotel Avenida, Calle San Pasqual, 3, via www.booking.com, 968 751215. There's a bar and restaurant downstairs too. Or the Hotel La Paz on Avenida de la Paz, 180, www.lapaz-hotel.com, 968 751350, which is a bit more pricey and also has a restaurant.

If you're on a budget then the youth hostel, Casa Rural Fuente Del Pinar, at km14 on the Yecla to Almansa road has 50 beds at a great price. www.webrural.com/España/Murcia-España/Yecla/Fuente-del-Pinar/

Eating

There are some restaurants around the town including a couple of Chinese.

You might want to try Restaurante La Paz, Avenida La Paz, 180.

Or enjoy a glass or two of wine at the restaurant at the Barahonda Bodega, www.barahonda.com, on the Pinoso Road, 968 753604. This restaurant has excellent food in a great location, and did I mention they have wine?

Essential Information

Brexit

In March 2019, Spain issued a royal decree guaranteeing the rights of 365,967 Britons who are registered as residents. Effectively, this means they can still enjoy the same rights to healthcare, to work and freedom of movement as before Brexit.

Others who do not currently have residency permission have until the end of 2020 to apply.

However, the Spanish deal is dependent on Britain bringing in a reciprocal agreement for about 150,000 Spaniards living in the UK. So far, the UK has brought in its settled status scheme for current EU residents but no bilateral deal exists. The transition period ends on January 1st, 2021.

Brexit: The rules for driving, passports, cards, pet travel and more may change from 1 January 2021. Keep informed.

Spanish nationality: If you've lived here for more than 10 years you can begin the process of applying for Spanish citizenship. It's complicated and costly, and takes quite a while (2 years plus). In addition Spain does not allow double nationality, so you also must renounce your British nationality. Take legal advice.

We are not going to cover any more details about Brexit, it's a moving target, with too many ramifications. Keep informed. Listen to and read factual sources of information. Check on the Government's website (semi-factual!): https://www.gov.uk/

Students

So what is the key to making a successful move? This obviously depends on your age and the degree to which you wish to integrate. If you are young(ish) and still in a position to decide where your life wants to go there are a number of options open to you.

- Undergraduates. The ERASMUS programme (www.erasmusprogramme.com), which has operated since 1987, gives students the chance to spend 3 to 12 months in a foreign country continuing their education and gaining all-important credits. Exchanges are usually organised by the home university so everything is set up before you leave.

> **How will Brexit impact the Erasmus+ programme?** The Withdrawal Agreement foresees that the UK will continue to participate in the current 2014-2020 EU programmes, including Erasmus+, as if the UK was an EU Member State until the closure of the programmes. The possible participation of the UK in future programmes after 2020 will depend on the outcome of the overall negotiations on the future relationship between the two parties. Source: https://ec.europa.eu/

- Postgraduates. Don't underestimate the broad range of courses on offer for Master's degrees and the excellent level of tutoring for doctoral theses in Spain. You would be mad to even think about it without a competent level of Spanish.
- English Teaching. Long gone are the days when you could turn up and get a job just because you spoke English. You will need a CELTA (the basic teaching certificate available through Cambridge TESOL) which can be obtained in several cities around Spain (https://www.studycelta.com/tefl-spain/). Once qualified you'll be able to apply for jobs from websites like www.tefl.com

Retiring

After a life of working, what better way to enjoy your hard-earned rest than in a year-round, sunny, warm climate? There are health spas in places like Fortuna, Archena and the Mar Menor, providing specialised treatments. There are already many ex-pats here so a thriving social life is assured.

Ensure you have excellent financial advice from someone who understands the issues of pensions and transferring money from the UK.

Pensions after 31 January 2020: There will be no changes before 31 December 2020 to the rules on claiming the UK State Pension in the EU, EEA or Switzerland as a result of the UK leaving the EU. Keep informed: https://www.gov.uk/guidance/living-in-spain#pensions

Working

Whilst many older people will come to Murcia to spend their retirement, this group has been joined by an increasing number of young professionals who, often as a result of the Internet, are able to continue their career in sunnier climes. If you belong to one of these groups you will have an independent income. But even so making Murcia your permanent home requires a great deal of thought, planning and research. See the moving section for more information.

If you work for an international company with offices in Spain, you could join the increasing number of workers who take advantage of a secondment abroad. Your company's Human Resources department should be able to organise everything for you. Bear in mind that a move might also involve a drop in salary.

Going Native: Georgie Foster Makes It Work

My name is Georgie Foster, I am originally from Stoke on Trent in Staffordshire and more recently from Somerset. I currently live, on a permanent basis, in Puerto De Mazarrón. I chose to live here in the port because I am passionate about the sea and I love the vibrancy the place offers me. (My apartment is a minutes' walk to the beach) I have no transport so living here affords me the luxury of having everything I need on my doorstep. I have shops, bars and restaurants all within walking distance of my home, it's perfect! The people here are very friendly, its multi-cultural which I love, and I know if I need help there is always someone I can call on.

I absolutely love Cartagena it just has a beautiful feel to it with the stunning marble Plaza Major, the little restaurants tucked away in the back streets, amazing waterfront and the wonderful Roman Amphitheatre.

One of my favourite beaches must be Bahia, there is something very tranquil and soothing about it and I always have a sense of calmness when I visit there. Living in the port I get to see our beautiful beach every day. I also love to visit the beaches of Bolnuevo and Isla Plana. I have always enjoyed a lovely meal at La Chara in Isla Plana, it's a family run restaurant and they offer a good Menu Del Dia. I also love the Restaurante Avenida in Puerto de Mazarrón, a Spanish run restaurant with very good food, with an A La Carte menu and also Tapas and the typical Menu del Dia/Noche. The lovely Oasis Cafateria in Bolneuvo is a great place to hang out for food/drinks/music and in the summer they have the Chiringuito beach bar which is fab.

I love waking up with a smile every day and none of the stresses of the UK! And most days to sunshine… Sometimes I can't quite believe this is my life now.

I originally came out here 3 years ago and a big part of me wishes I had not returned to England as I feel I would have been so much more established now with work, language and lifestyle. However, on the flipside by taking myself back it made me realise that Spain was my passion and how much I wanted this life. So, it was now down to me to come back and fight for it and make it work. So last year that's what I did and what I am currently doing right now... working hard to make my dream a permanent reality!

From a work perspective it can be tough, so you need to be mentally and financially prepared for that. I have had good and lean times. You just have to ride it out and weather the storm. My advice is to come out here with a positive attitude but be prepared that its not always as easy as you think it's going to be. Get things in place, get your NIE (Social Security Number) as future employers are going to ask for it.

I had previously worked in Sales/Training or Holistic/Beauty roles. Last year I took myself out of my comfort zone and put myself into a Spanish restaurant into a role I have never done before. It was challenging, crazy, busy, frustrating at times but I loved every minute of it and smiled/laughed my way through it and survived to tell the tale! I am looking forward to starting a new role soon in a newly refurbished bar/restaurant in the Puerto, so am feeling very excited to be a part of this new venture. Happy times ahead!

There is a growing tourism industry with many tourist related job opportunities. Opportunities exist in the property trading business throughout the area. Many expats offer their services to one another using the housing estates as hubs for networking. **For your own protection make sure you are a legal business in Spain and that you only contract with other legal businesses.**

Murcia and Cartagena are well–developed business cities with many opportunities for people who speak Spanish. There are some major employers in the area including SABIC Innovative Plastics (formerly GE Plastics). Sport related work is available along the coast. Internet access isn't a barrier to home working as fibre optic Internet has reached most towns in the area.

If you want to run your own business you will need to set up a company in Spain. Now, I am not qualified to give you legal advice about this process, but I am qualified to tell you what happened to me and how I managed to get a limited company set up in Spain and why. So I researched online, read the books, asked my friends, learnt all I could about the process, the pros and cons, the ins and outs and then decided that I would get someone else to do it for me!

I thought it was a hassle in the UK but Spain really takes bureaucracy to a new level of inventiveness. Now if you've already done this you might be thinking I'm making a montaña out of a colina but bear with me on this, the 'official' steps and my experience of them are a story to be told!

Should You Move To Spain?

For those of you thinking of making a move then you might like to consider what makes a successful expat:

- Adaptable and tolerant, taking the initial culture shock and different way of doing things in your stride.
- Independent, able to enjoy difference and diversity while retaining a strong sense of your own identity.
- Language learners, apply yourself to learning Spanish with commitment and enthusiasm.
- Flexible, able to make changes to plans without regrets.
- Positive frame of mind, there'll be good days and bad days. The trick is to focus on what you like about being here.

Not everybody wants to spend the rest of their life away from their home country. A short stay of a few months to a couple of years can be fulfilling and rewarding and will be an experience that will stay with you forever. However, there are certain people that seem doomed to fail. You can normally spot them a mile away and I suggest you avoid them.

- Criticisers, they arrive rubbishing everything they've left behind. Within a few months they'll be rubbishing the life they've built around themselves.
- Escape artists, some shady characters go to live in far-flung lands, but a more common example is couples who think a change of air might sort out their marital problems.
- Assumers, who expect you to be their new best friend, help them with their language difficulties and drive them around everywhere.
- The homesick, they may miss many aspects of their old life, but if things were so great back home, why did they leave in the first place?

Buying a House

For a full in depth look at the property market in Murcia and detailed buying, renting and selling guides then read

Buying Property in Murcia: Insider Tips on Buying, Selling and Renting Property in South East Spain, you can get details from http://www.NativeSpain.com This book is quite old now, but the vast majority of the information is still valid, except of course my predictions!

Developments

King Felipe VI officially opened Corvera Murcia Airport on 15th January 2019. The long-awaited inauguration opened up the Murcia region to an extensive network of international flights and destinations after several years of administrative delays. As of writing the number of flights is down a little in respect to San Javier, but it is still early days.

The government also plans to link Murcia up to the high speed national rail network, called AVE trains (see section for more details) ensuring trips from Murcia to Madrid will be reduced from 4 hours to just 2.5 hours. Again this is a project that has been talked about for years but work finally got underway in 2019.

Murcia has a great motorway network, although the section of the AP-7 from Cartagena to Vera is a toll road. Greater water capacity has been provided in the area through desalination plants.

Buy in Haste, Re(pe)nt at Leisure - Rent First!

Many people advise that before you decide to buy a property in Murcia you should rent a house in a location close to your chosen destination. This way you'll get a much better idea if the location will be right for you.

Also, if at all possible, don't sell up in your home country but rent that house out. You'll often find that the rental prices in Spain are much lower than the income you could get from renting your home in the UK, leaving you with some positive cashflow to help finance your plans.

Going Native

There are parts of Murcia that have yet to be inundated with Brits and these are the places where you will need to speak Spanish; your neighbours will be Spanish, the shops will be owned and run by Spanish people and most of your friends will only speak Spanish.

By selecting this option you will not only benefit from the wonderful climate of Murcia but also from the rich and fantastic culture. If you're looking for a real change and challenge then this is the way to go. You must be prepared to work hard at integrating in your new community.

Countryside Properties

Renovations, fincas, village and town houses can all be found. In Murcia it's possible to find properties that are up to 20km away from the nearest civilisation. Often they will be up country tracks with subsequent challenges in reaching them! I know, here at the #DisasterFarm we have 5km of track to traverse, and during the few times of the year when we get a downpour our track is impassable.

This brings its own benefits and challenges: fantastic views and peace, but the drawbacks include, fixing punctures on your car and the lack of some services like water, electricity and drainage, which you will have to make arrangements for yourself.

In Murcia you may well find that you need to take special care that these properties are not in protected areas. The best way to discover this is from an independent architect.

There are also properties within just a few kilometres of charming villages where you get the best of all worlds, peace and quiet, easy access to services and the village lifestyle.

Many Murcian villages have traditional single storey houses, most of which were built about 100 years ago, with a central reception area and doors leading off to bedrooms, living rooms and kitchen. They are usually dimly lit, with small windows and thick walls for warmth in winter and coolness in summer.

Cities and Larger Towns

The majority of people living in Murcian cities and more modern towns live in apartments. This seems an aspirational lifestyle choice, though many people also own a weekend hideaway in the countryside!

Choose your district with extreme care, spending some time in the locality to get to know it well will pay off in the long run and help you avoid expensive mistakes.

Living in the city in summer can be noisy; you have to be happy to sleep with earplugs! The youngsters on mopeds with helmets on elbows and the late night revelry can be exhausting. Of course you may wish to join in!

For those who crave daily access to their own stretch of beach there are some fantastic beachside towns with an authentic Spanish feel such as Águilas. There are also a small number of houses near the protected coastlines where new builds are prohibited.

Home Comfort

For those of you for whom learning a new language is daunting and you are really looking at Murcia's sunshine as its principal benefit, there are plenty of opportunities. From the coastal new–build housing estates and Campos de Golf, to the villages that have a high ex–pat population, home comforts can be found aplenty.

Within the newly–built housing estates you can find a range of properties from one bedroom apartments through to 4 bedroom detached houses, with as many bathrooms and a swimming pool too! Almost all of the new housing estates built for non–Spaniards have an en–suite golf course. In addition most estates have shops catering for all the Brit needs, including British staff and goods.

You'll also find bars and restaurants selling British beer by the pint, pie and chips and other such British gourmet fare! There are plenty of social clubs in Murcia, set up by and catering for Brits, from bridge to badminton; cricket to crochet!

Take care when choosing an urbanisation, in particular be sure that all permissions are in place, that services are provided, that there is a sensible community charge and management committee. Whilst an urbanisation will provide you with a home, resources, shops and fellow countrymen you won't be getting the authentic Spanish lifestyle.

Holiday Home

If you're looking for a property that you will only sporadically occupy such as a holiday home then it's best to buy somewhere with higher regular occupancy. This will ensure people are around to watch over your home and minimise your fear of bandits, raiding and looting (a popular concern in rural, remote areas).

For Investment & Rental

Just three words here: Location, Location, Location. Murcia really comes up trumps in this regard, with new regional developments (trains, planes, roads etc), superb weather, glorious countryside and unspoilt beaches.

Standard of Living

You'll save on eating out here. Our last three course evening meal for three people, with drinks beforehand, wine with the meal and coffees etc, totalled just €60. That's just fifteen pounds each! The daytime set menu can be as low as €9 per person.

The days when prices for everything in Spain were incredibly cheap compared to the UK are long gone and now you can expect to pay a similar amount for most things as you'd expect to pay in the rest of Europe. The following items are generally cheaper to buy in Murcia: cigarettes, food and alcohol. It's also a little cheaper to rent a property. With these items more expensive: cars, white goods, internet access and telephones. And about the same: electricity, gas and water.

The region of Murcia covers an area of just over 11,000 km2, with a population of a little under 1.5 million, that's just 136 people per sq km compared to the UK's official number of 272.

Murcia has 18 hospitals, four international schools and three universities. Murcia University was founded more than 700 years ago, making it one of the oldest in Europe.

Looking

Never buy in Spain without first viewing the property.

Make sure before you even start looking that you have an idea of what you want. What will you use your property for, how many rooms do you need, how much land, how often will you stay there, do you want to make money from your investment? Most often things go wrong when there aren't strong criteria for selection.

Draw up a wishlist, give this to your agents. This should mean that when you go to view they will only be showing you what you want and can afford, if they're not, stop viewing with them!

Estate Agents

Estate agents in Murcia are little different from those in the UK, except that they should be treated with even less trust than those you left behind in Britain. The local Spanish press has run some amusing articles on how some of the estate agents operating in the region can totally misrepresent what's being sold and put on a price tag that no local Spaniard in their right mind would consider. Estate agents take an even greater cut of the sale in Spain so will pursue a sales lead with rabid persistence. Therefore, bear in mind that local estate agents perceive British buyers as having more money than sense and there seems to be a never–ending supply of these walking cash dispensers.

All that aside, there are good estate agents who are interested in your well being as well as their own. Just not too many of them! Make sure you check out the history of an estate agent, visit their offices and meet the staff, and most importantly ask for references.

You can look on the Internet (Facebook has plenty to choose from) and in the local expat press for their adverts for buying in the new Brit–oriented housing estates and local papers such as La Verdad for buying in the cities.

Private Sales

If, and only if, you have a really good command of the Spanish language and have spent years in Spain, could you consider going 'off piste' and buying privately. However, never,

never shake hands, pay anything or commit to anything before you have engaged the services of a local solicitor. The vendor will treat this with a great deal of suspicion since "that's not how they would do it" and "they aren't necessary and are a waste of money and time". You need to just play dumb at this stage and just say you need them to translate the paperwork for you and to understand the process, and the vendor should be a little more understanding. Usually the vendor will already be well–known to your future neighbours and probably related to them, so it pays to keep them sweet.

Developers

Our best tip here is that you will probably have the least grief if you buy a property that has already been built, either resale or from stock. Fortunately there's plenty of that about in Murcia right now, especially in an expat–oriented housing estate.

Purchasing a new property, New Build / Off Plan

If you have to pay the full purchase price before the property has been completed, by law, you must have the benefit of a bank guarantee to ensure that if the developer goes bankrupt before the completion of the building work, you do not lose your money. In some parts of Spain developers try to ignore this legal requirement.

You also need to make sure that the property specification is agreed in detail with the builder and that the property will be delivered to you complete with the necessary licence to occupy it as a home.

Don't buy off-plan, there are plenty of empty built homes to buy. If you really want a new house take a look at the banks' website's, many of them are auctioning off newly built properties that they've been unable to sell. Do your due diligence before making an offer!

Bank websites offering repossessed properties in Spain:

Bankinter: https://www.bankinter.com/www/es-es/cgi/ebk+inmuebles+home

BBVA: https://www.bbvavivienda.com/

BMN: https://www.bmnviviendas.com/

BNP Paribas: https://www.real-estate.bnpparibas.es/bnppre/es/inmuebles/

Solvia: http://www.solvia.es

Official national property auctions website, "Portal de subastas BOE": https://subastas.boe.es/

Fincas and Rural Properties

The building rules in Murcia change depending upon which municipality you happen to buy in. For example the rules in Fuente Álamo are different to Alhama de Murcia. Often an estate agent will have properties in multiple municipalities so you must take care to know what the rules for each are. Your estate agent may not know and assume blanket rules.

Before deciding to buy ensure that you will be able to rebuild by running your own check using your gestor, abogado and architect. Never trust the word of the estate agent.

Moving To Murcia

There are a number of things you will need when you move to Murcia, including:

NIE, Número de Identificación de Estranjero, this document is for resident and non–resident foreigners, acting as both a social security number and an identity document. You will need this to open a bank account.

Taxes, Income tax rates are currently similar to those in the UK. If you live in Spain (resident) and own more than one house, or don't live in Spain and own any house in Spain, then you need to pay tax on the 2% of the value of the house. This is because the government assumes you'll be renting it out.

Another tax that will be unfamiliar to Brits is the wealth tax (patrimonio), which is levied on all of your property and possessions. Finally, there is a tax that is similar to the British Council Tax, called the IBI. This is used to pay for services in your locality.

Use a local accountant to make the arrangements and ensure you pay your taxes.

Padrón, this is the Spanish electoral role. As soon as you've bought a property or begin renting in Murcia, it is highly advisable to put yourself on the electoral role. This will enable you to have a say and make your voice count in local elections. It has an added benefit of encouraging Telefonica to get your phone connected and enabling you to buy a car with Spanish plates.

Registering on the Padrón has no affect whatsoever on your tax status. The benefits are that the local council gets state aid depending on the number of people registered. This affects the number of local police, the infrastructure, waste disposal etc.

There are some areas where the actual population is 4 times the registered population and as a result the facilities are totally inadequate. Get down to the Ayuntamiento and register! It's free!

Make sure you are legal: Find out more and keep informed at: https://www.facebook.com/CAB.Spain

Residencia, Residents Permit. In general Brits who are employees or self-employed in the UK do not need a residencia. However, if you want to start a business you do need a residencia. The best advice is if you want to live in Spain for more than 6 months in the year then apply. For more details about the complicated rules, take a look at David Hampshire's book. There is also a wealth of information available on the Citizens' Advice Bureau Spain's website (https://www.citizensadvice.org.es/).

The UK Government also offers advice. Remember the UK's withdrawal from the EU will cause changes. For the most up-to-date information: https://www.gov.uk/guidance/living-in-spain

---

The Withdrawal Agreement: The Withdrawal Agreement sets out the terms of the UK's withdrawal from the EU and provides for a deal on citizens' rights. It sets out a transition period which lasts until 31 December 2020. During this time you can continue to live, work and study in the EU broadly as you did before 31 January 2020.

If you are resident in Spain at the end of the transition period, you will be covered by the Withdrawal Agreement, and your rights will be protected for as long as you remain resident in Spain.

Any rights that are not covered by the Withdrawal Agreement will be the subject of future negotiations.

Keep informed!

Living in Murcia

Kids, School

Spain, Murcia included, did not used to have a good track record of basic education. Things have improved dramatically though, and the Programme for International Student Assessment (PISA) now rate Spain just a few points below the UK in core skills.

For basic education there are state funded and private funded schools. Most villages and towns have their own schools providing there are enough children to justify opening. Otherwise there is a school bus to take them to the nearest school. Private schools include:

El Limonar International School, Calle Colonia Buenavista, El Palmar www.ellimonarinternational.com, 968 882818, Vocational Training, Primary or Secondary Education.

El Limonar International School is a private fee-paying bilingual school founded in 1990 and governed by a permanent Board of Directors. The School is accredited by the Middle

States Association and by the Spanish Ministry of Education. The student population is comprised of over 15 nationalities including, English, German, Japanese, French, American and Russian.

Shoreless Lake School, Totana, Murcia, www.slsonline.org, 968 424386, Primary and Secondary Education.

Shoreless Lake School (SLS) at Murcia is the Spanish branch of SLS of New Jersey (USA), an American school established in 1991. SLS is a private, non–profit organisation accredited by the Middle States Association of Colleges and Schools (MSA); authorised by the Spanish Department of Education; all boys school for American, Spanish, and foreign students.

New Castelar College, C/ Teruel N°47, San Pedro del Pinatar, www.newcastelar.com, 968 178276.

New Castelar College offers a bilingual international education. The school offers education from infants through to baccalaureate level.

King's College The British School of Murcia, Calle Pez Volador, Urbanización La Torre Golf Resort, Roldán, www.kcmurcia.es, 968 032500, Nursery to Year 11 UK Education.

The school follows the National Curriculum for England and Wales in the same way that has been established at Kings College, Madrid, which has gained an enviable reputation not only in Spain but in Europe and the wider world for the high quality of education offered to its pupils. Caters to a maximum of 750 pupils.

Big Kids, Colleges & Universities

Universidad De Murcia, Avenida Teniente Flomesta, 5, www.um.es, 868 363000. The variety of courses offered by the University of Murcia is organised into official degrees (diplomas, degrees, engineering and technical engineering), Undergraduate and Postgraduate degrees, independent degrees, academic specialisation and extracurricular teaching.

Although its origins date back to the thirteenth century, the University of Murcia as we know it was founded in 1915, which makes it the tenth oldest university in Spain. The majority of the University's facilities and buildings are spread over two campuses: the older is La Merced, situated in the town centre and the larger is Espinardo, just 5km to the north of Murcia.

Universidad Politecnica De Cartagena, Plaza del Cronista Isidoro Valverde, Edificio La Milagrosa, 30202 Cartagena, www.upct.es, 968 325400.

Cartagena University started out as a mining school in the late 19th century, but didn't gain status as a technical university until 1975. The university retains a strong technical orientation focusing on engineering, agriculture and science. Cartagena has also built a good foundation of business studies teaching over the past 85 years. More recently, Cartagena has added tourism to the portfolio of courses.

Conservatorio de Música Narciso Yepes, Abad de los Arcos, 2, Lorca, Vocational School or Career College for Music, http://www.conservatoriodelorca.com, 968 441514.

ENAE Escuela de Negocios de Dirección y Administración de Empresas, Campus Universitario Espinardo, Espinardo, Business Administration, Vocational Training, www.enae.es, 968 899899

Inforges, Calle Vicente Alexandre, 13, Murcia, Information Technology, Multimedia, Computer Programming, Independent Private College, www.inforges.es, 968 350011

Building Work & Permissions

In Spain you need building permits for just about anything you do to the fabric of your house. This also includes lots of things that you might be considering doing in the garden. While in the UK you can build a patio, build low decorative and boundary walls, ponds and sheds as well as install or remove partition walls inside without planning permission, technically all of these things might need a building permit in Murcia.

Much of Murcia's inland area is covered by Natural Parks and protected zones (such as official forest areas). If you are fortunate enough to live out in el campo think twice before approaching the Ayuntamiento for building permits. Even if you are out of a protected area, but not in an official urbanised area, you will probably need over 2.5 Ha (~ 7 acres) of land to start any major building work. In protected areas this limit rises to 50Ha (over 100 acres!). Two things that you definitely want to avoid are: alerting the Ayuntamiento to something trivial and noncontentious beforehand and the other is forging ahead with major work only to be stopped half way through.

There are two classes of permit that are needed for building work in Spain, depending on the scale of the work involved and its potential impact on your neighbours. The larger works require that you have drawings professionally prepared and submitted along with full project costings including all labour (even if it's your own time!) and materials required. Smaller things (including most of the things that you would be allowed to do in the UK without planning permission) are covered by the term obra menor. The decision as to what category of work your job will fall into is ultimately the decision of the Technical Architect at the Ayuntamiento. If you are doing all the work yourself the Technical Architect will use some rules of thumb as to the costings.

The building licence fee is a percentage of the quotation, and for obras menores this is often a very small percentage. For these smaller works, once you have the license fee established with the Ayuntamiento's Technical Architect, you will then be given a form to take to another department of the Ayuntamiento. Here you will be given another form to take to the bank and pay a few Euros by way of a down payment on the final fee. Once the bank has taken your money and stamped the form you take it back to the Ayuntamiento. Within a few months you will get your permit in the post and an invoice for the remainder of the fee.

For larger projects you will need to submit much more information to the Technical Architect at the Ayuntamiento. You will need architect's drawings and costings (the proyecto) which must have been stamped by the College of Architects. A contract with Aparejador (Technical Architect), a copy of the escritura showing ownership of the land and copies of NIE certificates.

The drawings have to be authorised by the college of architects (the authorising body), who will ensure that it all meets building regulations, before being stamped and returned to the architect. He will then hand it all over to you and you must submit it to the Ayuntamiento with an application form. Most people have had to enter into a contract with an Aparejador (technical architect) who gets paid 30% of the architect's fee for overseeing the build, which is a similar role to the old building inspector in the UK. They should check steelwork, drainage, structure, roof slab etc.

It can take up to 4 months to receive the licence. You must start work within 12 months and are not allowed to stop work for more than 6 months otherwise the licence becomes invalid.

With a new build you really do need a licence and if the finished building is not as per drawings and licence details you may have difficulties getting the certificate of occupation. However, once signed off most people feel at liberty to, for example, add permanent roofs to terrace beams etc.

If you're not sure whether to apply for a license then it might be best to talk to a few of the neighbours and get their opinions, they should know how things operate, or you could ask at local builder's merchants or a friendly local solicitor/abogado.

Alternatives

Wooden Houses do require planning permission in Murcia. Installing a wooden house without permission will result in a fine proportional to the size of the house and dependent upon its location. You may also receive a demolition order.

For caravans there is no specific law, yet, in Murcia that prevents you from parking a caravan on any piece of land that you own. This is the loophole that many Brits have to use (once they've been sold a dodgy piece of land by a dishonest estate agent) in order to live there and remain within the law.

DIY

For basic tools and materials you should try your local hardware shop (ferretería or almacén). From these shops you should be able to get sand, cement, bricks, hand tools, basic plumbing fittings, some paints, floor and wall tiles, etc. We would encourage readers to use their local ferretería regularly since you'll regret it sorely if they go out of business!

For more weird stuff, like fibreglass septic tanks, water pumps for your downstairs deposit, a wider selection of bathroom taps, etc., you will be better off going to your nearest large trading estate (polígono). The best ones for electrical, building and plumbing supplies we have found are to the west of Murcia (San Ginés), to the north east of Cartagena and to the west of Lorquí.

You will find that suppliers on these trading estates usually have what you need ex–stock, at a good price and they often deliver a decent-sized order for free. Be aware that most of the trade counter outfits only accept cash, but this offers a good opportunity for substantial savings compared to the equivalent item ordered locally.

If you are looking for the warm feeling that UK DIY superstores offer then you need to visit Leroy Merlin (Murcia and Cartagena). This out–of–town shop has just about everything, but as with UK DIY retail outfits expect to pay over–the–odds for your individually shrink–wrapped widgets.

The Garden

There are several good books on the market that cover gardening in Spain where you'll find most of the information you need to design and maintain your garden in Murcia. In particular, we found the following book excellent: Campo, A Guide to the Spanish Countryside, Sandy Walker, Santana Books.

There is one topic of particular interest to Murcian gardeners, however, that we didn't find covered very well in other books, how to make best use of your water! Read on…

You probably know this already, but it's pretty sunny here in Spain, particularly in Murcia. For gardeners on anything but the smallest scale that's a problem. You only need to glance online and the chances are that the headlines are about water, or more precisely, the lack of it. Farmers in particular are taking the brunt of the war for water (although somehow the property developers always seem to find a supply for that new golf course!) The desalination plants make water that costs them at least four times that which farmers in other regions have to pay. Drip irrigation is how all farmers around here make the best use of this most precious resource.

Drip irrigation can be useful for your garden and smallholding too! Since your water will be on the meter here you too will be looking for ways to save it. Not only can drip irrigation save water it can save you time and also keep your plants alive when you're away from home.

For more information on drip irrigation and a full installation guide, including useful Spanish words take a look here: www.NativeSpain.com

Pets (Mascotas) & Animal Ownership

There are specific rules for importing different kinds of pets. In general, pets may be imported to Spain if they are accompanied by their owners or their representative and have a certificate of origin and health (if they are more than three months old). These are valid for ten days only and must state that the pet has been under the owner's supervision for three months before being imported. They must also include a declaration that the pet is not intended for trade.

In the case of dogs the certificate must show that the pet has had valid anti–rabies inoculation in the last twelve months (six in some cases). Certificates should be obtained from the nearest Animal Health Divisional Office in England. A full list of these offices is available by calling 08459 335 577 and at www.defra.gov.uk

Birds, monkeys and other species will need a certificate stating that there has been no local outbreak of disease that would affect the species for the last 60 days. For more advice contact the nearest Spanish Consulate.

Owners who intend to take their pets back to England must comply with the Pet Travel Scheme (PETS) for their pet to be able to enter the UK without going into quarantine. For information on PETS, see: www.defra.gov.uk

BREXIT: Current pet travel rules will stay the same until 31 December 2020. Keep informed.

The tick and tapeworm certificate and the declaration of residence have been replaced by an EU pet passport. Only dogs, cats and ferrets (!) require a passport.

The general opinion is that Spanish people have less respect for dogs than Brits (have for dogs!). Whilst this may be true for working dogs (and you can always find lots of newspaper coverage in the English speaking press about cruelty to working animals) many Spanish people devote as much care and attention on their beloved pets as we Brits do.

There are lots of kennels in Murcia that collect stray and abandoned animals. The most well known is Noah's ARC. You will find their most up to date contact details in any of the English press or try this number 699 352 818. Noah's ARC is run by volunteers, with a distributed kennel structure. If you want to home (or foster) a stray or abandoned animal get in touch and make a donation. Be generous! www.noahsarcmurcia.com

Other charities to visit when looking for a pet or you have some spare cash: www.perrosdelsol.es, www.petsinspain.info and www.andreasanimalrescue.com

Cats can be found wild in almost all towns and villages, especially around fish restaurants! There are plenty of cat rescues now too, which is a lovely advance.

HE'S VIBRATING! My thirteen year old Spanish friend from the riding stables came to visit one summer. She took one look at the six cats and hid behind me, "Will they bite?" she squeaked. After some reassurance she eventually allowed them to come near her. An hour later I found her on the settee with Randy our biggest cat on her lap, she suddenly shouted "Oh, he's vibrating!"

You'll find at least one vet in every town. Many vets speak English and the standard of Spanish veterinarians is considered to be very high.

The Law

All domestic pets in Spain must be identified by microchip or by a clearly readable tattoo. The tattoo was only accepted as a means of identification until 3 July 2011.

Vaccination against rabies is compulsory. It is also advisable to have dogs vaccinated against other diseases such as distemper and hardpad. Cats should be immunised against feline gastro enteritis and typhus.

There is no law against dogs fouling public places, however people are becoming increasingly sensitive about it and there are specific rules within certain places, such as urban parks.

Dogs should be kept on a lead in public places.

The Spanish authorities have declared the following breeds or cross–breeds as potentially dangerous dogs when over 3 months of age: American Staffordshire Terrier, Staffordshire Bull Terrier, Mallorcan Bulldog, Bullmastiff, American Pitbull Terrier, Rottweiler, Bull Terrier, French Mastiff / Bordeaux Bulldog, Japanese Tosa / Tosa Inu, Argentinian Mastiff, Doberman and Neapolitan Mastiff.

You must apply to the town hall (ayuntamiento) if you wish to keep or breed a potentially dangerous dog.

Stray dogs, if taken to the municipal refuge will be put down after 2 weeks if they are not claimed.

Horses and donkeys are popular with Spanish families here in Murcia. If you want to own a horse or donkey take a look at www.easyhorsecare.net and www.andreasanimalrescue.com

Smoking

Spain banned smoking in public places and work places in January 2006. The new law that came into effect on 2nd January 2011 was much stricter and outlaws smoking in all bars and restaurants. Smokers are also prohibited on television broadcasts, near hospitals or in school playgrounds. Hotels may have 30% smoking rooms; mental hospitals, jails and old people's residences may have public rooms where smokers cannot enter.

If you want to smoke in a bar or restaurant you will have to move outside to the terrace or street. When the ban came into effect many bars and restaurants ignored it, leading to hefty fines. Although most places are complying, you may still find the odd bar where smoking is tolerated despite the laws! (Like my accountant's office!)

The law for marijuana in Spain is complicated and less than crystal clear. It is legal to cultivate and smoke cannabis for your own personal use. It is, however, illegal to sell or traffic. It is also illegal to smoke marijuana in public places, but there are "cannabis clubs" where members can go to smoke marijuana. In Spain, drug laws cannot reach into homes and privately owned spaces, so if one was to grow their own marijuana at home and smoke it at home, they would be out of reach of Spanish law. It is only consuming in public or selling to others that will get you into trouble. The general rule of thumb seems to be that if you have only one or two plants at home, out of sight of prying eyes, you will be ok.

Entertainment

Radio

There are hundreds of national and regional Spanish radio stations, many of which can be found online at www.tunein.com. For those who prefer to listen through a radio, whether in the house, in the car, or on the beach, there are many options depending on your taste. The latest hits, plus local adverts and news in English can be found on Spectrum FM (90.3 or https://costacalida.spectrumfm.net/) and Bay Radio (89.1 or http://www.bayradio.fm) whilst Talk Radio Europe (96.3 or https://www.talkradioeurope.com/) offer English language chat throughout the day. Fans of the BBC World Service may be disappointed to learn that it is no longer broadcast on short wave in Europe. It can still be found online at http://bbcworldservice.radio.net/.

Television

National Spanish TV is TVE1, La2, Antena3, TELE5, Canal+, great for football and sport, lots of talking heads political programs, many cheesy soaps (just like in Britain!) and even the Simpsons, dubbed into Spanish.

Local TV is CanalSur, Canal9, Canal21, TVMurciana, TVEMurcia, 7RM and has lots of local talking heads, local news, local tourist programs which are very good and some rather dubious content in the small hours (take care with children in hotel rooms!)

You can watch UK TV stations with satellite or internet TV solutions. There are plenty of small businesses set up to help you get connected. Or you can DIY and buy the equipment and set yourself up. You will need good internet connection for best results.

Books

At many of the expat oriented bars along the coast you can find a book exchange program or second hand books for sale. If you want to buy new books then the most economical way is to visit amazon.co.uk or amazon.es, which both have a huge selection although you may find the UK version of the site cheaper than the Spanish one.

If you want to visit a library then there's a large one in Murcia city, Biblioteca Regional de Murcia, Avenida Juan Carlos I, 17, 968 366601, which has all the usual library services. There are also bibliobuses that come out to many towns during the week. Ask at your local town hall.

Cinema

All of the films will be in Spanish, including the Hollywood blockbusters which will be dubbed. You'll pay around €8 to watch a film. All big shopping malls have multiscreen cinemas and it is becoming increasingly common for them the have the occasional showing subtitled rather than dubbed. Cine Las Velas in Los Alcázares certainly do. See https://www.cinelasvelas.es/original-version-english/ for more information.

In January 2020, Totana's Cinema Velasco started showing English films. It's the largest cinema in Murcia, with beautiful architecture, and can hold 750 people. The price is around 5 euros. Find out what's showing: **Telephone: 629 070 263, info@cinemavelasco-totana.com, www.cinemavelasco-totana.com Facebook: Cinema Velasco Totana**

Law & Order

There are three police forces in Murcia. The Policía Nacional are tall, fit, jackbooted criminal police and wear dark blue uniforms and drive around in blue and white cars. Their official duties include, issuing of identity documents (ID cards and passports), to control receipts and outgoings of foreign people and Spaniards, immigration law, refuge and asylum, extradition and expulsion, drug enforcement, collaboration with Interpol and Europol and general law enforcement.

The Guardía Civil are the green-clad civil guard, and are primarily responsible for policing and/or safety regarding the following areas: highway patrol, protection of the Royal Family and the King of Spain, military police counter-drugs operations, anti-smuggling operations, customs and ports of entry control, weapons licenses and arms control, security of border areas, security in rural areas, intelligence and counter-intelligence gathering, cyber- and internet crime; hunting permits and environmental law enforcement.

The Policía Municipal are the local police and officially answer to and are paid for by the Town Hall, and performs functions such as, protecting local government authorities, and supervision or custody of their buildings and facilities, managing urban traffic, in accordance with the rules of the road, dealing with traffic accidents within the town, carrying out preventive measures against criminal acts and assisting in the resolution of private disputes when requested to do so.

Respect Spanish laws and customs. Spanish law defines anyone under 18 to be a minor, subject to parental control or adult supervision. Any unaccompanied minors that come to the attention of the Spanish authorities (for whatever reason, but particularly in connection with criminal incidents or when in hospital) are judged to be vulnerable and may face being taken into a Minors'

Centre for their protection until their situation is resolved and a parent or suitable guardian can be found.

You must provide ID, for example your passport, if requested by a Police Officer. The Police have the right to hold you at a police station until your identity is confirmed.

Being caught in possession of even a small quantity of drugs can lead to arrest and detention. Possession of large quantities will probably result in prosecution and a custodial sentence if convicted.

It is illegal to smoke in indoor public places i.e. bars, restaurants, airports, shopping centres etc. Smoking is also illegal outside hospitals, schools and children's play parks. Fines for breaking laws range from €30 to €600k and are being strictly enforced. There are also strict controls on drinking and sexual activity in public places, including beaches, where regulations have increased significantly. Fines range from €30-€1,500.

Hotels have a legal duty to register the passport details of tourists when they check-in. Wait until the hotel staff have registered your passport details or taken a photocopy of your passport, rather than leaving it in reception to collect later. It may help to take your own photocopy.

For more information take a look at www.fco.gov.uk or call the Foreign and Commonwealth Office on +44 20 7008 1500.

Crime

The vast majority of visits made to Spain by Brits are trouble-free. Be alert to the existence of street crime, especially thieves using distraction techniques. Thieves often work in teams of two or more people and tend to target money and passports. In many cases, one person distracts the victim while the accomplice(s) perform the robbery. When carrying valuables (e.g. credit cards or cash) don't keep them all in one place, and remember to keep a photocopy or photograph on your phone of your passport.

A significant number of Emergency Travel Documents issued by consulates in Spain are as a result of travellers having their passports stolen while passing through the airport, when arriving in or departing from the country. Special care should be taken to guard passports, money and personal belongings when collecting or checking in luggage at the airport and also while arranging car hire. I lost my driver's licence this way and found that a Spanish licence with my name had been issued in Spain!

In some city centres and resorts, thieves posing as police officers on foot patrol may approach tourists and ask to see their wallets for identification purposes. If this happens to you, be careful. First establish that the officers are genuine. If the police request ID, either show them your passport, driver's licence or other photographic identification. Genuine police officers do not request to see wallets or purses.

If you are a victim of crime call 112. To report all crimes, ring 902 102 112: you can explain the case over the phone (in English) and you will then be directed to your nearest police station to sign the police report (denuncia). If you have had belongings stolen, you will need to keep the report for insurance purposes. If your passport is lost or stolen, keep the police report for insurance purposes and in order to apply for an emergency travel document from your nearest British Consulate.

Personal attacks, including sexual assaults, are infrequent but they do occur. Be alert to the possible use of 'date rape' and other drugs including 'GHB' and liquid ecstasy. Buy your own drinks and keep sight of them at all times to make sure they are not spiked; female travellers should be particularly watchful. Alcohol and drugs can make you less vigilant, less in control and less aware of your environment. If you drink, know your limit, remember that drinks served in bars are often stronger than those in the UK.

Make sure that your accommodation has adequate security measures in place and ensure that all doors and windows are locked at night or when you are not in. It is advisable to ensure the security of your valuables including your passport.

When driving, be wary of approaches by bogus police officers in plain clothes travelling in unmarked cars. In all traffic-related matters, police officers will be in uniform. Unmarked police vehicles have a flashing electronic sign on the rear window which reads Policía (Police) or Guardia Civil (Civil Guard), and normally have blue flashing lights which they will activate when they stop you. In non-related traffic matters, police officers may be in plain clothes but you have the right to ask them to identify themselves. The Civil Guard or Police will only ask you to show them your documents and will not ask for your bag or wallet/purse. If in any doubt, you should talk through the car window and contact the Civil Guard on 062 or Police on 112 and ask them to confirm that the registration number of the vehicle corresponds to an official police vehicle.

Be aware of 'highway pirates' who target foreign-registered and hire cars, especially those towing caravans. Some will (forcefully) try to make you stop, claiming there is something wrong with your car or that you have damaged theirs. If you decide to stop to check the condition of your/their vehicle, stop in an area with lights/people, e.g. a service station, and be extremely wary of anyone offering help.

Quick Tips:
- Don't keep all money & credit cards together.
- Keep a photocopy of your passport somewhere safe and a photograph of it on your phone.
- Drink sensibly, take care driving and let people know if you plan to go off the beaten track.
- If you take a taxi make sure it is officially registered/licensed.

The British Consulates overseas can provide a British national with:

- Emergency passports and information about money transfers.
- Support if you have been a victim of crime, hospitalised or arrested.
- Special arrangements in crises e.g. acts of terrorism, civil disturbances or natural disasters.
- Details of local doctors, lawyers, interpreters and funeral directors.
- Facilities to contact your family or friends.

More information on the full support and services the consulate provides is on: www.ukinspain.fco.gov.uk.

Useful words:

Help! = ¡Ayudame! or ¡Socorro!
Look out! = ¡Cuidado!
Ambulance = Ambulancia
Police = Policía
Fire! = ¡Fuego!
Firemen = Bomberos
Do you speak English? = ¿Habla inglés?

CAR CRIME: I visited Orihuela Costa a couple of years ago (I know, crazy, but I wanted to see for myself if it was as horrid as people say!) I overheard two English women speaking: "So, what's the crime like out here then?" Her friend replied, with no sense of irony, "Oh, not that bad, I only had my car broken into three times last year."

Health

If you are visiting Spain, you should obtain a free European Health Insurance Card (EHIC) before leaving the UK. The EHIC is not a substitute for medical and travel insurance, but it entitles you to state provided medical treatment that may become necessary during your trip. Any treatment provided is on the same terms as Spanish nationals so if a Spanish national is required to pay a fee towards their treatment, you would also have to pay the same fee. The EHIC will not cover medical repatriation, ongoing medical treatment or non-urgent treatment. Apply for a free European Health Insurance Card to be able to access emergency medical treatment: www.ehic.org.uk, +44 (0) 191 218 1999.

Healthcare during the transition period: There will be no changes to healthcare access for UK nationals visiting or living in the EU, Iceland, Liechtenstein, Norway and Switzerland before the end of 2020. You can continue to use your EHIC during this time, as you did before. If you're visiting Spain on 31 December 2020, you can continue to use your EHIC until the end of your visit to that country. Source: https://www.gov.uk/guidance/healthcare-for-uk-nationals-visiting-spain (February 2020)

In 2021, make sure you are covered, check carefully on the Government's website.

An EHIC is not a replacement for travel insurance. Make sure you have both before you travel.

You should also make sure you have adequate travel health insurance and accessible funds to cover the cost of any medical treatment abroad and repatriation. If you are referred to a medical facility for treatment you should contact your insurance/medical assistance company immediately. As a general rule, if you require hospital treatment in Spain you are more likely to receive appropriate care in a public healthcare facility although in some tourist areas there may be no public healthcare facility nearby. Your insurance/medical assistance company will be able to provide further details.

Pharmacies will be able to provide you with any medications you need whilst you are here, often at a much reduced price compared to a UK prescription charge. Take your packaging to a pharmacy and ask them.

Driving

You drive on the right in Spain (opposite to the UK). Take care when driving in Spain as the accident rate is higher than in the UK, especially on motorways. In 2017 there were 1,827 road deaths in Spain (source: www.dft.gov.uk). This is 3.9 road deaths per 100,000 of population compared to the UK figure of 2.8 per 100,000. After many years of continual decline this number is sadly on the increase again.

It is a legal requirement for motorists travelling to or through Spain to carry two red warning triangles which are to be placed, in the event of an accident or breakdown, in front of and behind the vehicle. Drivers must also have a spare pair of glasses (if needed for driving), and a spare wheel if one is fitted, or a puncture repair kit. If at any time you have to leave your vehicle due to an accident or breakdown or while waiting for the arrival of the emergency services, you must wear a reflective jacket or you may face a heavy fine. There should be one jacket in the car for ever occupant.

Carry a certificate of insurance in case you are stopped. You should be given documentation if you have hired a car and bought insurance. If you are using UK insurance, always carry your certificate with you. Remember that this certificate is generally only valid for a stay of less than three months. Contact your insurer if you are staying longer. UK provisional licences are not valid for driving in Spain.

Spain has stricter drink driving laws than many other countries including the UK. Penalties include heavy fines, loss of licence and imprisonment. Our advice is that you simply do not drink and drive. The police are cracking down on drivers taking drugs and then driving too so be aware of what you are smoking.

Seat belts are required for all passengers in the front and back seats. No children under the age of twelve should be in the front seat and small children must be in an approved child safety seat in the back seat. Your car hire agency will be able to provide a seat so let them know you need one when you reserve the car.

Talking on mobile phones when driving is forbidden, even when pulled over to the side of the road. You must be completely away from the road. Using an earpiece is also prohibited but you are allowed to use with a completely hands-free unit. This is being policed using cameras so you may not even be aware that you are being watched. You shouldn't even use mobile phones for navigation, but as long as there is no interaction between the driver and the phone, this should be ok. Radar detectors have also been banned under Spanish law.

While it is not illegal to drive in flip flops, if it is thought that an accident was caused as a result of you wearing them, you will get fined. It is dangerous to drive wearing flip flops as they may slip off and distract you. Traffic police have sole discretion as to whether they can fine you or not if they believe that an accident was due to the wearing of flip flops!

A group of Spanish traffic police offers now have a very good website offering information about road safety and regulation in Spain IN

ENGLISH! Take a look at http://www.n332.es for the most up-to-date information.

Driving in Spain: Driving licence rules will stay the same until 31 December 2020.

If you are resident in Spain, exchange your UK licence for a Spanish one. You can still use your Spanish licence in the UK for short visits or exchange it for a UK licence without taking a test if you return to live in the UK. If you hold an old UK licence that doesn't have a 10-year validity period, you must renew or exchange it for a Spanish licence once you've been a resident in Spain for 2 years.

Keep informed!

Shopping

It's easy to do some fun shopping in Murcia, from the large shopping centres to old style family shops, from the craft markets to trendy retail outlets. And of course, the weekly markets where you can buy the best products that the area produces. Souvenirs, fashion, gifts, accessories, textiles, handicrafts, art, cuisine, whatever you're looking for you can find it. Even essential expat products like Marmite can now be found in large supermarkets like Carrefour!

In the Region of Murcia there are many commercial establishments awarded the Compromiso de Calidad Turística (Tourism Quality Commitment), issued by the Ministry of Industry, Tourism and Trade of Spain. So look out for the sign!

Opening hours in the large chain stores are generally from 10:00 to 20:30. In the shopping malls this time is extended until 22:00h. Traditional shops open from 10:00 to 14:00 and from 16:30 to 20:30. On Sundays and holidays the shops are usually closed except some shops around the tourist areas (like Dos Mares).

The sales for the winter season usually begin on 7th January and last to late February while the summer sales start on 1st July to late August. Most shops accept credit cards with Visa and MasterCard accepted in almost all shops.

Residents outside the European Union with purchases over €90.15 are entitled to a refund of Value Added Tax (VAT).

Location Report: Shopping!

Most people think of beautiful beaches and calm water when they visit the Mar Menor area but there will always be people who also want to do some serious shopping. The area around the Mar Menor will not disappoint them with shopping malls, shopping centres and individual shops throughout the towns and villages in the area.

One of the closest and oldest shopping malls to the Mar Menor is called Dos Mares which means Two Seas. It is in San Pedro del Pinatar and can be seen from the AP-7 motorway. It was built around 2006 and caused quite a stir among the locals as it is the first time the area had seen a proper American style shopping mall. It contains numerous clothing shops, gift shops, electrical shops and places to eat. It also houses a multi-screen cinema complex, but films in English are a rare event. It is well known locally for its Carrefour hypermarket which, like the mall, is open every day of the year except Christmas day. This is very handy to know as there is always the time when you have run out of some essential ingredient on a fiesta day! Like most shopping centres and malls the parking is free, although not endless and it can get very busy on Sundays and fiestas. It is not a huge mall but it will satisfy most shoppers who just want to have a mooch about and pick up the odd item. www.centrodosmares.com

More serious shoppers need to head to the Parque Mediterraneo which is a large shopping mall and centre located off the A-30 heading into Cartagena. Here you really are spoilt for choice with clothes shops galore, including a C&A which always attracts nostalgic British buyers. There is a large Carrefour, Toys-R-Us, a DIY superstore called Leroy Merlin, Decathlon and various other huge stores including a big shoe shop and a very popular electrical store called MediaMarkt. There is plenty of parking both over and underground so in the summer months you can keep the car cool while you shop.

If you are looking for the iconic Spanish shopping experience, El Corte Inglés, you need to head into Cartagena city itself (or Murcia). This is one of the best El Corte Inglés stores I have visited as it is light and modern with six full floors packed full of clothing, household goods, food and sporting equipment. On the top floor is a café and restaurant which has stunning views over Cartagena. It is always worth popping up there for a coffee break to enjoy the first class service and the panorama! There is a multi-storey carpark beneath the store but do note that parking is not free.

If you are looking for individual shops and some fresh air then Cartagena's main shopping area is hard to beat. It runs up from the port and this is the best place to stop and park. Head for the beautiful old town hall and you will find Calle Mayor, the principal street which houses shops such as Zara and Mango. Further shopping streets branch off from this and there are many back streets where small independent shops are hidden. Much of this area has now been pedestrianised and it does mean you can have a relaxed car-fume free stroll among the shops followed by well earned refreshments in one of the many cafes and restaurants located in the port area.

Martine Cherry, www.rhumbhor.com

Shopping Malls

Centro Comercial Y De Ocio Águilas Plaza, Avenida del Hornillo, Águilas, www.Águilasplaza.es

Centro Comercial Y De Ocio Espacio Mediterráneo, Calle Londres, Polígono Industrial Cabezo Beaza, Cartagena, www.espaciomediterraneo.com

El Corte Inglés, Alameda San Antón, Cartagena, www.elcorteingles.es

Parque Comercial Y De Ocio Mandarache, Avenida Ronda Ciudad de La Union, 30, Cartagena, www.mandarache.es

Parque Comercial Y De Ocio Almenara, Camino de en Medio, Campillo, Lorca, www.parquealmenara.es

Centro Comercial Y De Ocio Las Velas, Calle Catamarán, 1, Los Narejos, Los Alcázares

Centro Comercial Vega Plaza, Avenida de Granada, Molina De Segura, http://centrocomercialvegaplaza.com/

El Corte Inglés, Centro De Liquidación La Serreta, Carretera de Madrid, Cartagena, km377, Molina De Segura, www.elcorteingles.es

Centro Comercial Atalayas, Calle Molina de Segura, Murcia, http://www.centrocomercialatalayas.com/

Centro De Ocio Zigzag, Avenida Juan Carlos I, Murcia, www.zigzagmurcia.net

El Corte Inglés, Avenida. Libertad, 1, Murcia, www.elcorteingles.es

El Corte Inglés, Gran Vía Escultor Francisco Salzillo, Murcia, www.elcorteingles.es

Parque Comercial La Noria (Outlet), Centro Comercial La Noria Outlet Shopping, km5, La Ñora, Murcia, www.lanoriaoutlet.es

Parque Comercial Nueva Condomina, Carretera Nacional A-7 Salida D. Juan de Borbón, Churra, Murcia, https://nueva-condomina.klepierre.es

Parque Comercial Thader, Avenida Juan de Borbón, Churra, Murcia, www.thader.net

Centro Comercial Dos Mares, Carretera Nacional 332, Cruce El Mirador, San Javier, www.centrodosmares.com

Markets

There are plenty of markets around. Most towns have a particular market day, some of which are included here. The markets in Murcia sell everything from fruit and vegetables, fish and meat to hair dryers and CDs. Check https://www.mercadillosemanal.com/en.murcia for up-to-date information.

Monday

Beniel, Caravaca de la Cruz, Cartagena, Lorquí, Lobosillo, Monteagudo, Puente Tocinos, San Pedro del Pinatar, Sucina, Ulea

Tuesday

Alhama de Murcia, Alguazas, Bullas, Cabezo de Torres, El Palmar, Los Alcázares, Los Barreros, Los Belones, Los Garres, Jumilla, Molina de Segura, Molinos Marfagones, Murcia, Ricote, Sangonera la Seca, Santiago y Zaraiche

Wednesday

Alcantarilla, Balsapintada, Cartagena, Cieza, Cehegín, Churra, Santiago de la Ribera, Santomera, San Javier, Totana, Yecla

Thursday

Albudeite, Aljucer, Balsicas, Blanca, Ceutí, La Aljorra, La Azohía, La Palma, Lorca, Los Dolores, Lo Pagan, Los Urrutias, Librilla, Mazarrón, Murcia, San Javier

Friday

Abarán, Beniaján, Calasparra, Cartagena, El Algar, Islas Menores, Isla Plana, Llano del Beal, Pliego, Pozo Estrecho, Puerto Lumbreras, Murcia, Valladolises

Saturday

Águilas, Abanilla, Archena, Dolores, Los Narejos, Fortuna, Fuente Alamo, Mazarrón, Torre Pacheco, Molina de Segura, Moratalla, Mula, Sangonera la Verde

Sunday

Aledo, Cartagena, Cabo de Palos, Corvera, Los Nietos, Ojós, Puerto Mazarrón, Purias, Roldán

Artisan Markets

There's a growing artisan community. Check out https://www.murciaturistica.es/es/mercadillos/ and http://www.medievalesartesanos.com/ for the latest information. Another great source is www.murciaartesana.es.

Mercadillo Del Lloro, Paseo de la Ermita, Abarán, 968 770040.

Mercadillo De Antigüedades De Águilas, Plaza Alfonso Escámez, Águilas, 699 049187.

Mercadillo Artesanal De Los Mayos, Parque De La Cubana. Avenida De La Constitución, Alhama De Murcia.

Mercadillo De La Feria, Calle Casa De La Cultura. Concejalía De Festejos, Alhama De Murcia, 968 631985.

Mercadillo El Zacatín, Plaza Vieja Y Del Castillo, Bullas, 968 652244, http://elzacatin.es.

Mercado Medieval La Encomienda, Plaza Corredera, 27, Calasparra, 968 745325, www.calasparra.org

Mercado Del Peregrino, Plaza Del Arco, Caravaca De La Cruz, 968 701003, www.caravaca.org

Mercado Medieval De Caravaca De La Cruz, Caravaca De La Cruz, 968 701003, www.caravaca.org

Mercadillo Artesanal El Mesoncico, Plaza Del Castillo, Cehegín, 968 723550.

Mercadillo De Los Frailes, Calle Los Frailes, Cieza, 968 453500, www.cieza.es

Zoco Del Guadalabiad, Entorno Del Templete Del Parque De La Compañía, Molina De Segura, 968 388665, www.molinadesegura.es

Mercadillo De Las Cuatro Plazas, Plaza Del Ayuntamiento, Mula, 968 661501.

Mercado De Artesanía De Puerto Lumbreras, Pasaje De La Reina, Puerto Lumbreras, 652 902282, www.puertolumbreras.es/turismo

Mercado De Artesanía Navideño, Via Calle Lorca, Puerto Lumbreras, 652 902282.

Mercadillo De Artesanía La Sal, Parque De Los Reyes De España Y Explanada De Lo Pagán, San Pedro Del Pinatar, 968 180600.

Mercadillo Medieval De Torre Pacheco, Avenida Torre Pacheco, 968 579937, www.torrepacheco.es

Mercado Artesanal De Dolores De Pacheco, Plaza Nicolás De Las Peñas, Dolores, Torre Pacheco.

Mercadillo Artesanal De La Santa, Plaza Paraje De La Santa, Totana, 968 418151, www.totana.es

Mercado Medieval De Totana, Plaza De España, Totana, 968 422817.

Mercadillo Artesanal De Yecla, Parque De La Constitución, Yecla.

Emergency Telephone Numbers

All emergencies – 112

National Police – 091

Local Police – 092

Guardia Civil – 062

Fire Service - 085

Local Police:

Águilas	968 493062
Alhama de Murcia	968 630001
Cabo de Palos	968 337300
Cartagena	968 128877
Fuente Alamo	958 598500
La Manga	968 570880
Los Alcázares	968 171919
Mazarrón	968 591496
Molina de Segura	968 939900
San Javier	968 570880
San Pedro del Pinatar	968 188092
Torre Pacheco	968 585151
Totana	968 418181

Medical Centres:

Águilas	968 446014
Alhama de Murcia	968 631700
Cabo de Palos	968 145151
Cartagena	968 123601
Fuente Alamo	958 598507
La Manga	968 142125
Los Alcázares	968 575800
Mazarrón	968 592388
Puerto de Mazarrón	968 595342
San Javier	968 191866
San Pedro del Pinatar	968 182062
Torre Pacheco	968 579311
Totana	968 421111

Miscellaneous:

Iberdrola	900 225235

Social Services (Murcia)	968 358600
British Consulate (Alicante)	965 216022

Airports:

Corvera	913 211000
Alicante	966 919100

Bus Stations:

Águilas	968441961
Cartagena	968 505656
Murcia	968 292211
San Pedro del Pinatar	968 182942

Trains:

RENFE Customer Services	912 320320
Cartagena	968 502214
Murcia	968 252154

Local Charities

To support the local charities we've listed the main legal ones here. Most of them can be found on Facebook.

Access for All Group: 968 185 008: Project in San Pedro, San Javier, Los Alcazares and beyond encouraging better design of highways and building entrances for the disabled, elderly and families.

Age Concern Costa Calida: 634 310 216: For expatriates over the age of 50 offering information and assistance with health or economic problems.

Aglow International: 690 089 109: Women only meeting to support encourage and care for one another. Open to Christians and non Christians alike.

Alcoholics Anonymous Cuevas de Reyllo: www.aaspain.org: 646 290 420: Meetings are held on Thursdays at 18:00 at Socio Cultural, Avenida Principe de Asturias (MU-602), Cuevas de Reyllo, Nr. Fuente Alamo 30333 Murcia.

Alcoholics Anonymous Los Alcazares Step Meeting: www.aaspain.org: 679 385 105: Step meetings are held on Mondays at 11:00 to 12:30.

Alcoholics Anonymous Mazarron Group: www.aaspain.org: 646 290 420: Topic meetings are held on Mondays at 19:30. First Monday of each month is a Step Meeting. Pastrana Centro Social, 10km South-West of Mazarron.

Alpha Leos Mazarrón Bahia: The group focus on practical activities which involve young people in their local community.

Andrea's Animal Rescue: 690 90 65 65: www.facebook.com/pg/andreasanimalrescue: We will rescue any animal that we can, however we do give priority to donkeys, we also have details of other organizations that may be able to help you if we can not.

Animal welfare charity shop Los Narejos, Los Alcázares: 634 352 621: www.facebook.com/Animal-charity-shop-1413875975529728: An animal welfare charity shop in the Los Narejos area of the Los Alcázares municipality supports two charities which focus on rescuing, rehoming, training, neutering and educating within the Spanish community, where the biggest problems exist, Galgos del Sol, which cares for greyhounds and hunting dogs and Asociacion Unicos in San Javier which focuses on neutering and rehoming.

Asociación Únicos charity shop Los Alcázares: https://asociacionunicos.wixsite.com/asociacionunicos: 608 239 333: www.facebook.com/asociacionunicos: Asociación Únicos currently cares for 15 abandoned dogs at Paraje La Condesa, nro. 3. Los Infiernos, 30592, Torre Pacheco and is constantly seeking loving and caring homes for them.

Camposol Kitty Kitty: www.teaming.net/camposolkittykitty-ckk: www.facebook.com/groups/CamposolKittyKitty: We are a TNR - Trap, Neuter, Return group. We trap feral cats, test and treat them for any ailments, neuter, flea and worm and return to their original location - we then manage the colonies and keep track of any new cats and monitor illness etc.

Cancer Buddies Network: www.cancerbuddiesnetwork.org: On-line support network for anyone affected by cancer with a forum and private messaging system for chatting.

Cruz Azul: http://cruzazulmurcia.com: 693017616: www.facebook.com/pg/cruzazul.murcia: Cruz Azul exists to provide veterinary care for the sick and injured pets of people in need and to promote responsible pet ownership.

DGenes Asociacion de Enfermedades Raras: www.dgenes.es: 690 945 233: Providing information, support and guidance to improve the lives of patients suffering from rare diseases and their families. Including neurological and psychomotor disorders, autism, hyperactivity, hearing and language difficulties.

Expatriate Ostomates of Spain (EOS): www.ostomyinspain.org: 966 460 063: Provides support and improves the standard of public health care for all ostomates in Spain (particularly expatriates). Contributes to international efforts to relieve distress for ostomists in countries where there is no adequate public health care.

FAST - EMERGENCY FIRST RESPONDERS: www.fast2016.org: 968 970 626: FAST is a fast response medical emergencies team operated by trained volunteers on Camposol.

Forget-Me-Not Mazarrón: 626 734 922: Forget Me Not was set up to help those in the Mazarrón area suffering from long term illnesses such as dementia and Alzheimers.

HAH Help at Home: 633 673 034: Provide a little help at home in a time of need with voluntary carers (some medically qualified). English/Spanish translators for patients, hospital sitting, home help, drivers, mobility equipment, etc.

Help Murcia Mar Menor: www.helpmurciamarmenor.es: 654 632 077: Registered charity offering practical assistance to anyone of any age or nationality, at any time.

Helping Hands for Animals & People Aguilas Murcia: 634456701: Protector of Animals and assistance for humans wherever possible in emergency situations.

JJs Puppy Rescue Association: 618034921: The Association has rescued over 500 abandoned puppies and cared for them until new homes were found.

Los Reyes Kids In Need Golf Society: 642583864: The members of Los Reyes Golf Society are, in their own words, predominantly in the more mature age group and feel that life has treated them quite well and they would like to give something back in life, to others less fortunate than themselves.

MABS (Cancer Support Group) Murcia: 693275779: Offer practical help to local people who have been diagnosed with or are being treated for cancer by providing transport to appointments, translators, travel escorts and befrienders.

MABS Mazarron: https://mabscancerfoundation.com: 620 42 24 10: www.facebook.com/MABSinMazarron: Providing practical help and support to people who have been diagnosed with cancer.

MABS North West Murcia: 629225598

Making A Difference (MAD): 678 598 677: www.facebook.com/mad.mazarron: Christian based charity helping those in need with food, clothes, shoes, furniture.

Mazarron Animal Medi-Aid: 666186037: Their aim is to provide a source of funding towards the essential care and well being of domestic animals such as cats and dogs.

National Domestic Violence Helpline: 016: Free and confidential helpline for victims of domestic violence in Spain. Information about existing domestic violence related services and specialised legal consultancy is available.

Noah's ARC Animal Rescue: www.noahsarcmurcia.com: 603 20 63 63: www.facebook.com/NoahsArcMazarron: To help sick, injured and mistreated dogs in the Mazarron area of Murcia, Spain and to find caring, loving homes for them.

Refugio del Viento, Totana: http://protectorarefugiodelviento.org: We take dogs from Kill Stations, those injured in traffic accidents, mal-treated and off the streets and also those that are handed in by owners due to changes in circumstances etc. and endeavor to find homes for them.

Samaritans in Spain: www.samaritansinspain.com: 902 883 535: www.facebook.com/Samaritans-in-Spain-342312575891259: Volunteer organisation providing telephone emotional support to anyone in Spain in distress or with suicidal feelings.

Swap Tears for Smiles: https://swaptearsforsmiles.wixsite.com/swap-tears-4-smiles: 659 270 885: www.facebook.com/Swaptearsforsmiles: The Charity helps anyone of any creed, race or colour. In this world today there is enough food, enough houses and enough clothes that no one should be hungry, no one should be homeless and no one should be walking around in rags.

The Lions Club of Mazarron Bahia: 605112205: www.facebook.com/Mazarron-Bahia-Lions-106038586400701: Assists with disaster relief, curing preventable blindness and hearing problems, provision of clean water and youth education & guidance programmes.

Welcome Group Mazarron: 620 105 179: This group provides a social scene at a low cost where people can meet up and make new friends with a full programme of events taking place throughout the year.

Home Comforts

Home Sickness

No matter how well thought out your move to Murcia may have been there may be times when you feel a touch of home sickness. You may miss your old friends or the speed at which your post arrives, the theatres and shows or the reliable electricity supply. You may even miss the cold drizzle on a Monday morning and the warmth of a good curry on a Friday night.

Home sickness feelings don't usually last for too long and often only strike when you're feeling low. Having a good strategy in place to ward them off and deal with them if they do strike will keep you from feeling blue.

Wisdom has it that there are three common stages of homesickness:

1. Exaltation. Everything is so new, fresh and exciting. You're living in what amounts to an entirely new world and every day is an adventure. This is kind of like the natural high that occurs to holidaymakers. It usually lasts for several weeks or even several months in certain cases; but unlike the tourists, you're not going back home after soaking in a few days' worth of cultural sightseeing.

2. Frustration. Every high has to end sometime and usually it comes down with a bump. What am I doing here instead of going back home where I belong? I miss my friends and family. I miss wandering round my hometown and reading the local paper.

3. Acceptance. Well, things aren't perfect here, but things aren't perfect anywhere. By this stage you've learned to settle in and accept this society and your role here as it is. It begins to feel like home sometimes. You start to make a few friends among the locals, learn the language a bit and adapt to the customs and social norms.

Here are some ideas to help speed up the process:

Talk About It

Don't think you're the only person feeling sad. Your partner or neighbours may also get the blues occasionally too. Sharing your feelings will help and you may be able to come up with ways to reduce them in the future.

Keep In Touch

Having a good connection with old friends and family enables you to keep informed about their lives and will also remind you of what you've got now. Keep in touch:

- Phone - make sure you get a good international cheap call supplier and call home as often as your friends and family can put up with you.
- Letters - the post in Spain is even slower than in Britain and can sometimes be quite erratic. Don't feel too heartbroken if you think everyone has missed your birthday, the hundreds of cards may just be enroute or mislaid!
- Email - an infinitely more sensible and potentially more reliable solution to keeping in touch with friends and family. You also reduce the risk of becoming a pest as your loved ones can respond in their own time. Most modern mobile phones have email capability and Internet connection built in. Smart phones, of course, are capable of much, much more.
- Internet - Keep in touch with other expats through online forums or social events. Facebook is a growing resource for expats, see me at www.facebook.com/debsjenkins

Think Positive

Make a list of all the reasons you came here in the first place, make the list long and elaborate, with all the reasons why you left the UK and all the reasons why you chose Murcia. Really make an effort with this, include all your feelings and thoughts no matter how mad they might seem to someone else.

Then the next time you're feeling down review your list. Some friends of ours have scrapbooks with clippings and photos to remind them of their reasons for leaving and why it's so great in Murcia, they add to them on a regular basis as new thoughts occur.

Get Involved in Your New Culture
One of the fastest and most long lasting ways to beat the homesickness blues is to make Murcia your home. Get involved in the culture, the day-to-day living, the fun and fiestas. Make friends in the ferretería and the fish shop. Gossip with the gas man and the girls in the sausage shop.

It can be tempting to only mix with Brits, especially if you're living on a housing estate. This could be a mistake. Many Brits on the estates are only there sporadically and seeing them go 'home' may make you feel worse. Ensure you get a good grounding in the real Murcia.

Finally, if you're still feeling unhappy, then you may need to make the decision to return to the UK. Excellent resources can be found here. The discussion is a few years old but the advice still holds strong:

www.britishexpats.com/forum/showthread.php?t=267933

British Food

It's sacrilege I know, but now and then a bacon sarnie with tomato ketchup on fluffy, cheap, white Homepride is just what the doctor ordered. If you get sick of eating freshly prepared Spanish food a quick drive to one of the larger supermarkets or the small specialist shops in the housing estates can give you your quick fix of fast British food.

And, if like us, you're missing something hot and spicy, take a look here: www.spicesofindia.co.uk They source and import ethnic food into Spain, including Patak's curry sauces, spices and tea bags!

In San Javier there's an Iceland store where you can get all your frozen needs met, plus lots of store cupboard items too. In Puerto de Mazarron, the largest British-style supermarket in the province has opened. The Food Co Store, https://www.thefoodco.es/made a deal with the UK giant, and Tesco-branded products are now available, including ready-made curries, and bargain packs of tea.

Most major supermarkets are moving towards the homogenisation of our food buying habits, making almost anything you can buy in the UK available here in Spain. This process has increased exponentially in recent years with aisles of non-Spanish products available in many locations now.

Internet Shopping

We buy many items on the Internet, using ebay.com, amazon.es and other online shops. We have had few problems with delivery to Spain. We've found the price of some items when bought in Spain can be two to three times higher than if bought elsewhere in Europe and shipped over.

For almost anything unusual (dentistry kit for example, don't ask!) then eBay is your best bet. There are tens of thousands of sellers, just look for ones with good ratings and use your credit card or PayPal to increase your chances of not having a bad experience. (NOTE: We've bought hundreds of things from eBay and haven't had one bad experience.)

Other than the postal service here in Spain, which is quite good, the best delivery company is MRW. If you need to have something shipped to you or you need to ship something then try MRW at www.mrw.com. All other well known delivery companies work here in Spain, but with varying degrees of efficiency.

Resources

Food & Drink Cheat Sheet

A printable version of this cheat sheet can be found on the www. NativeSpain.com website

Food & Drink Cheat Sheet

Spanish	English
Comedor	Dining room
Carta	Menu
Menú del día	Fixed price menu
Comida or Almuerzo	Lunch
La cuenta	The bill
Platos combinados	Mixed plate
Cucharra	Spoon
Cuchillo	Knife
Tenedor	Fork
Vaso/Copa	Glass
Taza	Cup
Camerero/Camerera	Waiter/Waitres
Cena	Dinner
Desayuno	Breakfast
Frío	Cold
Caliente	Hot
Hielo	Ice
Entradas	Starters
Sopa	Soup
Sopa de cocido	Meat soup
Sopa de gallina	Chicken soup
Ensalada	Salad
Ensalada Mixta	Mixed salad
Aceitunas or Olivas	Olives
Primeros Platos	Main Courses
A la plancha	Grilled
A la brasa	Grilled
A la parilla	Grilled
Al horno	Baked/Roasted
Crudo	Raw
Asado	Roasted
Frito	Fried
Cocido/caldereta	Stew
Arroz	Rice
Paella	Famous rice dish
Verduras	Vegetables
Patatas	Potatoes
Patatas Fritas	Chips
Judías	Green beans
Zanahorias	Carrots
Guisantes	Peas
Ajo (al ajillo)	Garlic (in garlic)
Tomates	Tomatoes
Pimientos rojos	Red Peppers
Pimientos verdes	Green Pepers

Spanish	English		Spanish	English
Pollo	Poultry		Almejas	Clams
Pato	Duck		Langostinos	Crayfish
Pavo	Turkey		Langostas/ Bogavante	Lobster
Pechuga	Breast of poultry		Postres	Desserts
Perdiz	Partridge		Helado de Chocolate	Chocolate ice cream
Pollo	Chicken			
Carne	Meat		Helado de Vainilla	Vanilla ice cream
Cabra/chivo	Goat/baby goat		Tarta	Flan / Cake
Caza	Game		Flan	Crème Caramel
Cerdo	Pork		Frutas	Fruit
Cochinillo	Suckling pig		Manzanas	Apples
Conejo	Rabbit		Naranjas	Oranges
Cordero	Lamb		Uvas	Grapes
Solomillo	Fillet Steak		Ciruelas	Plums
Entrecot	Sirloin Steak		Melocotones	Peaches
Lomo	Pork loin		Cerezas	Cherries
Ternera	Beef, veal		Fresas	Strawberries
Pescado	Fish		Piña	Pineapple
Dorada	Sea Bream		Plátanos	Bananas
Atún	Tuna		Bebidas	Drinks
Anchoa/ boquerones	Anchovy		Vino Tinto	Red Wine
			Vino Blanco	White Wine
Bacalao	Salted cod		Cerveza	Beer
Lenguado	Sole		Zumo de naranja	Orange juice
Emperador	Swordfish		Agua	Water
Mojama	Cured tuna		Zumo de Manzana	Apple juice
Mariscos	Shellfish		Sangria	Red wine spritzer with fruit juice
Gambas	Prawns			
Mejillones	Mussels		Tinto de verano	Red wine spritzer

Alimento General	General Food
Aceite	Oil
Ajo	Garlic
Arroz	Rice
Azúcar	Sugar
Huevos	Eggs
Mantequilla	Butter
Miel	Honey
Pan	Bread
Pimienta	Pepper
Sal	Salt
Vinagre	Vinegar
Salsa	Sauce

Learning Spanish

Useful Web Links

Spanish phrases with audio: www.quiz–buddy.com

Dictionary: www.diccionarios.com

Spanish lessons online: www.wikibooks.org/wiki/spanish

Perhaps the best online language learning resource, which is also free, is: *www.duolingo.com*

Language Schools

Instituto Cervantes is an organisation that lists over 1700 Spanish courses in Spain. Take a look here: https://eee.cervantes.es

The following Instituto Cervantes accredited school in Murcia is worth trying: Instituto Hispánico de Murcia, Calle Enrique Villar, 13 www.ihdemu.com 968 900 325 They offer courses for different levels, special courses for teachers, and a wide range of activities and excursions. Accommodation in Spanish families or pensions.

It is best to find a school with CEELE accreditation, Certificado de Calidad en la Enseñanza del Español como Lengua Extranjera. Bit of a mouthful!

CEELE is a Certificate of Quality in the Teaching of Spanish as a Second Language and is granted by the Spanish Department of University of Alcalá de Henares and the Association of Spanish Economic Resources.

CEELE, Central de Reservas, Calle Talamanca, 10, 28807 Alcalá de Henares (Madrid), www.escuelai.com, 918 831264

Oxford Academy, Calle Miguel Hernandez, San Pedro del Pinatar, www.academiaoxford.net, 968 180297

Funcarle, Calle Jara, 28, Palacio Molina, Cartagena. www.funcarele.com/en/ 968 128953

In addition, the majority of towns offer free Spanish lessons to foreigners who are keen to learn. The quality of lessons may vary but it's worth checking them out. Go to your town hall for more information.

Going Native: Jax Moves To Murcia

I'm Jackie Ward, aka Jax. I'm from Stratford Upon Avon, UK, but relocated from South Tenerife after almost 7 years to Mazarrón.

I had planned to live on the Peninsula once my teaching days were over, but where and which location was the ultimate question. My eldest son lives near Málaga. In November 2018, I came to dog sit here for some friends who had relocated from Tenerife. I had visited the province many years ago on holiday, and I fell in love with the natural, unspoiled coastlines and the ruggedness of the Sierra Espuña.

I am passionate about everything outdoors. Here, I have the best of all worlds, the coast and mountains. Trekking, scuba diving, camping in my van. Beach days and chilling by my pool.

I love visiting Bolnuevo and La Azohía, and Cartagena as a city is full of interesting historical architecture as well as great variety of places to have a coffee or a tapas lunch and while away the time people watching. I keep going back to the beaches on my doorstep at Bolnuevo, there are so many to choose from and their individuality and uniqueness makes them all special. I also love travelling in my camper van and exploring new locations.

The chilled out pace of life and obviously the sunny days are wonderful. I don't have to plan and can just going with the flow. It's a powerful and liberating feeling after being so governed by the intensity of working in school.

The move from the familiarity of Tenerife, leaving good friendships, my son and a support network weren't easy, especially on my own. Learning to communicate in Spanish is so important, and another reason for my move to the mainland was to become more fluent. I am pretty independent so getting into the local community to get to know people is really important. I joined the local gym, and I have some good friends here that showed me the ropes. The logistics of travel is sometimes a challenge.

I do lot of volunteer work here in Spain supporting Spaniards learning English. I also enjoy supporting families on school issues.

My advice is to not try to do everything at once. Live in your new home and then decide on how you want things. I am living my dream, enjoying every day. A big birthday is coming up, so I plan to make some amazing memories, with great friends in fabulous places. Nowhere better than here.

Recommended Reading

Anthony I. Foster, The Complete Guide to Buying a Property in Spain 12th Edition, 2016, Self Published, ISBN 978-8494027031

David Hampshire, Living and Working in Spain 2009, Survival Books, ISBN 978-1905303656

Alec and Erna Fry, Finca: Renovating an Old Farmhouse in Spain, Santana Books, ISBN 8489954267

Sally Roy, The AA Map & Guide to Costa Blanca, AA, ISBN 0749543353

Juan Pablo Avisón, Guía Viva Murcia, Anaya Touring Club, ISBN 8481659983

Collins Bird Guide, Collins, ISBN 0007113323

Teresa Farino and Mike Lockwood, Travellers' Nature Guides Spain, Oxford University Press, ISBN 0198504357

Golfing Guide to Murcia: An Insider's Guide To The Best Golf On Spain's Costa Cálida, NativeSpain.com, ISBN 978-1905430550

About The Authors

Debbie Jenkins began writing the first edition back in 2003, and it was published in 2005, after years of hard work, lots of driving and eating to check out the restauarants. For this fourth edition she has been assisted by Russ Pearce, who took on the monumental task of fact checking and removing all the references to anything that had gone out of date or disappeared.

Debbie Jenkins

Debbie Jenkins has a 1st Class Degree in Electronics Engineering and has run her own businesses for the last 25 years. She was the co-owner of a marketing and publishing company where she commissioned, edited and published 80 books in the coaching, self-improvement and small business development fields. She now runs www.chaosification.com an online resource for creative people with too many ideas and not enough time.

During her career she has interviewed over 1,000 engineers, managers and directors helping companies such as Siemens, Mitsubishi and Toyota find the right people for their projects.

She has authored or co-authored books on marketing and business, including *The Gorillas Want Bananas* and *The Wealthy Author*. She has written hundreds of articles on Spain at her blog www.NativeSpain.com. Her most recent books are a dual-language cookery book, *Spanish Village Cooking – Recetas Del Campo* and *The Little Book of Big Decisions* – available on Amazon.

Debbie has lived in Murcia since 2005, when she moved with her husband to a cave house in La Murta, near Corvera. In 2015, they separated and later divorced. She now owns the #DisasterFarm in the foothills of the Algarrobo mountains near La Pinilla.

Debbie is bilingual (English & Spanish) and lives in Spain with her cats, dogs, goats and horses, and Italian partner Giorgio.

Russ Pearce

Russ Pearce lives with his wife Trish in Guardamar del Segura, Alicante. A keen photographer and writer of the blog www.anythingbutpaella.com, Russ sustains his life in Spain by teaching English, mostly online. A former air traffic controller, his specialisation is helping fellow controllers and pilots from around the world to improve their English in the aviation field.

After giving up controlling in 2003, Russ went off to university to gain a degree in travel and tourism management. With Trish also at a career crossroads, they made the decision to pack everything up and go to Argentina where they gained TEFL certificates and embarked on a journey of adventure around the world for the best part of a decade. Teaching assignments in Syria, Azerbaijan, Tunisia, Libya and even Scotland were all negotiated before an opportunity came up to work in Pamplona. A year later they left for Barcelona before fate drew them down to the Alicante province. Five years on and Guardamar is firmly their home, but travel remains their passion.

Giving their itchy feet the occasional good scratch, they have travelled extensively throughout Spain. Of course, there is still a longing for the exotic from time to time so trips to South East Asia or backpacking around southern Africa are still frequently on the agenda. If you want to read more about their global travels, take a look at www.mytb.org/rrruss.

Maps

Águilas Map

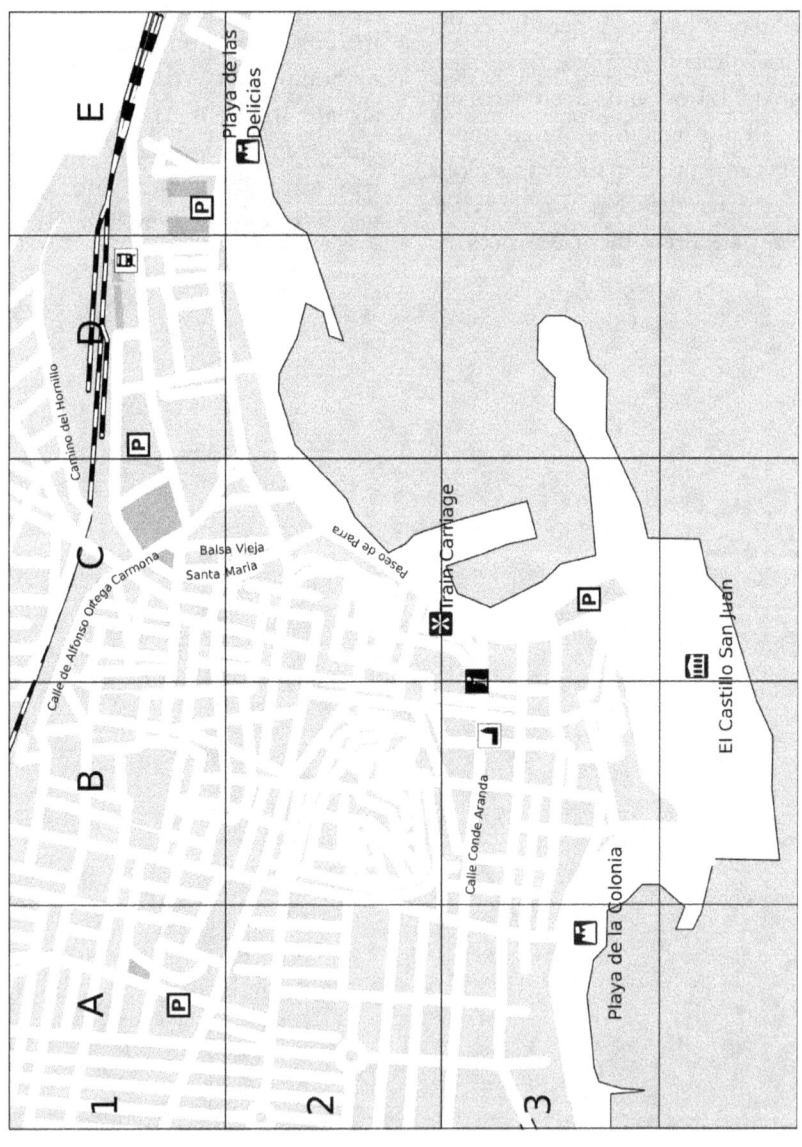

Caravaca Map

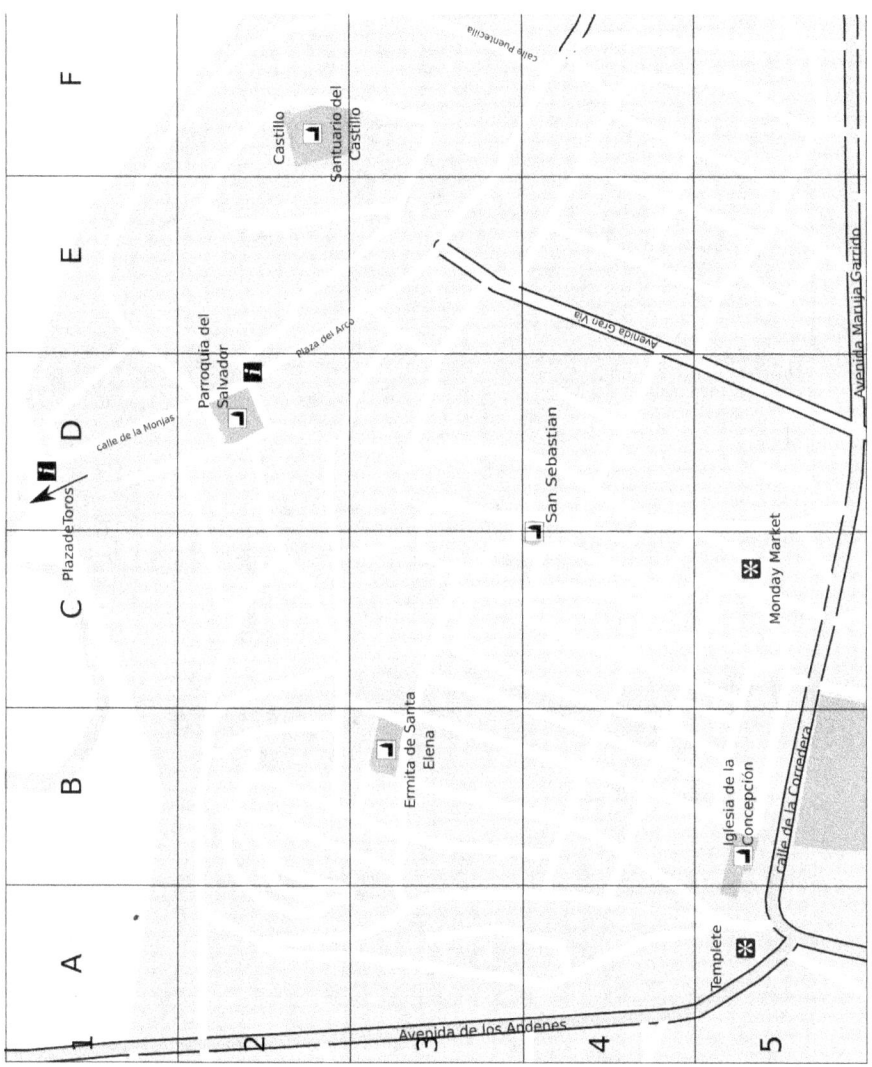

Cartagena Map

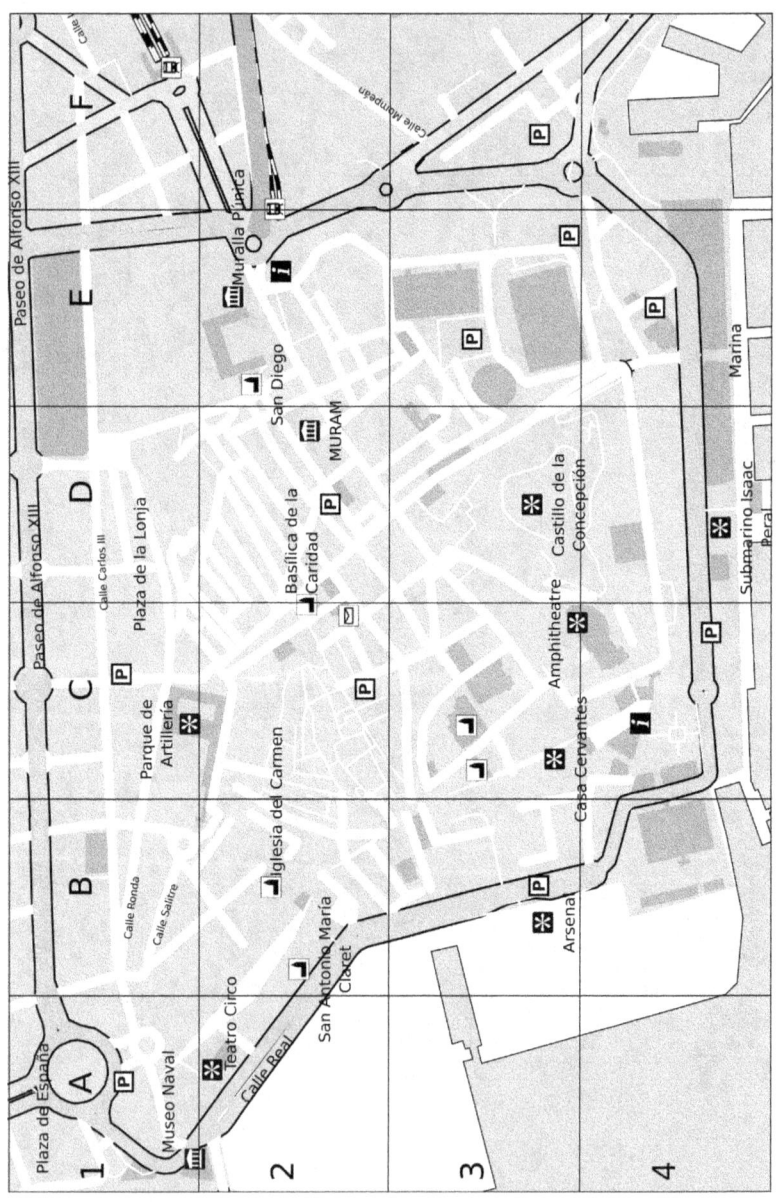

Lorca Map

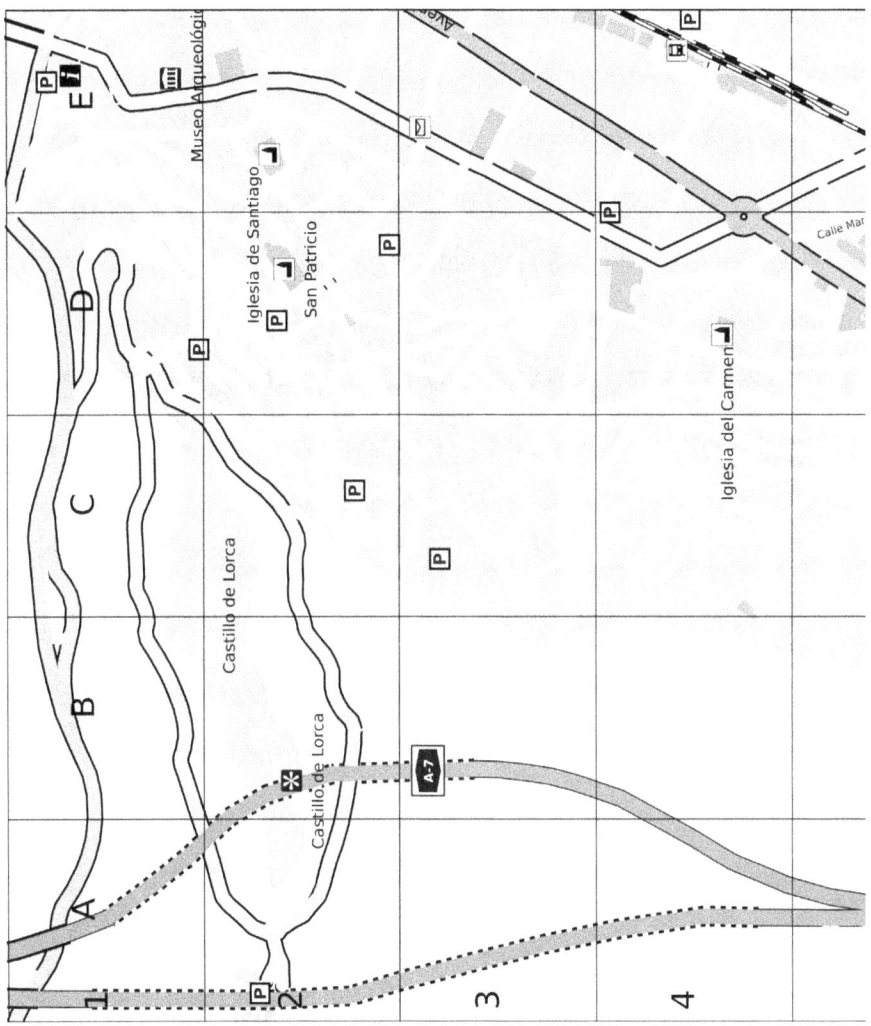

Moratalla Map

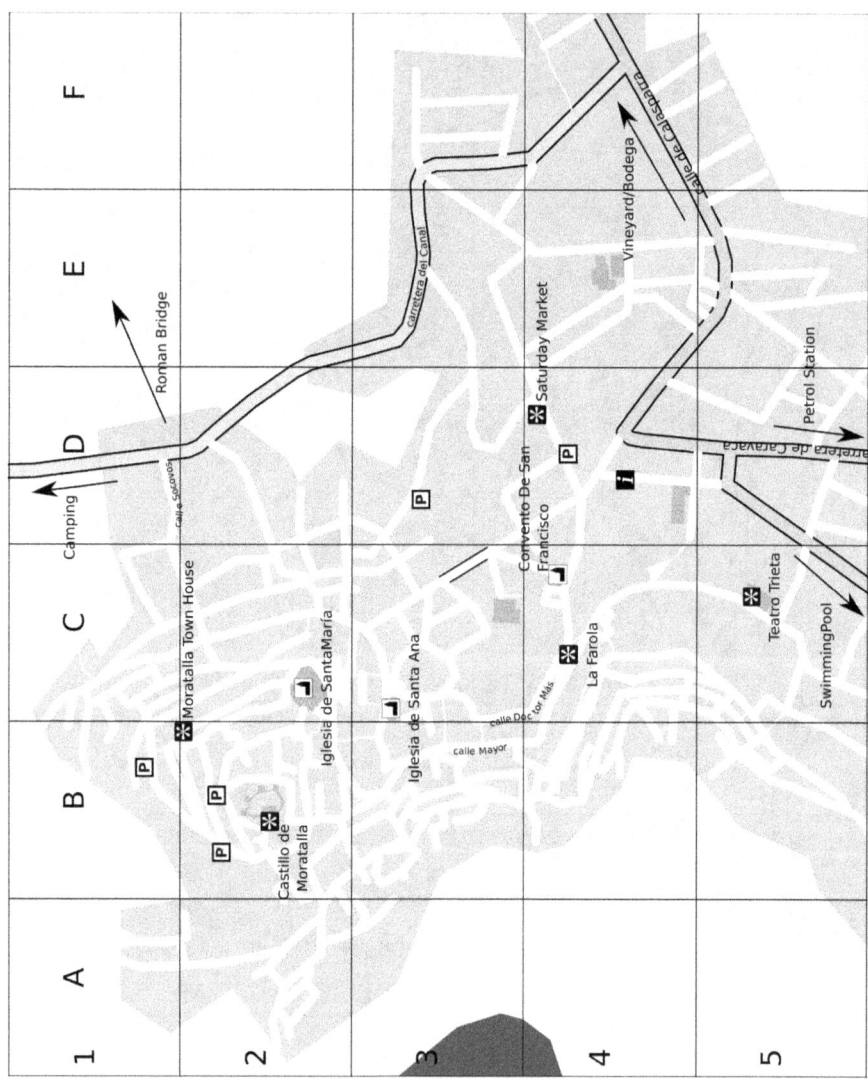

Murcia Map

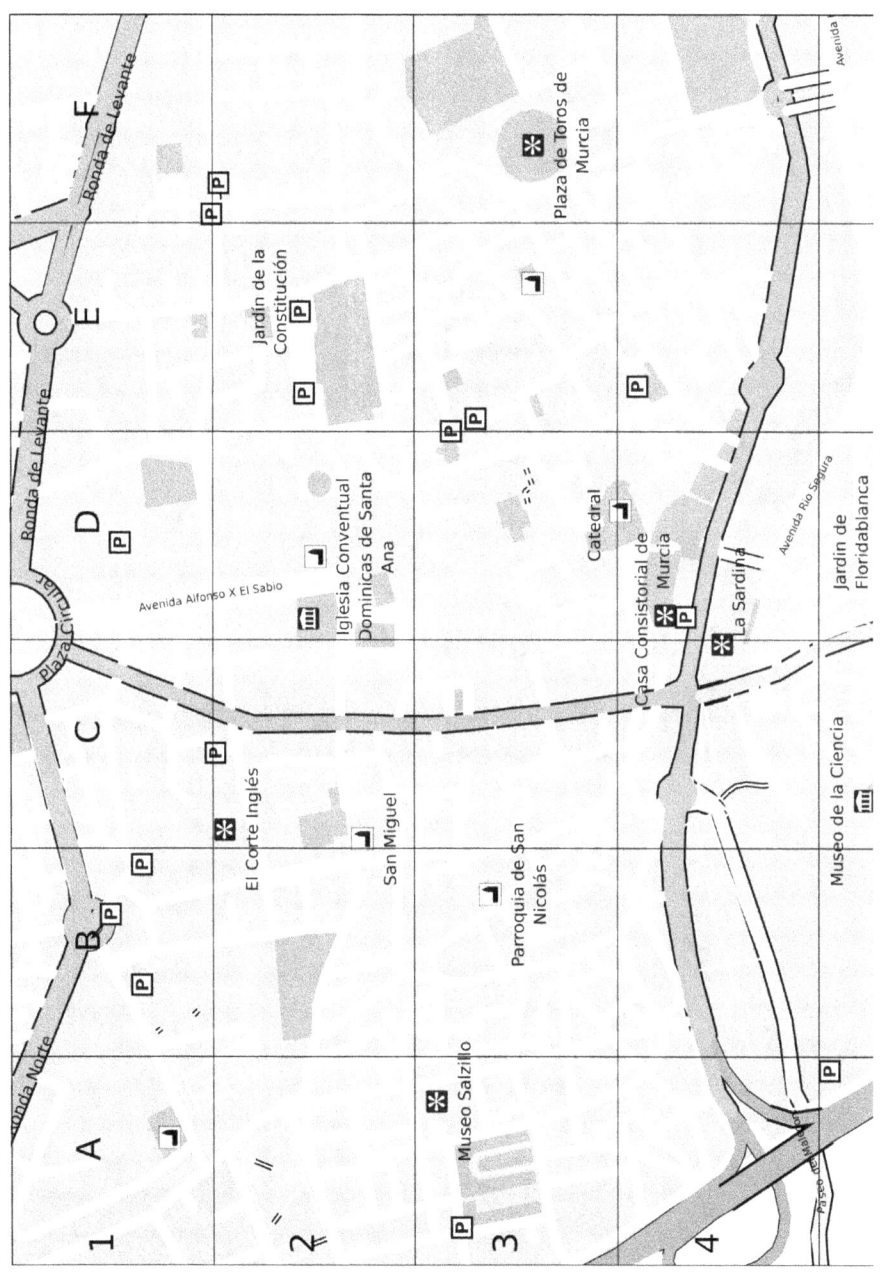

Connect with us and keep in touch at:

www.NativeSpain.com

www.facebook.com/debsjenkins

www.DebbieJenkins.com

And finally...

If you enjoyed our book please add a book review to amazon.co.uk or amazon.com – this would really help us and help other people who are also looking to enjoy the area.
Thanks in advance for doing so!

Full Table Of Contents

NativeSpain.com, 3
Praise for Going Native in Murcia, 4
Contents, 8
Foreword, 13
About This Book, 14
Updates, Changes and Your
    Feedback, 16
More For You!, 16
What do *you* want? The Highlights!, 17
Overview, 19
    A Brief History, 20
        Famous People, 21
    Language, 22
    Culture, 23
        Religion, 24
        Bull Fighting, 24
    Food and Drink, 24
        Eating Like A Spaniard, 25
        Breakfast, 25
        Lunch, 26
        Supper, 27
        Tapas Guide, 27
        Rutas de Tapas, 29
        Local Food Specialities, 29
        Vegetarians, 31
        Local Drinks, 31
    Wine Guide, 32
        Jumilla, 33
        Bullas, 33
        Yecla, 33
        Campo de Cartagena, 33
    Flora and Fauna, 33
        Mammals, 33
        Birds, 34
        Reptiles, 34
        Amphibians, 35
        Fish, 35
        Trees & Herbs, 35
        Protected Zones, 36
    Transport, 37
        Road Network, 37
        Airports, 37
        Car Rental, 38
        Car Hire Companies, 38
        Trains, 38
        Buses, 39
        Taxis, 39
    Climate, 39
    Fiestas, 40
        Going Native: Magenta
            Slipperz Entertains
            The Crowds, 42
        How To Fiesta, 43
    Activities, 44
        Special Report: Football, 44
        Rugby, 45
        Motor Sports, 45
        Walking, Trekking & Hiking, 45
        Going Native: Bob Walks For
            Charity – Join Him!, 46
        Segways, 46
        Horse Riding, 47
        Cycling, 47
        Location Report: Athletics
            Tracks & Sports
            Facilities, 47

Gliding, Paragliding and Skydiving, 49
Shooting, 49
Go Karts, 50
Scuba, 50
Watersports, 51
Fishing, 51
Sailing, 51
Golf, 52
Health & Beauty, 55
Thalassotherapy Centres, 55
Balnearios, 55
Spas, 55
Location Report: Spas, Balneariums, Thalassotherapy And The Mar Menor Mud, 56
Fitness, Aerobics, Dance, Yoga & Pilates, 57
Location Report, Geocaching: What To Do When It's Too Cold To Go To The Beach, 57
The Game of Caliche, 59
A Selection of Beaches, 59
Town & City Guide, 60
Where To Stay And Eat, 62
Águilas, 63
Location Report: Day Out In Águilas & Diving With Dolphins, 66
Los Arejos, 67
Los Geráneos, 67
Calarreona, 68
Calabardina, 68
Cope, 69
Todosol and Los Collados, 69
Hornillo, 69
Aledo, 71
Alhama De Murcia, 73
Archena, 76
Balneario Archena, 77
Bolnuevo, 79
Location Report: Bolnuevo, 79
Bullas, 80
Bodegas, 82
Cabo de Palos, 83
Scuba Diving, 84
Calasparra, 86
The Rice, 88
Calblanque, 90
Location Report: Calblanque Revealed, 90
Caravaca De La Cruz, 91
Archivel, 93
Barranda, 93
La Almudema, 93
La Encarnación, 94
Cartagena and Surrounds, 96
Location Report: Tentegorra Park, 97
Archaeological Route, 98
Baroque and Neoclassical Route, 99
Location Report: The Spanish Army, 100
Modernist & Eclectic Route, 101
Contemporary Route, 102
Location Report: The Spanish Navy, 102

Shopping, 103
Activities, 103
Location Report: Romans, Dining, Geocaching & Diving, 104
Fiestas and Festivals, 105
Location Report: Cartagena, 106
Beaches, 108
Baterías, 108
Location Report: The Guns Of Cabo Tiñoso, 109
Castles, 110
The Surrounding Area Of Cartagena, 110
El Albujón, 110
Beal, 111
Canteras, 111
Location Report: Batería De Roldán, 111
Escombreras, 112
Location Report: Diving Around Isla De Escombreras, 113
Lentiscar, 114
Los Puertos, 114
Perín, 115
Location Report: La Azohía, 115
Pozo Estrecho, 116
Rincón de San Ginés, 117
San Antonio Abad, 117
Location Report: Diving Around La Algameca, 118
San Félix, 119

Santa Lucía, 119
Going Native: Writer, Poet, Shrimper!, 120
Location Report: Cartagena Tapas Trail 1, 123
Location Report: Cartagena Tapas Trail Revisited, 125
Cehegín, 126
Wine, 128
Ceutí, 128
Cieza, 130
Costa Cálida, 133
Fortuna, 133
Going Native: Angela, Mick and Two Black Labradors, 134
Leana Balneario, 135
Almazara Ramón Pérez, 135
Location Report: Embalse De Santomera, 135
Fuente Álamo, 138
Balsapintada, 139
Cuevas de Reyllo, 140
El Escobar, Los Almagros and Los Paganes, 140
El Estrecho, 140
La Pinilla, 140
Las Palas, 141
Los Cánovas, 141
Location Report: Eating At The Motorway Ventas, 142
Jumilla, 143
Jumilla Wine and Bodegas, 145
Location Report: Tapear In Jumilla, 147

La Manga del Mar Menor, 149
　Location Report: La Manga Strip, 150
　Beaches, 151
　Ports, 152
La Unión, 153
Lo Pagán, 155
　Beaches, 156
Lorca, 157
　Beaches, 160
Los Alcázares, 162
　Los Narejos, 163
　Beaches, 164
　Location Report: Enjoying Los Alcázares, 165
　Location Report: Eating In Los Alcázares, 167
Mar Menor, 169
　Special Report: Serious problems in the Mar Menor, 169
　Beaches, 170
Mazarrón, 170
　Cañada del Romero, 171
　Gañuelas, 171
　La Majada, 172
　Going Native: Jennifer & Graham Devote Themselves to FAST (First Responders on Camposol), 172
　El Saladillo, 173
　El Mingrano, 173
　La Atalaya, 173
　Leiva, 173
　Pastrana, 174

Cañada de Gallego, 174
Las Moreras, 175
Balsicas, 175
El Alamillo, 175
Location Report: 5 Top Night Spots In Puerto De Mazarron, 176
Molina De Segura, 177
Moratalla, 180
　Location Report: Around Moratalla, 183
　Benizar (La Tercia, Mazuza, Otos), 184
　San Bartolomé (El Sabinar, Calar de la Santa), 185
　Campo de San Juan (Casicas de San Juan, Zaén de Arriba, Zaén de Abajo, Casas de Aledo, La Ribera), 185
　Cañada de la Cruz (and Los Odres), 185
　La Rogativa, 186
Mula, 188
　Yéchar, 190
　Los Baños de Mula, 190
　El Niño de Mula, 190
　La Puebla de Mula, 191
　Fuente Librilla, 191
Murcia and Surrounds, 192
　What is there to do in Murcia City?, 193
　La Huerta (agricultural countryside), 196
　The Silk, 197
　Museums, Exhibition Centres & Theatres, 198

Walking Around The City, 200
Fiestas, 201
Location Report: Bando De La Huerta, 204
Shopping, 204
Markets, 206
Location Report: Eating And Drinking, 209
Around Murcia, 211
    La Alberca, Santo Ángel and Algezares, 212
    Carrascoy-La Murta, 214
    Corvera, 216
    Guadalupe and La Ñora, 216
    Javalí Viejo, 216
    Monteagudo, 217
    El Palmar, 218
Ojós, 218
Pliego, 219
    Location Report: Vías Pecuarias And The Transhumance Routes, 220
Portmán, 221
Puerto Lumbreras, 223
Puerto de Mazarrón, 225
    Going Native: Paul and Gill Clarke on 'A Place in the Sun', 226
    Beaches, 228
    Fiestas, 229
    Location Report: Bahía De Mazarrón, 230
Ricote Valley, 232
    Abarán, 233
    Albudeite, 234
    Blanca, 234
    Location Report: River Rafting / Kayaking, 235
    Campos del Rio, 236
    Ricote, 237
    Ulea, 237
    Villanueva, 238
San Javier, 239
    Location Report: San Javier Jazz, 240
Santiago De La Ribera, 242
    Beaches, 243
San Pedro del Pinatar, 245
    Ports, 246
    Location Report: The Salinas, 246
    Beaches, 247
    Location Report: The Spa, 248
    Going Native: Cath Duhig Joins The Spanish Masters Athletics Squad, 250
Sierra Espuña, 251
    Location Report: Downhill Mountain Biking in the Sierra Espuña, 253
Torre Pacheco, 254
    Location Report: Cabezo Gordo, The Murcian Mountain Of Secrets, 255
Totana, 258
    Location Report: La Bastida De Totana, 260

Yecla, 262
Bodegas, 263
Essential Information, 265
Brexit, 265
Students, 265
Retiring, 266
Working, 266
    Going Native: Georgie Foster Makes It Work, 266
Buying a House, 269
    Developments, 269
    Buy in Haste, Re(pe)nt at Leisure - Rent First!, 269
    Going Native, 270
    Countryside Properties, 270
    Cities and Larger Towns, 270
    Home Comfort, 271
    Holiday Home, 271
    For Investment & Rental, 271
    Standard of Living, 271
    Looking, 272
    Estate Agents, 272
    Private Sales, 273
    Developers, 273
    Purchasing a new property, New Build / Off Plan, 273
    Fincas and Rural Properties, 274
Moving To Murcia, 274
Living in Murcia, 275
    Kids, School, 275
    Big Kids, Colleges & Universities, 276
Building Work & Permissions, 277
Alternatives, 278
DIY, 278
The Garden, 279
Pets (Mascotas) & Animal Ownership, 279
Smoking, 281
Entertainment, 282
    Radio, 282
    Television, 282
    Books, 282
    Cinema, 283
Law & Order, 283
Crime, 284
Health, 286
Driving, 287
Shopping, 288
    Location Report: Shopping!, 289
    Shopping Malls, 290
    Markets, 291
    Artisan Markets, 292
Emergency Telephone Numbers, 293
Local Charities, 295
Home Comforts, 298
    Home Sickness, 298
    British Food, 300
    Internet Shopping, 300
    Resources, 300
        Food & Drink Cheat Sheet, 300
    Learning Spanish, 304
        Useful Web Links, 304
        Language Schools, 304
        Going Native: Jax Moves To Murcia, 305
Recommended Reading, 306

About The Authors, 306
   Debbie Jenkins, 307
   Russ Pearce, 307
Maps, 308
   Águilas Map, 308
   Caravaca Map, 308
   Cartagena Map, 308
   Lorca Map, 308
   Moratalla Map, 308
   Murcia Map, 308
   Connect with us and keep in touch at:, 308
   And finally..., 308

www.ingramcontent.com/pod-product-compliance
Lightning Source LLC
Chambersburg PA
CBHW071556080526
44588CB00010B/926